The Russian Church
and the Soviet State

The Russian Church and the Soviet State

1917-1950

by

JOHN SHELTON CURTISS

GLOUCESTER, MASS.

PETER SMITH

1965

To
John Sutter Curtiss
and
Anne Curtiss

Preface

ALTHOUGH this study was begun in 1941, little could be accomplished on it until the years after the war. Its progress was greatly stimulated by a Senior Fellowship for the year 1947–1948 from the Russian Institute of Columbia University, with funds provided by the Rockefeller Foundation. Thanks to this, intensive work was done in major libraries along the Eastern seaboard, followed by several months of research abroad, notably in the British Museum, the Bibliothèque de Documentation Internationale Contemporaine in Paris, and the Russkii Zagranichnyi Arkhiv in Prague. The trip to Europe was made possible by a grant from the Carnegie Foundation for the Advancement of Teaching through the Research Council of Duke University. Additional work was done subsequently in American libraries, including a fruitful summer at the Hoover Library on War, Peace, and Revolution at Stanford, made possible by a second grant from the Duke University Research Council.

The author acknowledges his debt to many persons who rendered assistance. Professor G. T. Robinson of the Russian Institute gave liberal encouragement and advice, and without his support the project could not have been brought to completion. Professor Philip Mosely of the Russian Institute, Professor George Vernadsky of Yale University, and Dr. Vladimir Gsovski of the Library of Congress have also been very helpful. Valuable suggestions were received from Professor Alfred Levin of Oklahoma Agricultural and Mechanical College and Dr. Fritz Epstein of the Hoover Library. Professor N. S. Timasheff of Fordham University loaned the author important periodical items not otherwise obtainable. Dr. Paul B. Anderson of the International Committee of the YMCA and Dr. Donald Lowry of the Paris YMCA gave invaluable aid, supplying helpful materials and making possible interviews with leaders of the Russian Orthodox church in Paris, especially Professors A. V. Kartashev and L. Zander of the Russian Theological Institute, both of whom permitted the author to use important materials in their possession. The Russian Research Center, "Istina," of the Dominican Order in Paris also supplied valuable source material. Especial thanks go to Professor Fritz Lieb of the University of Basel, who granted access to rare items from his private library. Finally, warm thanks to Edna Sutter Curtiss for her unfailing encouragement.

As originally planned, this study was to end with 1928 and was first written in that form, but later it became desirable to bring it down to 1950. For this reason the second part may appear less thorough than the first, although in large part it lacks completeness because of the less abundant sources, almost all of which, during the 1930's, came from the Soviet side alone. Only from 1943 on are church publications available. Perhaps some of the gaps might have been filled if it had been possible to gain access to Soviet libraries, but that could not be done. On the whole, the material has been fairly complete, so that there are no serious lacunae.

The transliteration system has been based upon that of the Library of Congress, without diacritical marks.

Some of the translations in Chapters XII and XIII were supplied by Dr. Paul B. Anderson, notably from *Krasnaia Gazeta, Bor'ba, Proletarskaia Chernomorka, Brianskii Rabochii,* and some of those from *Bezbozhnik.* The other translations are mine, except as otherwise noted.

In conclusion, it should be emphasized that none of the persons mentioned above necessarily shares the conclusions and the opinions set forth in the succeeding pages, for which the author assumes full responsibility.

JOHN SHELTON CURTISS

Duke University

Contents

ix

The Russian Church
and the Soviet State

Introduction

As THE TITLE INDICATES, this study deals with the relationship between the Russian Orthodox church and the Soviet state; no attempt has been made to discuss other religious denominations. The period under consideration closes with the end of 1950. By that time the revolutionary aspects of the relationship had ended and, after the striking developments during World War II, a *modus vivendi* that promises to have considerable duration had been established. As no significant changes appear to be in prospect, December, 1950, has been chosen as the terminal date.

Throughout its pre-1917 history the Russian church as an organization had been noted for its close bonds with the civil authorities. It was originally established as the official religion by the Grand Prince Vladimir against the opposition of considerable elements of the population. At first a branch of the Greek Orthodox church of Constantinople, it was thoroughly imbued with the Greek tradition that the church should be submissive to the civil power. When the Russian state grew in strength, the grand princes and later the tsars inherited the position of the Greek emperors as heads of the church. Thus, while the claim of ecclesiastical supremacy was raised in the seventeenth century, the history and the traditions of the Russian church strongly upheld civil control.

In the early eighteenth century the power of the tsars over the church was further increased as a result of the ecclesiastical innovations of Peter the Great. This strong ruler, resenting the opposition of leading churchmen to his program, after a study of Western Protestant examples instituted a Holy Synod as head of the church in place of the Patriarch, its former head. Inasmuch as the Synod was picked by the tsar from among the episcopate and its activity was subject to his veto, the creation of this institution further increased civil control over the church.

Subsequently the weight of state control over the Russian church grew heavier. In the nineteenth century the tsar's lay representative in the Synod, the over-procurator, assumed the position of minister in charge of the administration of the church. In the name of the tsar the over-procurator ran the ecclesiastical administration, choosing, promoting, or removing bishops, picking the members of the Synod, and approving or disapproving the rulings of this body. The lay officials of the Synod were responsible to him and did his will, so that the princes of the church could do little contrary to his wishes. Even in the dioceses the over-procurator was all-powerful, for the secular officials of the diocesan administration were similarly devoted to him; and the bishop, whose tenure in the diocese was often brief, was not a free agent. Popular control of the church was still more out of the question. Thus the Russian church organization was thoroughly under the power of the government of the tsar.

The imperial government was not averse to using the church in its own interests. Through the catechism, through teaching in the schools of the church, through prayers for the tsar and through the sermons of the clergy, as well as in many other ways, the church sought to preserve and stimulate loyalty to the civil power. Enemies of the tsar, who was "the Anointed of God," were condemned by the clergy, while his triumphs were hailed with solemn *Te Deums.*

In return for this support, the government bestowed favors upon the Russian church. Its interests were considered in legislative and administrative matters, while its competitors were not favored. Economic assistance in the form of modest appropriations for episcopal salaries, administrative expenses, and church schools were provided by the Treasury, and the state naturally protected the church in the possession of its lands and other property. Moreover, the Russian church enjoyed a privileged position in respect to indoctrination and the winning of converts. According to law, the Russian subjects of the tsar were members of the Orthodox church and were not permitted to join any other. The clergy of other denominations were forbidden to seek converts from the Orthodox, and those who did so — especially the Old Believers, a dissident Orthodox group, and the sectarians, resembling the Protestants in their theology — were punished by arrest and exile. In some cases small children were taken away from sectarian parents so that they might be brought up in the Orthodox faith. In addition, it was difficult for these denominations to secure permission to establish churches or prayer houses, and often those that they opened without permission were sealed by the police. In contrast to this restricted status, that of the Russian Orthodox church was favorable. Its missionary activities were given official encouragement and support, and by law the children of mixed marriages had to be brought up in the Orthodox faith. A wide network of Orthodox parochial schools received financial support and favor from the government, and Orthodox religious instruction was required in all schools except those of recognized religious minorities.

In spite of its privileged position, however, in the first years of the twentieth century conditions were not entirely favorable to the Russian Orthodox church. Although, in spite of the vitality of the Old Believers and the sects, it still enjoyed the allegiance of the great majority of the Russians and the Ukrainians, it at times had passive acceptance rather than sincere support. The peasantry, traditionally devout as they were, were inclined toward lack of respect for the clergy, who were not always worthy of the cloth. Not only the drunkenness of some of the priests, but also the financial relations between priests and peasants, produced a lack of mutual esteem. By custom the clergy were usually paid for their ministrations — christenings, marriages, funerals, the blessing of homes or of fields, and prayers for the departed. As no fixed rates were set for these services, they were often preceded by hard bargaining between priest and peasant, which was not conducive to respect; religious though he doubtless was, the peasant all too often regarded the priest as a man prone to make exorbitant demands. Moreover, the priests often lacked zeal. On the whole they felt oppressed by their superiors, especially the bishops and the lay administrators, and dissatisfied with their often meager financial status. In addition, many of the priests had taken orders, not out of conviction, but because, as sons of priests themselves, they saw no other opportunity. Lacking the funds necessary for a university education, the sons of the priests usually resorted to the free theological education that led to the priesthood. The frustration of the seminary students was notorious, and, by testimony of the bishops themselves, radicalism and unbelief were widespread in their ranks. From such candidates came a clergy uninspired and apathetic, although rarely rebellious. They did, however, nurse a bitter hatred for the bishops and for the monastics in general, from whose ranks the bishops were traditionally always drawn. Thus for the parish priests, who were required to marry at ordination, access to the episcopate was closed. Because of this fact, and because of the often haughty attitude of the bishops toward them, the parish clergy generally bore strong resentment toward the bishops and toward all monastics.

The Revolution of 1905 inevitably affected the Russian church, as well as other parts of Russian society. In his effort to placate the people the tsar gave religious concessions, including the right to change religions. The administration also moderated its treatment of dissenting groups, especially the Old Believers. Furthermore, in response to wide demand in church circles, the tsar promised to call a church council or Sobor — there had been none since the seventeenth century — to institute fundamental reforms in the structure and the administration of the church. Little came of these concessions, however, for when the revolutionary tide ebbed the tsar indefinitely postponed the Sobor.

While this failure to achieve basic reforms doubtless discouraged and alienated some of the public, a more important reason for loss of prestige by the church was the fact that its administration and many of its leading members gave active support to the government of the tsar, to which large sections of the public had become hostile. The Synod condemned the revolution and all its works, terming those who rose against the Anointed Tsar sacrilegious foes of the church. By pamphlets against socialism, by proclamations and by sermons the leaders of the church sought to quiet the unruly and to discredit the rebellious. In addition, many of the most noted ecclesiastics played an active role in the extremely reactionary Union of the Russian People, a violently chauvinistic and anti-Semitic organization responsible for terrible acts of violence against those it hated. And when the revolutionary period was followed by the quasi-parliamentary regime of the Duma the influence of the church was thrown behind the government and against the realization of the reforms that great portions of the public felt were necessary. Undoubtedly, during these years the church lost in influence through the fact that to many it was identified as a supporter of the government.

Between 1905 and 1917 little was done to remedy defects in the state of the church. While the persecution of sectarians was less rigorous than before, it continued in spasmodic fashion with no objection from the church leaders. The position of the parish priests was not improved, and even more than before it became difficult to obtain suitable candidates for the priesthood, as the seminary students sought other careers. Above all, nothing was done to free the church from domination by the government. In fact, the civil control became more onerous through the advent of Rasputin.

This adventurer, a debauched peasant who managed to gain a mystical influence over the empress and the tsar, soon exerted power over the church hierarchy. So open was the secret that scandals caused by him were aired in the Duma and the press, but without result except to impair the authority of the church. For a time in 1914 Rasputin was in eclipse, but in 1915 he regained his influence at court. In addition to dominating the government through the empress, he held full sway over the Synod, promoting his friends to the top positions in the hierarchy and subduing his opponents. The scandal of his degrading power over the church perhaps did not reach the peasant world to any great extent; but to those who did learn of it, it must have been a damaging blow to the prestige of the church.

Its ties with the government of the tsar also led the church to give wholehearted support to Russia's participation in the First World War. In the early months public opinion apparently did likewise; but as the disastrous mismanagement and the resulting slaughter became known opposition to the government was voiced in wide circles of the politically minded, while the masses grew more and more eager for an end to the war at all costs. The church heads, however, continued to support the government and the war without cavil, vehemently condemning those who opposed. Thus, when the crisis came in 1917, the church as an institution was strongly committed to the discredited government and to the unpopular war. When the government fell, almost without a struggle, the church was in a very vulnerable position.

CHAPTER I

The Russian Church and
the February Revolution

On the eve of the fall of the tsar the Russian Orthodox church was a powerful organization. It was the church of the bulk of the population of the empire — nearly one hundred million Russians, Ukrainians, and Belorussians (White Russians) — and by law and by force of tradition it had no dangerous rival for their allegiance, as both the Old Believers and the sectarians were still relatively small groups. The other religious denominations within the empire were largely confined to the minority peoples: Catholicism was strong among Poles and Lithuanians, Lutheranism was prevalent among the peoples of the upper Baltic, the Armenian Gregorian and the Georgian churches were in the Caucasus area, and the Moslem faith was found in southern and eastern regions of the empire, while some of the Mongolian subjects of the tsar were Buddhists. Judaism, while important in some parts of the empire, had no followers among the Russian inhabitants. Thus the Russian Orthodox church had historical justification for claiming to be the predominant religion of Russia. As such, it enjoyed the political support of the government and received an annual appropriation, which in 1916 amounted to 62,920,835 rubles; more than half was used for the schools of the church.

In 1914, the last year for which full statistics are available, the Russian church had a widely developed network of parishes throughout the empire. In the 67 dioceses there were 54,174 churches of all types; many of these, however, were institutional chapels attached to public establishments, or monastery churches, while some were in

9

non-Russian dioceses (Warsaw, Grodno, Kishinev, Lithuania, Riga, Finland, and the Exarchate of Georgia). Allowance must also be made for 5830 churches not in use. Thus the functioning parish churches in the predominantly Russian dioceses numbered 40,437. Within the empire as a whole there were 50,105 deans and priests. There were 1025 monastic institutions — 550 for men, with 21,330 monks and novices, and 473 convents, with 73,299 nuns and novices.[1]

In spite of its apparent strength, however, all was not well with the Russian Orthodox church. Particularly during the Revolution of 1905 there had been signs that many of the Russian people were not as fully under the influence of the church as the latter might wish. Nevertheless, in the last months of the imperial regime the church supported it strongly and opposed the foes of the tsar. In January, 1917, Metropolitan Makarii of Moscow told the people: "Fear God and honor the tsar. Honor the tsar as the Anointed of God. . . ." He went on to urge national unity in no uncertain terms: "Let us unite around our mighy Orthodox tsar! Let us stand in defense of the divinely established authorities appointed by the tsar!"[2] Commenting on this message, *Seiatel'* (*The Sower*), a church periodical, declared that it was timely, as shown by the government's message regarding the arrest of the workers' group of the Central War Industries Committee.[3] A few days later Metropolitan Vladimir of Kiev warned the press: "We are Orthodox Christians, members of a monarchical state, to the bottom of our souls loving our tsars. . . . The waves of party strife must not undermine love and respect for the ruling house."[4] Similarly, the clergy of the diocese of Kiev, meeting a few days before the outbreak of revolution, adopted a resolution urging dismissal of the Duma as necessary for putting down the revolutionary movement.[5] And on February 25, when the waves of revolution were rising, the official journal of the church prominently printed an address by a bishop condemning the dangerous tendencies then manifest and calling on all to "hasten . . . to the aid of the local representatives of the Autocrat. . . . Now . . . let the cathedral bell call all Rus together under the one great and holy banner, on which in fiery words is written: For faith, tsar, and fatherland!"[5]

Except for these gestures, however, the Synod played no role in the February Revolution that overthrew the tsar. Indeed, it was careful not to commit itself further, for on February 27 it rejected the proposal of Over-Procurator Raev to condemn the revolutionary movement.[6]

The bishops also for the most part seem to have done nothing in the face of the revolution. Archbishop Arsenii of Novgorod is reported to have said: "There is no tsar, there is no church!" and when his clergy asked him what they should do, he allegedly told them: "I don't know! I know nothing! Do whatever you want." [7] One of the first commissars of the Provisional Government tells of encountering a bewildered priest who sought advice as to whether to continue to say prayers for the imperial family. "It seems that under present circumstances one should not, but I am afraid to omit them. But there are no instructions from my superiors." [8] Even Archbishop Antonii Khrapovitskii of Khar'kov (formerly of Volhynia), an outstanding reactionary, dared not speak out, but indirectly showed his sympathies by recommending to his clergy the book of the reactionary Dean Butkevich, *Lessons of the French Revolution*.[9]

While the clergy remained passive during the events of the February Revolution, some of them proved reluctant to recognize it as an accomplished fact. Prayers for "the most Orthodox, most autocratic tsar" were continued in many places. In several cities priests refused to read the abdication manifesto of Nicholas II. Moreover, on March 1 solemn requiems were said for the departed Alexander II in the cathedrals of Sevastopol and Kiev, as though the revolution had never occurred.[10]

Protopresbyter Shavel'skii, chief chaplain of the armed forces, who emigrated from Russia after participation in the White movement against the Soviets, stated that in the first days of the revolution the clergy, both hierarchs and priests, "had an expectant, cautious attitude toward it." This watchful waiting was caused by the fact that the clergy, "in great measure, formed an especially conservative part of Russian society. . . . There were even priests who, even after the abdication of the Sovereign, stubbornly continued to mention him in the divine service." While others obeyed the instructions of the Holy Synod and proclaimed "long life" to the Provisional Government, "the thoughts of both [groups] continued to tend in the same direction." [11] In March, 1917, the moderate newspaper *Rech'*, organ of the Constitutional Democratic (Kadet) party, printed an editorial, "The Tragedy of the Church," expressing the hope that in spite of the Black Hundred (ultrareactionary) activities of clerics like Father Vostorgov and Metropolitan Vladimir, the rank and file of the clergy would assume a more liberal attitude.[12] In April, however, *Rech'* expressed regret that so few priests had taken a liberal stand, and cited several instances where pastors had incited their parishioners against the Provisional Government.[13] Similar testimony is given by a Soviet historian of the revolution in the province of Samara. In April a priest agitating against the new government threatened the revolutionaries with the gallows. Other priests, according to the local press, spread reactionary ideas in the villages; one such priest was said to be carrying on "agitation against the new government, threatening its supporters with the torments of Hell." [14]

The Synod perforce had to accept the new order of things. Raev, former Over-Procurator, who with his assistants had fled, was replaced by V. N. L'vov, active in the Duma on church affairs, and a determined foe of Rasputin. On March 4 L'vov met with the Synod and announced that for the church this revolution meant the approach of freedom from domination. At his suggestion the Synod issued an appeal to the people terming the revolution "the will of God" and urging that they for the sake of the successful prosecution of the war, "in this great historic time put aside all quarrels and dissensions, unite in fraternal love for the good of Russia, trust the Provisional Government. . . ." [15] The Synod also eliminated all mention of the tsar and his dynasty from the ritual of the church, substituting prayers "for the divinely protected Russian Power and its true-believing [that is, Orthodox] Provisional Government." A special commission was appointed to revise the service books in keeping with the spirit of the times.[16]

The harmony which the Synod enjoined did not, however, long endure. L'vov, once a strong foe of the power of the over-procurator, in the face of the reactionary Synod quickly assumed dictatorial powers over the church, repeatedly insisting that the bishops appointed by the influence of Rasputin, several of whom sat in the Synod, could not be trusted. Metropolitan Pitirim, thoroughly compromised as a Rasputinite, was quickly removed and retired to a monastery in the

Caucasus. Metropolitan Makarii of Moscow did not want to retire, but as many of his clergy asked L'vov to remove him from his see, the Synod was forced to sign the order for his retirement. Before he left, the irate Makarii forbade the hostile clergy of his diocese to perform mass; this ban, however, was generally ignored.[17] Bishop Varnava of Tobol'sk, another intimate of Rasputin, was also retired; the fiery Bishop Hermogen, who had been disgraced for opposing Rasputin in 1912, was installed in Varnava's place.[18]

L'vov, instead of sweeping out the remaining members of the Synod, tried to work with them. His headstrong and erratic personality, however, was not conducive to harmony, and for their part the appointees of the old regime had little inclination toward co-operation. A bitter conflict developed when he turned the conservative organ of the Synod, the *Vserossiiskii Tserkovno–Obshchestvennyi Vestnik (All-Russian Church–Social Messenger)*, over to an editorial board of liberal professors of the Petrograd Theological Academy. The Synod's refusal to modify the antiquated divorce rules of the church was another cause of friction. L'vov went over the Synod's head on two other important questions, thereby angering the embattled ecclesiastics. Thus by April L'vov, realizing that his program of reforming the church by means of a church council or Sobor could not be achieved in the face of the hostile Synod, used his power as over-procurator to dismiss it, calling a new one. Only the capable Archbishop Sergii of Vladimir (formerly of Finland) and Platon, Exarch of Georgia, were retained from the former Synod. The new members — three bishops and four deans, two of them professors of theology — proved to be co-operative, and church matters proceeded more smoothly after that.[19]

L'vov, however, did not long retain his powers. When a new government was formed in July, he was replaced by A. V. Kartashev, of a more tactful character than L'vov. Kartashev served as over-procurator for only ten days; on August 5 his title was changed to that of Minister of Confessions. Until the Constituent Assembly should decide the final form of the government he was to possess the powers of over-procurator, although he did not make real use of them. One of his first acts was to tell the Synod that he regarded that body as autonomous and that the Provisional Government eagerly awaited the Sobor, which would set up a regular administration for the church.[20]

In general, there was little change in the relations between church and government during the first six months of the Provisional regime. The only important innovation was the law of July 14, 1917, providing for freedom of religious profession and the right to change religions or to profess none at all.[21]

Within higher church circles the dominant view was that the Orthodox church should enjoy autonomy in its internal affairs, while receiving the special position due the church of the majority of the nation's inhabitants. The courts of the church, its marriage and divorce rules, its record books and its holidays were to be recognized by the state. Its schools were to remain intact, and compulsory Orthodox religious instruction, supported by the government, was to be retained in all schools. In addition, the government subsidies to the church were not to be disturbed. Such was the content of the resolution adopted on July 13, 1917, by the Pre-Sobor Council, the preparatory commission for the Sobor to be held later in the year. The minority group of reformers felt that there should be full separation of church and state, to be realized, however, after a considerable preparatory period.[22]

For a time after the fall of the tsar it appeared that a liberal reform movement might sweep the Russian church. To the unleashing of repressed forces during the revolution was added the encouragement of L'vov's removal of the worst reactionaries from the Synod. In addition, his action in turning over the official church journal to the liberals of the Petrograd Theological Academy helped the reform movement.[23]

Petrograd was the stronghold of the church liberals. Here, as early as March 7, there appeared the League of Democratic Clergy and Laymen, headed by Deans Popov, Egorov, and Vvedenskii; some of its members had belonged to "the Thirty-two," a liberal group of priests in the period from 1902 to 1905. The new body took a strong stand against the monarchy, which it termed harmful for both church and people, and declared for a republican form of government. Even more significantly, it condemned capitalism, demanded the giving of the land to the peasants, profit sharing for the workers, and other radical measures. For the church it advocated a program of democratic reforms intended to increase popular participation in control of the church and to lessen the power of the upper clergy.[24]

This radical movement did not take root in Moscow; although Vvedenskii addressed a group of Moscow clergy, they did not commit themselves to the cause. In the Crimea and the Urals, however, groups did affiliate with the Petrograd liberals. The latter held many public debates on religious matters and published brochures on the revolution, socialism, and similar problems.[25] Vvedenskii, the most advanced of the group, held that the principles of the early church fathers were close to socialism and that the church must now win over the workers by espousing the principles of the Marxists. "We have a similar principle — equal distribution of worldly goods — but a different method: moral action."[26]

Other groups of liberal churchmen were formed; so keen was the zeal for reform (chiefly among members of the priesthood) and so strong the fear of episcopal reaction, that in March, 1917, clerical and lay members of the Duma and certain other leaders of Russian society formed a Council for Affairs of the Orthodox Church; its existence, however, was brief.[27]

In addition to these organizational manifestations of church liberalism, in the first months after the February Revolution a number of diocesan gatherings of clergy adopted liberal resolutions supporting the Provisional Government and favoring a Sobor. Occasionally these resolutions touched upon special topics. For example, the Ekaterinoslav diocesan congress asked that bishops be elected by the clergy and laymen of the dioceses, from candidates from the parish clergy as well as from the monastics.[28] This same gathering asked that all privately owned land above a maximum amount be confiscated for distribution to the peasants; church lands, however, should not be confiscated, as the clergy needed them for support. For the workers this gathering favored the eight-hour day and a wide program of social legislation.[29] The diocesan congress of Kishinev advocated a democratic republic; it strongly urged that the clergy be permitted to enjoy the use of church lands, but made no recommendation as to the holdings of private landowners.[30] Liberal resolutions were also adopted by church gatherings in Petrograd, Kiev, and Tver,[31] and probably in other dioceses.

Fearing reaction on the part of the upper clergy, the liberal clergy, in order to demonstrate their strength, organized an All-Russian Congress of Clergy and Laymen in Moscow in the first days of June, attended by twelve hundred elected delegates. L'vov and Exarch Platon attended to show their support. The assembly, which met for ten days, passed strong resolutions urging that church reforms of a more democratic nature be adopted by the Sobor. It advocated popular sovereignty in church and state; it urged the handing over of the land to the cultivators and just treatment of labor by capital. On the other hand, its insistence on special prerogatives for the Orthodox church[32] suggested a tendency of the clergy as a whole to turn away from radicalism — a trend that soon became evident.

The radicalism among the lower clergy immediately after the fall of the tsar also took the form of settling accounts with hated bishops. According to Protopresbyter Shavel'skii, in Kiev a religious directory of five men was set up to seize power over the religious administration of the diocese, in spite of the efforts of Metropolitan Vladimir. "In several dioceses, such as Orel, Tula, Tver, there were stormy diocesan congresses headed by liberal, 'free' priests. The congresses deposed their bishops." Archbishop Tikhon of Voronezh, who was suspected of counterrevolution, was even arrested and sent to Moscow in a prison car.[33] In the case of Archbishop Serafim of Tver, the clergy of his diocese sent a delegation to the Synod asking his removal; L'vov supported this demand, but the Synod succeeded in delaying action for some time.[34] The removal of Bishop Nikon of Enisei diocese also was asked by a vote of 101 to 7 in the diocesan congress.[35] When a bitter quarrel broke out between Bishops Paladii and Leontii of Saratov, the diocesan congress voted unanimously to remove both bishops.[36] In January, 1918, Bishop Efrem told the Sobor of 1917–1918 that the clergy had been infected by the spirit of revolution as much as the lay intelligentsia had been. "Raging in their gatherings and congresses, they greeted with telegrams the lay wreckers of the church [Kerenskii and L'vov] and at the same time with furious wrath threw themselves upon the bearers of church authority — the bishops. . . . And how many religious persons left their service to the holy church and went off to the service of the revolution?" He stated that the attitude of the lower clergy was shown by the violence done by one priest to his bishop, and the arrest of a bishop in his quarters by a priest leading an armed band.[37] Even Archbishop Vasilii of Chernigov was retired as a result of rejection by his clergy, even though he was a member of the Synod.[38]

After these episodes, the Synod, urged by L'vov, adopted a rule that bishops should be elected by the clergy and the laymen of their dioceses. In the elections that followed the incumbent was usually re-elected, with only a few rejected by their flocks. In Petrograd Bishop Veniamin, vicar of the diocese, was chosen to fill the vacancy left by Pitirim; in Moscow, Archbishop Tikhon of Vilna, who had had to flee from his see to escape the Germans, was elected.[39]

The ousting of bishops actually was not widespread, and indeed, after the first outburst of excitement, the clergy, as will be shown later, turned to conservatism. Most of the bishops retained their dioceses, including many who had strongly opposed liberal trends in the church. As the Synod interpreted the absence of effective opposition in their dioceses as tacit approval of the conservative prelates, they were in a stronger position, and began to assert themselves once more.[40]

While dissension did for a time appear in the ranks of the clergy, with negligible exceptions they supported the war effort. The Synod urged energetic propaganda on behalf of the Provisional Government's Loan of Freedom and sent the local clergy two obligatory sermons advocating subscriptions. Although the liberal All-Russian Congress of Clergy and Laymen opened with "eternal remembrance for the fallen fighters for freedom" (the revolutionaries), it gave a ready ear to Prince Eugene Trubetskoi, who told the members that to save Russia fiery patriotism was needed, like that of the medieval St. Sergii.[41]

Repeatedly during 1917 the church undertook to stimulate enthusiasm for the war. On March 12 in the Kazan Cathedral in Petrograd the popular young Bishop Andrei of Ufa preached to a vast crowd that they should pray to God and He would give them victory. He deplored the lack of discipline and of respect for elders, and went on to say: "Esteem your officers, be submissive to them, and the enemy at the front will be broken." [42] On June 4 in Red Square in Moscow, a special *Te Deum* was said "for victory and the internal well-being of the motherland." [43] The church's enthusiasm for the cause was fervently expressed by *Golos Svobodnoi Tserkvi* (*The Voice of the Free Church*), which printed a telegram sent to Kerenskii, Minister of War, on the eve of his summer offensive: "Call yet louder into the holy battle, into the last decisive battle, so that war, the shame of the whole world, may be conquered by war." [44] In Petrograd, "on the day of the Holy Trinity there was performed a nation-wide prayer to the All-Highest, with religious processions from the capital's churches to the Isaac Cathedral asking victory over the enemy for our warriors and the assuaging and ending of hostility and internal disturbances." [45]

The aid of the church was directly invoked by the Russian army. On May 9, at the request of General Alexeev, Commander in Chief, three noted Petrograd priests from the League of Progressive Democratic Clergy, Deans Vvedenskii, Egorov, and Boiarskii, went to the front to tour the lines and to raise morale by urging discipline and by warning of the falsity of the Bolsheviks.[46]

The church authorities also aided the cause by printing leaflets containing appropriate verses from the Bible: "I came not to send peace, but a sword" (Matt. 10:34); and "he that hath no sword, let him sell his garment and buy one" (Luke 22:36). Some inspirational verses written by a priest were widely reprinted by ecclesiastical journals. The church was repeatedly urged to help distribute the pamphlets of the War Industries Committee, and the official church periodical printed several such appeals to the clergy, in large type, on its front page. It stated that the publications of the committee, "unlike party speeches, attempt to promote unity and solidarity among the people." [47]

But while there was unity of purpose between government and church on most matters, they differed sharply about the 37,000 parochial schools of the church — one third of the nation's schools. Public opinion, even in the moderate parties, had long favored nationalization of the parochial schools, and the Duma had repeatedly urged it, so that when on June 20 the Provisional Government put them under the minister of education, on the grounds that they were largely supported by public funds, the move was welcomed by much of the public. Indeed, the All-Russian Teachers' Congress in May had urgently demanded the nationalization,[48] and a meeting of parochial school teachers in April had sent a declaration to L'vov stating: "We, teachers in parochial schools, warmly welcome this undertaking and hope for your co-operation in the speedy creation of a unified, secular school." [49] The clergy, however, had come to regard these schools as an important form of missionary work and were indignant when they were secularized. The All-Russian Congress of Clergy and Laymen protested, and the Synod sent a delegation to the Provisional Government, terming the action "impossible." "It deprives the Orthodox church of one of the means of exerting a religious enlightening influence upon the Russian people, who, because of the great historic significance of the Orthodox church in the Russian state, are accustomed to draw the seeds of faith and their ideals of life from the church." The government tried to explain the reasons for its action to the indignant churchmen, but the latter were not mollified.[50]

The question of compulsory religious education in the secular schools was another contested point. The state committee on public education was strongly in favor of making it voluntary. The teachers of religion raised heated objections, however, and the church authorities and the Pre-Sobor Council, formed on April 29 to prepare for the Sobor, insisted on making it obligatory and giving it "full and proper attention and the proper amount of time." [51] In this case the clergy were temporarily victorious, for religion continued to be a compulsory subject in the schools. Only one concession was made: if neither the pupil, at the age of fourteen, nor his parents wanted the religious lessons, the pupil might be excused upon written request of the parents.[52]

The religious program of the Provisional Government was far from radical, and in most respects the church still enjoyed its honored position; nevertheless, the measures respecting the church's educational activities dampened what little enthusiasm the churchmen had had for the revolution. Another influence that caused the majority of the clergy to veer sharply to the right in the summer of 1917 was the fact that the influence of the church among the masses was visibly declining.

Even in the first days, before the radical wave had gained strength, many parish priests felt the force of the revolutionary elements; a number of pastors were ousted by their parishioners, often led by the deacon or the psalmist. In some dioceses hundreds of priests were so dealt with.[53] A certain Father Chel'tsev described the situation as follows:

> From everywhere comes exceedingly grievous news. Here the *muzhiks* [peasants] in a meeting have established such low rates for services that even the least exacting person, with a small family, cannot live on them. There they have decreed that none of the peasants shall work for the priest, by the year or by the day. . . . In some places they deprive them of the right to perform divine service in church, they drive them out of the parsonages, drive them out of the villages.[54]

Similar developments occurred in the Ukraine. In the province of Kiev it was found necessary to "inform all village and hamlet committees that they should not take independent measures against persons of religious calling, and in cases where it became necessary to remove undesirable persons of religious calling, they should turn to the provincial executive committee." In Volhynia action against priests abounded; late in April the church press reported that within two weeks over sixty agreements for the expulsion of priests had been made. In the diocese of Khar'kov there were so many "self-willed outbursts . . . of irresponsible persons and groups against church institutions and the clergy, expressed in demands to religious persons to remove themselves immediately from the parish without trial and investigation, in deprivation of their freedom, in subjection to arrest and imprisonment, in forbidding them to perform religious service in church, in closing the churches themselves . . . ," that the ecclesiastical authorities had to appeal to the provincial authorities for aid against such manifestations.[55]

The authority of the army chaplains was also low. Protopresbyter Shavel'skii, writing in 1922, recalled that after March, 1917, agitators had gone to the troops to promise them peace and land — an appeal that the chaplains had great difficulty in countering. " 'We are follow-ing the *via dolorosa*,' the preacher of the Third Army said to me in the summer of 1917. 'To what abuse we are subjected!' " When the priest tried to explain to the soldiers the nature of duty and the cor-rect interpretation of freedom, "suddenly a soldier dashed up to . . . [him], holding out his rifle. 'If you want to fight, take the rifle and go into the trenches, for we're going home!' " [56]

Even for many Russians who were not directly drawn into the revolutionary current, the church and religion had relatively little influence during 1917. The liberal, popular Dean Vvedenskii stated that at Easter the Petrograd churches were rather poorly attended and after Easter were almost empty. Vvedenskii's church, with a capacity of one thousand, had only a few score worshipers, and in other churches the same situation obtained. [57]

The state of affairs was summed up by the leading church organ in August, 1917. It declared that the hopes of the church that its influence might restrain the masses intoxicated by new-found freedom had proved vain; the moral restraint of the church was of no avail. "Evidently what has been repeatedly said in our cultural history has been said once more: that religion consists almost entirely of ritual and the apparent religiosity had beneath it no moral basis. . . . The 'Christ-loving' people not only did not love, but did not know Christ: here is the long-standing tragedy of our Russian reality." [58]

Thus by midsummer, 1917, the leaders of the Russian church, and with them most of the priests, were becoming greatly disturbed by the situation that faced them. The Provisional Government, in which they had placed such high hopes, had taken a stand that many felt was hostile to their interests; and, even more important, they saw that their influence was declining as radicalism mounted. As their dismay at the course of events increased, the clergy turned from their former liberalism and displayed more conservatism in word and deed.

The All-Russian Congress of Clergy and Laymen, a stronghold of the liberal churchmen, was not immune to this influence. At its last meeting, on June 12, it opposed separation of church and state as synonymous with persecution of the church. It also condemned the seizure of church and private lands, holding that the agrarian prob-lem should be left to the Constituent Assembly; it urged the factory workers to work harder and longer hours, in order to save the country from disaster.[59]

In the light of this, it is not surprising that the conservatives, who were probably closer to the rank and file of the clergy than was the Congress of Clergy and Laymen, again raised their heads. They formed reactionary groups such as the League of Church Unification, which took an uncompromising stand on parochial schools and urged excommunication of the liberal Petrograd clergy who had claimed that there was much similarity between Christianity and socialism. In part owing to the efforts of the conservatives, Dean Egorov was publicly insulted because of a liberal sermon, and some of the clergy tore down posters advertising Vvedenskii's lecture "Christ and Marx." [60]

After the July Days — a great demonstration in Petrograd led by the Bolsheviks — the Synod attacked the latter as representative of evil. On July 15 a ceremonial funeral was held in Petrograd for the Cossacks killed in the street fighting. Archbishop Platon, chairman of the Synod, preached the sermon in the great St. Isaac's Cathedral, comparing the Cossacks to the martyrs of old and terming the Bolsheviks German agents. "Blessed, a thousand times blessed are those whom God hath chosen to receive the martyr's crown. To die for one's own people — what a glorious death. . . ." "What a striking difference between those whose loss we now mourn and those who, . . . clothed in the holy name of Russian soldier, promote the betrayal of the native land . . . ! The Holy Synod has commissioned me, with prayer to God, to forward into eternity these heroes of duty. . . ." [61]

At the same time the Synod issued a proclamation to be read in all churches, calling for prayer and repentance. It stated that the country had had hopes of a better day, but that

a new and evil foe has come amongst us and has sowed tares in Rus, which have not failed to send forth leaves which have stifled the growth of the desired freedom. . . . The country has set forth upon the path of ruin, and in future there awaits it that frightful gulf which for all of us is full of horrifying despair, if only "the trouble and treading down and perplexity by the Lord God" (Is. 22:5) does not cease.

. . . .

Archpastors and pastors of the church of Russia! Fulfil your duty before the country. . . . Call the people to prayer and heartfelt repentance. Instruct, inspire, convince — especially the bringers of dissension, that they defile not their consciences with malice and do not fill the country thirsting after real peace with abominations; beseech the citizens with your words, that they may love in holy brotherhood, that the sons of Russia may give their hearts over to submission to the truth of God, and their strength and labor to the benefit of the suffering native land.

Arise then, Rus, with thy spirit in repentance, with thy love in brotherhood, . . . and "The Lord will raise thee up, and will spare thee from the evil one and will release thee from the hand of the oppressor. . . ." [62]

After the July Days the Synod recommended singing a prayer in all churches "for saving the Russian Power and for assuaging therein division and strife." The prayer stated that the people were come before Christ with heavy hearts, confessing before Him "their sins and unlawfulness" with which they had affronted the Lord. The antiphonal response asked God to alleviate "wavering and dissension in our land, remove from us envy and ambition, killing and drunkenness, destruction and temptation," so that men might love each other as He had commanded. God was asked to strengthen and make wise those in power, to make strong the warriors and to save them from all onslaughts of the foe. The prayer asked that He bring to the people "strong men and wisdom, and give to us all the spirit of wisdom and the fear of God, the spirit of steadfastness and righteousness." [63]

On August 2 the Synod, in a message designed to increase the patriotism of troops and populace, warned that the enemy was using all means to "weaken in our troops the feeling of patriotic duty and the Christian viewpoint." The pastors were urged to make great efforts to imbue the military with Christian principles, paying especial attention to the enlisted men of reserve battalions, in order that the new troops sent to the front should bring "high religious and patriotic inspiration." This was to be accomplished by scrupulous performance of the religious rituals, instructive talks by priests, formation of groups of strongly religious persons to influence the reservists, and dissemination of the Gospel and of religious and moral tracts among the troops and the people.[64]

The church press also began to call for distribution of antisocialist printed matter originally published after the Revolution of 1905. Even the once-liberal ecclesiastical journals declared that the Bolsheviks were in touch with agents of the Germans and did their bidding. One periodical stated: "The work of traitors and betrayers who have received German money and who call themselves Bolsheviks has borne its fruit. . . . Those who promised the people all sorts of blessings and called for peace with the Germans have sold Russia." [65] The clergy, according to a church magazine of this period, should influence the people by sermons as well as by printed matter. At parish meetings the priest could manifest a purely political and social activity, preparing for the Constituent Assembly and the local elections, and imbuing his flock with the feeling of civic duty and responsibility to the native land.[66]

This call for political action was by no means an isolated instance, for in the summer and fall of 1917 the clergy felt a need to participate in political life. While many old-line churchmen were still doubtless covertly loyal to the tsar, the realities of the times made a large part of the clergy side with the Party of National Freedom — the Kadets. The diocesan congress of clergy of Voronezh said that they found the desired principles only in the Party of National Freedom. Bishop Serafim of Cheliabinsk publicly joined this party, and in the city elections the clergy of Orenburg sided with it. *Propovednicheskii Listok* (*The Leaflet of Preaching*), published in Kiev, said that only the Kadets were taking a serious attitude toward the problems of the church. The influential liberal, Professor Titlinov of Petrograd, stated in his church periodical that "the party of the church is the Party of National Freedom" and that "Christian sympathies will be on the side that prefers evolution to revolution." Only a very few of the ecclesiastics, such as Bishop Andrei of Ufa (at that time quite liberal) spoke favorably of the Socialist Revolutionary party.[67]

In August the elections to the Sobor and the preparations for the elections to the Constituent Assembly caused a heightened interest in politics in extensive circles of the church. An article in an official church publication stated: "At the elections to the Constituent Assembly the church electors will doubtless be guided in their political orientation by a community of interests, and the attention of the

Party of National Freedom to the church question may bring it practical election results." [68]

Thus on the eve of the first All-Russian Sobor since the seventeenth century the church hierarchy was tending strongly away from radicalism. The liberalism and even radicalism that had appeared in sporadic outbursts in the first flush of the revolutionary spring had disappeared by midsummer, and with few exceptions churchmen frightened by an army in revolt, an insufficiently sympathetic government, and a massive agrarian movement, sought security in more conservative political circles. Just when the overwhelming masses of the people, urged on by the Bolsheviks, were beginning to demand an end to the war and a drastic solution to the agrarian situation, the church was taking a firm stand for the rights of private property and for energetic prosecution of the war. Such clerical conservatism in the face of the rapidly growing secular radicalism boded no good for the peace of the church.

CHAPTER II

"To Save the Russian Power"

THE All-Russian Council or Sobor of the Russian Orthodox Church in 1917 was not a new institution in Russian history. Before Peter the Great there had been a number of Sobors, and although there were none after 1681, the idea remained alive. Indeed, the idea of *sobornost'* is basic in the Russian church — namely, that the church consists of the sum of its members, both lay and clerical, and that supreme ecclesiastical authority resides in councils representing all the faithful, and not merely in the hierarchy. During the Revolution of 1905 hope of a Sobor grew strong; although frustrated by a suspicious Autocrat, it reappeared after his fall. Over-Procurator L'vov obtained wide support for his projected Sobor from the numerous diocesan congresses in the early months of 1917, and after the old Synod had been dismissed the way was clear. At L'vov's request, on May 8 the Synod issued a call for a Pre-Sobor Council to consider a wide range of church problems, from the election and functioning of the Sobor to religious education, the organization of the diocese, the parish, and similar matters. This body, composed of bishops, clergy, and laymen, included the best minds of the church, drawn chiefly from the theological academies.[1]

On August 12, with the permission of the Synod, the Pre-Sobor Council issued a long list of problems for solution by the Sobor. A final, lengthy paragraph dealt with "the difficult circumstances now experienced by our Fatherland. . . ." The situation was serious, it declared, and "only the voice of the Mother-Church could bring people to their senses. . . . The work of bringing the Russian land to sanity, so necessary at present, is possible only on a religious basis. From the Sobor is awaited a mighty call to the people to turn to God and the

26

establishment . . . of a day of public prayer to the Lord for saving
the Fatherland and bringing the erring to reason. . . ."[2]

While the Synod announced on April 29 that the Sobor would
meet, in Moscow, the call for the elections was issued on July 15.
Most of the members were elected, two ecclesiastics and three laymen
from each diocese, by indirect voting. Delegates were also elected by
the monastics, by the theological academies, the army and navy chaplains, and the universities. In addition, the bishops of the dioceses and
the members of the Pre-Sobor Council were ex officio members. In
all there were 265 clerical members and 299 laymen.[3]

The elections began late in July, at a time when most Russian
churchmen were turning strongly to conservatism. The collapse of the
army's morale, the rise of Bolshevik influence, and the growing agrarian disorder, by which not a few priests had been personally affected,
had convinced most members of the church community that the revolution was going too far and that the church should exert a calming
influence. According to Kartashev, Minister of Confessions at the
time, at the election meetings the speeches were predominantly conservative and the electors and delegates chosen were for the most
part men of moderate or Rightist views. The split between lower and
upper clergy had largely disappeared, and the Sobor represented a
conservative church opinion, which was becoming more and more
conservative.[4]

Most of the clergy in the Sobor were from the upper levels of the
church organization — metropolitans, archbishops, bishops, abbots,
priors, and deans; only 91 out of the 265 ecclesiastics were simple
priests or lower. As for the laymen — professors and instructors,
chiefly from theological institutions, were the most numerous category, with officials not far behind. There were 11 military men, 9
counts and princes, and 8 capitalists. Forty-three of the members were
listed as peasants; only 6 were workers.[5] Thus the Sobor, whose members frequently claimed to speak for all the one hundred fifteen
millions of Orthodox inhabitants of the empire, actually was heavily
weighted in favor of the upper strata of society.

Although the Sobor had been called primarily for ecclesiastical reasons, from the beginning it was of political importance. More and
more, conservative citizens, and many of the Sobor itself, felt that it

should serve as a rallying point for those who wanted to preserve military discipline, uphold law and order, and fight agrarian and political extremism. At the service opening the Sobor on August 16, Protopresbyter Liubimov delivered the sermon, in which he stated that it was the duty of the Sobor to give wisdom and inspiration to the people. "For our mother is being ruined, our native, Russian fatherland, not so much overcome by a ferocious foreign foe as storm-swept from within by various winds of false teachings, unbelief, rebellion, and passions. . . . Where to seek salvation from the storms of life and liberation from those grievous failings that gain control of it? Where, if not in the church of Christ? . . ." [6]

After the religious ceremonies, various greetings to the Sobor were read. Metropolitan Tikhon, speaking for the diocese of Moscow, said: "Now our native land is in ruin and danger, almost on the verge of destruction. How to save it — this question is the subject of hard thinking. The many-millioned population of the Russian land trusts that the Church Sobor will not remain inactive regarding that grievous condition which our native land now experiences." [7] S. K. Rodionov, speaking for the Moscow zemstvo, warned of the mutinous state of the army, the "selfishness, the thirst for power" of many in the rear. "Where is the voice that might stop the Russian people, unbridled in their lusts, where is the voice to say: 'Halt, brothers, we are being ruined in the frenzied dance of riotous passions!' Let this sobering voice speak out here, within the walls of the church, . . . let this voice powerfully proclaim: 'Stop, join together as one in the name of salvation of the Native Land. . . .'" [8] Similar speeches were made by Dean Lakhotskii, who said, "May the Lord grant that the Sobor be the beginning . . . of reuniting the sundered and ruined greatness of our fatherland," and by M. V. Rodzianko, former president of the Duma. A representative of the League of Officers of the Army and Fleet declared: "The All-Russian Church Sobor should help, and should be able to awaken the true sons of Russia from the terrifying nightmare. We officers believe that they will awaken and that Russia will be saved." [9]

As a result of these appeals for action, on the following day the chairman, Metropolitan Vladimir of Kiev, called for national unity in the face of internal disorder. V. N. Shein, a noted conservative, asked the Sobor to utter a flaming prayer for setting the church in order and for the salvation of Russia. He suggested prayer by the whole people for victory for the Russian army and for salvation for the Russian church and the Russian land. A similar speech was made by Prince A. G. Chagadaev, Shavel'skii followed, with a long speech about the collapse of the army, to which the Sobor should appeal "with a most fiery and decisive proclamation." He also suggested an uninterrupted flow of leaflets to the army and that preachers be dispatched to the Moscow garrison and populace. Finally, he suggested that on August 28 a day of nation-wide prayer be set, for saving the fatherland and for bringing the erring to their senses.[10] This proposal was supported by Count Apraksin, Professor Abramov, and Prince E. N. Trubetskoi.[11]

On the next day, August 18, an impassioned appeal for such a proclamation was made by the famous preacher, Father Vostokov:

> When children see their mother wounded, it is no time for juridical considerations. Our native land has been poisoned, beaten, and lies in blood. There are her wicked children, who divide her bloody garments. But among the Russian people there are also valiant, honorable sons, who perform their deeds of love. They suffer for their motherland, they die for her. Our obligation is to uphold her honorable children and clearly, decisively, to rebuke her criminal children. . . . If we should speak, then we should speak as spoke the saints of old. . . . We should call by their right names the phenomena that are destroying our motherland.[12]

As no opposition to these proposals was voiced, on August 24 the Sobor issued two messages: one to "the All-Russian Christ-loving troops and fleet," and the other to "all Orthodox Russian people." The first of these painted a black picture of the military situation, with whole regiments deserting and turning upon the defenseless civilians, abandoning their positions to the foe. "German spies and hirelings and our betrayers and traitors from the rear have poisoned the mind of the army and have torn its heart." Appeals were made to these betrayers of the nation to return to duty, with grim threats of the people's eventual vengeance if they did not. To the men who had listened to temptation or who had succumbed to cowardice, a special plea was made, to be worthy of the name of Russian soldier. "The foe is at the door. . . . Great Rus is at the verge of destruction. The native land calls you — save her!" "Go, brothers, to save her! Forget party quarrels and feuds. . . . Merge into one united family, mighty in love for the native land, and in the name of Christ ready for all sacrifices for her salvation." [13]

The second message — "For Saving the Russian Power" — likewise stressed the calamities Russia was suffering and begged the people: "Orthodox! In the name of Christ the Sobor beseeches you. Awaken, take thought, cast aside your mutual hatred and internal strife, stand up for Russia. . . . Do not permit the Native Land to be outraged to the shameful end." Finally, after appeals to all classes and groups of citizens to contribute to the nation's cause, the message ended with the words: "May holy Rus again rise up in a great deed of self-sacrifice and of Christ's love." [14]

Undoubtedly the Sobor's keen interest in restoring military discipline and in checking the drift toward radicalism was heightened by the growing political crisis. When the Sobor met in mid-August, the great Bolshevik demonstration of July was still fresh in men's minds, and, although the radical wave had been checked, the conservatives had little confidence in Kerenskii's ability to control the country. At the Moscow State Conference, which coincided with the opening of the Sobor, there was a sharp split between the moderate supporters of Kerenskii and the conservatives who advocated a dictatorial government under the fiery General Kornilov. Archbishop Platon, chairman of the Synod, speaking as representative of the church, immediately after Kornilov had demanded vigorous steps to restore order, optimistically stated that, in spite of the decline of the army, "God is with us." Three centuries ago, he said, Russia had been similarly threatened, but "its best people gave to their chosen one [the first Romanov tsar] autocratic powers. . . . By this their act our fatherland, our people, testified to their political maturity and to their coming of age." [15] Although the archbishop did not mention Kornilov by name, he was obviously pleading that he be granted dictatorial powers.

At the session of the Sobor on August 17, Prince G. N. Trubetskoi read a message from Kornilov, asking that the Sobor support the army with its prayers.[16] In answer, the Sobor sent him a telegram calling

. . . the blessing of God upon you, the valiant Russian army, and fleet.

We pray to the All-Highest for reviving the spirit of limitless love for the church and the native land among our Christ-loving warriors, for giving victory to the Russian arms. May rear and front unite in prayer for long-suffering Russia and in firm hope of God's aid! May the revival of the conciliar principle now beginning in the Russian church serve as a guarantee of the strength and firmness of the Russian Power!

Chairman of the Sobor, METROPOLITAN
TIKHON OF MOSCOW[17]

A few days later Kornilov launched his attempt to capture Petrograd; according to two liberals active in the church at the time, the Sobor, filled with joyous expectation, debated in closed session the question of declaring for him. As, however, the first reports indicated that the attempt was not succeeding, the Sobor decided to await developments rather than take a position of outright support for him. Afterward, however, it showed its sympathy with Kornilov's undertaking by asking the Provisional Government to show mercy to those involved.[18] Protopresbyter Shavel'skii, a member of the Sobor, wrote in 1922: "The attitude of the church toward the revolution was clearly expressed at the All-Russian Church Sobor. . . . The intercession of the Sobor for Kornilov is doubtless also remembered, as for a fighter against the collapse of the army and of the popular masses." [19]

Although the failure of the Kornilov coup left the Sobor with only the Bolsheviks and Kerenskii to choose between, its relations with the Provisional Government were not cordial. To be sure, Kartashev, Minister of Confessions, told the Sobor that his right of control would remain largely nominal,[20] and the Provisional Government granted one million rubles to the Synod for the expenses of the Sobor (much as it had aided other all-Russian congresses of that summer),[21] but the Sobor felt that the government was not sufficiently sympathetic. For one thing, a law of July 20 put the parochial schools under state control, much to the anger of the churchmen. Also the Ministry of Education showed a tendency to slight religious education in the public schools, whereas the Sobor felt it should be compulsory. In September the Sobor voted to send a strong telegram to Kerenskii asking the government to defer action on religious teaching in the schools,[22] and soon after voted to ask the government to return the parochial schools to the church.[23] These representations achieved little, so in October a deputation from the Sobor went to Kerenskii to present their petition in person. Although the appointment had been carefully arranged, the premier kept them waiting for forty minutes, and when he did receive them, failed to display the respect for the clergy the delegation felt was proper. While he expressed willingness to compromise on religious teaching in the schools, he refused to return the parochial schools. The members of the delegation felt that the government was no longer sympathetic. "The Russian state is breaking the ties with the church of Christ." [24]

In spite of the lack of cordial relations with the Provisional Government, however, the Sobor continued to be even more disturbed by the unsettled political and agrarian situation and to issue proclamations, prayers, and appeals, with the object of quieting the populace. Thus late in September a group of members proposed a message to the workers, beseeching them, in the name of the church, to renounce class conflict, social hostility, and exaggerated demands for benefits for themselves, to the detriment of all the rest and, above all, of the state. The Sobor voted for the message, which, without condemning socialism, warned against extremes and distortions, "to say nothing of manifestations of violence. . . ." The message, to be read the following Sunday in churches in workers' settlements, was to point out "the necessity of subordinating private interests to the good of the fatherland and to the highest national problems." [25]

Although appeals such as these had important political implications, the Sobor always regarded them as nonpolitical in character. Consequently, when fifty-two members signed a petition urging that the Sobor take the frankly political step of publishing a message asking the election of "men loving the holy church and their native land" to the Constituent Assembly, it touched off a long debate. Most of the speakers favored the proposal, feeling that, provided no political party was endorsed, the Sobor should speak, as it could not leave the Orthodox without guidance.[26] Count Apraksin made a characteristic speech for the measure: "The village is being flooded with agitators and party literature; a mass of proclamations comes from various nationalities, and only the Great Russian nationality is silent. . . ." Abbot Matfei declared: "The Sobor looks with hope at the firm tie of church with state, and stresses the bond for the future as well." After mentioning the services of ancient churchmen in helping to found the Russian state, he concluded: "I beseech the Holy Sobor that we . . . should emulate their labors and deeds in founding the might and the glory of Russia." [27]

Voices were raised in opposition to the proposal. The liberal Professor Titlinov, speaking for a group, warned that the Sobor was called for church matters, not for political problems. F. G. Kashenskii, who recalled that the clergy had incurred public disfavor by their role in the Third and Fourth Dumas, added: "The Lord has already saved the Sobor from speaking out in respect to the Kornilov affair. May He also turn the Sobor from this political step, which may be ruinous for our Orthodox church. . . ." [28]

These warnings received scant consideration, as the Sobor believed that it was entitled to give advice to the faithful. One speaker struck a popular note by saying: "Oh, if only it [the message] might bear the signature of a Patriarch! " [29] The proposal was adopted, and a commission of five was named to prepare the message. [30]

The proclamation, read to the Sobor on September 30, stated: "We believe that the Russian Power will stand only as long as it has not been false to the faith of Christ and has not set itself apart from its basic principles," and warned, "It is known to all how stubbornly the spirit of the prince of this world struggles against . . . [faith], attempting to establish its kingdom by the lure of earthly, temporal blessings." To this Professor S. N. Bulgakov, who read the message, added his hope that the Russian people "may not fall into the all-destructive power of the spirit of Antichrist. . . ." [31] These veiled references were undoubtedly directed against the Bolsheviks and other radical groups.

Not long after this, the Sobor published its proclamation to the people concerning agrarian attacks, calling on them to obey the laws and to wait for the Constituent Assembly to solve the land problem. After citing a number of attacks on churches, monasteries, and estates, it warned against the incitements of "sly false-teachers, who egg people on, one against the other, and against their spiritual fathers." [32]

The Sobor printed these proclamations in considerable quantity. In October the members were told that there were available numerous copies of these messages (including forty thousand of the appeal concerning the Constituent Assembly), as well as a "Ruling of the Sobor concerning the Fratricidal War Threatening the Native Land," and a sermon by Dean Spasskii.[33] In addition, members of the Sobor were sent to the fighting fronts in October, to distribute its proclamations and persuade the men to follow the advice given. Dean Rozhdestvenskii, sent to the Caucasus front, found the soldiers at Tiflis so suspicious and hostile that he sent the proclamations to the front by a chaplain and returned to Moscow.[34] Two others, sent to the Northern front, were eagerly met by the commanders, but, in spite of earnest appeals, they accomplished little with the enlisted men.[35]

Still another method was used by the Sobor to combat radicalism. On October 20, 1917, a leading Petrograd newspaper reported that, in expectation of armed outbreaks by the Moscow Bolsheviks, the members of the Sobor,

> in view of the evident disturbed attitude and the special significance at present of prayer by the Sobor for peace and love, have decided to take part in this church ceremony for strengthening and encouraging the people, in full array, including the hierarchs. The religious procession will pass out through the Spasskii Gates of the Kremlin, across the whole Red Square, earlier proclaimed as the place of Bolshevik assembly, to the Kazan Cathedral, where before the miracle-working image of the Mother of God, which will be brought out of the church, a *Te Deum* will be performed, for saving the fatherland from internal factions and from all foes and adversaries.[36]

The same newspaper reported two religious demonstrations in Petrograd. One of these had by chance encountered a Bolshevik procession with revolutionary banners and songs, whereupon part of the religious procession spontaneously turned toward the Bolsheviks, singing a strongly monarchist hymn as they advanced. The radicals at once scattered. The other procession, scheduled for October 22 at the request of Cossacks of the Petrograd garrison, was ordered by Metropolitan Veniamin, who was to participate. A *Te Deum* in the cathedral square was to be sung for saving the country, with special prayers "for ending internal faction and averting internecine strife." Later, a requiem was to be sung at the graves of the Cossacks who fell during the July Days.[37]

While the Sobor was thus strongly conservative in political and economic matters, it was also growing increasingly conservative toward church problems, to the dismay of the liberals in the church and the joy of the bishops. The right wing, with the conservative bishops headed by the ardent reactionary, Archbishop Antonii (Khrapovitskii) of Khar'kov, had great influence, although the center, led by Professors E. N. Trubetskoi and S. N. Bulgakov, did not always accept its program. The weak left wing comprised a few churchmen liberal in church matters, although conservative politically, such as Protopresbyter Shavel'skii and Bishop Andrei (Prince Ukhtomskii) of Ufa, and a group of professors from the theological academies, who were relatively liberal in both ecclesiastical and political matters.[38] The liberals were not united and had little following among the masses of believers, who were imbued with church tradition. Hence the upper clergy, aided by the growing fear of further revolution, were able to dominate the Sobor.[39]

The struggle between liberals and conservatives at times grew bitter. Bishop Andrei of Ufa, eager for church reform, was checked and denounced as a Bolshevik by the dominant element.[40] By the end of September the press was speaking of "the characteristic symptoms of turning to the Right" on the part of the majority,[41] and on September 27 in the debate on a message concerning the Constituent Assembly the Right defied all efforts of Professor Titlinov's forces to guide them along a liberal course.[42] Later the conservatives proposed to deprive Titlinov of the editorship of the *Vserossiiskii Tserkovno-Obshchestvennyi Vestnik,* official organ of the church. The debate grew heated and personal, and after hearing a bitterly sarcastic speech against him Titlinov allegedly expressed a desire to use his fists on the speaker. He was removed as editor, and not long afterward he resigned from the Sobor.[43] V. N. L'vov, writing in 1922, stated that during the Sobor the oppression of the liberal clergy reached such a degree that he and sixteen priests left the Sobor, followed by the representatives of the League of Deacons and Psalmists.[44] Such resignations naturally increased the predominance of the conservative element.

The main struggle in the Sobor, however, was over the patriarchate.

The restoration of this office, abolished by Peter the Great, was a favorite project of many of the upper clergy, who regarded it as a guarantee of their rights against the civil power. Archbishop Antonii of Khar'kov was especially eager for it and was believed to have hopes of becoming patriarch himself. The liberals, however, and many of the lower clergy, viewed the patriarchate as a threat to the conciliar principle and feared that it would result in monastic absolutism in the Russian church, resembling the Roman papacy. The question was debated, first in the Pre-Sobor Council, and then in the Sobor's committee on the higher administration of the church, where the chairman, Bishop Mitrofan, secured a vote of 56 to 32 in favor of the patriarchate.[45]

Although the Sobor received the project on September 11, it postponed debate until October 14. At that time a lengthy and heated discussion was held, with a number of professors advancing historical and theoretical arguments against the patriarchate, while the conservatives stressed the need for a strong head for the church. More and more it was argued that in that troubled period the church required a strong figure at its head, to protect its interests and even to serve as leader for the nation. "Undoubtedly, as was openly stated in speeches, many hoped to obtain in the Patriarch not only a head of the church, but also a national leader, whose living person might be a sort of center of attraction and unification of the raging elemental forces of the populace." [46] In presenting the proposal to the Sobor, Bishop Mitrofan argued: "In all disturbed times, in epochs of political storms, the idea of the patriarchate has revived with especial strength." Archbishop Anastasii of Kishinev stated: "A pastor is needed, to unite and bless us for undertaking deeds. . . . the head of the church is most of all in this world. Our church should gird on all the weapons of God, should become truly a militant church. . . ." [47] Bishop Mitrofan declared: "When war is going on, a single leader is needed, without whom the troops fall into disunity; we need an instrument for gathering together, for unifying Rus." [48] Father Vostokov and Prince Trubetskoi strongly urged the need for a Patriarch under the troubled circumstances then existing: "A Patriarch can have special and powerful means of influence upon the decisions of the government." [49]

The liberals continued to fight strongly, with Professor Titlinov (who had not yet resigned) delivering the chief speech on October 21, in which he again expressed fear that the patriarchate would lead to church absolutism. But neither he nor his supporters could sway the impatient majority.[50] Much more to the taste of the Sobor was the remark of Abbot Matfei, made at the session of October 25: ". . . winged by faith and grace, we shall confidently follow him [the Patriarch] into spiritual battle with Satan and his servants."[51]

On the same day the Provisional Government in Petrograd was overthrown by the Bolshevik forces; when the Sobor next met, on October 28, the fighting in Moscow was in progress. The chairman, Metropolitan Tikhon, performed a *Te Deum* asking "the bringing of peace to the Russian Power," and afterward urged the Sobor to continue its work, "as an aid to pacifying Russia."[52] He suggested that debate on the patriarchate stop, in view of the crisis, but strong protests caused him to permit speeches for and against the proposal. Finally, the Sobor voted that the highest authority in the Russian church would belong to All-Russian Sobors, to meet at fixed intervals; the patriarchate was to be established; the Patriarch was to be first among the bishops, with the others equal to him; and the Patriarch and the organs of the church administration would be responsible to the Sobors.[53]

Even these proposals, which were calculated to disarm the objections of the liberals, failed to mollify them. At the session of October 30, in spite of the sparse attendance caused by the firing in the streets and the belief of many members that no important business would come up, the proposal was made to begin immediate voting for the Patriarch. This, however, met with considerable opposition. The question of a quorum was raised, but Metropolitan Tikhon declared that there was a quorum and referred to the election of patriarchs in the past, when as few as 220 votes had been cast. The proposal to proceed immediately to elect the Patriarch then carried by 141 votes to 112, with 12 abstaining. Thus less than half of the Sobor, or less than a quorum, was present, and the vote in favor of immediate election was carried by less than one quarter of the Sobor's original membership.[54]

Nomination of candidates took place on October 31. On the first ballot Archbishop Antonii of Khar'kov was first, with 101 votes;

Archbishop Arsenii of Novgorod was second, with 27, and Metropolitan Tikhon of Moscow third, with 23. On the second ballot only the three leading contenders were considered; Archbishop Antonii received 159 votes, or more than the 155 necessary for nomination; Arsenii and Tikhon received 148 and 125, respectively. On the second round of balloting Arsenii was nominated, and it was not until the third vote that Tikhon was chosen to stand with the other two.[55]

The actual choice of the Patriarch was delayed until November 5, at which time an aged monk selected by lot the name of Metropolitan Tikhon from the urn in which the names of the nominees had been placed. Tikhon was at once proclaimed Patriarch.[56]

The choice of Tikhon seems to have been a great surprise to most members of the Sobor, for Archbishop Antonii, and to a lesser extent Archbishop Arsenii, had been looked upon as the logical candidates, as they were strong personalities and ardent reactionaries, in sympathy with the dominant attitude of the Sobor. Kartashev, Minister of Confessions under Kerenskii, calls Tikhon "modest, good-natured, not learned and not proud, but shining with Russian popular simpleness and modesty." [57] Dean Vvedenskii, writing when in bitter opposition to Tikhon, described him as "this humble man, definitely not noted for anything, soft, characterless, poorly educated. . . ." [58] While this estimate seems somewhat unfair, the new Patriarch apparently was not an outstanding or an aggressive man, although there is reason to think that his character was not weak.

Tikhon, who was born in 1866 near Pskov, had had a long career as a bishop, including eight years as Bishop of the Aleutian Islands and North America and seven years as Archbishop of Iaroslavl. In 1913 he became Archbishop of Vilna, but was forced to leave his see in 1915 by the German invasion. In 1917 he was elected Metropolitan of Moscow in place of the Rasputinite Makarii.[59] According to his foes in 1922 and 1923, during his stay in Vilna Tikhon had given considerable support to the violently reactionary Union of the Russian People.[60] In September, 1917, however, he was regarded as a possible candidate of the moderates for the patriarchate, as he was not identified with any of the factions.[61] He was not entirely unknown, for in August he had been elected chairman of the Sobor by a vote of 407 to 33; the "stars of the first magnitude," such as Archbishops Antonii of Khar'-kov and Arsenii of Novgorod, became merely vice-chairmen.[62] It seems probable, however, that by November the Sobor favored a more aggressive candidate, so that Tikhon was not the real choice of the gathering.

Nonetheless, the Patriarch was accepted by the church at its leader. After his installation on November 21, in a magnificent ceremony in the Uspenskii Cathedral in the Kremlin,[63] numerous ceremonial greetings were sent to him. The Petrograd Theological Academy expressed confidence that the helmsman of the ship of the church would guide it to a safe haven and that he might "inspire a spirit of unity and fraternal harmony in all sons of our suffering fatherland, in order that holy Orthodoxy and the Russian name . . . shall again shine forth upon the basis of the true foundations of the divinely protected Russian power." [64] Dean Khotoviskii, in an address after the ceremony, said that it was only the dawn of victory, "and the road to victory is still a long and very painful one. For never yet did a Russian Patriarch go into battle against so great a multitude of hostile forces that have taken up arms against the Lord and His Christ." [65]

During the interval between the Communist uprising and the installation of the Patriarch on November 21, the Sobor, in keeping with its earlier attitude, showed open hostility toward the revolutionaries. On November 1, while the fighting was still raging in Moscow, the Sobor sought to put the onus for the bloodshed upon the insurrectionists by sending a delegation, led by Metropolitan Platon and Bishop Nestor, to the Military Revolutionary Committee to ask that the fighting cease; "the delegation moved like a religious procession: bishops in mantles, ikons, lighted candles." [66] En route, some of the citizens crossed themselves and showed respect, but most of the soldiers and the Red Guards were openly hostile. "Why did you come to us? Go into the Kremlin, there is your kin, there the priestlings are fighting. They shoot from buildings, from belfries. We are many, but they are few." [67] Metropolitan Platon told the Sobor: "The soldiers, as was clear from the conversation, were disturbed by the fact that machine guns were set up in belfries. . . . At the time of my talk with Soloviev [the Soviet commander] an officer ran up and said: 'They found a machine gun in a church.' " [68] The Red leader at the committee head-quarters told the churchman that the Junkers (military cadets) hold-ing out in the Kremlin were the sole obstacle to peace and sent him back to the Sobor with a safe-conduct and a guard to protect him.[69]

When Metropolitan Platon reported his experiences to the Sobor, a proposal, signed by thirty members, including Archbishop Evlogii, advocated that the Sobor go in a great religious procession around the area of fighting, to bring it to an end. Several speakers made impas-sioned appeals for action. Father Nezhintsev said: "We must help our native land. . . . If a strong man should appear, who in an authorita-tive, mighty voice would say to all Rus: 'Stop, German, and stop, you internal enemies . . .,' millions of Russian people would hear his voice, and peace and quiet would be established in Rus." He urged a proclamation calling for a national mobilization to save the coun-try and appealed for a great sacrifice of treasure for the cause. "Don't say that this is politics! Forward for the salvation of the native land!" Prince Chagadaev spoke in the same vein: "Go, save Moscow, Holy Sobor! Show your face before Holy Rus, Holy Sobor, and justify the trust of the Russian people! This is our duty." Another speaker begged: "I ask you not to put off the religious procession for a min-ute. . . . Tomorrow, in the morning, let us go to the noble work of saving Russia!" [70] Cooler counsel prevailed, however, and the Sobor contented itself with an appeal to both sides to cease fighting and to refrain from acts of vengeance, as well as to spare the holy places of the Kremlin from artillery fire.[71]

As the fighting ended shortly thereafter, on November 4 the Sobor commissioned Metropolitan Platon and two lay members to negotiate with the Military Revolutionary Committee concerning neutraliza-tion of the Kremlin, the committee's co-operation in arranging the installation of the Patriarch in the Cathedral of Christ the Savior, and the right of the church to help protect the holy things of the Kremlin. On November 8 Metropolitan Platon reported that he had done so with complete success.[72]

This moderate attitude upon the part of the Soviets did not, how-ever, deter the Sobor from issuing a new proclamation stating that great calamities had come upon Russia as a result of unbelief and hearkening to the promises of false teachers. For such men the fatherland did not exist, and they became capable of the foulest betrayal of Russia and her allies. Only repentance and prayer could redeem the nation from the evil ways into which it had fallen. The message closed with the words: "May God arise and scatter His enemies and may all who hate Him flee from His countenance!" [73]

This message had little effect against the new Soviet regime. Neither did it irritate the Bolsheviks. On November 13 Metropolitan Platon visited the commandant of the Kremlin, who treated him courteously and tentatively approved his proposal for a religious service over the graves of the Junkers killed in the civil strife. The commandant also agreed to place guards over the sacristy of the Uspenskii Cathedral, and when Metropolitan Platon expressed grief at the posters displayed there, the commandant agreed that they were not suitable for that place. [74]

The requiem over the graves of the Junkers was duly held. Some of the people attending, however, felt that it was discrimination for the Sobor to pray for the fallen Junkers and not for their opponents. Remarks were overheard by members of the Sobor: "They came to the rich, but refused to come to us." [75] When this was reported to the Sobor, there was a heated debate over the question of whether to say a requiem for the fallen Reds. Finally it was decided to do so, and Metropolitan Platon asked the Military Revolutionary Committee whether such a service would be permitted. The Presidium of the Moscow Soviet replied that it regarded such a service as a private matter in which it did not propose to interfere. Consequently the Sobor arranged the service and issued a proclamation stating that, although it regarded the nonreligious burial of men who had profaned the holy things of the Kremlin, had raised the banner of fratricidal strife, and had disturbed the popular conscience, as "an open and conscious outrage to the church and a lack of esteem for holy things," nevertheless the Sobor did not wish to deprive relatives of the departed of the consolation of the prayers of the church. Hence it was arranging a funeral service over the graves. [76]

In spite of the relative ease with which the Bolsheviks had seized power, apparently the Sobor felt that the Soviet regime was merely a passing episode, for on November 17 it voted that the members should distribute the proclamation concerning the elections to the Constitu-

ent Assembly.[77] Several days were spent in preparing recommendations for the Constituent Assembly concerning relations between
church and state. These desiderata held that while the Orthodox
church should be internally free, in its relations with the state it should
enjoy special prerogatives. The church's rulings on marriage and
divorce should receive state sanction; church property should be in-
violable and free from taxation; the church was to have parochial
schools, and religious instruction was to be compulsory in all schools.
In addition, the church was to receive financial support from the
state.[78]

The Sobor further displayed its contempt for the Soviet regime. On
November 17 it issued a message to the people concerning peace, stating that certain men, who had seized power by force of arms, had
had the audacity to open peace talks with Germany on the eve of the
Constituent Assembly. The members of the Sobor, "as lawfully
elected representatives of more than one hundred millions of the
Orthodox population of Russia," felt it necessary to repudiate such
action. Russia was eager for peace, but these persons had not been
elected and were not empowered to make peace. The war could
be ended only in agreement with Russia's allies; a peace made
on any other basis "would be treason to our allies, betrayal
of our coreligionist peoples, and might plunge Russia into
most bitter calamities, from which may the Lord God preserve
her." [79]

This venture of the Sobor into the field of international relations
did not bring retaliation from the Soviet authorities, who apparently
had more important matters to deal with. They had issued no legislation relating directly to the church or to religion (although some of
their early measures, such as the Land Law, affected the interests of
the church). Moreover, they showed no intention of dispersing the
Sobor, and, as already stated, on November 21, several days after the
above proclamation, the Moscow Soviet permitted the installation of
the Patriarch to take place in the Uspenskii Cathedral in the Kremlin,
the military center of Moscow. Nevertheless, the utterances of the
churchmen on that occasion (which have been discussed above), like
the earlier actions of the Sobor, suggest that the leaders of the church

had no intention of accepting the Soviet regime. The Communists, on the other hand, were fundamentally hostile to religion. Consequently the future would certainly bring a contest between the new government and the church.

CHAPTER III

Decrees and Anathemas

THE POSITION of the churchmen toward the revolutionaries had been clearly defined by the time of the installation of the Patriarch: The Bolsheviks were German hirelings, betrayers of the fatherland, men who led the simple people astray by false promises of worldly blessings, haters of Christ. For their part, the Communist leaders had a definitely hostile attitude toward religion and the Orthodox church in particular, formulated well before the October Revolution.

In a famous passage Marx states: "Religious belief is at one and the same time an expression of real poverty and a protest against real poverty. Religion is the sigh of an oppressed creature, the soul of a heartless world, the spirit of timelessness. It is opium of the people." [1] Engels wrote in *Ludwig Feuerbach:* "Christianity has entered its last stage. . . . It has become more and more the exclusive property of the ruling classes, used by them as a bridle for the lower classes." [2] In *Deutsch-französische Jahrbücher* he wrote: "We wish to make a clean sweep of all that presents itself as supernatural and superhuman. . . . We have then declared war once and for all on religion and on religious conceptions. . . ." [3]

Similarly, Lenin was outspokenly hostile to religion. When a conservative Moscow newspaper declared that religion made it easier for people to perform obligations without complaining and gave courage to bear grief and privation, Lenin gleefully stated that that was just what he had been saying; when the masses have to bear heavy burdens and a tiny minority enjoys wealth and power, "then fully natural is the sympathy of the exploiters for religion, which teaches us 'uncomplainingly' to bear the earthly hell for the sake of the alleged heavenly paradise." [4] Or as he wrote in another context, "Who con-

44

soles a slave instead of raising him up to an uprising against slavery, helps the slaveholders." [5] When the Social Democrat Surkov, speaking in the Duma against approval of the Synod budget in 1909, declared that many of the reactionary churchmen "both by word and by silence sanctified the soaped noose, shootings, the scaffold, the gallows, butchers," [6] Lenin declared that ". . . the speech of Comrade Surkov is excellent and should be distributed by all organizations." [7]

It was not, however, only the Orthodox church that Lenin opposed. He wrote that Tolstoi's "new, purified religion" was "a new, purified, refined poison for the oppressed masses." [8] As he explained in 1909,

> Marxism is materialism. As such, it is mercilessly hostile to all religion. . . . We struggle against religion. This is the ABC of all materialism and consequently of Marxism. But Marxism is not materialism that stops at ABC. Marxism goes further. It says: you must know how to struggle against religion. . . .[9]

On the other hand, the infrequent references to religion in Lenin's writings indicate that he regarded it as of secondary importance. Indeed, in the 1909 article quoted above he expressly warns against exaggerating the importance of the religious struggle; it should always be viewed in relation to circumstances. If hostility to religion is stressed during a strike by both religious and nonreligious workers, many of the religious will be alienated. An anarchist who preaches war against religion at all cost aids the clergy. The Social Democrats had correctly stated in the Duma that religion is the opium of the people. "Should we go further, developing more in detail our atheistic conclusions? We think not. This might threaten us with exaggerating the struggle against religion on the part of the political party of the proletariat. . . ." [10]

In view of this doctrinal position, it is not surprising that the Soviet leaders were slow to move directly against the Russian church, but that when they did they showed no tenderness for it. The first blows at the church were indirect. No attempt was made to disperse the Sobor as the Constituent Assembly was dispersed, nor was the Patriarch interfered with. But on December 4, 1917, the decree nationalizing all land, including that of the church and the monasteries, damaged the church's economic interests. Actually this was largely a statement of principle, for by this time the peasants had seized much of the land, and the Soviet authorities could not exert effective control over this "national property"; but the legislation gave legal sanction to the seizures. Other laws followed rapidly: a decree nationalizing all schools, including church secondary schools and the theological seminaries and academies, which the Provisional Government had not touched; and another law reserving legal recognition to civil marriage and divorce only; the record books on births, marriages, and deaths were ordered turned over to governmental bureaus. Finally, on January 23/February 5, 1918, a decree on separation of church and state established the principle of the completely secular state, made religion a private matter, and deprived all religious bodies of their property, their legal status, the right to maintain schools, and all subsidies from the government.[11]

This law, like many others of the early Soviet period, was only partially enforced. The government immediately eliminated all religious ceremonies and objects from state life and stopped the state payments to the church, while the parochial and other schools were at once taken over. The ending of religious teaching in the schools was immediate. The action of the peasants wiped out much of the church's landholding, while the confiscation of the banks and the repudiation of the state debt and private securities annihilated most of the financial resources of the church. On the other hand, the new government had neither the personnel nor the organization to take over the registration of births and marriages, and the nationalization of the church buildings remained largely a dead letter for some time. Even the theological academies and seminaries were not interfered with, but continued to function until financial straits caused them to close.[12]

Some of these measures had long been demanded by Russian liberals and were actually in effect in progressive countries of the West — notably freedom of conscience, secular education, civil marriage and divorce, and withdrawal of state subsidies. The application of these measures, however, began suddenly and with little or no period of adjustment, so that the church received an abrupt shock. The cessation of financial subsidies meant little to most of the parish clergy, but the diocesan and central administrations of the church felt it keenly, as at the same time the church's investments and its cash reserves were confiscated,[13] and the seizure of monastery lands decreased the amounts received from these institutions. It is not surprising that the Sobor and the Patriarch, already bitterly opposed to the Soviet regime, displayed still more hostility.

In addition, individual churchmen suffered at the hands of revolutionaries. It was later charged by a special investigating commission of the anti-Soviet regime that in the restive Don Cossack region at least fifteen priests were killed between January and July, 1918 — usually by returned soldiers, Red Army units, and the like, rather than by orders of the Soviet government. Often these priests had "openly stood up against Bolshevism," or were charged with sympathy for the Cossacks and the Kadets. In the diocese of Stavropol likewise, the authorities, at least in the first months, did little against the church, although outrages against priests, defilement of churches, and similar abuses were allegedly perpetrated by sailors released from penitentiary battalions, by convicts, or by similar persons. Many of the clergy were arrested and some of them were killed. In one village Red Army men allegedly killed a priest because he had said a *Te Deum* asking salvation from the Bolsheviks; another, because he had preached that they were leading Russia to destruction.[14]

Elsewhere there were arrests of bishops, usually in connection with anti-Soviet demonstrations; in most cases the ecclesiastics were soon released. It is impossible to determine the basis for these arrests, but doubtless in some cases at least, local Soviet officials acted arbitrarily. The diocesan congress in Orel was banned in March, 1918. In several cities the authorities interpreted the law as banning all religious organizations, as, for example, in Smolensk, where the consistory was disbanded. There were cases where clergy were arrested for refusing to marry persons divorced by the civil courts or for refusing to give up church record books.[15]

An incident that especially shocked the church world was the killing of Metropolitan Vladimir of Kiev on January 25/February 7, 1918. Although he was living in the Pecherskaia Lavra (a famous monastery in Kiev) among eight hundred monks, a small band of men penetrated into his quarters, abducted him, and killed him, undeterred by the monks. In fact, although the Red commander Muraviev had instructed the monks to warn him at once of any such visitation, they made no attempt to give the alarm.[16]

These consequences of the revolution further antagonized the churchmen, who reacted strongly. Petrograd was the scene of one of the first tests of strength. In December, 1917, the Soviet authorities seized the Synod printing plant and closed chapels in two palaces and two government buildings; also a noted shrine was broken into (apparently by thieves). Metropolitan Veniamin called a protest meeting on December 11 and published a letter in local newspapers to the Council of People's Commissars, warning them "that the people would stand like a wall in defense of their holy things." A second meeting issued resolutions of protest and arranged for a religious procession to march on January 21, 1918. On January 13 a detachment of sailors sent by Mme. Alexandra Kollontai, Commissar of State Welfare, came to requisition the great Alexandro-Nevskaia Lavra (a famous monastery) but were induced to leave. Finally, after long negotiations, the government, in the face of opposition from the monks and lay supporters from the vicinity, merely sought to take part of the Lavra buildings for asylums for war invalids. When, on January 19, a commissar came with troops, pealing bells summoned a crowd and in the resulting confusion a priest was killed by one of the Red Guards. The sailors and the Red Guards were forced to leave, and not even the threat of machine guns dispersed the crowd.[17]

The scheduled procession was held on Sunday, January 21; according to the churchmen, Metropolitan Veniamin organized it at the demand of the people. In spite of warnings of possible trouble, the crowd insisted on marching: "We'll go, even into rifle fire." But the government wished to avoid another Bloody Sunday; Bonch-Bruevich, a noted Communist, declared he was not an enemy of religion and issued orders for the arrest of anyone who violated order during the procession. Automobiles drove along the line of march, scattering printed copies of the order. Everything went smoothly; a crowd of several hundred thousand is reported to have assembled for a *Te Deum* in the Lavra square, at which the metropolitan read a message from Patriarch Tikhon. On the march back to the Kazan Cathedral, where the metropolitan preached, the marchers appeared to be greatly aroused; a bystander was struck in the face for not removing his hat, and others had their caps knocked off. In his sermon the metropolitan declared:

We feared when we organized the religious procession that it would turn out badly, but the Lord, Who sheds light on good and evil, has sent us a little sun, and we are all alive and well. Hence we will all stand in the faith in readiness to suffer until death itself, as Dean Skipetrov [the priest killed at the Lavra] has shown us. . . . The deceased pastor was killed on the threshold of his archpastor, and you should unite around your archpastor; in this is our strength and victory.

In answer to this the crowd sang: "May God arise and scatter His enemies." [18]

The Patriarch's message read at the gathering was one published on January 19/February 1, while the Sobor was away for the Christmas holidays. It told of the evils endured by the church at the hands of "the open and concealed enemies of Christ," who had aroused the people to crimes of violence and bloodshed, forgetting Christ's commandments.

Think what you are doing, you madmen! Stop your bloody outrages! Your acts are not merely cruel, they are the works of Satan, for which you will burn in hell-fire in the life hereafter and will be cursed by future generations in this life.

By the authority given me by God I forbid you to partake of the Christian Mysteries, I anathematize you, if you bear a Christian name and belong, if only by birth, to the Orthodox church.

I call on all of you, believing and true sons of the church, to stand in defense of our Holy Mother, now outraged and oppressed. . . . And if it should be necessary to suffer for the cause of Christ, we call on you, beloved sons of the church, we call you together with ourselves to these sufferings. . . .

And you, brother archpastors and pastors, without delaying in your spiritual action for one hour, with burning faith call our sons to defend the trampled rights of the Orthodox church, immediately organize religious leagues, call them . . . to range themselves in the ranks of the spiritual fighters, who to external force will oppose the strength of their holy inspiration, and we firmly trust that the enemies of the church of Christ will be broken and scattered by the strength of the Cross of Christ, for immutable is the promise of the Divine Cross-

Bearer Himself: "I will build My church; and the gates of hell shall not prevail against it" (Matt. 16:18).[19]

On the following day the famous reactionary priest Father Vostorgov spoke in the church of St. Basil on Red Square, promising to preach the next day, "if, of course, after service or during the night they do not arrest or kill me." He told them of the Patriarch's message calling them to "the holy struggle for the church," and counseled those determined to go "without trembling in defense of the church against bayonets and rifle fire" to confess and receive Communion.[20]

On the following day, in a sermon "The Struggle for Faith and the Church," he told them that the Patriarch was calling them to this struggle against the forces of evil.

> Then — all into the churches! All — to prayer meetings, . . . on streets and squares! By religious processions, petitions, declarations, protests, resolutions, messages to the authorities — by decisive force, by all that is permitted by Christian conscience, we can and are obliged to fight in the holy fight for faith and church, for the trampled treasures of our soul. . . . Let them then cross our dead bodies. Let them shoot us, shoot innocent children and women. Let us go with crosses, ikons, unarmed, with prayers and hymns — let Cain and Judas kill us! The time has come to go to martyrdom and suffering![21]

The Sobor reopened on January 20, 1918, with general expressions of approval of the Patriarch's utterance. Apparently the members believed that the Soviet regime, opposed by all the experienced public leaders and officials, could not endure, and, now that the Constituent Assembly had failed to galvanize opposition to the Communists, there doubtless was hope that the Patriarch and the church might do so. D. I. Bogoliubov said that the people were turning against the Bolsheviks and were willing to support the church. "And I pray to the Lord God that the Patriarchal message may serve as a sort of church tocsin, as that trumpet call which may turn public attention to the criminal actions among the people. . . . I welcome the Patriarchal message as a great national work, as a bright dawn of a better future in our life." In like fashion Prince E. N. Trubetskoi urged the Sobor to speak out. "Here is an open war against the church, not begun by us. On our part silence and inaction would be criminal. We must loudly raise our voices and arouse all the Orthodox people to the defense of the church. . . ." Dean Khotovitskii believed that this message might well lead to the arrest and execution of the Patriarch, but felt that the church should lead the people into the fight; ". . . for the people with us thirst for deeds no less than we; they already call us and ask how to save the native land. The hour has come when, following our Most Holy Father, the Holy Sobor should, offering themselves as a sacrifice, inform the people how they should act and whom they should follow." [22]

At its session of January 22 the Sobor approved the message of the Patriarch, expressing full unity with him and calling on the Russian church "to unite around the Patriarch, in order not to give our holy faith over to abuse." [23]

This resolution, however, did not satisfy the members, and they quickly proposed that the Sobor itself should issue a message regarding the decree of separation of church and state. Dean Tsvetkov, who made the proposal, expressed a wish that "the first encounter with the servants of Satan may serve as the beginning of the salvation of the native land from destruction and of the church from its foes. Finally, I would propose to name Bolshevism itself 'Satanism' or 'Antichristianity.' (Voices: 'Correct!')." [24] Several similar speeches were made, the most striking by the noted priest, Dean Vostokov. He declared that the Sobor must speak out concerning the ruinous nature of socialism and charged: "We have cast down the tsar and subjected ourselves to Jews. (Voices: 'True!' 'True!')." The chairman asked for quiet, and Vostokov continued: "The only salvation of the Russian people is an Orthodox, Russian, wise tsar. Only through the election of an Orthodox, wise, Russian tsar can we put Russia on the good, historic path and re-establish good order. As long as we do not have an Orthodox, wise tsar, we shall have no order, and the blood of the people will flow. . . ." Finally, he urged the Sobor to speak out against socialism and to say "that the Russian people have now become the plaything of Jewish-Masonic organizations, behind whom is seen Antichrist in the form of an international tsar, that . . . they are forging for themselves Jewish–Masonic slavery. If we say this openly and honorably this very hour, I do not know what will happen to us, but I know that Russia will be alive!" [25]

Shortly after this the decree on separation of church from state was issued, which further aroused the ire of the churchmen. The Sobor hastened to condemn the new legislation in a message complaining of the violence of the persons in power, who were "attacking the very existence of the Orthodox church." Now, "in fulfillment of this Satanic intent," the government, in the guise of aiding freedom of conscience, had legalized open violence against all religious denominations. In particular, church property had been nationalized, which meant that the relics of the saints, the holy crucifix, the Gospel, sacred vessels, and miracle-working ikons, were now at the disposal of all — of Christians, Jews, Moslems, and heathen. Also the financial resources of the church were wiped out, which prevented the maintenance of monasteries, church, and clergy. The confiscation of the church's printing plant made the proper publication of the Gospels and the service books impossible. The demand that all must fulfill their civic obligations in spite of religious outlook meant that priests would be compelled to perform military duty, forbidden by the rules of the church. Religious education was banned and the state completely refused to have any religious rites in connection with state activities. Hence the Sobor decreed:

1. The decree issued by the Council of People's Commissars concerning the separation of the church from the state is, under the guise of a law for freedom of conscience, a malicious attack upon all the structure of the life of the Orthodox church and an act of open oppression against it.

2. All participation, both in publishing this legislation hostile to the church, and likewise in attempts to put it into effect, is incompatible with adherence to the Orthodox church and will draw upon the guilty persons penalties up to excommunication from the church. . . .

. . . the Sobor calls upon all the Orthodox people now, as of old, to unite around the churches and monastic cloisters for defense of the outraged holy things. Both the pastors and the sheep of the flock of Christ will suffer abuse, but *God may not be abused*. May the righteous judgment of God come to pass upon the impudent abusers and oppressors of the church, and let all loyal sons remember: we shall have to wage a fight against the dark deeds of the sons of destruction for all that is dear and holy to us Orthodox and Russians, for all without which life has no value for us.[26]

This formal message was also accompanied by a pronouncement "To the Orthodox People," for more popular consumption. It termed the decree "full violence against the conscience of the believing," which would be worse than the Mongol yoke. If put into practice, churches would be taken away, the silver adornments would be stripped off ikons, the sacred vessels would be melted down and cast into money, the performance of the sacraments would cease, and the dead would be buried without rites. "Unite then, ye Orthodox! . . . Do not permit this frightful sacrilege to take place. If it should occur, then Holy Orthodox Rus would be turned into the land of Antichrist. . . . Better to shed one's blood and gain the martyr's crown than to turn the Orthodox faith over to its foes for abuse." [27]

On March 5/18 Patriarch Tikhon issued a new message, condemning the Peace of Brest Litovsk, just concluded with the Germans. The Russians had thirsted for peace, he said, but this was not the peace desired, as it left tens of millions of Orthodox people under foreign domination. At the same time, civil war and fratricidal strife were continuing, hunger grew worse, and robberies and killings were frequent. Consequently, he declared: "We are called by our conscience to raise our voice in these frightful days and loudly to proclaim before the whole world that the church cannot bless the shameful peace now concluded in the name of Russia. . . ." He urged his followers to hearken to the command of God, "which will correct the evil work that has been wrought and will return what has been torn away and will collect the scattered," and issued a call to "peace, quiet, to labor, love, and unity." [28]

In this message the Patriarch claimed to speak as representative of the Russian people and especially of those under German rule. While his position as head of the church gave him a legitimate interest in the matter, the propriety of his pronouncement on a political matter in the field of international relations is open to question, since the treaty could be undone only if the Soviet regime were overthrown. To the Soviet leaders this message of the Patriarch, like several of his utterances, probably seemed better calculated to weaken and subvert their power than to serve the vital interests of the church.

The latter conclusion is strengthened by the fact that on April 29, 1918, when Hetman Skoropadskii took power in the Ukraine with the aid of German bayonets, one of his first acts was to have a religious ceremony in the Kiev Cathedral in which Bishop Nikodim, a subordinate of the Patriarch, blessed and anointed the hetman and then went in a solemn procession into the cathedral square, where a *Te Deum* was sung, as well as "long life" to the hetman.[29] As far as can be determined, the Patriarch did not punish Bishop Nikodim for this pro-German act. Nor did he rebuke Archbishop Antonii Khrapovitskii when the latter, elected Metropolitan of Kiev during the hetman's puppet rule, according to Soviet writers, warmly supported the hetman's regime.[30] Indeed, the indictment of Patriarch Tikhon, drawn up in 1922 and published in 1923, and which the Patriarch admitted was basically true, charged that he was in close communication with Skoropadskii through one Krivtsov, agent of the Patriarch.[31]

Whatever the validity of the charges that Metropolitan Antonii and Patriarch Tikhon collaborated with the Germans in the Ukraine, it seems clear that, by the proclamations and messages cited above, the Sobor and the Patriarch declared open war on the Soviet regime and called on the faithful to fight it. Actually the measures of the Soviets were not as drastic as the churchmen alleged: while they did close churches or chapels in government buildings and in palaces, they closed few parish churches,[32] so that fears that they would be turned over to Jews, Moslems, or heathen were baseless. Priests were not drafted into the army, services continued in parish churches, and little was done to halt religious indoctrination.[33] The Sobor, however, continued to take such a militant tone and to sponsor measures so challenging to the Soviet authorities that it seems probable that these actions were intended to provoke violence and bloodshed, which might produce a great popular revulsion against the Soviets and sweep them away.

One such move was the organization of a great religious procession on January 28/February 10 to Red Square in Moscow, where the Patriarch was to perform prayers asking that the religious persecutions cease. The priest who told the plans to the Sobor stated: "We believe that there will be displayed a religious upsurge that will serve as a definite warning to the usurpers. . . ."[34] The Sobor discussed at some length the preparations for this demonstration; the members were urged to participate and to get the church brotherhoods, religious societies, and similar groups, to assume a leading role in it.[35] A special prayer was adopted for reading to the procession, asking God to save His true church from oppression and abuse and "to protect now our fatherland from the foes destroying it. . . ." An appeal to the people was also approved. "Be courageous. Rus is holy. Go to your Golgotha. With you is the Holy Cross, an invincible weapon. . . . 'Be ye faithful unto death, and I will give you a crown of life.' " [36] The procession was held as planned, with a great crowd participating, but no excesses occurred; the Soviet authorities did not accept the challenge.[37]

Samples of church propaganda for mass distribution also called for a struggle against the Soviets. A leaflet of this period warned the people that the Bolsheviks, not content with usurping the government, were laying their hands on the church: "According to their new decree, the Cross no longer belongs to the Church, nor the Chalice, with the Holy Sacraments, nor the ikons, nor the relics of the Holy Saints. All this belongs to the Bolshevik Commissars, who profess no religion themselves, and recognize no sacraments." It ended with the words: "They will abuse all holy things. Will you let them do this? Will you not now defend them, Russian people?" [38] A poster which was found on the walls of Petrograd on February 1/14 made an especial appeal to soldiers and Cossacks. "You ungodly ones, stop! . . . Consider well before you raise your hands against the Holy Cross! Know that no Christian soldiers will pierce the side of the Savior. . . . The hour is not far off when the wrath of the Almighty will descend upon you." *"You, soldiers and Cossacks, stand for the Orthodox faith just as your ancestors did in days of old. . . ."* [39]

The members of the Sobor felt that their defiance of the Soviet authorities and their calls to action would produce stern retaliation. Consequently, at the session of January 25/February 7 Prince E. N. Trubetskoi announced a proposal that the Patriarch be empowered to name his deputies, who should take his place if he were arrested and no Sobor could meet to elect a successor. These deputies were to be appointed by the Patriarch rather than elected, in order that their names might be kept secret. This proposal, occasioned by "the extraordinary events we are experiencing," was approved by the Sobor.[40]

The Patriarch also issued detailed instructions to the local churchmen concerning opposition to the decree of separation of church from state. The clergy were told to unite the believers and to encourage them to defend the church, chiefly by forming organizations of laymen to protect the holy things; these leagues were to be organized by parishes, and also by monasteries and religious educational institutions. If violence was done to the clergy, the parish was to be punished by being left without a priest. Church vessels and other valuables were to be protected against "outrage and theft," and whenever possible were to be kept in the church strongboxes, in well-concealed places. They should not be voluntarily given up, as they were consecrated. "In cases of attack of plunderers and robbers upon church possessions, call the Orthodox people to the defense of the church by ringing the tocsin, sending out messengers, and so on." When seizures occurred, the persons guilty were to be excommunicated and priests permitting the confiscations were to be unfrocked. Finally, marriage, divorce, and record books were matters for the church to control, although the civil authorities might be permitted to inspect the books and make copies.[41]

As a result of this urging, leagues of laymen were formed in many places. In Petrograd a Brotherhood for the Defense of the Alexandro-Nevskaia Lavra was organized, and parish brotherhoods with a total membership of 60,000. In Moscow similar groups were united under a general council. The person of the Patriarch was protected by a guard maintained at all hours by twenty-four picked defenders.[42] With the coming of Lent there were claims in the church press of a great rise in religious feeling; there were strong protests when the government finally carried out the law banning religious instruction in schools, and the religious press claimed that the Soviets would have to go to Canossa. Even Maxim Gor'kii's leftist newspaper *Novaia Zhizn'* (*New Life*) stated that the decree of separation on January 23 had gone too far and that the Communist leaders had not taken account of reality.[43]

Church agitation spread rapidly to the provinces. In Samara the clergy declared a three-day fast against the decree, whereupon the local Soviet jailed them for preaching against the authorities. In Iaroslavl a meeting of parish councils resolved not to let the authorities inventory the nationalized church property, and when attempts were made to do so, disturbances occurred, leading to martial law. In Voronezh the attempt to inventory a monastery caused the beating of a commissar and numerous demonstrations. In Orel there was an exchange of shots. In Tula a religious procession held in defiance of an official ban was fired on with 13 killed and many wounded. Religious processions in Khar'kov, Saratov, Nizhnii Novgorod, Orel, Viatka, Vladimir, and many other cities were accompanied by conflict. In Voronezh the churchmen defied an official prohibition against a procession; feeling ran so high that the authorities withdrew their opposition and issued a strong decree guaranteeing order, thanks to which violence was averted.[44] In the rebellious Don Cossack country Bishop Hermogen of Aksai sided so ardently with the Cossacks that he was arrested by the victorious Soviet forces, but was amnestied on the anniversary of the fall of the tsar.[45] A Soviet antireligious publication later declared that in the period from February to May, 1918, there were 687 victims killed in religious riots, to say nothing of persons wounded or beaten.[46]

These demonstrations of religious strength were impressive, but they failed in the larger objective. The Soviet government avoided a head-on collision with the church, and in spite of the fact that blood was shed, the masses of the people did not support the Patriarch and the Sobor in their hopes for a crusade that would compel the revocation of the decree of separation and might even "save the Russian Power." Indeed, the populace was not infuriated. The churches were still open, most of the priests were unharmed, the sacred articles were not abused, and the authorities showed no desire to make martyrs of ardent churchmen; even the Patriarch and the Sobor were not molested. So the confiscation of the church's land and investments did not arouse the masses to fighting pitch. Indeed, as the Soviet authorities gradually established their administrative machinery and brought the country under their control their position respecting the church tended to improve.

A curious episode in March, 1918, seemed to indicate a possibility of compromise, in spite of the innate hostility of church and state. On March 15/28, 1918 the Sobor heard a report on a visit by seven persons (four of them members of the Sobor), who had conferred in the Kremlin with three representatives of the government. When Samarin, former Over-Procurator, called the decree of separation of church from state an outrage to the church, one of the commissars said that they were not hostile to religion but in general benevolent toward it, including the Orthodox church, and that incidents harmful to the church were not intended by the commissars. They could not, however, annul the separation of church from state. The commissars welcomed the discussion with the churchmen and expressed the hope that by negotiations on the basis of the decree of separation the many mistakes that had occurred might be cleared up. The churchmen complained of several acts — the seizure of Synod capital, the closing of diocesan courts dealing with marriage and divorce, and the prohibition against teaching religion. For their part the commissars complained of the reactionary preaching of Dean Vostorgov and some of the bishops. But the meeting was remarkably amicable. The commissars expressed belief that the differences could be compromised, and one of them said: "We are attempting to construct socialism in Russia. Christ Himself was a socialist, and the only difference in our attempts lies in the fact that we are promoting socialism by means of compulsion." [47]

This interview made a strong impression on the delegation. Professor Kuznetsov said that the talk affected him more favorably than the discussion with Kerenskii in October, 1917, when their pleas had "bounced off him like peas off a wall." Kuznetsov told the Sobor that it

> should not ignore the Council of People's Commissars, as the *de facto* rulers of Russia, and [it is] . . . obligated, through negotiations with them, to do, in the interests of the church and the clergy, everything that appears possible. To judge otherwise means to summon the church to remain outside the real conditions of life and to repeat the mistake to which the Russian intelligentsia are so prone. The church, of course, should not take part in the political struggle; it should only pursue its higher ends, independent of any party program, and, of course, take account of the tasks of the moment.[48]

Malygin, another church delegate, also was struck by the attitude of the Soviet officials: "My impression from the talks with the People's Commissars was this: their attitude toward the church and its interests is benevolent."[49]

Several members of the Sobor were highly critical of the report of the delegation and their recommendations, but after the intervention of Metropolitan Arsenii of Novgorod, the Sobor gave them a vote of thanks.[50]

According to Professor Titlinov, who favored moderation toward the Soviet authorities, the talks continued for some time. A second note of the Sobor, after complaining of the nonreligious character of the government and insisting that it be Orthodox, dealt with specific grievances: the ban on religious teaching in schools, the loss of the church's juridical rights, the nationalization of church property, and the prohibition of subsidies to the church from local governments. The government was disposed to compromise on some of these issues, but it felt that nationalization of church property was part of the general revolutionary program concerning property and must stand.

It was conceded that the clergy might receive land for their own use on the same basis as other agriculturists, and that monastics who actually worked the land might form agricultural communes, but without special privileges. On the other hand, the invested capital and the taper factories of the church could not be returned without violating the general principles of the revolution. These limited concessions proved unacceptable to the church authorities; the talks were soon broken off, and the conflict was resumed.[51]

Apparently, however, the number of those who hoped for a *modus vivendi* with the Soviets was not insignificant, for on April 6/19, 1918, the Sobor issued a decree against those bishops, clerics, monastics, and laymen who, disobeying their superiors, had in church matters turned "to the civil authorities hostile to the church," thus bringing it harm. The Sobor admonished them to repent, condemning them as opponents of God, and threatened the ecclesiastics with unfrocking and the laymen with excommunication. Parishes displaying a hostile attitude were to be put under a ban, while recalcitrant dioceses were to lose the right to elect bishops.[52] Dean Vvedenskii, one of the liberal priests, says, however, that the Patriarch never dared enforce this ruling.[53]

The leading churchmen continued to oppose the Soviet government. In April Patriarch Tikhon proposed a special day of repentance for the people's sins, "expressing complete confidence that our great native land, through Christ and His church, must without fail be reborn and rise again to a new, free life." [54] In Petrograd a series of lectures by the author Merezhkovskii, Professor Bulgakov, and others close to the church hammered on the theme that "the hope of resurrecting Russia lies in a firm alliance of conscience and reason, of church and society, of religion and culture." [55] On April 13, 1918, the Petrograd diocesan journal called for the formation of a network of parish co-operatives, schools, and even courts. According to churchmen, "the general opinion was that the Bolsheviks would break their necks on the church." [56]

The Sobor supported this campaign by publishing, on April 5/18, "Measures Produced by the Persecution of the Orthodox Church now Occurring." Special prayers and requiems, on a nation-wide scale, were urged for those who were persecuted or had died as martyrs; religious processions were to go to the burial places, where the requiems were to be sung. Measures were suggested for recovering confiscated church property — churches, monasteries, theological schools — or for preserving what remained. Special brotherhoods of loyal men were to be formed, bound by written agreements to defend the church and its property; these organizations were to be united through an All-Russian Council of parish congregations. Efforts were directed toward greater dissemination of the propaganda of the church. Finally, the Sobor's message proclaimed that only the Sobor and the Patriarch might administer or dispose of the property of the church; no one else might do so — especially not "persons who do not even profess the Christian faith, or who even openly declare themselves to be unbelievers in God. . . ." [57]

On April 7/20 a new proclamation of the Sobor announced that the intended celebration of May Day would outrage the feelings of the Orthodox, as it coincided with Wednesday of Holy Week. Hence the faithful were instructed not to participate, but instead to fill the churches.[58]

In May, 1918, the Patriarch paid his first visit to Petrograd. The *Messenger* of the diocese, in a long editorial on his coming, stated that it brought a ray of hope amid the encircling gloom, for the Patriarch had repeatedly prophesied better things. The *Messenger* confidently predicted: "The dark cloud will be scattered," and "The holy fire of faith will save the native land." "Rise up, Russian people, like Job from his sores." The editorial prophesied a great miracle which would unite "fragmentary, sundered, and endlessly warring Rus." [59]

The Patriarch was warmly received by the Petrograd churchmen, who organized processions, *Te Deums,* meetings of the Brotherhood of Parish Councils, and similar activities. At a special service held at the Alexandro-Nevskaia Lavra he addressed the multitude, lamenting the low state of the northern city. "Great Rus, which astounded the whole world with her deeds, now lies helpless and suffers humiliation." Salvation would come, however. He reminded his audience of the deeds of their patron saint, Alexander Nevskii, who, too, had suffered humiliation, but had defended his fatherland against nonbelievers, winning brilliant victories over the foe. "Remember our land, once so abundant, . . . and now so poor. O Saint of God, by thy intercession before the throne of God save thy true servants. . . ." [60]

These and other militant utterances did not produce the desired effect. In spite of the elaborate preparations, there was no great outburst of popular fervor. The miracle hoped for did not occur, and the Soviet government was not compelled to change its methods.[61]

On the contrary. When the infant Soviet state had to fight for its life against uprisings, counterrevolutionary armies, and Allied intervention, its measures grew more drastic, both in respect to the church and regarding hostile secular organizations. The Constitution of the R.S.F.S.R., adopted by the Fifth Congress of Soviets on July 10, 1918, provided in section 12: "To secure for the toilers real freedom of conscience, the church is separated from the state, and the school from the church, and freedom of religious and antireligious propaganda is recognized as the right of every citizen." Furthermore, along with capitalists, merchants, former members of the police, criminals, and imbeciles, the clergy were deprived of the vote and the right to be elected — [62] which relegated them to the category of second-class citizens and entailed serious limitations as to rations, housing, and other matters.

These provisions doubtless indicated that the Soviet leaders felt that compromise with the church, which was clearly hostile, was now impossible. In the same spirit, on August 24 the People's Commissariat of Justice issued a long Instruction for carrying out the decree of "Separation of the church from the state and of the school from the church." The main part of this Instruction dealt with church and religious societies, which were to be deprived of all rights of juridical persons in accordance with the original law of January 23. Property for use in religious ceremonies was to be turned over to the local Soviets, which, after receiving an inventory of the property from the religious representatives, were to turn the property back to them for free use, provided that twenty persons were willing to assume responsibility for the property and its upkeep. The construction of new churches was to be freely permitted; but they would also become national property. One of the most drastic provisions of the law instructed the local Soviets to confiscate the funds and investments of the religious organizations and to receive their bank accounts from the State Bank within a two-week period. All the operations of nationalizing the churches were to be completed within two months.[63] Thus the churches lost all their savings and financial resources and were made entirely dependent upon the current donations of the parishioners. Subject to this limitation, however, the parishes had full opportunity to maintain services in their churches.

Other provisions of the Instruction provided for immediate taking over of the parish record books by local record offices known as ZAGS, and for the elimination of all religious services and objects such as ikons from state and public buildings. Public religious processions might be held, however, with the permission of the local Soviet. Finally, the Instruction ordered that all religious instruction cease in all public or private schools except in special theological institutions and that all buildings of theological and parochial schools be taken over by the local soviets or by the Commissariat of Education. These buildings might, however, be rented to religious groups to serve as theological institutions.[64]

This Instruction actually did little to change the legislation concerning the church; now, however, the Soviet authorities began actively to enforce it. Although, as will be shown, enforcement frequently lagged, thenceforth the measures of the government tended to become more rigorous, and while the parishes that complied functioned freely, the diocesan authorities and the monastic institutions found their position increasingly difficult. The willingness of the government to compromise concerning the legal position of the church, as professed in March, 1918, was now a thing of the past.

The increasing rigor of the Soviet measures, as well as the intensifying political struggle, moved the church leaders to issue new appeals to the Russian people. One such message, issued by the Patriarch on July 25/August 8, laid Russia's miseries to sin, which had called forth Satan out of the pit. Because of this the "once mighty and powerful Russian Orthodox people" was lying "stricken in the dust, trampled on by . . . enemies, burning with the flames of sin, passion, and fratricidal fury." To redeem the nation, the Patriarch named August 2 and 3 as days of nation-wide prayerful repentance. "May all the Russian land be washed as by living dew, by tears of repentance, and may it flourish again with fruits of the spirit." [65]

On August 30/September 12, 1918, the Sobor issued its final ruling, "Concerning the protection of the church's holy things from sacrilegious seizure and blasphemy." Contrary to the legislation of the Soviets, churches and the articles therein were termed the property of God, "in exclusive possession of the Holy Church of God." Forcible confiscation of this property was called "blasphemous seizure and an act of violence," which each Orthodox Christian was obliged to prevent "by all means available to him and not contrary to the spirit of the teachings of Christ." Those who aided such seizures or who were careless of their duty were threatened with excommunication. On the other hand, the parish meetings were permitted to present to the civil authorities inventories of the churches and their belongings, provided that those who came to verify the inventories did not enter the chancels, which would be blasphemy.[66]

The rules for the administration of church property adopted by the Sobor on August 24/September 6, 1918, also went counter to Soviet legislation, stating that church property was subject to the rules of the church and might be used only in accordance with its decisions. One section even provided: "Sums assigned for the needs of the Orthodox church out of the state treasury are expended according to the appropriation." [67] It is impossible to determine whether the Sobor expected the Soviet government to reverse itself and provide the church with state funds, or whether it was hoping that a new government would arise in place of it which would give the church the financial aid to which the Sobor felt it was entitled. It seems probable that the Sobor had in mind the latter contingency. In any event, this pronouncement did not indicate a spirit of conciliation toward the Soviet regime.

Late in August the Sobor, of late poorly attended, dissolved "because of lack of funds." While it was implied that another would convene inside three years, no provision for another Sobor was made. [68] Thus the Patriarch was left to struggle against the Soviet government with the aid of the new church administration created by the Sobor: the Synod, with members chosen for three- or one-year terms, and the Higher Church Administration, named for three years. [69]

In the greatly strained situation in the summer of 1918 many churchmen, disturbed by the arrests of clergy on charges of counter-revolutionary activity, looked to the Patriarch for salvation. An article in the Petrograd diocesan periodical declared: "We must at all costs recover our fatherland — this is our first and basic problem. You ask: 'But is such a task within the power of the church?' Yes, unconditionally, it is within its power, if only its children wish to help it. . . ." [70]

The Patriarch sought to perform this task. On October 13/26, 1918, he issued a message to the Council of People's Commissars, in which he used the text "All they that take the sword shall perish by the sword" (Matt. 26:52). In it he summarized a year of Soviet rule: a country running with blood, a shameful peace, ferocious civil strife, class hatred. "No one feels himself in safety; all live in fear of search, plunder, dispossession, arrest, shooting." He accused the authorities of unjustified arrests, of seizure and arrest of hostages, the execution of bishops, priests, monks, and nuns "not guilty of anything, but simply on the wholesale accusation of some sort of vague, indefinite 'counter-revolution.'" He also charged the commissars with encouraging people to plunder or confiscate lands, estates, factories, cattle, and personal belongings, and with misleading the ignorant into hoping for easy and unpunished gain, too often accompanied by killing and looting. "Where is freedom of word and of press? Where is freedom of preaching in church? Already many bold church preachers have paid with the blood of martyrdom. . . ." Particularly he complained of abuses against the church and the clergy: priests were mistreated, bishops were compelled to dig trenches, monasteries and institutional churches were closed without cause. The Soviets were blamed for a long list of calamities afflicting the country — the decline of once mighty Russia, breakdown of communications, starvation and cold. "Yes, we are now experiencing the frightful time of your overlordship, and for long its image, which has darkened in the souls of men the image of God, and which has impressed thereon the mark of the beast, will not vanish from it." He closed with a strong indictment:

> It is not our work to judge the earthly power; all power permitted by God would draw upon itself our blessing, if it verily showed itself to be "God's servant," for the good of those under it. . . . Now then, to you, who use power for persecuting your neighbors and for wiping out the innocent, we extend our word of admonition: celebrate the anniversary of your taking power by releasing the imprisoned, by ceasing bloodshed, violence, havoc, restriction of the faith; turn not to destruction, but to organizing order and legality, give to the people their wished-for and deserved respite from fratricidal strife. Otherwise all righteous blood shed by you will cry out against you, and with the sword will perish you who have taken up the sword (Matt. 26:52).
>
> TIKHON, *Patriarch of Moscow and All Russia*[71]

This message — according to Professor Miliukov, more passionate than his preceding ones — was almost completely political in character, and "undoubtedly was not of his own composition."[72] An appraisal of it written under the anti-Soviet government of General Denikin stated: "Every word of this message threatened death to the Patriarch, but he fearlessly sent it to Lenin and took all measures for its wide distribution." The Soviets put Patriarch Tikhon under house arrest, but took no other steps against him.[73]

There was basis for many of these charges. In the fall of 1918 Russia was in desperate straits, faced with all the horrors of civil war, hunger, and economic dislocation. The attacks on Lenin and Uritskii had started a wave of reaction, the Red Terror, and Soviet measures were marked by a ruthless severity not previously shown. The Cheka (Extraordinary Commission for Struggle against Counterrevolution and Sabotage) was taking hostages from unfriendly elements, to be shot at the first outbreak of counterrevolution; among them were priests and monks. Some ecclesiastics were shot on charges of having incited counterrevolution.[74] Possibly some were guilty of these charges; but, as the Soviet prosecutor Krylenko later stated, until November, 1918, the Cheka was not governed by any set rules as to jurisdiction or method of deciding cases. Especially during the frenzied period of crisis in the summer of 1918 it was "fully understandable that in the atmosphere of this unlimited power there could arise a number of excesses and abnormalities in the work of these commissions, which in their turn could not but produce a righteous reaction."[75] At this time Bishop Andronik of Perm met his death, cursing his diocese for not having defended him; also Bishops Hermogen of Tobol'sk and Efrem of Seleginsk, Father Kudriavtsev, and others — [76] whether for cause or not cannot always be determined.

In addition, according to a periodical of the Commissariat of Justice, in the early months local officials sometimes used unwise methods in dealing with the church. In one locality county officials had a troublesome priest arrested and the church sealed — a very incorrect procedure. As a result, the tocsin was rung and at the subsequent mass meeting speeches were made about "the Jews, the sellers of Christ"; the only Jew in the village was beaten, and the whole village marched in a procession to the county seat to protest the closing. A worker in Moscow reported in the press that in the province of Moscow religion was being fought by compulsory and undesirable means; people were compelled to renounce attendance at religious ceremonies under threat of dismissal from their jobs. When the clergy agitated against the secularized schools and induced peasants to keep their children at home, one locality imposed fines for unexcused absences and ordered the guilty persons turned over to revolutionary tribunals.[77]

Even more outrageous was the sacrilegious conduct of some Soviet supporters.

Thus, for example, they took away from churches church vestments, episcopal mantles, altar cloths — all these were sewn up into revolutionary flags and as if intentionally to outrage the feelings of the believers, were hung out in squares and in the busiest streets of city and village settlements. In Petrozavodsk, in the building of the former diocesan church, late in January a masquerade was held, at which two masked persons appeared in priestly robes, bishops' miters, with crucifixes and censers in their hands and cigarettes in their mouths. . . . In one city draperies from the biers of relics, as it were publicly, with the aim of discrediting the Soviet Power, were hung up to decorate the walls of the local office of Public Education. The removal of ikons from public places was sometimes performed at the time of special assembly of people, and this removal was accompanied by entirely senseless attacks against one cult or another.[78]

But, while some of the Patriarch's charges are thus substantiated by admissions of the Soviet authorities, the latter also preferred charges against high ecclesiastics, among them Patriarch Tikhon. Latsis, a Latvian high in the Cheka, alleges that in August, 1918, when a Latvian commander of Red troops in Moscow pretended in discussions with the British spy Sidney Reilly to agree to a *coup d'état,* he discovered that the heads of the church had agreed to sanctify the overturn by nation-wide *Te Deums* and sermons.[79] The indictment of Patriarch Tikhon mentioned above charged that in 1918 he was in close contact with the leaders of the counterrevolutionary conspiracies of the "Tactical Center" and the "National Center" and had blessed their work. It was also alleged that the Patriarch had had several interviews with the French agent René Marchand and with Oliver (Wardrop?), British Consul, in which he approved anti-Soviet plans, including the landing of Allied troops in northern Russia.[80] Another charge was that he had been a party to the plot to kill Lenin in 1918.[81]

In addition to accusations against Patriarch Tikhon, charges of counterrevolutionary activity were laid against many other ecclesiastics. A search of the quarters of the retired Metropolitan Makarii allegedly disclosed his ties with subversive societies and a proclamation calling on the people to rise.[82] Metropolitan Iakov of Kazan is said to have carried on agitation against the Soviets, including a message urging funds for the national (anti-Soviet) army and asking all able-bodied men to enlist.[83] In Nizhnii Novgorod, with the encouragement of Bishop Lavrentii, several of the monasteries allegedly became centers of counterrevolution and distributed anti-Soviet leaflets. Violence occurred at one institution, with one killed and four wounded, when officials attempted to inventory its property, and not long afterward the diocesan congress voted to print a proclamation urging the population to rise against the confiscation of the lands of the clergy. As a result, the bishop, who had approved the resolution, was arrested.[84]

Counterrevolutionary activity was also alleged at the parish level. In Riazan a priest was said to have ascribed a severe influenza epidemic to the wrath of God because He had been driven out of the schools. In Penza leaflets were distributed. "About the great new martyr, Nicholas" (the tsar), and "the sons of Satan — the Bolsheviks." In Tver twenty priests were arrested on charges of speculation, agitation against the government, and distributing reactionary literature. When Father Gal'kovskii, former chairman of the Union of the Russian People, was arrested in Vitebsk, many counterrevolutionary pamphlets, as well as weapons, were allegedly found in his rooms.[85]

There is no doubt that church leaders, secular and clerical, sought to combat the regime by publishing anti-Soviet literature. In June, 1918, Professor E. N. Trubetskoi, a leading figure in the Sobor, published a book *The Meaning of Life,* in which he termed the Soviet dominion "the kingdom of the Beast," and declared that the stronger the attempts to establish such rule, "the more must we Christians attempt to keep the state in our hands, to make it a serviceable weapon in the struggle against the principle of the Beast in the world." He went on to discuss the efforts of St. Sergii when the Mongol rule lay heavy on the land. "Did he prescribe to endure patiently the yoke of the men of violence . . . ? No, he blessed the leader of the Russian armies against the Tatars [Mongols]; he appealed to Dmitrii Donskoi: *Go boldly against the godless and thou shalt conquer!*" [86]

Even more incendiary was the message allegedly written by the reactionary Dean Vostorgov and printed in the official organ of the Synod for obligatory reading by the clergy to their parishioners. According to Soviet sources, it explained the rigors of Soviet rule "by hatred of the Jews and the Judaized, which is especially evident in the Lassalles, Marxes, Kautskys, Engelses abroad, and those with us who now control the fate of the church and of Russia. . . . By this is explained the ferocity and extremism — qualities always displayed by Jewish psychology." He asked whether the people would long tolerate such a government, and, answering in the negative, urged them: "Bless yourselves, beat the Jews, overthrow the People's Commissars." [87]

It is impossible to determine the truth of all the Soviet charges; it is, however, certain that during the imprisonment of Nicholas II and his family in Tobol'sk in 1918 the Patriarch was in touch with the former tsar through Bishop Hermogen of Tobol'sk and sent Communion bread and his blessing to the deposed ruler. The bishop was involved in monarchist plots to rescue the prisoners, although there is no proof that the Patriarch was also a party to them.[88]

When the tsar and his family were killed by the Soviets in July, 1918, the Patriarch announced to the crowded Kazan Cathedral in Moscow that "the killing of the Sovereign without a trial was the very greatest of crimes, and . . . those who do not condemn this crime will be guilty of his blood." Shortly thereafter the Patriarch, together with members of the Sobor, performed a requiem for the deceased.[89]

Even after this action, however, the Soviet rulers did not, as many churchmen expected, arrest the Patriarch. Dean Rozhdestvenskii, who was in Moscow at the time, states that the Patriarch drove freely around the city and performed service in various churches. Even after the Iaroslavl uprising in July, a critical time for the Soviets, he was permitted to visit the ruined Volga city; the Red commanders attended the reception for him, dined with him, and were photographed with him.[90]

When the Dean visited the Patriarch before leaving Moscow in December, 1918, he found that, as a result of his message condemning the Council of People's Commissars, the Patriarch was living in his own quarters under house arrest, with three Red Army guards on the ground floor. Tikhon was permitted to officiate only in his own chapel; later, apparently, he was permitted to go for drives and to walk in the garden.[91]

Unquestionably, during 1918 the Russian church fought the Soviet regime as a deadly enemy and sought its overthrow. The Soviets proceeded to enforce their measures affecting the church, but made no attempt to abolish the church or religion. If one may judge by the original objectives of the contenders, the church was the loser and the Soviets the victors, for the latter had accomplished their purpose of secularizing the state, and in so doing had not aroused the great popular revulsion the churchmen had confidently expected. The Patriarch and the Sobor at the very least had counted on compelling the Soviets to reverse their religious policy, while the major objective desired by many, of "saving the Russian land," likewise had not been achieved. Thus in the year of struggle the Soviet government had gained strength in relation to the church, but the latter was in a worse position than before. The struggle, however, was not yet ended, for while the Patriarch did not again seek to challenge the regime directly, the hopes of many of the churchmen were now centered in the civil war being fought in Siberia and in the Ukraine, and it was there that the next phase of the struggle took place.

CHAPTER IV

Soviet Measures Respecting the Church during the Civil War

From midsummer of 1918 until the end of 1920 the Soviet state was fighting desperately for survival against hostile Russian armies and troops of many nations. On several occasions its overthrow appeared imminent, and it was not until 1920 that the Soviet leaders could feel safe, although even then economic collapse made their position far from enviable.

At the height of the conflict, in 1919, appeared the first issue of a periodical, *Revoliutsiia i Tserkov'* (*Revolution and the Church*), published by the Eighth Division of the People's Commissariat of Justice, whose function was to "liquidate" the bonds between church and state. This organ became the medium for publishing legislation, administrative orders, interpretations, and similar documents affecting the church, and an expression of the official attitude toward it. Hence the first editorial, "Soviet Policy on the Religious Question," is a document of some importance.

The editor declared that religion was a tool used by the bourgeoisie to keep the masses in subjection, particularly under the tsar. The revolution, however, had ended this state of affairs by breaking the bonds of the state with the church and by encouraging the peasants to take the church lands. The decree of separation of church from state now regulated the position of the church, providing for freedom of cult and of belief and also free use of religious property. But the church had lost its special privileges and its economic position. Hence the religious organizations — especially the Orthodox church through Patriarch

71

Tikhon — had declared a crusade against the workers and peasants and appealed to "Kerenskii, Kornilov, Skoropadskii, the Constituent Assembly, the Czechoslovaks, the Germans, the French, the English, Zulus and Hottentots, Kolchak and Denikin." Anathema and war were proclaimed against the Soviets; the church joined the counter-revolutionary efforts of the White Guards.

In spite of this, Soviet policy was defensive. Churchmen were punished only for open counterrevolutionary activity. Education had been taken away from the church, but the parish churches were turned over to the believers for free use. The chief method of Soviet policy was to strip the church of economic power and to prevent it from organizing a capitalist, counterrevolutionary force. This defensive policy did not affect the mass of believers, but hit the upper clergy, many of them monarchist.

On the other hand, the struggle against "religious prejudices" was following a different course, as these could not be fought merely by decrees; the peasants were both revolutionary and religious. They would have to be taught to hold a materialistic outlook, for as long as they did not have this outlook, defeat for the new regime was possible. The backwardness of the Russian economy demanded more political understanding — hence the need to prevent the use of religion against the Soviet regime. Merely to combat the priests and to close churches would do no good, as the masses would be alienated thereby; rather the program should be to leave to the clergy their special function — the performance of divine service; all other functions must be taken over by the state.

The peasants and workers should be taught that there were two phases of Soviet religious policy: the positive enlightenment of the masses, which meant giving them modern technique and a materialistic outlook; and the crushing of the counterrevolutionary activity of the clergy.[1]

One aspect of the above program was the campaign to indoctrinate the masses with materialism — a long-term undertaking, which will be discussed subsequently. The effort to weaken the power of the church took the form of applying the decree of separation of church and state, which was done in the midst of the civil war; for while it had been issued on January 23, 1918, the detailed Instruction for enforcing it did not appear until August, and, in spite of the two-month time limit for putting it into effect, there was little systematic enforcement until mid-1919. After the publication of the Instruction, so-called "liquidation sections" of the Eighth (later the Fifth) Division of the People's Commissariat of Justice were attached to the executive committees of the provincial Soviets, but because of the size of the task, the shortage of proper personnel, the opposition of churchmen and believers, and sometimes sheer inertia, the work moved slowly. In the province of Tver a "liquidation section" was set up late in 1918, but its decree for carrying out the measure was not approved until two months later. Although the township executive committees were instructed to push the work, many of them failed to do so. In three cases peasants beat the officials who came to explain the decree. Nevertheless, early in 1919 a beginning was made; by mid-1920, however, the work was far from complete in this province.[2] In Petrograd also there was delay until the local officials appointed special instructors to each county executive committee for brief periods.[3] In Iaroslavl and Riazan,[4] as well as in other provinces, the progress was likewise slow.

By the time of the Eighth Congress of Soviets in 1920, however, the Eighth Division was able to report that this work was almost complete and had proceeded without real difficulty. The liquidation of the ready cash and the invested capital of the churches had produced a total of 7,150,000,000 rubles, according to preliminary figures from Russia, the Ukraine, the Caucasus, and Siberia.[5]

It should be stressed, however, that while the enforcement of the decree wiped out the investments of the church, the parish churches for the most part continued to function. A report from Moscow in October, 1919, stated that 534 groups of citizens had received for their use a like number of churches (probably of all denominations) and the religious articles therein. Over thirty million rubles in securities and cash, on the other hand, had been confiscated.[6] The nonreligious property of the church organizations in Moscow also was taken: 551 dwellings, 100 commercial buildings, 71 almshouses, 6 orphan asylums, and 31 hospitals.[7] In Krasnoiarsk, a city that returned to Soviet rule only in the winter of 1919–1920, by the end of 1920 some 262 out of the city's 520 churches (49 of them non-Orthodox) had been turned over to believers for use, while 22 institutional churches had been permanently closed. The remaining 236 churches, the greater part of them institutional churches, had not yet been dealt with. Most of the parish churches were among those functioning — [8] which fact seems to agree with the observation of the monarchist V. Shul'gin in 1920 that the Bolsheviks permitted all but the institutional churches of Odessa to be open.[9]

On the other hand, the Soviet authorities were not averse to closing parish churches if circumstances warranted. In 1919 the city and provincial authorities of Vologda appealed to the Eighth Division of the Commissariat of Justice for permission to requisition 20 of the city's 50 churches for use as schools. They stated that the growth of the city, the cessation of building during the war, and the needs of the military had caused a school shortage, so that the actual needs of the children could not be met in any other way, while the religious needs of the population could be met by the remaining 30 churches. The Eighth Division replied: "There can be no doubt, from the spirit of all Soviet legislation," that this was permissible, provided that there was no restriction of religious performance thereby. The local authorities were instructed to carry on the necessary propaganda among the local population, in order to prepare them for this step and to get them to adopt resolutions in favor of requisitioning the churches.[10] On another occasion, a general meeting of the citizens of Cheboksari voted to turn 8 of the town's 16 churches into schools.[11]

It is noteworthy, however, that occasionally the government even decided not to close institutional and monastery churches. Where the churches of monasteries or military garrisons were separate buildings and there was a popular demand for more church facilities, with groups of believers willing to sign contracts of responsibility for them, they might be turned over to the newly formed parishes. As for prisons and asylums, where the churches were always to be isolated, the religious needs of the inmates might be satisfied by permitting priests to come in to perform services at specially set times, using portable altars.[12]

Like the enforcement of the provisions regarding the parish churches, the turning over of the record books for births and marriages took some time. Although the original law decreed that the records were to be delivered to the civil record offices, this was rarely done, and, as before, most people went to the priests for recording marriages and births. Late in 1918 the record books were ordered turned over to the Commissariat for Internal Affairs, and by the beginning of 1919 they were firmly in the hands of the civil authorities.[13]

The question of marriage and divorce was more strongly contested. Although the Soviet government did not object to church marriages or to the refusal of priests to marry persons who had obtained a civil divorce,[14] divorce was made a civil matter. The Sobor had declared in June, 1918, that only the diocesan councils were entitled to handle divorce cases, which they continued to do. The Commissariat of Justice, however, ruled that by so doing these organs were assuming juridical rights denied them by law, and consequently the provincial executive committees were instructed on May 18, 1920, to close them, and when they did so, to bring the members to trial. Some of the bishops refused to give in, but the priests and the public seem to have accepted this ruling.[15] In February, 1921, the Novgorod Revolutionary Tribunal heard the case of Metropolitan Arsenii, Bishop Alexei, and the Novgorod Diocesan Council, on charges of carrying on counter-revolutionary propaganda through the diocesan journal and of violating the law by assuming juridical functions in divorce actions, charging fees, and similar acts. The court found the accused guilty and sentenced them to five years' imprisonment, but made the sentence probationary. The diocesan council was ordered closed.[16]

Shortly thereafter Patriarch Tikhon and the members of the Higher Church Administration and the Holy Synod gave a written pledge that, in accordance with the government's circular, "the carrying on of divorce cases and the trial, investigation, taxation, financial, economic, and administrative matters connected with them are discontinued in the diocesan councils, the Holy Synod, and the Higher Church Administration." [17]

Thus, although church marriages were still permitted and continued to be popular, the church was excluded from divorce cases; divorce was purely a civil matter.

Inevitably the question of religious education had to be settled. The decree of January 23, 1918, had laid down broad general rules, which still needed clarification: "Sec. 9. The school is separated from the church. The teaching of religion in state and public schools, as well as in private schools where general subjects are taught, is forbidden. Citizens may study or teach religious subjects privately." [18] The Instruction of the Commissariat of Justice of August 24, 1918, added little to this. It reiterated that religion might not be taught in any educational institution, but added "with the exception of special theological institutions." The Instruction further provided that all school buildings of the church should go to the local civil authorities. There was added, however, a Note stating: "These buildings may be turned over by the local Soviet . . . , on a rental or other basis, for special educational institutions of all religious faiths, . . . with the knowledge of the People's Commissariat of Education." [19] These two pieces of legislation, which expressly forbade the teaching of religion in the public schools and opened the way for special theological schools, merely mentioned private religious instruction as permissible for the general mass of Orthodox children. This important matter required further clarification.

Some light was given by an important circular of the Commissariat of Public Education on March 3, 1919, which stated: "Teaching religious doctrine to persons younger than eighteen years is not permitted." [20] This apparently contradicted the law of January 23, 1918, which provided that religious subjects might be studied or taught privately. Actually, what was apparently meant was that there should be no *organized* instruction in religion for the younger children, for a later ruling of the commissariat of Public Education, on April 23, 1921, ordered local officials of this commissariat "to take all measures to ensure that teaching of religion outside the walls of religious institutions to children up to eighteen should by no means come to assume the form of establishing regularly functioning educational institutions managed by the clergy." The educators were told to investigate the teaching of religion and to report to the commissariat. "The teaching of religion to children may not be permitted either in schools or in church buildings." [21]

To adults the law gave greater opportunities for religious instruction. The 1919 circular of the Commissariat of Public Education referred to above provided: "Special theological courses may be organized for persons of eighteen or over to prepare them for the priesthood, but these courses must be limited to special theological subjects.

For persons over eighteen separate lessons, discussions and readings on matters of religious doctrine are permitted, insofar as these do not have the character of systematic school instruction." [22] The Fifth Division of the Commissariat of Justice explained that the teaching of religion to persons of eighteen or over was not forbidden, but on the contrary was permitted outside schools and educational institutions. The local Soviet was to decide whether to grant the request of the believers for using a church for this purpose. The message gave the following suggestion: "If in the given locality the population is still embraced by religious prejudices, a direct prohibition leads only to unnecessary hostility." [23]

Apparently no theological courses were organized throughout the civil war period, for as late as 1923 the Fifth Division stated that, aside from a general decree in 1921, the question had not been dealt with by the legislative organs, so that it had to formulate the rules for opening such courses.[24]

The Soviet government does not seem to have encountered open opposition from the churchmen in respect to religious education. The school system was firmly in the hands of the government, and the church, after the confiscation of its capital, had no resources with which to create a new school system. The Russian Orthodox church had never been very successful in the field of teaching and, as the general public did not seem to be disturbed by the government's measures, the leaders of the church could do little. Undoubtedly the government's actions left the church in a weak position, for the religious instruction of children at the most impressionable age was now accomplished either in the home circle or by the clergy under most difficult circumstances.

Two examples indicate that this was the case. The Nizhnii Novgorod provincial educational authorities, when asked about permitting religious instruction in the churches, decided that "in view of the fact that the churches were built for prayer and are entirely unsuited for school needs, it was decreed to advise . . . that permission to teach religion in churches is not desirable." [25] In the province of Moscow a member of the United Council of Religious Congregations and Groups asked for permission to open a Sunday school, to have an official stamp for it, and to sell religious literature. He also asked to be allowed to use the building of the women's school for this purpose. The local authorities rejected the request, and the Eighth Division of the Commissariat of Justice confirmed the decision, as the decree of January 23, 1918, had taken school matters out of the hands of religious organizations and groups.[26]

The Soviet authorities were especially determined to bar the clergy from cultural activities. When the question of participation of clergy in the work of local cultural and enlightenment groups arose, the education officials ruled:

> Two years of revolution have disclosed with sufficient clarity the counterrevolutionary attitude and the hostility of the whole mass of the clergy toward the social overturn. Considering the damage that would be wrought by the activity of a minister of a cult in a village environment of little culture, the collegium regards the inclusion of ministers of a cult in the membership of cultural and enlightenment groups as unconditionally undesirable.[27]

M. N. Pokrovskii, Vice-Commissar of Education, ruled that priests might not teach or have any functions at all in any school, and even ex-priests might be permitted to teach only with the special authorization of the commissariat.[28]

In several other ways the Soviet government sought to limit the influence of the church. The rule against ikons in public buildings was strictly enforced. A meeting of rural inhabitants of Saratov county, in 1919, asked permission to have an ikon in their official building, as all citizens were Orthodox believers and wanted to have it. The request was supported by the provincial authorities, but the Commissariat of Justice declared that it was contrary to the law on separation of church from state, which provided that no religious emblems might be displayed in a public building.[29] It was, however, ordered by Moscow that the removal of ikons should not resemble an antireligious demonstration, but must be done when as few people as possible were present, in order not to create "a false impression in the minds of the populace regarding the methods of the Soviet authorities in the struggle against popular prejudices." Furthermore, the ikons so removed were not to be destroyed, but should be placed in churches already functioning.[30]

A ruling was also issued against the attempt of the church to make a nation-wide collection of the "church mite" authorized by the Sobor. Parish organizations were entitled to receive voluntary donations to acquire religious articles, to maintain the clergy, to buy firewood and other necessary articles for the church; the "church mite," however, was not regarded as a voluntary contribution, but one required by the church authorities, and was not for local purposes but for the needs of the Sobor and the Synod, and hence was illegal.[31]

Curiously enough, even the opening of the first crematory in Russia was hailed by the Commissariat of Justice as a means of freeing the people from their "religious prejudices," by breaking the church's control over the last rites for the dead.[32]

The treatment given conscientious objectors did not benefit the Russian Orthodox church. The law provided that such men might apply for exemption from front service and that, at most, in case of need they might be used in noncombatant capacities, as, for example, orderlies in hospitals for contagious diseases. In judging a man's appeal, however, the court was obliged to consider the previous record of his denomination toward war and its record of struggle for religious liberty under the tsars. This provision expressly worked to the detriment of denominations like the Orthodox church "which not only did not reject active participation in imperialist wars in the past and in the present, but which also took most active part in them." As the Orthodox church had never opposed war as such for pacifist reasons, the Orthodox clergy were not entitled to exemptions from service, but those of draft age might be mobilized for duty in the rear.[33] Izvestiia stated, in April, 1919, that the many requests from the clergy to be excused from duty in the rear were useless unless they were performing some other socially useful work, or the local authorities would testify that they did not belong to parasitical elements, but were doing useful labor.[34]

The Soviet government also acted to nationalize the church's sixty-one diocesan taper factories and to sell the tapers, incense, and olive oil they provided directly to the churches and monasteries for their own use, but not for resale at higher prices. In this way it was hoped to deprive the church of another fragment of its former economic power.[35] After this had been done, however, the churchmen bought the tapers and then sold them in the churches for higher prices; the government, although it forbade this practice, actually did little about it.[36]

While the Soviet regime obviously was not motivated by favor for the Orthodox church or for religion in general, there were repeated instances in which the central authorities frowned upon excessive severity of local officials toward the church. Thus, on January 3, 1919, the Commissariat of Justice reminded its subordinates that "free performance of religious rituals is guaranteed insofar as they do not violate public order and are not accompanied by violations of the rights of citizens. . . ." Arrests and searches might be performed at the time of religious service only in case of extreme necessity. In searches made in churches, and especially in the chancel, a representative of the religious denomination had to be summoned, and a correct attitude observed toward the feelings of the believers. Hence officials when making searches or removals were to avoid any actions that were unnecessary and might seem mortifying to the denomination.[37]

Not long after this the Commissar of Internal Affairs felt it necessary to issue a warning to the effect that "the Communists do not in any way insult and oppress religion." To his great regret, certain hooligans, provocators, and undesirables interpreted the law as giving them the right to exterminate the believers, to plunder churches and houses of prayer, and to appropriate the goods of religious communities; but it was admonished that "the great liberating decree" be interpreted "as it was written and understood by the government."[38] A circular of the Commissariat of Justice instructed that when dealing with members of the clergy, officials "should in no way permit their acts to show a feeling of hostility and scorn for the eternal assistant of all exploitation, which the clergy have been throughout history; it is necessary to avoid all treatment of individual persons which is unworthy of the Workers' Power and is in any way similar to abuse." The circular went on to say that it was entirely incorrect to compel ecclesiastics, as a special punishment, to perform labor duty by cleaning streets and bazaar squares, or doing other unseemly work.

The appearance of a minister of any cult, in his special costume, for compulsory common work on crowded squares and streets only arouses entirely unnecessary ill feeling, not only on the part of adherents of his religion, and as a result will give a pretext for portraying such ministers of cults as a sort of martyrs to an idea; moreover, this, a distortion of the idea of labor duty, is directly in contradiction to the decree of . . . December 10, 1918.[39]

Some especially flagrant actions of local officials were condemned in the circular of the Eighth Division of the Commissariat of Justice of January 3, 1919. It insisted that when inventories of articles for religious service were made, they must be handed over to the groups of citizens who had made agreements for their use; the material of which the articles were made did not matter.

> . . . it is completely incorrect to take away church vestments, bishops' mantles, altar cloths, bishops' ceremonial rugs, other coverings and objects for divine service, and to use them for antireligious purposes (sewing them into flags, and so on); the removal of silver frames and adornments from ikons, crosses, Gospels and altars is also not permitted.
> All these actions, in the first place, are not legal, as no general order about removing religious objects from churches, even though made of precious metals, has yet been published, and secondly, they are not expedient, as they irritate the religious feelings of some of the citizens, and, moreover, they damage and depreciate the articles themselves, partially destroying their artistic significance. Their use for antireligious emblems, flags, banners, and so on has no real significance.[40]

These were not the only instances in which the Soviet authorities found it inexpedient to push their hostility to religion and to the Orthodox church to its logical conclusion. When appeals were made from the refusal of local authorities to permit religious processions, the Commissariat of Justice replied that this was a matter for the local officials to decide, depending on the concrete circumstances. It did state, however, that a funeral procession carrying banners and accompanied by the tolling of bells was permissible.[41] In spite of the fact that the clergy were regarded as a parasitical class, the government permitted them to hold positions in state institutions and enterprises, with the exception of the Commissariats of Education, Justice, Agriculture, and two or three others; they were not permitted to work in township or village institutions, but only at the county or provincial level; and they were required to wear civilian clothes while at work.[42] When a priest aged sixty-five years applied for old-age benefits, he was told that he was certainly entitled to them on the same basis as other people over fifty-five years.[43]

Additional evidence indicates that the church did not always fare badly, even at the height of the civil war. In 1919 an indigant citizen complained that Moscow was literally plastered with posters of the churchmen announcing concerts of religious singing, prayer meetings, and lectures by former professors of theological academies. At the concerts they engaged the best opera singers, paying fees of from three to five thousand rubles for each performance. It was asked where they obtained the paper for the posters and whether it was proper for stars of the state theaters to perform at occasions of such a reactionary character.[44] At Easter, 1919, Lenin and the Central Executive Committee were in favor of opening the Kremlin churches for three days for the Easter services. Whether this request was actually granted, however, is not clear, as the government was warned by churchmen that the frescoes in the cathedrals might fall if the buildings were heated after having been cold all winter.[45]

Likewise at Easter, 1919, at the orders of the Moscow Cheka Bishop Nikandr and four other clerics were released in time for the holiday season, as they had already endured sufficient punishment.[46] The Commissariat of Justice cited this fact in a strong denial of persecution of the church and also announced that Patriarch Tikhon, who had been under house arrest, had been released and was still at liberty in spite of the complaints of various provincial officials that his influence was dangerous. The Synod and the Higher Church Administration were also permitted to continue their functions.[47] In the words of Professor Fedotov: "During the Civil War the Bolsheviks had little time for the Church. While by no means hiding their attitude toward it, . . . they did not undertake the struggle on a broad programme. Leaving the Patriarch in freedom, they even seemed to forgive him the anathema which he proclaimed in 1918." [48]

But while the government did not try to eliminate either the Patriarch or the parish churches, the policy toward the monasteries was more drastic. In 1920 the Eighth Division of the Commissariat of Justice stated its policy toward them: "Painless but full liquidation of the monasteries, as chief centers of the influence of the churchmen, as nurseries of parasitism, as powerful screws in the exploiting machine of the old ruling classes." [49] The Instruction of the commissariat, August 24, 1918, provided for the transfer of all monastery property not intended for purposes of divine service to the local soviets, which were to use it in the most rational manner for "socially useful ends," without, however, disrupting any functioning economic units of the monastery in question. The Instruction recommended beginning with those that were especially active centers of counterrevolution.[50] The disposition of the monastery buildings was left to the discretion of the local soviets, presumably for use as sanatoriums, asylums, schools, and similar institutions. Money from the sale of luxury goods (such as furniture) found therein was to be added to the income of the Republic. Any business or manufacturing property was to be taken over. For these measures no special permission of the central authorities was needed, and the monastics were not to claim the protection of the law guaranteeing freedom of worship. The organization of parishes around the monastery churches was not to interfere with the dissolution of the monasteries concerned.[51] In 1921 the Commissariat of Justice stated that in general the monastery church should be closed when the monastery was dissolved. Only in exceptional cases might the provincial authorities turn it over to a newly organized parish, and then on condition that the parish provided a separate entrance to the church, a fence or wall around it, and agreed not to ring bells.[52]

According to a Soviet writer, the monks and the upper clergy bitterly opposed the dissolution of the monasteries. Crowds of neighboring peasants were called together to defend them, by the ringing of the tocsin; the clergy made inflammatory speeches, and the mobs beat the Communists who had come to liquidate them; "thus died the best Soviet workers." Incidents of this sort occurred at Zvenigorod, Nizhnii Novgorod, and other places. Allegedly, Patriarch Tikhon sent instructions to Archbishop Ioanniki, head of the noted Novo-Ierusalimskii Monastery near Moscow, telling him when dealing with the authorities to seek the support of pilgrims and other persons who revered the monastery and to attempt the organization of a brotherhood of persons ready to defend it. In spite of these efforts of the churchmen, however, the dissolution of the leading monasteries had proceeded successfully.[53]

In 1920 official statistics showed that 673 monasteries had been dissolved and their capital of 4,247,667,540 rubles (probably current paper rubles) had been confiscated. Their land, amounting to 827,540 *desiatinas* (approximately 2,334,000 acres) of all sorts had been given to the peasantry, and a variety of other property nationalized: 84 factories, 436 dairies, 620 cattle barns, 1112 rented dwellings, 708 hostels, 311 apiaries, and 277 hospitals and asylums. Approximately 1,680,000 workers, soldiers, students, and children were housed in the buildings. The uses to which the buildings were put were as follows: sanatoriums and health centers, 48; "institutions of social protection" (apparently for the aged), 168; schools and courses of the Commissariat of Education, 197; hospitals, lazarets, sanitary settlements, 349; maternity homes and asylums for children, 2; Soviet institutions, 287; military establishments, 188; and concentration camps and places of confinement, 14.[54]

Numerous as these closings were, they did not by any means wipe out all the monasteries, for, as indicated earlier, in 1914 there were 1025 monastic institutions in the Russian empire, and, although some of these were in the lost borderlands, the monasteries in Soviet Russia doubtless numbered more than 673. Various evidence indicates that some of the monasteries survived. In 1927 a Soviet source reported that 6 out of the 47 monasteries in the Ural area were flourishing and that in those officially closed some 155 monks and nuns were living, so that in all there were some 305 monastics still living the cloistered life.[55] Professor Fedotov of the Theological Institute in Paris reported in 1928 that in many of the closed monasteries aged monks or nuns were left to live out their days as watchmen or in other nominal posts, while in many places, even including Moscow, there existed monasteries with regular ascetic life.[56]

Thus it is not strictly accurate to say, as did one monastic in 1926, that "the black clergy were scattered over the face of the Russian land, like cockroaches swept out from under the stove by the hand of a tidy housewife." [57] But while not all monastics were driven forth, for the majority the iron broom of the revolution was irresistible. Many of the monks and nuns drifted off as a result of their loss of financial support — some to the villages to farm; some of the novices even joined the Red Army. A few of the nuns married. Other monastics remained in their institutions, only to be drafted into labor battalions if able-bodied or to be placed in homes for the aged if infirm.[58] Even nuns were drafted for labor duty or sent to asylums, in the provinces of Tambov and Arkhangel'sk,[59] and perhaps in other places.

When the early attempts to fight the dissolution of the monasteries proved vain, at many institutions the inmates attempted to solve their problems by forming "working collectives," or farming communes. In one monastery the monks cut their hair, donned ordinary clothes, and took up farming as their sole means of support; wherever this occurred, the authorities approved.[60] In many cases, however, the authorities felt that these "working collectives" were a sham, as the monks or nuns continued to derive revenue from religious services, did little labor, and limited membership in the collective to Orthodox believers, usually of the same sex as before, and sometimes including aged monastics incapable of labor. The local officials were instructed to break up false communes of this sort.[61]

One result of the dissolution of the monasteries was the exposure of what the Soviet authorities called "relic frauds." It was a tradition in the Russian church that the absence of corruption in the body of a deceased churchman proved his holiness, and at a number of Russian monasteries the faithful came in multitudes to do reverence at the biers of holy men whose relics were regarded as incorruptible, especially when the occurrence of miracles near the tomb was reported. When, however, the property of the Alexandro-Svirskii Monastery was inventoried, the massive silver coffin of the saint was opened and allegedly found to contain, not a miraculously preserved body, but a wax effigy. This scandalous discovery was widely published, producing much excitement among the populace, many of whom demanded that other sacred relics be opened for inspection. This was widely done, so that by 1921 some sixty-three investigations had been made, many of which, according to Soviet reports, resulted in highly compromising disclosures.[62] The official reports stated that the magnificent coffins, encrusted with precious stones, had contained either rotting bones or — what was even worse — imitations of human figures made with iron framework, or bundles of cloth, batting, women's gloves, boots, cardboard, or other extraneous matter. One coffin contained a mixture of coal, rusty nails, and little bricks. Another was entirely empty.[63]

The Soviet leaders saw in these exposures a valuable means of weakening the influence of the churchmen and made sure that the opening of the relics took place under favorable circumstances. The local officials were instructed not to attempt it when the churches were filled with large crowds. On the other hand, they were advised to summon representatives from the provincial executive committee, from the Communist party, from workers' organizations, and peasant delegates. Doctors were to be summoned to inspect the contents of the bier and to sign the affidavit as expert witnesses. The actual process of exposing the relics was left to representatives of the clergy, who were compelled to be present. After the completion of the inspection, the affidavit was to be signed by the ecclesiastics present, in order to remove the possibility of charges of fraud or sacrilege on the part of the Soviet officials. If possible, moving pictures were to be taken of the whole proceedings.[64]

The Commissariat of Justice advised that after relics had been opened they should be displayed in the monastery church for a time and then placed in museums of the Commissariat of Health. It was termed inadvisable to leave them in the possession of the clergy and unwise to destroy them. Furthermore, "in all cases disclosing charlatanry, trickery, falsification, and other criminal acts, intended for the exploitation of ignorance, . . . the sections of the Commissariat of Justice shall start criminal proceedings against all guilty persons. . . ."[65]

Few such trials were reported in the publication of the Commissariat of Justice, but in 1920 a report of a trial in the diocese of Novgorod was printed. On November 1, 1920, Bishop Alexei and several abbots and priors were tried before the Revolutionary Tribunal on charges that they had secretly opened relics and had removed extraneous materials from the coffin. Bishop Alexei admitted that this had been done, but declared that this was purely a church matter of no special significance. The clergy all insisted that the holiness of the relics did not depend upon the absence of decomposition. The court, however, decided that the clergy had been guilty of deception by preparing the relics for inspection by removing objects that had falsely given the appearance of nondecomposition, and hence they were sentenced to five years' imprisonment. Amnesty was at once granted to all defendants, however.[66]

This merciful outcome is not to be regarded as fully typical of Soviet treatment of the clergy during the civil war period, for there is no question that, especially at the critical period of the conflict, the Soviet authorities acted rigorously. According to the anti-Soviet clergy outside Soviet-controlled areas, their conduct was marked by atrocities. The reports of the Special Commission of Denikin's government in 1919 listed a number of alleged Soviet outrages against the church and churchmen. Many of the latter, whose sole crime was said to have been sympathy for the White cause, were killed, often with torture or other abuse. Although the crimes were chiefly committed by mobs or irresponsible individuals, they allegedly were inspired by "unchristened Bolsheviks of another race." [67] In addition, there were the clergy shot within the interior of Russia by the Cheka and other authorities. According to the bitterly anti-Soviet publication of the *émigré* clergy in Yugoslavia, 23 bishops in all had been killed, some by torture; 4 others were listed as having died in prison from hunger and harsh treatment. Others were believed killed, although exact data were lacking. By 1920, over 1200 priests had allegedly been killed.[68] At the Sobor at Stavropol held during General Denikin's regime Archbishop Dimitrii replied to Father Vostokov's charge that the church had not taken a sufficiently strong stand against the Bolsheviks by reminding him of Bishop Andronik, of Bishop Hermogen of Tobol'sk, of Father Matvei and Dean Vostorgov, and of many other ecclesiastics killed by the Soviets.[69]

There is little in Soviet sources concerning execution of clergy during the civil war. As indicated previously, they admitted shooting Bishops Andronik and Hermogen for their open counterrevolutionary conduct, and Dean Vostorgov as well. While they freely admitted punishing other bishops and priests for alleged counterrevolutionary activity, in each case that they discussed the punishment was imprisonment or exile. Archbishop Varnava, friend of Rasputin, is said to have declared during his imprisonment by the Cheka that he was courteously treated and he had no complaints.[70] Archbishop Konstantin of

Mogilev, who had actively opposed the Soviet government, was sentenced in December, 1919, to loss of freedom until the end of the civil war.[71] Bishop Viktor of Ufa, tried in May, 1920, by the Viatka Revolutionary Tribunal, was charged with having told the people that a typhus epidemic was punishment for the sins of the Bolsheviks and that instead of using medical measures they should sprinkle themselves with holy water. The Tribunal ruled that he was a dangerous person and had him imprisoned in the Viatka Correctional Home until the end of the war with Poland.[72] Bishop Palladii of Zvenigorod, tried in October, 1919, was sentenced to five years on charges of counterrevolutionary activity and immoral acts with boys.[73] Bishop Avgustin of Ivanovo-Voznesensk, "as an active opponent of the dictatorship of the proletariat, was exiled from the city." [74] And after the defeat of Admiral Kolchak's forces three bishops who had energetically supported his movement were in prison in November, 1920: Archbishop Andrei of Simbirsk, Bishop Andrei of Ufa, and Bishop Nikolai of Zlatoust. All three wrote earnest appeals expressing full loyalty to the Soviet regime and asking release. Bishop Andrei even repented of his former attacks on the Soviets and expressed willingness to co-operate; as a result he was freed and sent to Ufa.[75]

One of the outstanding trials of churchmen during the civil war was that of Samarin, former Over-Procurator and head of the United Council of Parishes of Moscow; Professor Kuznetsov, of the same organization, and several monks. These men were tried and convicted of having systematically carried on agitation against the Soviet regime and of trying to stir up riots against it. The tribunal judged Samarin and Kuznetsov to be enemies of the people and sentenced them to be shot; but, because of the strong position of the Soviet regime, changed the sentence to imprisonment in a concentration camp; the term was not indicated. The others received lesser sentences.[76]

The Soviet press also reported that the Novgorod Revolutionary Tribunal had sentenced a group of persons to prison terms up to eighteen months for carrying on religious and anti-Soviet talks among school children. All but one of the accused, however, were put on probation.[77] Another report stated that the Cheka had tried four priests for counterrevolutionary activity and had sentenced them to five years in a concentration camp. The charges against three of them, if true, seemed to warrant this punishment, but the fourth was sentenced "because he tried exceedingly zealously to win back from the Executive Committee the church dwelling, which had been turned into a dining-room, in which lived the wife of the psalmist, who had fled with the Whites." [78] This conduct does not seem to justify a sentence of this nature.

A circular of the Commissariat of Justice for March 1, 1919, sheds additional light on Soviet punitive measures against the clergy. The circular stated that in some places the local Soviets in applying repression to counterrevolutionary clerics decreed administrative exile for life to monasteries or life exile outside the province. The central authorities termed this procedure incorrect in dealing with counterrevolutionary ecclesiastics, as it merely passed them on to another province; moreover, exile, especially for life, was not in keeping with Soviet principles and was not provided as a punishment by any decree of the government.[79]

It is very difficult to draw definite conclusions from the scanty and partisan evidence concerning Soviet treatment of the clergy during the civil war. A careful study, however, leaves the impression that the Russian church was a matter of slight concern to the Soviet authorities at this time and that they executed a relatively small number of clergy, and these only in cases where they believed that the conduct of the ecclesiastics was not only hostile but dangerous. This conclusion is supported by the words of Professor Fedotov cited earlier. For four years the Soviet regime was engaged in a desperate struggle for survival, during which its hostility to religion, and especially to the Russian Orthodox church, was a matter of minor importance. As will be shown in the succeeding chapter, this relative indifference to the church was not caused by any marked change in the attitude of the leading ecclesiastics.

CHAPTER V

The Russian Church during the Civil War, 1919–1921

As INDICATED EARLIER, the Russian churchmen, headed by the Sobor and the Patriarch, opposed the Soviet regime from its inception. The ecclesiastics and laymen gathered in the Sobor apparently felt that it and the Patriarch would serve as a national rallying point against the Bolsheviks and that the exasperated revolutionaries "would break their heads against the church." The incorrectness of these calculations was clearly shown in the summer of 1918, when civil war began on a substantial scale. The Communists struck back fiercely against their enemies and did not spare the church from retaliation and repression. To the surprise of the church leaders, in spite of their careful preparations, the general public did not support the church on a large scale. The anathema of the Patriarch, the bitter condemnation of the Sobor, the calls for repentance, and the requiem for the late tsar and his family did not arouse the populace against the Soviet regime, which was reducing the power of the church by its separation of church from state. The message of the Patriarch to the Council of People's Commissars in October, 1918, was the last manifestation of a policy that had proved ineffective.

From that time on the churchmen, seeing that the church could not hope to win singlehanded, apparently placed their hopes in the anti-Soviet "White" movements that appeared in Siberia and the south of Russia, with support from the Entente nations. As will be shown, this was especially true in the areas under the control of White armies. It is more difficult to determine the actions of Patriarch Tikhon during this time, as he ceased to issue proclamations and manifestoes against the Soviets and late in 1919 published a message to the Russian clergy (to be discussed subsequently) urging them to refrain from politics. Even at the end of 1918, according to Prince G. N. Trubetskoi, the Patriarch refused to send his blessing to General Denikin of the Whites.[1]

Soviet writers, however, charge that Patriarch Tikhon, who had allegedly supported various anti-Soviet plots in the spring of 1918 and who had been in contact with the imprisoned Nicholas II and his family, continued secretly to support the foes of the Soviets. In *Revoliutsiia i Tserkov'* an article was reprinted, allegedly from the White newspaper *Narodnoe Delo* of December 4, 1919, published in Siberia: "Bishop Nestor, who came to Kolchak [White dictator in Siberia] from Moscow, brought the blessing of Patriarch Tikhon and a verbal message to all the Russian people who are taking up arms to defend the holy city." [2]

Even more serious charges were made against the Patriarch when he was indicted in 1922 (a matter to be discussed later). The indictment, allegedly based largely upon documentary evidence and the admissions of Tikhon, charged that he, from 1918 to the end of the civil war, had been in secret communication with Metropolitan Antonii Khrapovitskii and other counterrevolutionary Russian ecclesiastics; that letters to and from *émigré* clergy were carried through the Latvian, Estonian, Finnish, Polish, and Czechoslovakian diplomatic missions and by a secret emissary, "Fedia" or "Fedor," who traveled back and forth between the south of Russia and Moscow during much of 1918 and 1919. The Patriarch allegedly was in touch with Metropolitan Antonii, with Archbishop Mitrofan of the Don, with the Stavropol Sobor held under Denikin in 1919, and with Archbishop Nafanail of Arkhangel'sk, who is reported to have told Tikhon of his intention to appeal to the Archbishop of Canterbury to secure the retention of British troops in Arkhangel'sk. Allegedly, the Patriarch also admitted having been in communication in 1918 and 1919 with representatives of anti-Soviet plots in Moscow and had blessed their activity.[3]

If all this was known to the Soviet leaders, why did they not punish the Patriarch? Krylenko, leading prosecutor at the time, gave one

possible answer to that question: ". . . the case of the chief offenders is closed, and it remains only to send it to the Revolutionary Tribunal. . . . [However,] on the principle of a careful attitude toward the insufficiently clear understanding of the wide masses of
workers and peasants, we leave these persons, our class enemies, in
peace. . . ." [4]

It has not been possible to obtain any primary evidence either to
corroborate or disprove the Soviet accusations against Tikhon, although such actions on his part would be in keeping with the
strong hostility that he displayed earlier toward the Soviets. Evidence
is not lacking that he retained his feeling of hostility toward them as
late as 1920. In February of that year British Captain Francis Mc-
Cullagh, who had been captured in Siberia while with Kolchak's
forces, made his way to Moscow and interviewed the Patriarch in his
spacious quarters. The visitor told Tikhon of the manner in which
the supporters of Admiral Kolchak and General Denikin had used as
propaganda the messages of the Patriarch anathematizing the Council of People's Commissars — which obviously delighted the churchman. "But," wrote Captain McCullagh, "I do not think he will write
any more encyclicals, being apparently satisfied that he has done all he
can, and that the rest is in the hands of God. On the other hand, the
Bolsheviks are not likely to trouble him as long as he keeps quiet." [5]

One action of the Patriarch in 1921 suggested that he had not
turned against the reactionaries of the church. On March 26, 1921, he
turned over the Russian churches abroad, which had been under the
jurisdiction of Metropolitan Veniamin of Petrograd, to two émigré
ecclesiastics: those in France to Archbishop Evlogii of Volhynia, and
those temporarily under the protection of the Patriarchate of Constantinople to Archbishop Anastasii of Kishinev.[6] Both these ecclesiastics had had reactionary records under the tsar and had actively
opposed the Soviet government during the civil war. The fact that
Patriarch Tikhon named such men as his subordinates, and that
Metropolitan Veniamin of Petrograd did not protest, brought no immediate reaction from the Soviet authorities, but it was duly noted,
and later formed part of the Soviet indictment against them.[7]

Actually, the Patriarch was merely recognizing an existing condition, and it is difficult to see what else he could have done if he

wished to retain authority over the church abroad. The Communists, however, took the position that this was clear evidence that the Patriarch, in spite of his apparent change of front in 1919, was actually unregenerate.

Even though in 1921 the Patriarch and his entourage probably had no more love for the Soviet regime than they had had in 1917, from mid-1919 on they no longer felt it wise to take an attitude of open condemnation. Whereas the message of the Sobor in the summer of 1918 minced no words regarding the revolutionary government, and the message of the Patriarch to the Council of People's Commissars in October, 1918, was unsparing in its condemnation, the next patriarchal proclamation, a year later, was quite different in tone. Unfortunately, no complete copy of it has come to hand; lengthy passages have, however, been quoted by Soviet writers, and they agree with anti-Soviet writers as to its nature. In it Patriarch Tikhon mentioned that numbers of clergy had been killed on the suspicion of covert counterrevolutionary activity. He denied the accusation of subversive acts; "the establishment of any particular form of government is not the work of the church, but of the people themselves."

He also denied that churchmen had supported the White cause. He went on to say that nothing would save Russia from disorder and destruction until the Lord changed His wrath to mercy and the people purified themselves in fonts of repentance. He did admit that ecclesiastics in some places had performed *Te Deums* in honor of the advancing Whites, but declared that this had been "either at the demand of the new authorities themselves or at the wishes of the masses of the people, and not at all at the initiative of the servitors of the church." He then warned the clergy against sympathizing with the White movements, as they should stand outside and above all politics and should heed the rules of the church forbidding its servitors "to intervene in the political life of the country, to belong to any party, and above all to make the divine rituals and priestly ministrations a tool of political demonstrations." In closing, he urged the clergy to follow the commandment of the Apostle to keep themselves "from those working dissension and strife" and to refrain from political parties and utterances.

"Submit yourselves to every ordinance of man" (I Peter 2:13), give no grounds to justify the suspicion of the Soviet Power, submit also to its demands, insofar as they do not contravene faith and reverence, for to God, according to the Apostolic instruction, "we must hearken rather than unto man" (Acts 4:19; Galat. 1:10).[8]

This message, while not an enthusiastic endorsement of the Soviet regime, was in effect a declaration of neutrality and showed that the Patriarch had learned that it was vain to fight the revolutionary regime.

On November 7/20, 1920, Patriarch Tikhon, with the Synod and the Higher Church Administration, issued another circular. This time he did not mention the Soviet regime, but confined himself to advising the diocesan bishops, if for any reason they should lose contact with the central administration of the church, to organize a temporary church administration through joint action with neighboring dioceses, and if need be, to divide their sees into several dioceses, to name new bishops or in other ways to provide for the continuity of church life.[9]

At the time this circular was issued, the Crimea, last stronghold of the Whites, was on the point of collapse, and the last of the strongly anti-Soviet clergy in that area were about to go into exile. It seems likely that this circular was issued with them in mind and that it served as the justification for setting up new church administrations abroad. But while this message was a last crumb of comfort to the anti-Soviet ecclesiastics, it is notable because of what was *not* said. There was no condemnation of the Soviet authorities or their methods, but tacit acceptance of the existence of the new government.

Another move, even more conciliatory than the Patriarch's proclamation of September, 1919, was made by Metropolitan Veniamin of Petrograd in 1919. On hearing that the Commissariat of Justice was planning to open the relics of St. Alexander Nevskii, he sent a delegation to appeal to Zinoviev, chairman of the Petrograd Soviet, not to do so. The delegation officially declared that the clergy of the diocese of Petrograd condemned the support of the Whites by individual ecclesiastics and that Metropolitan Veniamin had decided to unfrock clerics who gave assistance to the White cause.[10]

While the church leaders in Soviet territory were thus showing a decidedly conciliatory attitude, those in areas under White control were acting differently. Although Patriarch Tikhon in his message of 1919 insisted that religious ceremonies of welcome for the White armies were the result either of popular demand or the orders of the White leaders, Soviet spokesmen told a different story. They accused the clergy of having actively supported all anti-Soviet movements from Skoropadskii, the Germans, and the Turks, to the British and the Japanese, as well as the various White armies. Monasteries were said to have helped anti-Soviet officers to reach the White forces and to have stored arms and provisions for the Whites. Bishops and priests allegedly preached to inspire the White armies and even helped them secure information about their foes.[11] It has not been possible to obtain the documents on which the Soviet writers base many of these charges, so that it is impossible to determine the validity of the accusations. There is enough information, however, to demonstrate that many of the clergy were ardent supporters of the White cause.

While not much evidence has appeared concerning the actions of the Siberian churchmen during the anti-Soviet regimes there, the diocesan publication of Tobol'sk late in 1918 tells of the formation of a Temporary Higher Church Administration to function until communication with the Patriarch could be restored. Thirteen bishops, headed by Archbishop Silvestr, met in Tomsk on November 1/14, 1918, and issued a statement to the Orthodox of Siberia, in which they dwelt on the evils of Bolshevik rule. "With the help of God Siberia and the Ural region have now been freed from the bloodthirsty plunderers. Moscow and all central Russia continue to experience the horrors of that rule."[12] This message doubtless was intended to aid the White cause.

The Temporary Higher Church Administration soon followed this message with an appeal to the Archbishop of Canterbury, the Archbishop of Paris, the Roman Catholic Archbishop and the Protestant Episcopal Bishop of New York, the Pope, the Metropolitan of Athens (who was asked to forward it to the Eastern Patriarchs), the Metropolitan of Serbia, and the Metropolitan of Bucharest. The appeal narrated a list of alleged Bolshevik atrocities, including the killing of about twenty Orthodox bishops and many hundreds of priests — often accompanied by brutal tortures. Religious processions had been fired on in many cities. "Wherever the Bolsheviks are in power the Christian Church is persecuted with even greater ferocity than in the first three centuries of the Christian era. Nuns are violated, women are made common property, and everywhere death, misery, and famine." Only in Siberia had the people chosen the course of sanity, to cast out the Bolsheviks and establish law and order. "In the name of human solidarity, and in the spirit of Christian brotherhood, we trust that we shall be able to count upon your Grace's compassion." [13]

While these appeals gave moral support to the anti-Soviet cause, some of the Siberian clergy actually fought in the ranks of religious detachments called by the Bolsheviks "Regiments of Jesus." In the diary of General Pepeliaev, Minister of Interior under Kolchak, the entry for September 21, 1919, was: "Yesterday the first detachments of the Holy Cross and Moslems went off — in all 500 rifles and 100 sabers. On the 18th they were reviewed by General Dieterichs, which review coincided with a *Te Deum*. . . ." The entry also indicates that several of the ministers present at the ceremony had warned General Pepeliaev not to link his name with "these Black Hundreds." [14] Likewise, L. A. Krol', an important figure in the Kadet party in Siberia under Kolchak, wrote: "Detachments of 'Crossbearers' were formed, including Moslems with a crescent on their banners. A religious character was given to the struggle." [15]

In the light of this testimony, a grimly curious reminiscence by the antireligious leader Iaroslavskii becomes credible. To illustrate his statement that the peasants often had a dualistic attitude toward the church, he told of an incident known to him. A detachment of peasant partisans of the Altai captured one of Kolchak's "Regiments of Jesus," which contained many priests and monks. The peasants, most of whom were believers, chose out of the captured detachment the deacons and protodeacons with especially fine voices and set them to chanting in the churches; the rest they quickly executed. [16]

In the Don Cossack country in the south of Russia the clergy also supported the Whites. In his memoirs General Krasnov stated that shortly after the Revolution of November, 1917, there were frequent meetings in the cities of the Don, at which the clergy read proclamations of the Cossack generals and preached to the populace; "usually after reading the proclamations and the sermons they performed a *Te*

Deum, and after the *Te Deum* very many [Cossacks] went off to the front." [17] When some of the Cossacks were killed in the fighting, Bishop Hermogen of Ekaterinoslav preached at a requiem for them, laying a curse upon the opposing Red Guards — "those evil sons of Cain." [18] The Red forces proved too strong, however, and the Don fell for a time into their hands; "religious processions with prayers for salvation from the Bolsheviks" proved of no avail.[19]

Later in 1918 General Krasnov who, with German aid, had regained control of the Don, made Bishop Hermogen Bishop of the Don army and fleet, in which capacity he paid frequent visits to the front and distributed pastoral messages calling on the men "to hold fast to the holy things of their native land" and "to march against Moscow to liberate the native land and the outraged faith." [20]

General Denikin's Volunteer Army, fighting desperately during most of 1918, also enjoyed ecclesiastical support. Often when the White troops entered a town they were met by the clergy, who performed a *Te Deum* in their honor. Solemn requiems were said for the slain generals Kornilov and Markov.[21] Late in 1918, when British and French military representatives came to Novocherkassk, the Don capital, the clergy turned out in force. "From the cathedral came peals of bells: all the clergy in gold vestments awaited their liberators. As soon as the Allies had entered the cathedral . . . the *Te Deum* began, which Archbishop Mitrofan of the Don . . . performed, assisted by Archbishop Hermogen. . . . The Most Reverend Mitrofan made a short speech of welcome. . . ." [22]

In Odessa, Metropolitan Platon was active in the White movement. In December, 1918, after the evacuation of the troops of the Central Powers, he sent an earnest appeal to the Archbishop of Canterbury to save the church "from the frightful agonies it is enduring." [23] When, during the brief French occupation early in 1919, an attempt was made to organize a coalition government to replace Skoropadskii's fallen regime, Metropolitan Platon undertook to unite the lesser bourgeoisie, "in order to set them in opposition to the socialists from the workers' groups." [24]

The French soon left Odessa, but in the North Caucasus and the Don General Denikin grew rapidly in strength. When he set up his governmental machinery, at the suggestion of Protopresbyter Shavel'-

skii he proposed the holding of a local Sobor to arrange for the administration of the Orthodox church. This Sobor duly met at Stavropol in May, 1919, and elected a seven-man Higher Church Administration headed by Archbishop Mitrofan. Although provision was made for religious freedom, the Russian Orthodox church was granted a predominant position. The Sobor was glad to co-operate with Denikin's regime, for it addressed "an encouraging word to the people, to the leaders and to the Army, and an admonition to the Red Army men." [25] According to the Soviet writer Kandidov, who made a thorough study of the Stavropol Sobor, it sent the following message to General Bogaevskii, Ataman of the Don: "May your labors in defense of the outraged Orthodox faith and church, and for the sake of the revival of great, indivisible Russia, be blessed by God." [26] Its general message to the people, as cited by the same author, referred to "the heroic victorious advance" of the great Volunteer Army, which had given all believing Russians "feelings of burning trust in the speedy liberation, with God's help, of our brothers in the central provinces of Russia." [27]

Kandidov also cites the text of a message addressed by the Stavropol Sobor to "the Christians of all the world," which ended with the words: "We call on all Christians of the Western world: recognize the common danger threatening all Christianity, unite with us for joint struggle against the foe, to cast him down at the feet of Christ." [28] While it has not been possible to obtain a copy of this message from a non-Soviet source, a message of a similar nature was sent by the church of Ekaterinodar "to the Christian churches of the whole world." It listed a whole series of alleged Bolshevik outrages — sacrilege, defilement of churches, atrocities against the clergy, oppression of the church, a carnival of vice, including socialization of women and children — and warned that a similar fate might overtake the rest of the world unless they should "stand in defense of Christianity from its present oppressors and be . . . a timely defender from the threat of Bolshevism — the deadly enemy of Christ the Savior and of all Christianity." [29]

Further evidence of the ardent support of the Whites rendered by leading churchmen is given by the message of Metropolitan Antonii of Kiev to the Kuban Cossacks. After expressing his grief at the fact that the holy Russian people could let themselves be overcome by the godless fleeing from penal labor, by heathen Chinese, Jews, and heretic Latvians, he closed on a hopeful note: "But our common calamity will not last forever; the Russian people will throw off the hated yoke of the godless and again will take up their blessed labors and will defend their freedom." [30]

General Denikin states that, although the Stavropol Sobor was headed by moderates, it contained extremists like Father Vostokov, who founded the "Brotherhood of the Life-giving Cross," an extreme monarchist organization, whose real aims were largely political — to fight against "Jewish-Masonry." Although opposed by the church leaders, Vostokov was very active and published many leaflets and brochures and even tried to organize in the army secret fighting bands — "the Order of the Holy Cross." [31] Another scheme of some of the ardent nationalists in Denikin's camp was to make the parish the basic unit of political life. This idea was taken up by some of the priests, who "spread the purest demagoguery and political intolerance" in spite of the efforts of the church leaders to restrain them.[32]

Curiously enough, in spite of the zeal of the Whites for the church, when General Mamontov made his daring cavalry raid deep behind the Red lines in the fall of 1919, he wired back that he was bringing rich loot, including valuable ikons and church utensils, to adorn the churches of the Don — which produced great rejoicing in the region.[33]

Even when the collapse of Denikin's cause was evident, some of the churchmen continued to give it ardent support. In Odessa the monarchist Shul'gin found Metropolitan Platon organizing "Holy Detachments" to make a last-ditch defense of the city. Shul'gin, disapproving, warned the Metropolitan of the dangers of sponsoring such elements, as they were composed largely of "criminal elements." [34]

In Northern Russia also there was ecclesiastical opposition to the Soviets. In September, 1919, hearing that the British forces were to be withdrawn, the bishop and clergy of Arkhangel'sk sent a long telegram to the Archbishop of Canterbury asking the English Christians for aid. "In this solemn hour the Arkhangel'sk Christians ask the

Christians in England to ask their government to leave the British troops in Northern Russia until after the storm has passed and the position of the Russian people has become clear." [35]

The last stand of the Whites in Russia proper was that of Baron Wrangel in the Crimea, who whipped the beaten remnants of Denikin's armies into a fighting force again. In rebuilding the White army Wrangel received valuable help from Bishop Veniamin of Sevastopol, who was named Chief Chaplain in place of the dispirited Shavel'skii. On March 25, 1920, when Wrangel took command, there was a solemn *Te Deum* and a religious procession to the chief square, where Bishop Veniamin made an inspiring address, prophesying success for the White cause. After this message, which made a great impression, the bishop sprinkled the troops with holy water.[36] The bishop also traveled to all parts of the front and rear, gave out rewards to zealous priests, and blessed the faithful. In his sermons he sometimes went to such extremes that the officers objected, thinking that his outbursts would ruin their authority in the eyes of the Cossacks.[37]

At Wrangel's suggestion in September the heads of the church proclaimed three days of fasting and repentance. The church's message laid the calamities endured by Russia to the fact that the people had "overturned and killed the Lord's Anointed," and prayed that God might "unite all the Russian people as one and as soon as possible might entrust the guidance of the Russian people to His Anointed." The fanatical Father Vostokov led a religious procession to the Sevastopoi harbor, where he read the proclamation and then announced that he could actually see the tsar coming to save them.[38]

Father Vostokov's zeal went to such lengths that he even urged that the march against the Red Army be made, not by Wrangel's veteran troops, but by the clergy of the Crimea with ikons and banners. At the sight of this procession, he claimed, the Reds would take off their caps, plunge their bayonets into the ground, and fall before the ikons. This scheme, however, was rejected by the clergy and by General Wrangel.[39]

This priest was also noted for his anti-Semitic agitation. In October, 1920, an observer fresh from the Crimea reported that the pogrom agitation of Father Vostokov and Bishop Veniamin was unrestrained and that General Wrangel did not feel able to do anything to stop it.[40] Another observer told of the vehement anti-Semitic agitation of Vostokov in Simferopol, where he called for a fight against Jewry, which had enslaved the Russian people through the Bolsheviks. Immense crowds gathered, and under the influence of the preaching hysterical cries burst from the crowd: "Beat the Jews!" Finally, after representations had been made to General Wrangel concerning the danger of a pogrom, he issued orders against such agitation.[41]

Apparently, a considerable number of the Russian Orthodox clergy supported the White cause zealously. Their efforts were not confined to performing *Te Deums* of welcome to the White troops at the demand of the commanders or the populace, as Patriarch Tikhon claimed. Instead, they preached strong sermons hailing the Whites as liberators and condemning the Reds as enemies of the church. They published much anti-Soviet printed matter and otherwise tried to sway the populace toward the White side. In addition, they issued urgent appeals for aid to the Allied powers. Moreover, anti-Semitic agitation was not a rarity among the clergy under White jurisdiction, and some of the more extreme leaders of the church even tried to organize bands of men to fight the Reds under the sign of the cross. On the other hand, no direct evidence has been found to support the more extreme Soviet allegations against the clergy. In any event, the facts presented here show that the Soviets had some grounds for regarding the clergy as a group, and especially the upper clergy, as their enemies. The marked hostility of many of the Russian clergy toward the Soviet regime must have been evident to much of the Russian population, so that it doubtless affected the attitude of the people toward the clergy.

Unquestionably the Russian Orthodox church was weaker vis-à-vis the Soviet state in January, 1921, than it had been before the civil war began. Not only had the church's political, educational, and economic position been gravely weakened, but Soviet sources reported that there even were a few signs of weakness within the church itself. In 1919 Archbishop Vladimir of Penza proclaimed the founding of a "Free People's Church," entirely in agreement with the government of workers and peasants and opposed to the ruling hierarchy. This attempt came to little, for he was not supported by the believers; whether this was because he had a very bad moral record, according to the followers of the Patriarch, or for other reasons, cannot be determined.[42] In 1920 there appeared the so-called Executive Committee of the Clergy, headed by one Filippov, which demanded that Patriarch Tikhon cease his opposition to the Soviet regime in order to avert the danger of further severe treatment of the church by the government. The Soviet authorities, however, disapproved of Filippov's agitation, as he also sought to recover the confiscated taper factories of the church.[43]

There was rebellion against the Patriarch even on the parish level. In one village a widowed priest remarried, contrary to church rules; when the ecclesiastical authorities tried to unfrock him, he, with the support of his parish, defied them.[44] In another parish the believers chose the psalmist as their priest, in defiance of the bishop, as the psalmist said the service correctly "and prays aloud for the health of the Soviet government." When placed under a ban because of this, the parishioners declared themselves independent of both bishop and Patriarch.[45]

These, even if true, were exceptional cases. Perhaps more important (if correctly reported by the Soviet press) were the numerous instances at the close of the civil war where ecclesiastics renounced opposition to the Soviet regime and pledged it their loyalty. The case of Bishop Andrei of Ufa has already been mentioned; in June, 1920, all the clergy of Ekaterinburg, headed by Bishop Grigorii, declared at a solemn service that they were now on the Soviet side. The bishop made a long speech urging his followers to join the Soviet Power and bestowing his blessing on the Red Army.[46] Bishop Viktor of Viatka, imprisoned for anti-Soviet sermons, made a written statement renouncing his opposition to the workers' and peasants' government.[47]

As mentioned earlier, Metropolitan Veniamin of Petrograd had issued a similar statement, in which he promised to unfrock any of his clergy who opposed the Soviet government.

The lower clergy, according to Soviet sources, also began to express loyalty to the new regime. The famous monk Iliodor, once a friend of Rasputin, at Easter, 1921, appeared on the portico of the Tsaritsyn Cathedral and before a large crowd proclaimed "long life" to the Soviet Power and wished it victory over its enemies.[48] Likewise a considerable number of parish priests declared their loyalty, and some even gave active aid during the Polish war.[49]

In some cases the change of policy took the form of renunciation of the cloth. While most who took this step were members of the lower clergy, Bishop Zosima of Irkutsk was reported also to have done so, declaring that as a result of the conduct of the church during the civil war he was leaving it of his own free will.[50] An anti-Soviet writer in 1922 admits that "no small quantity" of ecclesiastics renounced their calling — most of them village priests. He adds, however, what was probably true — that the church benefited thereby, as these persons had no real vocation to the priesthood.[51]

While the church suffered little from the loss of those not strong in their faith, there are some slight and inconclusive bits of evidence suggesting that it had lost somewhat in influence during the civil war period. General Denikin, journeying incognito to the Don country in 1918, was struck by the readiness of soldiers and peasants to laugh at a sacrilegious parody on the litany.[52] Captain McCullagh, who visited Moscow after the fighting had ended, remarked on the decline in outward religious observance there. Cabdrivers and streetcar passengers did not, as formerly, pay reverence at famous shrines, and the worshipers at these shrines were only about 10 per cent of the former number. Fervently praying pilgrims were such a rarity that when in 1923 a man bowed to the ground before an ikon in Moscow, three youths were greatly amused and finally ran to fetch their sister to see the strange sight.[53] Naturally Communist writers rejoiced at such developments; they also claimed that not merely the city dwellers, but even some of the peasants, were turning against religion.[54]

Probably at this time few of the peasants had actually turned against the church. Iaroslavskii, leading antireligious spokesman, told of a group of Altai peasants who organized a ceremonial welcome when the Red Army came in in 1919; a divine liturgy was performed in the cathedral, at which all the clergy were compelled to be present.[55] Moreover, peasant girls continued to insist on church weddings in spite of the law making civil marriages sufficient. Indeed, so strong was the demand for church weddings that many Communist party members gave in to their brides on this matter, much to the disgust of the party authorities.[56] Finally, to stop such violations of the Communist party rules, on September 15, 1921, the Central Committee of the party ruled that, while such misconduct might be tolerated on the part of new members, responsible members should be expelled for such failings.[57]

Another sign of the influence of religion was the case of a Communist party member whose superiors rebuked him for playing his phonograph in his room during service in the local church, on the grounds that it might outrage the feelings of the believers.[58] An even more remarkable incident was reported from a county of the province of Tver, where the Executive Committee and all the other Soviet institutions made a mass pilgrimage of several miles to pray before the relics of a saint.[59]

These doubtless were exceptional cases; but certainly faith was far from dead in Russia. In fact, there were some indications of a distinct religious revival after the civil war. Especially marked was the new piety of the educated classes, many of whom had formerly been indifferent; now, apparently as a result of their sufferings and uncertainty, they flocked to the churches with new zeal. Some even joined the priesthood.[60] In addition, in considerable numbers the masses flowed into the churches — in part out of real piety, in part because the church was the only non-Soviet institution in existence.[61] The revival of religion was also helped by the fact that the church began to function more normally in time of peace. Exiled bishops returned to their dioceses, church discipline grew stronger, and preaching became more effective. One supporter of Patriarch Tikhon even claims that church life was on a higher level than before the World War.[62]

Data on the collection of vital statistics in the province of Altai (very isolated and by no means typical) indicate that there religious practices were widespread. While practically all births, deaths, and marriages were registered at the civil records office (ZAGS), almost all the children were christened in church as well, and most marriages were sanctified by a church ceremony. Of those who had turned away from the church, 67 per cent were Communists, who were only a small part of the population; few of the nonreligious were peasants.[63]

The Russian church apparently survived the period of revolution in a strong condition. Nonetheless, in the political field it had suffered a severe defeat. It had attempted to challenge the Soviet authorities over the separation of church from state and had been worsted on every point. The state controlled the schools and marriage and divorce, and the church had lost valuable economic resources. In addition, the unfriendly government that so many churchmen had hoped to unseat was more firmly in the saddle than ever, and to many of that government's supporters the church was clearly identified as an institution hostile to their interests, allied with their enemies.

On the other hand, the legend that the Russian Orthodox church was wiped out by the revolution and the civil war had no foundation. The vast majority of the population were still strongly religious, and although the government was against the church, it could do little in the face of the mass support for religion. The parish churches continued to function, and the dioceses and the central administration of the church were operating with some effectiveness. In spite of its extremely close ties with the defunct Romanov regime, the Russian Orthodox church had shown remarkable powers of adjustment to completely new and difficult conditions. The antireligious propaganda encouraged by the Soviet government had done little to break the religious authority of the church and in fact had hardly begun to reach the masses of the population. Thus, although the Soviet authorities had gained the advantage in the first encounter, the victory was so far from decisive that the struggle died down and was followed by a tacit truce in 1921 that gave promise of enduring for a considerable time.

CHAPTER VI

The Russian Church and the Famine of 1921

THE UNEASY TRUCE between government and church at the end of the civil war was not of long duration, for in 1921 Russia was afflicted by a new calamity, which before long involved the church. This calamity was a terrible famine, caused largely by drought, which lasted much of the summer over wide areas of the Volga region and in parts of the Ukraine. The resulting crop failure hit with intense force a population weakened economically by years of fighting, requisitioning of food and horses, a broken-down transportation system, and destruction of buildings. As the winter of 1921–1922 approached, millions of people, now destitute, abandoned themselves to despair or flocked into the desolate cities and, finding little relief, streamed on to seek it elsewhere. Typhus added to the horrors. For those who survived there was little help; some in desperation turned to cannibalism, and terrible stories appeared in the Soviet press. Even when spring came, the situation remained catastrophic. The survivors rarely had horses to work the soil or seed to plant; these had to be provided if another crop failure in 1922 was to be avoided.

The Soviet government early realized that relief on a colossal scale would be needed and took steps to aid the famine sufferers. Its resources were slight, however, and little gold-supported currency to buy grain abroad could be obtained, so that foreign aid was necessary. Charitable assistance was given by a number of organizations such as the American Relief Administration (ARA), the Quakers, the Papacy, the Nansen Committee, and various trade-unions, but as the disaster grew, even greater aid was needed.

As early as August, 1921, Patriarch Tikhon issued an appeal for help to the Eastern Patriarchs, the Pope, the Archbishop of Canterbury, and the Protestant Episcopal Bishop of New York, and with great urgency begged the members of the Russian church to contribute. An All-Russian Church Committee was formed for famine relief and money, and food collections were undertaken by the parish brotherhoods. The Soviet government, however, apparently distrusted this move of the church, which it still felt to be hostile, and insisted on centralized state control of the relief administration. The churchmen were obliged to turn the funds collected over to the official relief committee. The results of the church's collections, however, proved disappointing to the government,[1] as, according to Professor Titlinov, only nine million rubles were contributed during the last six months of 1921.[2] Since by that time the situation had become catastrophic, on December 9, 1921, the Soviet government reversed itself and ruled that the church organizations might make collections and that the Central Committee for Aid to the Starving (Pomgol) should "reach agreements with the religious societies as to the form of the donations and the method of forwarding what has been collected, having in mind the wishes of the donors."[3]

Six weeks later the Soviet press reported that such agreements had been made. The church organizations would collect the funds or supplies and turn them over to central or local organs of Pomgol at the place of collection, where they would be credited to the account of the religious organization. A plan of distribution would be worked out by the religious authorities together with Pomgol, at the various levels concerned. The local religious representatives were to be permitted to participate in the distribution of the amounts collected.[4]

It is highly significant that the above article raised a new point: the question of the use of church treasure for famine relief. It stated that the churchmen had been given plenty of opportunity to participate in famine relief and suggested that they draw upon the large amounts of gold, silver, and precious stones in the churches. While this was legally state property, according to the decree of January 23, 1918, the gov-

ernment had not used it, but had spent large sums otherwise obtained
for relief. "The religious societies should widely use this source of
funds for the starving of the Volga. With the gold and silver valuables
they could buy several million *puds* of grain and could save several
million of the hungry from starvation." [5]

By this time the Soviet leaders were becoming suspicious that the
leading churchmen were not sincere in their desire to help alleviate
the famine. Late in 1921 an event occurred that greatly heightened this
suspicion and convinced many that the Patriarch and his followers
were using the famine for political purposes. This event was the so-
called Karlovatskii Sobor.

The Karlovatskii Sobor was a congress of *émigré* clergy and laymen,
which met in the Serbian town of Sremski Karlovtsy under the chair-
manship of the ardent reactionary Metropolitan Antonii Khrapovitskii of Kiev and Khar'kov. Its ecclesiastical membership, consisting
of fifteen bishops and a number of lower clergy, included such strong
supporters of the White movement as Metropolitan Platon of Odessa,
Archbishop Feofan of Poltava, Bishop Veniamin of Sevastopol, Archbishops Anastasii of Kishinev and Evlogii of Volhynia (all of the
Higher Russian Church Administration Abroad), Dean Vostokov,
and Protopresbyter Shavel'skii. The lay members, in part elected, in
part co-opted, were largely representatives of the Russian nobility, the
army, and high official circles. There were at least nineteen generals
and many princes and counts. N. E. Markov, of the Supreme Monarchist Council, who had made himself notorious in the Third and
Fourth Dumas, was an outstanding figure.[6]

Although this gathering met ostensibly to decide questions of religious administration outside Russia, it quickly showed its political
coloration. Warm greetings were sent to the former Empress Maria
Feodorovna and to General Wrangel and his troops evacuated from
the Crimea.[7] The latter message, addressed to "the Christ-loving
Troops of the Russian Army and the Valiant Leader," urged them to
"expect the imminent salvation of Russia. . . . The motherland will
call her sons to the final struggle for her salvation. Be ready for it.
Transform yourselves, Russian Army, into truly cross-bearing troops.
Under this sign shalt thou conquer!" [8] The temper of the gathering
was also shown by a bitter personal attack on Rodzianko, former

chairman of the Duma, for his role in the abdication of Nicholas II. Although Rodzianko was a sincere monarchist, the attack was pressed so strongly by A. V. Trepov and other lay members that he resigned from the meeting.[9] Even more significant was the message to the Russian émigrés. Markov insisted that it must express hope for a monarch of the House of Romanov. Several of the clergy objected to specific mention of this dynasty, although all favored the monarchy and hoped for a Romanov tsar. Markov's proposal was adopted unanimously, with several of the bishops abstaining. The message to the émigrés voiced the hope that God might "return to the All-Russian Throne the Anointed, a lawful Orthodox Tsar of the House of Romanov." [10]

The Karlovatskii Sobor also considered the famine in Russia. Archbishop Anastasii urged that the churchmen make an appeal to the whole world not to permit the extermination of the Russian people; they should also say what the Patriarch could not say — "that the calamity experienced by Russia is the result of the wild, perverted, bloody regime of the butchers of Russia. . . ." If it were only possible, the churchmen should send missions to all parts of the world to open their eyes to Russian realities. He also proposed another appeal to the émigrés not to make peace with the Bolsheviks and urged that prayers be ordered in the churches "for all the martyred holy ones who have fallen for faith, Tsar and Fatherland, beginning with the Martyr Tsar Nicholas II." These proposals were unanimously adopted.[11] The resulting appeal, "To All Governments and Peoples of the Whole World Who Believe in God," supplemented Patriarch Tikhon's appeal, but declared it spoke for him, as he had been deprived of communication with the outside world. It stated that twenty-five million people in Russia had been ruined, as everything had been burned by the sun and vast numbers were dying of hunger and cholera. Hence the churchmen asked donations, to be sent to the Higher Russian Church Administration Abroad, or to frontier cities or ports, addressed to the Patriarch or to the bishops in Reval, Riga, and Helsingfors.[12] To the already suspicious Communists in Russia, this proposal undoubtedly suggested that an attempt would be made to use the donations to influence the masses against the Soviet regime.

Although, in spite of the claims of its members,[13] the Patriarch had not authorized the Karlovatskii Sobor — an *ad hoc* gathering — and had not formally recognized the Higher Church Administration Abroad, he was in touch with one of its leading members. In the spring of 1921 he had named Archbishop Evlogii as head of the Russian churches in Western Europe, and on January 17/30, 1922, he had given him the rank of metropolitan.[14] As indicated in a preceding chapter, authority over the Russian churches in Eastern Europe was delegated to Archbishop Anastasii. Thus Patriarch Tikhon was in relationship with two important members of the Karlovatskii Sobor, all of whose members recognized his authority as Patriarch. Moreover, the bylaws of the Sobor stated that its decisions were subject to confirmation by the Patriarch. The various decisions adopted by the Sobor were obviously important, so that the Soviet leaders had reason to believe that Patriarch Tikhon had sanctioned them. Even several members of the gathering were sure that its appeals had the Patriarch's approval.[15]

In spite of the rising Soviet suspicions, at first nothing was done by the government concerning its proposal to use church treasures for famine relief. Nevertheless, the Patriarch felt it necessary to authorize a statement by Dean Tsvetkov, his representative at Pomgol, to the effect that some church valuables had a ritual significance and were sanctified; but others, not sanctified, might be so used. Dean Tsvetkov added that the Patriarch was preparing a message to the faithful, urging them to donate gold and silver adornments on Ikons, old or discarded articles such as broken halos, vestments from which gold or silver might be reclaimed by burning, bracelets, medallions, and similar articles.[16] In mid-February the Patriarch's message appeared, proposing the donation of adornments given for ikons (rings, chains, bracelets, and necklaces) and of broken pieces of gold and silver.[17]

In view of the extreme need, these concessions apparently seemed small to the Soviet leaders. Already a number of proposals to make wide use of church treasure had appeared in the Soviet press. The appeals were said to have come from Simbirsk peasants who had come to Moscow to appeal to Kalinin for help; from inmates of an old people's home in Moscow; from a group of believers; and from some Moscow transport workers.[18] Moreover, the press reported that some of the clergy, especially in the stricken Volga valley, had proposed donating church valuables. In Saratov Bishop Dosifei as early as January 31 expressed willingness to contribute church utensils, and on February 10 Archbishop Evdokim of Nizhnii Novgorod published an appeal to the believers to donate the church's wealth. A number of instances were reported where churchmen, nuns, and congregations donated valuables, and the Dean of Saratov Cathedral made a speaking tour in the Ukraine, where he obtained considerable quantities of plate for the sufferers.[19] In addition, the press began to express indignation against the Patriarch and his followers, who seemed unwilling to grant real aid. One such article stated that many of the village clergy were willing to give up the church's wealth, but feared the Patriarch; hence a revolution should occur in the church similar to the revolution in the political sphere.[20]

The increasing demands for the use of the church's treasure indicated that the government was planning to act. Its policy, however, did not at once crystallize. On February 11 *Pravda* reported that the All-Russian Central Executive Committee had decided to begin immediately to confiscate the valuables and had instructed the Commissariat of Justice to prepare detailed work for this undertaking.[21] The following day, however, the more authoritative *Izvestiia* denied that the matter had been decided, saying that it would be considered at the next session.[22] Actually, it was not until February 24 that *Izvestiia* published a brief notice to the effect that the Central Executive Committee had resolved to order the local soviets to remove the valuables from the churches.[23] The decree itself followed two days later. It provided that the local soviets should, within one month's time, remove from the churches of all religions the valuables of gold, silver, and precious stones "whose removal will not essentially harm the interests of the cult itself," and turn them over to the Central Committee for Aid to the Starving (Pomgol). Special commissions should handle the work, in which the groups of believers should participate. The valuables were to be used for famine relief only, and periodic accountings of the confiscations and the use made of the valuables were to be published.[24]

Even before the publication of this decree the attitude of the leading churchmen had already grown less co-operative. Captain Francis McCullagh, who was in Moscow at the time, was told by a high ecclesiastic that the faithful had been offended by the Patriarch's willingness to use the adornments and broken metal for famine relief, as they felt that the proceeds would be improperly used by the government.[25] When the Soviet decree for confiscation of the treasure appeared, the Patriarch issued a message to the faithful recounting the church's actions to aid the famine sufferers and alleging an unco-operative attitude on the part of the government. In particular, he condemned the decree for taking sacred vessels and other articles used for divine service. "From the point of view of the church such an act is an act of sacrilege. . . ." He called for continued contributions for famine relief, but went on: "We cannot approve the taking away from the churches, even by voluntary donation, of consecrated articles, whose use for purposes other than divine service is forbidden by the canons of the Church Universal and is punished by it as sacrilege — for laymen, by excommunication, and for ecclesiastics, by unfrocking." [26]

Actually, according to Dr. Matthew Spinka, the canons of the Ecumenical Church do not expressly forbid the use of church treasure for secular needs, as it had been so used at various times in history. What is forbidden is the diversion of church wealth to personal use — something quite different from using it for national needs at a time of disaster.[27] Indeed, Soviet writers have claimed that churchmen proposed giving up treasure to the imperial government in time of war. According to *Pravda,* Metropolitan Antonii of St. Petersburg had proposed this to the tsar during the Japanese war,[28] and it was alleged that in 1916 Abbot Nikodim of the Iur'ev Monastery had made the same suggestion, referring to many earlier instances when churchmen had donated church treasure to the cause of the nation.[29] Nevertheless, it is understandable that churchmen who had lost invested capital, lands and other properties, and government subsidies, were extremely loath to surrender their remaining holdings of gold, silver, and precious stones, especially to a government they detested.

For obvious reasons the Patriarch's proclamation opposing the confiscation of the church's valuables was not published, but was secretly distributed by the churchmen. The government apparently did not at once learn about it. On March 10, however, *Izvestiia* stated that a copy had been sent in anonymously and commented that clerical levity of this sort could not be tolerated.[30]

The situation did not at once become critical. Although the Soviet press became increasingly hostile to Patriarch Tikhon, its tone was not extreme. On March 15 *Izvestiia* printed an interview with him in which he declared: "Remembering the words of Christ, if you have two shirts, give your shirt to your neighbor — the church cannot remain indifferent to those great sufferings which the starving are experiencing." He declared he favored donations of nonconsecrated church articles, but warned that the amount to be so realized would not be great.[31] On March 26, however, a report of an interview between five non-Communist peasants from the famine area and the Patriarch indicated that trouble was brewing. According to the account, the Patriarch was sceptical about the need for greater aid, expressed doubt that the government was doing its utmost, and held that the church was doing all it could. When the peasants remarked that even the tsars had taken church treasure in time of need, Tikhon answered: "The Tsars took, but they also gave." [32]

This Patriarchal attitude, while understandable, doubtless displeased the Soviet authorities; moreover, at approximately the same time a new move by the Karlovatskii Sobor must have greatly heightened their suspicion. The Soviet leaders at first paid little attention to the Sobor, but when Metropolitan Antonii, its authorized spokesman, published an appeal to the Genoa Conference, their wrath was aroused. This message warned the peoples of the world against recognizing or entering into relations with the Bolsheviks, as any strengthening of this vile regime would only facilitate the penetration of the Bolshevik infection into other lands. Failure of the Communists to achieve this depended "(1) upon nonrecognition of the Bolsheviks by all governments, and (2) upon the frightful calamities of hunger, cold, and epidemics raging over Russia because of the Bolshevik disorders." Hence if through trade Russia should be able to obtain transportation equipment and other goods, the Communist virus would spread to other lands. The message, however, did not merely advocate a continued quarantine of Bolshevist Russia; it also appealed:

> Peoples of Europe! Peoples of the World! Have pity on our honest Russian people, noble in heart, who have fallen into the hands of international evildoers! Do not support them, do not strengthen them against your children and grandchildren! Better to help the honorable Russian citizens. Give them arms in hand, give them your vol-

unteers and help them drive Bolshevism — this cult of killing, looting, and blasphemy — out of Russia and the whole world. Pity the poor Russian refugees. . . . They are more than half of them officers, generals, and soldiers, ready to take up arms and campaign in Russia in order to tear her out of the clutches of the shameful slavery to bandits. Help them to realize their patriotic duty, do not let your loyal ally go down. . . .[33]

This appeal, which was printed in *Novoe Vremia* (*The New Times*) of Belgrade on March 1, 1922, reached Moscow about the middle of the month and immediately aroused strong feeling.[34] It closely coincided with the first disorders attendant upon the confiscation of church valuables, which probably seemed to the Soviet authorities the first fruits of a widespread ecclesiastical plot. An article by Protopresbyter Shavel'skii at this very juncture showed the hopes cherished by *émigré* churchmen. He stated that the time would soon come when the Patriarch would temporarily assume power in order to transmit it to a newly formed government. This would come if a state of anarchy ensued in Russia after the fall of the Bolsheviks. Another possibility was that some form of national assembly would establish a new regime. The church should do its part to bring this about, although the collapse of the Bolsheviks would come of itself. The task of the church was to call the people to repentance, to pacify the hostile parties, and to exercise religious and moral influence over the people.[35] According to Stratonov, an ardent supporter of the Patriarch against the extreme clerical reactionaries, in certain politically minded circles of the church abroad the dreams went even further; these folk pointed out, citing several historical precedents, that the treasure of the churches and monasteries might have vast financial significance during the transition period of the Russian state after the Soviet regime should fall.[36]

Even before Shavel'skii's article was published the Soviet authorities reacted strongly to the appeal to the Genoa Conference. Krasikov, high official of the Commissariat of Justice, after characterizing the Karlovatskii Sobor as the quintessence of reaction, asserted: "To all it is known that the local church head, sitting in Russia, gave consideration to the Karlovatskii Sobor and was fully informed of all the 'acts' of this Sobor." He then posed a challenge to Patriarch Tikhon: either he was in organized, hierarchical conjunction with the *émigré* gathering, against the life of the Soviet state, or he must intend to excommunicate them "for rebellion and treason carried on under the flag of religion. Or are your anathemas hurled only against the workers and peasants who dare to take from the landlords and from you land, factories, and mills, which are drenched with their sweat and blood?" [37]

Another very bitter article, "The Most Holy Counterrevolution," by the antireligious writer Mikhail Gorev, was published in *Izvestiia* on March 28. It stated that at the time when the mass of the lower clergy welcomed the decree on confiscation of church treasure, a handful of princes of the church opposed this measure and carried on counterrevolutionary propaganda against it. "Who are they, these enemies of the people, these enemies of the starving, and, moreover, oppressors of our democratic clergy?" There followed a long catechism, which began, "Who, in 1918, after the Soviet Power took away the land and the capital from the landowners, factory-owners, and priests, cursed the workers and peasants?" with the response, "Patriarch Tikhon with all his church Sobor." Then, point by point, the upper clergy were accused of supporting the various counterrevolutionaries, from Skoropadskii to Kolchak and Wrangel, of encouraging pogroms, and, at the Karlovatskii Sobor, of plotting to use famine to starve out the Soviets, to the delight of "world capital." Finally, Gorev wrote:

> *What* should the workers and peasants do, if they do not wish the deaths of millions of dying peasants?
> *Give a rebuff to all this band of rabid "dignified" priests. Burn out "the most holy counterrevolution" with a hot iron. Take the gold out of the churches. Exchange the gold for bread. Save the starving with bread.*[38]

In this article are met two of the leading motifs of the Soviet policy of 1922 and 1923: support for the lower, "democratic" parish clergy, and concentration of the attack upon the opposing leaders of the church rather than upon religion in general. In fact, Gorev specifically warned against an antireligious approach to the removal of valuables from the churches. "He who turns the removal of church riches into an antireligious or anticlerical demonstration, he who carries out this removal with abuse or assault upon the religious feelings of dark but sincerely believing people, he spoils the work, is an enemy of the people! . . . To disclose the very roots of religion, to uncover all the unseemliness of religious prejudices — for that we have another time and another place." [39] Likewise, in an interview in *Izvestiia* Mikhail Kalinin stated that the removal of the valuables from the churches was not in any sense a struggle against religion or against the church. He also pointed out that the clergy had split into two groups: one which approved the use of the valuables for famine relief, and one which opposed and had taken a hostile attitude toward the Soviet government.[40] Furthermore, in May *Pravda* declared: "It is necessary that all honorable ministers of religion, who do not transform their God into a golden calf, who do not turn the work of helping the starving into a monarchist plot, should help in the struggle against the inhuman men of violence, who in the name of Christ bless cannibalism." [41]

In line with this policy, on March 28 Kalinin invited the liberal Bishop Antonin to join the Relief Commission as representative of the church. The government, he said, wanted to bring loyal priests to participate in order that the removal of the treasures should proceed properly, without acts that might irritate the believers. The split in the church over this matter was already an accomplished fact. Kalinin promised that there would be no mechanical, forcible crushing of religion or persecution of the religious feelings of the believers; there could be only a struggle of ideas, propaganda based upon science. Bishop Antonin accepted the proposal on this basis.[42]

As far as can be determined from Soviet sources, the policy of using church valuables for famine relief proved to be a success. The priests and the parishioners in most instances seem to have accepted the program, and a number of bishops chose to support it rather than to follow Patriarch Tikhon's lead. As indicated above, Archbishop Evdokim of Nizhnii Novgorod was one of the first to pronounce for the removal of the valuables; Archbishops Serafim of Kostroma and Tikhon of Voronezh, Metropolitan Sergii of Vladimir, and Bishops Feofan of Kaluga, Vladimir of Penza, Nikon of Kursk, Dimitrii of Stavropol, Melkhisidek of Minsk, Pimen of Podolia, and Fedosii of Khar'kov also came out in favor of the use of the church treasure for famine relief.[43] Likewise, many of the liberal deans and priests supported the proposal, among them Al'binskii, Boiarskii, Belkov, Vvedenskii, and Krasnitskii.[44] A report of the progress of removing the valuables, made on April 1, indicated that on the whole matters were proceeding well. The Relief Commission asked the government to appropriate one million gold rubles to buy food as an advance against the collections. The work was going ahead without opposition in the provinces of Nizhnii Novgorod, Voronezh, Tsaritsyn, Viatka, Arkhangel'sk, Kursk, Khar'kov, Kaluga, Ivanovo-Vozenesensk, Saratov, and Kuban. On the other hand, in some cases the valuables appeared to have been hidden or stolen from the churches.[45]

As will be seen, however, in a number of places strong opposition occurred, largely inspired by Patriarch Tikhon's message, so that suspicion of his connection with the Karlovatskii Sobor remained strong. To be sure, on May 5, 1922, the Patriarch with the Synod ruled that the Higher Russian Church Administration Abroad (which had called this Sobor) had no legal existence and that its acts, being purely political, had no ecclesiastical significance. It was declared dissolved, and the Synod was to collect evidence in order to consider whether to put its members on trial, after the Synod had again returned to normal and had its full membership. Also it was stated that Metropolitan Evlogii alone had jurisdiction over the Russian church abroad.[46]

This action of the Patriarch, however, was far from what the Soviet authorities had demanded: namely, full excommunication of the members of the Karlovatskii Sobor. About this Tikhon said nothing. Several months later, when the Patriarch was under arrest and indictment for counterrevolution (to be discussed subsequently) he allegedly admitted that he had been in communication with Metropolitans Antonii and Evlogii, who had informed him of their intention to call this Sobor, asked and secured his blessing upon it, and forwarded its resolutions to him. According to the Patriarch's admission, the correspondence was conducted through one of the foreign diplomatic missions in Moscow. The Patriarch's admission was allegedly corroborated by the testimony of a number of other witnesses.[47] As will be seen later, when he secured his release in the summer of 1923 the Patriarch signed a statement in which he admitted the substantial correctness of the charges against him — an admission which lends credence to these charges. Unfortunately, no other evidence on this point has come to hand.

But whether or not the Soviets actually had proof linking Patriarch Tikhon directly with the Karlovatskii Sobor, they apparently believed him to be in league with the *émigré* churchmen. His decrees condemning the confiscation of church treasure seemed to be in line with the *émigré* hope to utilize "the bony hand of hunger" to overthrow the Soviet regime; the disorders that occurred were apparently a planned attempt to implement that program.

The first violence occurred at Shuia, a town northeast of Moscow. Here the removal of the valuables began early in March and proceeded without difficulty in the smaller churches. When the commission came to the cathedral, however, according to the official Soviet account a hostile crowd beset them and some individuals who supported them were beaten. Action was postponed for two days, but when the second attempt was made, the violence grew even worse. Pogrom appeals were made, the tocsin was rung for over an hour, and six mounted militiamen were stoned. Half a company of soldiers was called out, with two machine guns. When they arrived, revolver shots were fired from the crowd and the mob pressed in on the Red Army men, trying to disarm them. After several had been knocked down by chunks of ice, the commander ordered a volley into the air; when the crowd still persisted he fired into it. Four persons were killed, ten wounded. Arrests were made as the crowd dispersed and no further difficulty was met.[48]

Similar developments were reported at Smolensk on March 28, although without fatalities. A number of Red Army men were disarmed and badly beaten, and the crowd, which numbered thousands, was dispersed with difficulty by blank volleys and rifle butts. At one time the mob beat two Jews and tried to start a pogrom, but was stopped by the authorities.[49] Other incidents were reported at Staraia Russa, Moscow, Petrograd, and elsewhere, although rarely with loss of life. In every case the government succeeded in quelling the disorders and in carrying out its intention to confiscate the valuables. It was not satisfied with this, however, but arrested many of the leaders and made careful investigations that resulted in trials and sentences.

The trial at Shuia, which ended on April 25, 1922, resulted in three death sentences, but no startling disclosures. The Smolensk trial did not take place until August, several months after the event. The opposition to the removal of the valuables in Moscow, however, which produced several violent encounters, led, early in May, 1922, to a sensational trial involving the Patriarch himself. According to *Izvestiia*, this hearing, known as the trial of the Fifty-four (there were fifty-four defendants) disclosed that early in March Archbishop Nikandr called a meeting of the district priests at which he read and distributed the Patriarch's proclamation against the confiscation of the consecrated articles and induced the priests to protest to the government. In turn, there were parish meetings a few days later, at which Patriarch Tikhon's message was read and incendiary speeches sometimes made, calling the confiscations "looting" and the officials "bandits." When the officials actually came to requisition the valuables, at some churches agitation by laymen or by priests stirred up the crowd summoned by the tocsin. False rumors were circulated to the effect that the treasure was wanted, not for the starving but for the Soviet officials to accumulate in foreign countries against the day of their expulsion from Russia. Cries were uttered: "Kill the Jewish plunderers! Kill the Communists!" Violence occurred in several places; troops were used and several individuals were wounded. As a result of these disclosures, the accusation was not merely of agitation against the requisitioning of the valuables, but of counterrevolutionary activities directed toward the overthrow of the Soviet Power.[50]

In keeping with this policy of considering the wider implications of the case, the prosecution introduced the testimony of Professor Kuznetsov, Bishop Antonin, and Priests Kalinovskii and Ledovskii concerning the propriety, according to church law, of using religious articles for purposes of mercy. All agreed that the canons cited by Patriarch Tikhon applied only to cases of putting church plate to personal use, not to using it for aid to the needy. All agreed that the latter use was not sacrilege nor blasphemy.[51]

After this expert testimony, the court next sought to show that the real responsibility for the Moscow disorders lay with the heads of the church. Archbishop Nikandr was unexpectedly brought into court from his prison cell and questioned concerning the meeting on March 7 with the district priests. He denied that he had read Tikhon's proclamation condemning the requisitioning, but said that he had merely discussed it with the priests and had encouraged them to organize protests to the government. He also denied having distributed copies of the proclamation. This testimony was rebutted by several district priests, who testified that he had both read the proclamation and given them copies of it for distribution.[52]

The next surprise witness was Patriarch Tikhon himself, who appeared on the stand after Archbishop Nikandr. He testified calmly and with dignity that he ruled the church and its property. He declared that he had only done his duty in issuing his proclamation, as he felt that the government had made a mistake in ordering confiscation of the church treasure, and it was his task to point out the canonical rules. As for those dying of starvation, he was quoted as saying that that was the affair of the government and not his concern. When asked about his responsibility for the clergy who followed his orders and opposed the removal of the consecrated articles from the churches, he stated that the clergy did not have to obey his commands; it was for them to decide whether to do so; his task was to point out the rules of the church.[53]

At this point the Soviet press turned all its guns upon the Patriarch, whose quarters were termed "the general staff of the counterrevolution." One editorial traced the thread of opposition from Archbishop Nikandr to the district priests, and then to the parish clergy, who received Tikhon's proclamation. Next, speeches of incitement, and "finally, stones thrown at the heads of Red Army men." Another stated that the church had consistently supported reaction and that, in spite of the Patriarch's denial of connections with the Karlovatskii Sobor, "for us there can be no doubt whether the 'Russian Pope' was informed of the deliberations and the resolutions that took place in the 'spiritual Genoa' at Karlovtsy."[54] Similarly, *Pravda* declared that the Moscow and Shuia trials had shown that the counterrevolutionary threads leading from the monarchist organizations to the Karlovatskii Sobor had extensions into Russia, used "to strike blows at the Soviets in the name of religion." It ended the editorial by saying that now it was clear who had incited the outbreaks. "The struggle was not for golden vestments — it was for the Tsar's crown, for returning their holdings to the landowners. . . . Under the black cassocks of the higher clergy were hidden the foulest, blackest foes of the working people and the revolution."[55]

Finally, the Moscow Tribunal ruled that the evidence at the trial had shown that the hierarchy, headed by Archbishop Nikandr and Patriarch Tikhon, had "worked out a plan of opposition to the removal of the valuables" and had distributed the proclamation against it, which had produced excesses. Hence Patriarch Tikhon and Archbishop Nikandr were to be indicted.[56]

Captain McCullagh, in Moscow at the time, was told by a high ecclesiastic close to Tikhon that the latter had had no intention of stirring up violence by his proclamation. In fact, the captain was told, the Patriarch condemned bloodshed and civil war; and on April 11, in a circular letter to the bishops he had condemned violent opposition such as flared forth at Shuia, Smolensk, Rostov, and other places, and earnestly begged the bishops to dissuade the faithful from violence.[57]

The Soviet authorities, however, seem to have been sure of themselves. The seriousness of the charges against the Patriarch was shown by the sentences handed out to the far lesser figures already on trial. Of the Fifty-four, ten men (mostly priests) and one woman were sentenced to be shot; ten were acquitted or released, and the rest received prison sentences of from one to five years each.[58] The sentences were appealed to the All-Russian Central Executive Committee, which after much deliberation confirmed the death penalty for five of the men and reduced the sentences of the other condemned to five years' imprisonment each.[59]

After the trial an additional charge against Archbishop Nikandr was made. During a search of his rooms made by Father Krasnitskii of the pro-Soviet Living Church group, a bag of empty foreign envelopes was allegedly found, indicating that he was in communication with the world abroad — presumably with enemies of the Soviets.[60]

An even more sensational trial occurred at Petrograd in August, 1922. During the period, the Soviet press reported nine violent incidents at Petrograd churches when the official commission came to remove the valuables destined for famine relief. Crowds, usually summoned by the tocsin, gathered and stoned the commission and the militiamen stationed for their protection; troops had to be called out to re-establish order. Although there were apparently no fatalities, the frequency of the disorders and the violence of the crowds indicated a serious situation.[61] The authorities, probably after long and detailed investigation, held a great trial of those accused of fomenting the disorders, at which Krasikov, head of the Fifth Section of the Commissariat of Justice, served as prosecutor. Ninety persons were accused, including Metropolitan Veniamin himself, Professor Novitskii, an important figure in the administration of the diocese, V. P. Shein, former member of the Nationalist party in the Fourth Duma who had become an abbot during the revolutionary period, and Professors Beneshevich and Petrovskii, theologians. The charge was participation in an organized counterrevolutionary plot to incite the masses to overthrow the Soviet regime; the inspiration for the plot allegedly came from Patriarch Tikhon and the Karlovatskii Sobor.[62]

During the trial the prosecution charged that in February and March secret meetings had been called by the metropolitan, at which a campaign of opposition to the removal of the church treasures was mapped out.[63] Shortly thereafter, the churchmen allegedly presented a series of impossible demands to the Petrograd Commission of Pomgol, and then without waiting for the Soviet reply, began to circulate their petition to the parishes, where its condemnation of the removal of consecrated articles as sacrilege was read to the parishioners. At this point the Soviet authorities conferred with the metropolitan, seeking to meet his demands for safeguards in the handling of the sacred objects. The metropolitan proved obdurate, however, and a second proclamation calling the requisitions sacrilege and blasphemy was circulated. The talks with the Petrograd Soviet were broken off, and the disorders began soon thereafter.[64]

The defendants claimed that they had favored turning over the valuables, but that the canons forbade this; they also claimed that the crowds had become violent because of sincere belief and not because of proclamations or clerical agitation; several of the priests declared that they had tried to calm the mobs.[65] An account of the trial published abroad, based on the statements of an anonymous observer, declared that Metropolitan Veniamin had not been hostile to the Soviets and had refrained from politics. He was willing to turn the church treasure over to Pomgol and had actually reached an agreement on the matter, when the central Soviet authorities, eager to smash the church, had ordered confiscation of the valuables. Even then, this account stated, the confiscation was achieved with little violence. The Moscow authorities, however, wanted to discredit the church and hence staged a demonstrative trial, accusing Metropolitan Veniamin of counterrevolution, with the verdict a foregone conclusion.[66]

Certainly the charge of counterrevolution was the essence of the trial. In his prosecutor's charge Krasikov dwelt upon the record of the church as an opponent of the Soviets and a supporter of the White movements; the Karlovatskii Sobor with its alleged ties with the Patriarch figured largely, and the connections of Tikhon and Veniamin were cited to show that the leading churchmen in Russia were in league with those abroad.[67] Sensational testimony was given by some of the Petrograd clergy, notably the priests Vvedenskii and Krasnitskii, who had broken with the Patriarch and had formed the new Living Church group. They declared that counterrevolutionary activity *was* carried on in the parishes and that Metropolitan Veniamin and other ecclesiastics were "conscious tools" of the counterrevolutionary clique of former bourgeois, officials, and other reactionaries who dominated the church. Although Metropolitan Veniamin had hypocritically pretended to approve the requisitioning of the church valuables, actually he had backed the anathema of the Patriarch and hence was responsible for the disorders.[68]

The defense sought to shake this testimony by charging that Vvedenskii had for some time been a special protégé of Metropolitan Veniamin and now was playing the role of Judas. (This led to an attack on Vvedenskii by a fanatical woman, who severely wounded him in the head with a stone.) Krasnitskii was allegedly much taken aback when the defense showed that ten years before he had written an article upholding the theory of Jewish ritual murder.[69]

The testimony of these dissident priests nonetheless produced a strong impression and played an important part in the decision. The court sentenced ten of the defendants, including Metropolitan Veniamin, to be shot "as dangerous and uncompromising foes of the republic." Upon appeal, the Central Executive Committee spared six, but Metropolitan Veniamin, Abbot Sergii Shein, Novitskii, and one other were executed.[70] Kalinin, chairman of the Central Executive Committee, expressly stated that the trial was held not merely on the basis of the disorders that had occurred, but on the grounds of counterrevolution. The government was not concerned with matters of faith, ritual, or the organization of the church, but could not remain indifferent when "the heads of the church declared civil war against the government." He concluded: ". . . there cannot and will not be mercy for those princes of the church, and also those laymen, archbourgeois politicians, who now, covering themselves with the organization of the church, raise the especially dark and perverted elements of the population against the Workers' and Peasants' Power, in league with their White-Guard co-thinkers abroad." He completely rejected the argument of the defense that the disorders resulted from spontaneous action on the part of devout believers whose faith had been outraged by the confiscation of holy things.[71]

In addition to these outstanding trials, the Soviet press reported a number of lesser magnitude, in which the results were usually less drastic, but still severe. The Smolensk trial was significant because Bishop Filipp, the central figure, admitted guilt, which he laid to the instructions of the Patriarch and his reactionary advisers, and renounced his allegiance to the Patriarch in favor of the dissident Living Church. In view of this repentance, the court merely reprimanded him; but four laymen involved in the disorders were shot and other defendants received prison terms.[72] At Rostov-on-Don Bishop Arsenii, with a long record of anti-Soviet activity, was sentenced to be shot, but in view of his repentance and the government's amnesty this was reduced to ten years' imprisonment.[73] Archbishop Anatolii of Irkutsk was likewise sentenced to be shot, but was permitted to appeal; the result of the appeal was not stated.[74] Bishop Viktor of Tomsk, who allegedly stirred up numerous disorders over church treasure, was also sentenced to death.[75] Other hierarchs who were punished were Archbishop Nafanail of Khar'kov, and Bishops Kirrill of Iaroslavl, Gennadii of Pskov, Zinovii of Tambov, Anatolii of Astrakhan, Boris of Penza, and Alexei of Kiev. Their sentences seem to have been varying terms of imprisonment.[76] Bishops Iuvenalii of Tula, Boris of Rybinsk, and Serafim of Uglich were also sentenced to prison terms.[77] There doubtless were others sentenced.

In addition to the clergy and laymen who were punished for contesting the requisitioning of the church valuables, there were others who were punished for allegedly stealing them or for concealment. *Izves-*

tiia reported the arrest on a train of two priests and the chairman of a parish council, who had boxes of chalices, crucifixes, censers, and other religious articles of gold or silver, which they admitted they were taking from Samara to Minsk to sell abroad.[78] Another report told of a group which had been stealing and melting religious articles into silver bars, which were then smuggled out of Russia in an Estonian diplomatic car.[79] On the other hand, anti-Soviet sources charged that the Soviet accusations against the clergy were in reality made in order to conceal their own theft and embezzlement of church valuables.[80]

It is difficult to determine how effective the use of the religious articles for famine relief turned out to be. In its report on its accomplishments Pomgol stated that as early as April, 1922, the sufferers were receiving grain from the proceeds. As of October 1, 1922, Pomgol reported that the local offices of the Commissariat of Finance had received 1217 lbs. avoir. of gold and 863,913 lbs. of silver, 4268 lbs. of other precious metals, and a great number of diamonds, pearls, and other gems. The gold had an approximate value of 600,000 gold rubles, while the silver was then worth approximately 18,500,000 gold rubles. As the gems were reported to be worth 211,563 gold rubles,[81] the total received from the gold, silver and gems amounted to some 19,300,000 gold rubles. These returns were not complete, as the task was not finished for some time thereafter. As far as can be determined, more exact figures were never published. The financial results of the confiscations certainly were unsatisfactory, for in December, 1922, *Izvestiia* stated so, blaming the poor showing in part upon undue mildness of the local authorities, who did not wish to irritate the believers, and in part upon concealment or theft by churchmen. It proposed that the total could be raised considerably by following the example of one province and proclaiming a week during which churchmen might turn in any additional valuables with no questions asked.[82]

It has frequently been asked why the Soviet authorities did not sell the Russian crown jewels before taking the property of the church. In October, 1922, Herbert Hoover of the American Relief Administration sent a telegram to Kamenev saying that it would be difficult to obtain charitable donations to aid Soviet famine victims unless the government made full use of the crown jewels, the church treasures, and other liquid assets. The Soviet government replied that it was willing to pledge its liquid assets abroad as collateral for a loan, provided that a guarantee could be given that the crown jewels would not be attached by foreign claimants against Russia. Dr. H. H. Fisher, historian of the American Relief Administration's operations in Russia, stated that "this condition removed this proposal from the realm of possibility, for to secure such a guarantee . . . would involve vast international complications. . . ." [83] Indeed, when the Soviets attempted to send gold to the United States to purchase grain it was difficult to get it accepted; affidavits had to be made that the gold had been in Russian possession before 1917.[84] Thus it was probably for practical reasons that the Soviet rulers did not use the crown jewels, and not in order to have an excuse to seize the treasure of the church.

The political results of the conflict over the use of the church's valuables cannot be determined with any accuracy. One Soviet writer does give statistics as to the sentences inflicted by 55 tribunals, but they are far from complete. Of the 738 persons tried, 149 were acquitted, 33 were shot, 75 were put on probation, and the others received prison terms (usually from two to three years) or other penalties. Of the condemned 181 were ecclesiastics, 408 were laymen.[85]

Undoubtedly these sentences, and any others that may have been imposed, were not explainable merely by the disorders that had occurred, if these be viewed as isolated instances of violence caused by outraged religious feeling. It is only when they are considered as incidents in a possible campaign to overthrow the Soviet regime and restore the monarchy that the Soviet severity becomes understandable. The government had just survived a long period of civil war and intervention; fighting was still going on, on Soviet soil with the Japanese and Finnish irregulars; banditry was still prevalent in Belorussia and in Soviet Central Asia, and the Caucasus was far from quiet. Under these circumstances there was grave doubt whether the Communist state could survive the famine. When the Karlovatskii Sobor openly called for renewed intervention in Russia and expressed hope that the famine would cause the collapse of the Soviets, and when, after the Patriarch's message of anathema, disorders broke out over the seizure of the church vessels, it doubtless looked to the Soviet rulers like a widely ramified plot. If, as they claimed, they had evidence linking Patriarch Tikhon with the Karlovatskii Sobor, it is not surprising that they struck with severity to scotch the plot.

Another possible explanation of the Soviet measures is advanced by anti-Soviet writers: namely, that the whole question of the church valuables was raised to provide an excuse for smashing the Russian church, which the Communists hated as the only institution in Russia that was not under their control and which, as good Marxists, they detested on ideological grounds. This theory, however, does not seem plausible, as even at the height of the civil war no attempt was made to destroy the church, and in 1921 its position was quite tolerable, with no efforts on the part of the responsible Soviet authorities to crush it. Only the coincidence of the Karlovatskii Sobor and the violent opposition aroused by the Patriarchal message brought about harsh Soviet action to eliminate hostile church leaders. Fear of a widespread ecclesiastical plot seems to be the more likely explanation.

It is impossible to determine the correctness of the Soviet charges that the Patriarch was the organizer of a plot whose ramifications extended to the Karlovatskii Sobor. It is clear that the latter explicitly asked for an insurrection and new intervention in Russia, but the connection of the Patriarch with such a scheme is uncertain. Undoubtedly, however, he was far from hostile to the *émigré* churchmen and he probably had never lost the antagonism that he had shown toward the Soviet regime in 1918. His message condemning the seizure of church vessels was a clear defiance of the government and its legislation of 1918 and 1922, and the circumstances under which this message was circulated indicate that it was intended and used to promote active opposition. Whether that opposition was merely intended to preserve consecrated articles from seizure or whether Patriarch Tikhon and his advisers hoped and expected, as did the members of the Karlovatskii Sobor, that the violent outbreaks would grow into outright rebellion that would cause the downfall of the Soviet state, cannot be determined here.

In either case the Patriarch failed. The danger to the government does not seem to have been extreme at any time, and the opposition did not embrace any large fraction of the population. Indeed, public opinion seems to have supported the authorities in holding that the starving of the Volga had greater need of the valuables than did the church and that to oppose their use upon legalistic grounds was far from Christian. Although public interest in the trials of those who opposed the seizure was apparently great, there is no evidence to show that there was widespread displeasure at the sentences imposed. In addition, the trials seem to have eliminated, either permanently or temporarily, many of the hierarchs most hostile to the Soviet regime, while numerous members of the parish clergy were now ready to repudiate the ecclesiastical leadership that had caused many of them to suffer punishment for obeying the Patriarch's instructions. Thus the Patriarch, who in May was put under arrest and indictment, was soon faced by a wide revolt within the church. The circumstances of that revolt and its outcome form the subject of the following chapter.

CHAPTER VII

The Church Revolution of 1922

THE REVOLT in the Russian Orthodox church against Patriarch Tikhon in May, 1922, had deep roots. During the Revolution of 1905 the Thirty-two, a group of progressive clergy, had formed in St. Petersburg, and a few liberal priests appeared elsewhere. Bishop Antonin was one of the few liberal bishops. Nevertheless, the liberal movement made little progress under the tsar. After the February Revolution, as indicated earlier, a reviving liberalism, encouraged by L'vov, gave hope that the church, which had long followed a reactionary course, might now enter the liberal path. The calling of the Sobor seemed a victory for the League of Democratic Clergy, led by Vvedenskii, Boiarskii, Egorov, Popov, and others. But the rising tide of revolution frightened many of the once progressive priests, so that the conservatives were able to dominate the Sobor, in spite of a few liberals headed by Professor Titlinov. An attempt was made by Protopresbyter Shavel'skii, Vvedenskii, and others to organize an underground movement of progressives within the church, but nothing came of it.[1]

By 1919–1920, however, the progressive spirit was again strong, much to the dismay of Patriarch Tikhon, who issued a decree in the fall of 1921 forbidding any innovations in the practice of the church, under threat of severe penalties. In Petrograd, however, Metropolitan Veniamin was induced to protect the liberals, so that Vvedenskii, Boiarskii, and others were able to survive unscathed.[2]

Another factor in the presbyterian revolt in 1922 was the hatred of many parish priests for the monastic bishops. This class feeling of white (nonmonastic) clergy against black had flared forth in the diocesan congresses that had turned on their bishops in the spring of 1917; and it remained a latent force. It was the combination of these two influences within the church that produced the movement against the Patriarch in 1922.

The famine of 1921 and the question concerning the use of the treasure of the church became the catalyst that crystallized the amorphous discontent. Late in March, 1922, after the Patriarch's message opposing surrender of the valuables, Dean Vvedenskii and eleven other clerics appealed to the believers to surrender them, and Father Kalinovskii wrote that those who refused to give up the treasures were disobeying Christ. He closed his appeal with a significant prophecy that time would soon show whether conservatives or liberals were correct. "We are on the eve of great events in the church, we are on the eve of a revolution of the church." [3]

At the same time the Soviet leaders, who in 1919 had rejected a proposal for supporting pro-Soviet clergy, now were ready to help their friends among the clergy as well as to punish their active foes. An editorial in *Izvestiia,* "Princes and Plain People," in March, 1922, expressed the belief that the government should aid "that more democratic part of the clergy that finds within themselves some sort of common feeling with the suffering masses, and protect it against the violence of the group of commanding church heads, who are definitely hostile to the laboring masses and dream only of bringing back the old order." [4] This course of action, which was repeatedly advocated in the press, was obviously becoming official policy. Doubtless this fact, as well as the fear felt by some priests that they might be punished by a Soviet tribunal if they obeyed Tikhon's orders, played its part in strengthening the movement away from the Patriarch.

The connection between the trials of the churchmen and the rise of the new movement is inescapable. On May 9 Patriarch Tikhon, who had just testified before the tribunal in the case of the Fifty-four, was indicted and placed under arrest. The following day, *Pravda* contained an interview with Father Kalinovskii, one of the liberal leaders, in which he stated that the movement away from Patriarch Tikhon had begun long ago in Petrograd and Moscow and that the conflict over the church's valuables had merely impelled them to act at that moment. [5]

Developments now came in rapid succession. On May 12 a group of clergy, headed by the priests Kalinovskii, Krasnitskii, and Vvedenskii, visited Patriarch Tikhon, who was under house arrest in his quarters, and had a long talk with him. According to the statement issued by this group, they charged the Patriarch with responsibility for the low state of the church, with its leaders under arrest, some of its clergy under sentence of death, and a complete breakdown of church authority imminent. They accused him of following a consistently counterrevolutionary policy from his anathema in January, 1918, throughout the civil war, and charged him with sheltering a number of counterrevolutionary persons who wished to use the church as a center of opposition to the Soviets. They declared that the church, whose authority among the masses had been undermined by the opposition to the removal of the church valuables, had fallen into a state of anarchy, and that this could only be remedied by the calling of an All-Russian Sobor and by the temporary elimination of the Patriarch from the administration of ecclesiastical affairs. After some discussion the Patriarch signed a renunciation of his authority, which he turned over to one of the other hierarchs.[6]

Two days after this conference, the same group of clergy, plus Bishop Antonin, published an appeal "To the Believing Sons of the Orthodox Church." It stated that the workers' and peasants' government, which existed by the will of God, had sought to combat the famine, epidemics, and other disasters afflicting Russia, but the leaders of the church took the side of the enemies of the people, as shown by the outbreaks when the church's valuables were requisitioned. By so doing the churchmen had tried to create a state overturn. "The proclamation of Patriarch Tikhon became the banner around which flocked the counterrevolutionaries. . . ." The people, however, did not support this program of the hierarchs, but condemned those "who wished to use the national calamity for their own political ends." Likewise the clergy signing the appeal condemned these prelates and called for a new Sobor to pass judgment upon those guilty of the ruin of the church as well as to set in order the administration of the church and re-establish good relations with the Soviet government. "The civil war of the church against the state, which is guided by the upper hierarchy, should be ended."[7]

Patriarch Tikhon carried out the agreement to give up his authority by a letter to Metropolitan Agafangel on May 16, in which he stated that the circumstances of his arrest had made it desirable to turn the administration of the church over to Agafangel until a Sobor could be called. He therefore asked the latter to come to Moscow without delay; according to his report, he stated that the authorities had agreed to this.[8]

According to Captain Francis McCullagh, who seems to have had close connections with the Orthodox leaders at this time, on May 12 the liberal priests got the Patriarch out of bed to demand that he appoint Bishop Antonin as his successor. He was told that the eleven Moscow churchmen condemned in the trial of the Fifty-four would be shot if he refused, while there might be a pardon for them if he consented. When Tikhon sternly refused, it was suggested that he name as his deputy either Metropolitan Veniamin or Metropolitan Agafangel. Agafangel was named, because of the Soviet attitude toward Metropolitan Veniamin.[9]

To the group of liberal churchmen, however, it probably seemed not enough to replace the Patriarch by the conservative Metropolitan Agafangel. Consequently on May 18 three of them, in another interview with Tikhon, presented a request that, in view of the interregnum between Tikhon's arrest and the coming of Agafangel, the administration of the church business, then at a standstill, be temporarily entrusted to them. They promised to obtain bishops in Moscow to help in the work in the patriarchal chancery and agreed that the Patriarch's deputy should at once assume the functions assigned to him upon his arrival in Moscow. The Patriarch discussed this proposal with them for over an hour and finally agreed to it. He wrote the following note upon the top of the petition:

> The persons named below are ordered to take over and transmit the Synod affairs to the Most Reverend Agafangel upon his arrival in Moscow, . . . with the assistance of Secretary Numerov; the Moscow diocese to the Most Reverend Innokentii, Bishop of Klin, and before his arrival to the Most Reverend Leonid, Bishop of Vernensk, with the assistance of the Department Chief Nevskii.[10]

A year later Patriarch Tikhon, upon his release from imprisonment, gave out a statement concerning this incident in which he declared that he had merely permitted the priests in question to attend to the classification of incoming correspondence of the chancery.[11] For the ambitious group of priests, however, this limited task was far from sufficient. Father Kalinovskii told a reporter that they had reached an agreement with the Patriarch that for the present the authority in the church should go to the "Temporary Higher Church Administration" — a self-constituted body consisting of Bishops Antonin and Leonid, Dean Vvedenskii, Fathers Krasnitskii, Kalinovskii, and Belkov, Deacon Skobelev, and Khlebnikov, a layman. They would take over both Synodal and diocesan affairs and would shortly take steps to call a Sobor. As Patriarch Tikhon had moved from his quarters in the Troitskoe Podvor'e to the Donskoi Monastery, the administration of the church concentrated in the Podvor'e was now in the hands of the new group.[12] Short notices in the press on the following day stated that the new board had actually started to administer the church.[13]

Thus by a bloodless coup the insurgent clerics seized control of the administrative machinery of the church; there was no one to say them nay, for the Patriarch was under arrest, Metropolitan Veniamin also was in the toils, and Metropolitan Agafangel never came to take over his charge. For some time the leaders of the new movement insisted that they had taken power legally by permission of the Patriarch and that they were the properly instituted authority in the church. Obviously this was far from accurate. The Patriarch had merely permitted them to handle the current correspondence of the Synod until Metropolitan Agafangel might assume his duties — something quite different from appointing them to administer the church in his place. Indeed, Professor Titlinov, one of the more sober leaders of the movement, later admitted that this was not a legal change of heads, but a revolution in the church — a much needed one, which in his eyes was sufficient justification.[14] Likewise Vvedenskii, one of the guiding spirits of the movement, later stated that "it began its existence by breaking with the Patriarch" and sneered at casuists who "mumble something about a canonical succession from Patriarch Tikhon." [15]

In the meantime, Metropolitan Agafangel, named as deputy for Patriarch Tikhon, did not come to Moscow. According to one of the liberal priests, he was approached by Dean Krasnitskii, who summoned him to come to Moscow, only to receive the reply that he could not come, as he had to put his affairs and those of his diocese in order.

Later the local clergy asked him why he had done nothing about assuming his new duties, whereupon he calmly explained that he could do nothing from Iaroslavl, and could not leave, as he was under house arrest. He told his questioner that there was no hurry — within a month the new ruling body would collapse, and then he might rule the church from Moscow.[16] The patriarchal party, on the other hand, explained his failure to come to Moscow as due to the interference of the government, which allegedly wished to help the reforming group. Shortly thereafter Agafangel was arrested and exiled to the Narym region in the far north.[17] In June he had issued a message to the faithful which was secretly circulated, calling on them not to recognize the unlawful acts of the new figures at the helm of the church but to remain true to the Orthodox faith and its Patriarch. In the interim he urged the bishops to rule their dioceses in autonomous fashion until the restoration of the true church authorities. He appealed to the pastors to hold to the true faith and asked the flock to have nothing to do with those who had fallen into the snares of the tempters.[18] His proclamation was posted in a number of churches in Moscow. A few days later *Pravda,* stating that he was under house arrest for violating article 12 of the new criminal code, referred to him as "the Black Hundredite and counterrevolutionary, Metropolitan Agafangel — the same Agafangel who posted on the Church of the Savior in Moscow reactionary proclamations demanding the nonrecognition of the Higher Church Administration and all sorts of opposition to the liberative movement . . . in the lower levels of the church and the clergy." [19]

The arrest of Metropolitan Agafangel removed the last important obstacle to the new orientation in ecclesiastical affairs. The Soviet government always claimed impartiality in religious matters, asserting that its punishment of churchmen was for counterrevolutionary activities, not for adherence to the wrong grouping. Nevertheless, there is strong reason to believe that on occasion membership in the patriarchal party came to be regarded as evidence of counterrevolutionary intent and was punished accordingly. On the other hand, the new group, which called itself the Living Church, received full freedom to carry out its plans. The government, which had long followed a policy of armed neutrality toward the Orthodox church, was now co-operating with its friends within the church and punishing its enemies. In spite of variations and wavering, the latter course has been followed by the Soviet authorities down to the present time. Whether, as the anti-Soviet *émigré* clergy claim, this was a subtle way to discredit the church in the eyes of the people by enslaving it to the Soviet regime, or whether the Soviet leaders were merely seeking a *modus vivendi* with a troublesome, influential organization, cannot be determined.

A highly significant expression of the hopes of the liberal churchmen appeared in the first issue of their new journal, *Zhivaia Tserkov'* (*The Living Church*), which was published on May 12 or 13, 1922, at the time of the first meeting with the Patriarch. This program took the form of a memorandum to the All-Russian Central Executive Committee from "the Initiative Group of the Orthodox church." It stated that the difficulties and conflicts over the use of church treasure showed that under certain conditions the government could not remain aloof from the Orthodox church, but had to take positive action concerning it. The Soviet constitution provided no legal organs for carrying on negotiations with the church, so that when the government acted to take the valuables, physical conflict resulted, which was bad for the nation. Hence the group proposed that a special All-Russian Committee on Affairs of the Orthodox church be formed of Orthodox clergy and laymen, headed by an authorized person of episcopal rank, which should be under the All-Russian Central Executive Committee. The function of this new body should be to organize those clerics and laymen "who recognize the righteousness of the Russian Social Revolution and are loyal in respect to the Soviet Power," to protect them against the patriarchal administration and unite them on a nation-wide scale for development of a general program on church matters and relations with the state. It should keep watch over the patriarchal administration, and its local organs should do the same in the dioceses. Finally, it should further the peaceful and lawful carrying out of governmental measures that did not violate the religious beliefs of the Orthodox.[19a]

This issue also contained editorials by leading figures in the Living Church movement. Father Kalinovskii, the editor, and Father Krasnitskii both stressed that the church was in a parlous state as a result of the follies of "the old bureaucratic order." Bishop Antonin, characteristically, urged more spiritual and religious life in the church in order to bring it out of its state of paralysis. Dean Vvedenskii also held that the church was paralyzed, spiritually dead. To recover, it must stop expecting the return of a tsar and must take to its heart the interests of the poverty-stricken, as church fathers like St. Cyprian of Carthage, St. Basil the Great, and St. John of Damascus had strongly urged.[19b]

Upon the pronouncements of the Living Church *Izvestiia* turned a somewhat jaundiced eye. The editor said that while the movement represented an attempt on the part of progressive or merely honorable clergymen to adjust themselves to the catastrophe that had struck the church, the real question was whether the ecclesiastics merely sought to ease the contradictions of their counterrevolutionary leaders, to get them out of an impossible situation, or wanted to break with the counterrevolutionary hierarchy and to recognize and uphold the social revolution.[19c]

One of the first moves of the Living Church was to appeal to Kalinin on behalf of the Moscow priests condemned in the trial of the Fifty-four, asking that an act of mercy mark the beginning of the new period of church life.[20] Later Bishop Antonin told a turbulent audience that he had appealed for the clergy under sentence, and had been told that some, but not all, could be pardoned. He stirred up a storm by saying that the government hit the churchmen because they were counterrevolutionary and by expressing his opinion that if General Wrangel marched to Moscow the clergy would greet him with banners. Antonin also accused his audience of displaying an anti-Soviet frame of mind at two earlier lectures, which attitude had not eased the state of the accused. "When orators poked fun at us for our attempts to make contact with the authorities, you applauded them." [21]

While the first issue of *The Living Church* had merely suggested an ecclesiastical steering committee to exercise a check upon the patriarchal administration, by the time of the second issue, as a result of the success of the Living Church group in gaining control of the church organization, their program was much more ambitious. An editorial now blamed the low state of the church upon the patriarchate, which had been foisted upon the church at the Sobor of 1917.

Hence the new Sobor should consider the feasibility "of abolishing the very institution of the patriarchate," which might be replaced by a collegiate administration. As for the relation of the church to the government, the Sobor must definitely and without reservation recognize the separation of church from state. Furthermore, the editor stated that the church could not remain indifferent to the struggle against social and economic injustice, "against the fact of the existence of capitalism in the Christian world." [22]

Once the Living Church movement had gained the seats of the mighty in Moscow its manifesto received considerable support, chiefly among the parish clergy, although some bishops also approved. Part of the clergy of Kiev and Archbishop Amvrosii of Briansk were reported as early as May 20 to be in favor of abolishing the patriarchate and unfrocking Patriarch Tikhon.[23] Many signatures were reported to have been placed upon the proclamation of the Living Church group, with calls for a Sobor and for trying the Patriarch. Archbishop Evdokim of Nizhnii Novgorod, who had taken the lead in proposing the use of church treasure for the famine sufferers, issued a statement condemning the policies of the Patriarch.[24]

A great moral victory was won by the Living Church when, on June 16, 1922, the revered Metropolitan Sergii of Vladimir and Archbishops Evdokim and Serafim of Kostroma issued a joint proclamation stating that, after considering the platform and the legality of the Temporary Church Administration,

> we entirely agree with the measures of the Temporary Church Administration, we regard it as the only, canonical, legal higher church authority, and all dispositions proceeding from it we regard as fully lawful and binding. We call all true pastors and believing sons of the church, both of the dioceses entrusted to us and of other dioceses, to follow our example.[25]

Later, additional bishops, whether leaderless and frightened or convinced of its correctness, declared for the Living Church. Bishop Filipp of Smolensk, tried for inspiring the disorders in that city, declared that he repented of the counterrevolutionary past that he and the church had had in common and expressed the belief that through a new Sobor the church should achieve wide reforms and declare itself on the Soviet side.[26] Bishop Ierofei of Ivanovo-Voznesensk and Bishop Benedikt of Viazma also declared themselves for the Living Church.[27]

The formal organization of the Living Church group took place on July 4 in Moscow, with forty-two persons present. Father Krasnitskii stated that they had already organized the Central Committee and the Moscow Committee; now they planned to organize similar committees all over Russia. The gathering adopted bylaws for "the Group of Orthodox White Clergy, the Living Church," which stated that its purpose was to free the pastors "from the economically dominant elements of society." At the coming Sobor, they were to secure for the white clergy the right to become bishops and to participate in the Higher Church Administration and the diocesan administrations along with the bishops. Members must recognize "the justice of the Russian social revolution." [28]

Thus the Living Church movement at this time was chiefly a sort of trade-union movement of the parish priests, although it also stood for a pro-Soviet policy. For most of its members its chief purpose was to break the domination of their foes, the monastic bishops. They also wished to free themselves from the counterrevolutionary stigma resulting from the policy of the bishops. Other considerations were of less significance.

The expected opposition from the bishops was not long in coming. As soon as the Temporary Higher Church Administration was formed, Metropolitan Veniamin (who had not yet been arrested) excommunicated three members from Petrograd without a hearing, and Dean Vvedenskii was ousted from his church by his parishioners. Moreover, at a pastoral meeting on June 5 the Petrograd clergy completely refused to recognize the overturn in the church and sent two conservative clerics to Moscow to get in touch with Patriarch Tikhon. Bishop Alexei, to whom Veniamin turned over his diocese when he was arrested, stated that he scorned the social revolution.[29] Late in June, however, the aggressive Father Krasnitskii was sent to Petrograd by the new church administration. He found the local clergy disorganized by the numerous arrests among them and was able to induce Bishop Alexei to resign as administrator of the diocese. On June 28 a meeting of the district priests recognized the Living Church and the social revolution and the new diocesan administration, composed of presbyters only, that was set up the same day. Dean Sobolev was put at the head of the diocese; on July 9 he was consecrated bishop in Moscow — the first non-celibate bishop — and was raised to be Archbishop of Petrograd. He at once asked pardon for the eleven sentenced to death in the trial of the Fifty-four.[30] The situation in Petrograd was further simplified for the new administration of the church by the unfrocking of a number of Petrograd clerics and the excommunication of several of the most reactionary laymen.[31]

The new central body of the church also moved to gain control over the other dioceses. To each was sent a delegate with plenipotentiary powers, who helped organize local units of insurgent clergy, dissolved the old diocesan councils, and in some cases ousted the bishops by sending them into exile (apparently to distant monasteries). The proclamation circulated by Metropolitan Agafangel hindered this work, as it showed that the purge did not have the sanction of Patriarch Tikhon as had been claimed. But the work went on. The congress of the Living Church in August voted to ask the diocesan and county church administrations to take "most decisive measures" against the opponents of the renovation of the church, not excluding removal from office and expulsion from the diocese. Responsibility for the exact performance of these measures was placed personally upon the deputies of the Higher Church Administration.[32] Later a report was made to the congress stating that of the 143 bishops of the church, 37 had announced their support for the Higher Church Administration, 36 were entirely against the renovation movement, and the remainder had not declared their positions. Father Krasnitskii told the meeting that the 36 ardent counterrevolutionary bishops would be removed from their positions but would be permitted to live where they could lead a monastic life. The congress demanded that the noncommittal bishops be required to state their positions.[33] A few days later the congress was told that 24 bishops already had been retired in addition to the 36 removed by the congress — making 60 in all.[34]

The followers of Patriarch Tikhon have repeatedly charged that the deputies of the Living Church used intimidation and force in conducting their purges in the dioceses. Especially after Metropolitan Agafangel's proclamation had shown that they lacked the support of the Patriarch and his appointed successor, the reformers allegedly obtained the open collaboration of the GPU (the political police), who on occasion arrested stubborn ecclesiastics and sent them into exile. While documentary proof of these assertions has not been presented, there is reason to believe that the police — sometimes with cause — at times viewed the enemies of the Living Church as counterrevolutionaries and dealt with them as such, thereby giving aid and comfort to the liberal churchmen. This question of governmental support for the Living Church movement will be considered later in more detail.

The congress of the Living Church in August, 1922, was a small, highly selected gathering, which, in view of the hostile attitude of many laymen in the chief cities, was open only to ecclesiastics; since, however, many laymen had come from the provinces for the gathering, an exception was made in their favor by Father Krasnitskii, the dominant figure.[35] On August 6 it was reported that 154 delegates had arrived, of whom 3 were bishops and 24 laymen. Additional delegates were expected.[36]

The keynote of the congress was hostility to the monastics, from Patriarch Tikhon down, and the desire of the white clergy to obtain a dominant position in the church. Although the monastics Evdokim, now Metropolitan of Novgorod, and Bishop Antonin spoke, and thanks were voted to those monks who upheld the Living Church, the congress adopted a resolution asking the closing of all urban monasteries; those in rural areas should be made into working brotherhoods. In addition, it demanded the unfrocking of Patriarch Tikhon and the cessation of prayers for him. Other hostile monks should be removed from their posts; monks who submitted to the new order in the church were merely to be moved to another diocese.[37]

The enmity toward the monastic bishops was also shown by the adoption of a resolution that a married priest might become a bishop and that a widowed priest might remarry. Both of these acts had by long custom been forbidden, and many persons held that they were banned by the canons of the church. Hence this resolution was a revolutionary measure. That it was so intended was shown by the speech of Bishop Ioann, a married priest who had recently been consecrated bishop. He hailed the gathering because it had "finally decided to overturn the burdensome, medieval monastic domination" that had turned the parish clergy into cannon fodder in the futile struggle against the Soviet regime. Likewise V. N. L'vov, Over-Procurator in 1917, thanked the white clergy "because they have finally raised the banner of rebellion against their oppressors. . . ." For this rebellion to succeed, however, the church must be purged of the reactionary monastics and the secular counterrevolutionaries who dominated the parishes. "Then down with the cowls and the counterrevolutionaries! Long live the white clergy, who are carrying on the fight against them and are achieving the renovation of the church!" [38]

The Living Church congress also indicated that it favored close relations with the Soviet government. It issued an appeal to bishops, priests, and believers, saying that capitalism was the highest form of godlessness and that the faithful should follow the new dispensation in the church, which was fighting capitalism and the kulaks. On the other hand, Krasnitskii told the meeting that they should accept the fact that the church was separated irrevocably from the state and that "no sort of bridge has been laid between the Soviet Power and the church. Each will go its own road." [39] Krasnitskii himself, however, showed that this statement was not entirely accurate. He reported a visit to Kalinin, whom the delegation told that the foes of the government and of the Living Church were the same; the Living Church opposed capitalism, and the bishops who fought the liberals were counterrevolutionaries. Krasnitskii, who asked Kalinin for aid in gaining control of the Church of Christ the Savior in Moscow, was told to present a special petition asking the All-Russian Central Executive Committee to cancel the existing agreement with the parish council. When the delegation spoke of their difficulties in gaining control in the Ukraine, Kalinin told them to take the matter up with the head of the Ukrainian government. They also asked a ban on church congresses without the permission of the central authorities of the church, in order to prevent counterrevolutionary elements from holding local church gatherings. [40] The result of this request was not indicated.

Except for approving more "creative activity" in the performance of service, chiefly in making the service more understandable to laymen, [41] the reforming churchmen made little change in theology, claiming to be more Orthodox than the Patriarch. Krasnitskii ad-

vised the members of the Living Church congress not to be hampered
by the canons, many of which were obsolete and would be repealed
at the coming Sobor.[42] Nevertheless, the Living Church claimed to
be fully Orthodox, although the followers of the Patriarch regarded
them as schismatics.

Schism within the ranks of the reformers themselves was not long
in appearing. In August Bishop Antonin formed a new group, "the
League of Regeneration of the Church," which placed much emphasis
on the spiritual side of religion.[43] The split, however, did not wreck
the reforming movement, as both groups felt the need for unity in the
face of the patriarchal party and continued to collaborate in the
Higher Church Administration.[44] In October, 1922, a third group,
"the League of Congregations of the Ancient Apostolic Church,"
headed by Dean Vvedenskii, was formed.[45] Later, two small denominations were formed: "the Russian People's Church" in Vologda, and
"the Free Laboring Church" in Penza.[46] All these groups were pro-
Soviet.

These repeated fissions indicated that the Living Church suffered
from internal weaknesses. This was the case, for it represented the
special interests of the parish priests to the exclusion of those of other
groups. Above all, it had only a small following among laymen, who,
since the revolution, had had an important role in parish affairs. It
was relatively easy for the reformers to win the priests, who were
pleased by the weakening of the bishops, by the permission to remarry
if widowed, by the possibility of entering the episcopate, and by other
points in the program. The bishops could either be won over by
threats or promises or replaced with new bishops from the white
clergy or with subservient monastic bishops. But to control the parishes, which depended on the laymen who had signed contracts for
the use of the church buildings and who alone could provide the
priests with income, was more difficult. The laymen were often quite
conservative and had no love for the religious innovations of the reformers. In addition, they in large part still revered Patriarch Tikhon
and resented the harsh things said about him. Finally, many of the
leading laymen seem to have been the richest peasants of the community, who disliked the Soviet regime and those priests who praised it.

At the August congress of the Living Church the parish priests were urged to win independence from the parishioners by gaining control of the parish finances — the proceeds from the sale of tapers and the contributions for parish needs. The priests were told to seek the support of the diocesan commissions so that the power of the laymen might be broken and the priest might rule the parish.[47] Another proposal was that only those parishioners who professed canonical obedience to their pastors and who put into practice the rules of the Living Church should be regarded as laymen with full rights in the parish.[48] The Living Church congress adopted a resolution urging the administrative organs of the church to "take the most decisive measures in respect to opponents of the renovation of the church up to and including dismissal from office and expulsion from the diocese." Where opposition was found in the parish councils, steps should be taken "to dissolve such councils immediately, instructing the pastors . . . to present to the diocesan organs for confirmation new lists of candidates for members of the parish council from persons who preserve canonical submission to their priest." Those who opposed this measure were to be subject to church punishment, even excommunication.[49] Another method was tried in the diocese of Tomsk; a new parish code was adopted, providing for the election of the elders by a parish meeting at which the voting age was reduced to eighteen. In this way the influence of the parish kulaks was broken and the poorer peasants were put in power.[50]

Some of these measures were obviously hard to enforce and might prove deadly for the priest unless he could make them succeed beyond question. The dangers of alienating the parishioners by attempts to dissolve the parish councils and to create new ones that would support the priests proved great and were one of the leading reasons for the split in the ranks of the reformers.[51] Nevertheless, the new movement could hope to succeed only if the parishioners supported it, so that the attempt had to be made to win them over. For years the struggle between the new church group and the old was waged at the parish level, and it was there that the fate of the rival parties was decided. At first, with the leaders of the old church faction in confinement and with the central power in the hands of the new faction, the laymen who clung to the old orientation had nowhere to turn. Later, however, after the Patriarch again appeared on the scene, the weakness of the reformers at the parish level proved serious.

Even without effective leadership the opposition to the reforming movement continued strong. Titlinov states that so inflamed were the masses of believers that in some places they used physical violence against the Renovationist leaders. The stoning of Vvedenskii has been noted. Many others were threatened with violence and escaped it only thanks to police protection. The clergy of the Living Church often could not perform service in peace nor appear on the streets or even in church without having hostile remarks and sometimes curses cast into their faces. Rumors circulated about the appearance of Antichrist; gossip in Petrograd had it that Vvedenskii was using an automobile with "the number of the Beast" upon it — the mystic number "666" — as his car had a license plate numbered "999," or "666" inverted. At public meetings and debates the hostility to the Living Church was plain to see.[52] In Saratov the Renovationist clergy were threatened with violence, so that the provincial executive committee had to warn that the religious contest must proceed without violence.[53]

Another method adopted by the followers of Patriarch Tikhon was to form autocephalic dioceses as Metropolitan Agafangel had instructed them to do. In December, 1922, Father Krasnitskii told the Higher Church Administration that such independent dioceses, hostile to the Renovationist movement, had been attempted in Petrograd, Moscow, Kaluga, and half a dozen other places. Krasnitskii proposed that strong ecclesiastical punishment be inflicted upon participants in this opposition and that the Soviet government be informed of the views of the church administration and "of the political character of this church phenomenon."[54] In Minsk Bishop Melkhisidek and his supporters declared themselves independent of Moscow as early as September, thereby provoking a bitter struggle with the Renovationist forces.[55]

Even more significant was the loss of a sincere supporter of church reform, Metropolitan Sergii of Vladimir. Apparently not long after his adhesion to the Living Church movement he wrote to Archbishop Evdokim: "We wish renovation, but we wish it to be accomplished in harmony with the divine traditions of our Holy Church."[56] Later in the year he wrote to the Higher Church Ad-

ministration protesting against the resolutions of the Living Church
congress abolishing basic rules of church discipline and also the resolutions on matters of faith. Some of these rulings he termed unconditionally unacceptable; while others were beyond the competence of
a Russian Sobor. He particularly listed the removal of the excommunication of the late Tolstoi, the permission of a second marriage
for widowed priests, and the consecration of married priests as bishops. He declared that he could not permit such practices within his
diocese or be in communion with those who permitted them elsewhere.[57]

In the Ukraine the ecclesiastical picture was even more confused
than elsewhere, with a three-cornered conflict in progress. The Ukrainian nationalists, who had tried in 1917 to set up their own church, in
1921 succeeded in holding a church Sobor at Kiev, at which Dean Lipkovskii was consecrated as bishop by the gathering, although no bishops were present. He was proclaimed Metropolitan of Kiev, head of
the Ukrainian Autocephalous church. Because neither Patriarch Tikhon, nor the Georgian Patriarch, nor the Patriarch of Constantinople would consecrate their bishops, they remained without episcopal
sanction and hence lacked the apostolic succession.[58]

Although the Sobor's Preparatory Commission adopted a message
of thanks to the Soviets for the freedom to meet that had been ac-
corded them,[59] the Soviet authorities remained highly suspicious of
and hostile to this Ukrainian church, whose head had been a strong
supporter of the anti-Soviet nationalist Petliura. In March, 1922, the
Ukrainian Commissariat of Justice asked its local subdivisions to
provide periodic reports concerning the Autocephalists, especially on
their strength and social influence, and to state: "Is there not some
open or secret connection with the Petliurites? If there is, how is this
connection with the Petliurites manifested?"[60]

The formation of the Autocephalous church led to bitter hostility
between it and the old Russian Orthodox church, whose center was
Kiev. The Ukrainian Commissariat of Justice found it necessary to
instruct its officials that the Autocephalists had no right to impose
their authority upon a parish that did not want to accept it or to compel a parish to use the Ukrainian language in service. Instead, the
question of parish control should be decided by conducting a census

of the believers. In one case it was suggested that the two factions should use the parish churches on alternate weeks.[61] When the split in the Orthodox church in Moscow occurred, the new schism spread to the Ukraine. The followers of Patriarch Tikhon, led by Metropolitan Mikhail of Kiev, fought back fiercely, allegedly beating several Living Church priests. The Soviet press reported that many of the Tikhonites took a strongly anti-Soviet, reactionary stand, which led to the arrest of Metropolitan Mikhail, Bishops Nafanail and Pavel in Khar'kov, and others. Apparently the Living Churchmen and the Autocephalists got on with less friction, with the latter concentrated chiefly in the western Ukraine, and the Living Church in the eastern part.[62]

During all this contest and struggle, the Soviet policy toward the various factions as expressed by the authorities of the Commissariat of Justice, remained one of neutrality, although it continued to deal severely with those guilty of "counterrevolutionary actions." An attitude of "loyalty" in the observance of Soviet laws respecting religion became an important factor in the decisions of the authorities, so that the neutrality professed in religious matters was at times affected by the official reaction to the political views of the churchmen.

In 1923 the Commissariats of Justice and Internal Affairs issued Instructions for the enforcement of religious legislation under the new conditions, reiterating that no church or religious society might enjoy any privileges or subsidies from the government. Hence all governmental agencies were forbidden to support by administrative intervention any cult or denomination to the detriment of other cults or religious groups. Moreover, "the exiling of counterrevolutionary servitors of cults, like that of other citizens, may take place only in accordance with the decree of the Council of People's Commissars concerning administrative exile . . . on the general basis." Likewise, no religious organization had the right to intervene in the activity of any other such organization. "In general the local authorities should protect the quiet and free performance of religious services in that loyal form that is pleasing to them and should bring to responsibility persons who violate the laws of the R.S.F.S.R." [63]

How these rules were applied was shown in August, 1923, when Bishop Nikolai Solovei appealed for reductions in his rent and taxes.

The Fifth Division of the Commissariat of Justice replied that in such matters all ministers of religion paid on the same basis as members of free professions. "Your petition for granting the so-called Renovationist clergy special exemptions and privileges in comparison to all other ministers of religion cannot be satisfied," as the law forbade the granting of special privilege on the basis of religious adherence.[64]

Likewise, the cases cited in Soviet lawbooks reveal that the Fifth Division, in deciding which faction was to possess parish churches, did not by any means give complete support for the Renovationists, although they were regarded as the more trustworthy. In October, 1923, several groups of Tikhonites of Vladivostok complained that the local authorities had canceled all their agreements for the use of parish churches and had turned them over to the diocesan administration of the Living Church. To this the Fifth Division replied that if the facts had been correctly reported, the actions of the Vladivostok officials were incorrect, as diocesan administrations were not entitled to possess churches, which were to be given over only to parish groups.[65]

Early in 1924 the Fifth Division was called on to hear complaints from six different parts of the country that the local authorities upon various pretexts had canceled all agreements with the parish groups and had given the churches over "to sometimes extremely insignificant groups of Renovationists," although the overwhelming mass of the population, which belonged to the Tikhonite section, was thus completely deprived of facilities for satisfying their religious needs. The Fifth Division, acting under the instructions of the Central Executive Committee, informed the local officials that they should divide the churches in each locality between the groups of the old and the new denominations as far as possible according to the size of the denominations, and in any case so that each group received one church; both groups should be obliged to live peacefully and not violate public order. The local authorities were told to see that "the agreement should be concluded exclusively with citizens inspiring trust. . . ." The latter rule could easily have been used to veto the composition of the group who contracted for the use of the parish church, and even to bar completely a denomination regarded as "untrustworthy." Another complaint from seven different localities brought a ruling that clarified this point. The plaintiffs, charging that all churches in their localities had been given to the Renovationists, asked that they be given one of the two churches in each village. The Fifth Division explained that if, according to law, the local officials felt it necessary to cancel the agreements for the use of the churches and to turn them over to more trustworthy groups, then each denomination might receive only one church. Hence the Fifth Division asked a speedy review of the decision granting both churches to one denomination and the allotment of one of these churches to each denomination, "in order not to arouse unnecessary brawls and conflict among the peasant population by deprivation of the right to perform their religious rituals in the old manner." [66]

Somewhat similar cases arose over the use of urban churches, except that here the petitioners asked that the old group be permitted to possess one floor of the church in question. The Fifth Division approved this scheme and ordered that in dividing the church the arrangements be in conformity with the number in each group — that is, the lower floor to the old group, the upper to the new. The running expenses of the building — taxes, insurance, and the watchman's pay — should be divided proportionately according to the amount of floor space occupied by each group. In other instances, the petitioners requested that the churches be divided vertically instead of horizontally. This Solomonic decision was also approved on the same basis as above. [67]

The Soviet authorities also acted to limit the power of the local authorities to take away churches from parish groups. It was pointed out that the congregation had full control over the church and could engage and discharge the priest at their discretion (a rule that many of the Living Church priests found inconvenient). A church might be taken away and put to nonecclesiastical use only if there were not enough parishioners to guarantee its maintenance or if there was a great need for buildings for other purposes. In the latter case, the provincial officials were required to see to it that the religious needs of the believers were not adversely affected. [68] The agreement with a parish group should be canceled if the church groups participated in counterrevolutionary manifestations or if there was abuse or loss of church property; in either of these cases, the provincial authorities should both cancel the agreement and bring the guilty to trial. The ruling of the Central Executive Committee called for "extreme circumspection" on the part of the local authorities when deciding the fate of church buildings.[69]

Two other decisions also reveal that the central Soviet authorities did not always favor the Renovationist clergy in their dealings with the old or Tikhonite group. When a group of believers of Iaroslavl complained that the local authorities would not let them have a religious procession without a permit from the Renovationist authorities, although the petitioners were not of this denomination, and "form the predominant majority of the population of the city of Iaroslavl," the Fifth Division decided that to require such a permit would be a violation of the decree of separation of church from state and of subsequent legislation.[70] To another complaint that the Renovationist clergy did not permit the clergy of other groups to accompany the bodies of departed believers to the cemetery or to perform service there, the reply was given that the clergy of all cemetery churches would be informed that the cemeteries were no longer monopolies of the clergy of those churches.[71]

On another matter, however, the Soviet authorities took a much stiffer attitude — namely, on the question of public prayers for Patriarch Tikhon after he had been indicted. In July, 1923, the Petrograd provincial prosecutor issued a ruling in reply to an inquiry from a Petrograd church, in which he stated that public recognition of the Patriarch as their leader and also public prayers for him at divine service "may give grounds for starting criminal prosecution against the guilty persons for complicity in counterrevolutionary acts" — an obviously serious charge. In a similar case the Novgorod provincial prosecutor held that, while prayers in church as a religious act were outside the competence of the civil authorities, solemn prayers for "former Patriarch Tikhon" at important parts of the service exceeded the limits of a mere prayer and were in reality "a public manifestation of praise for known enemies of the Soviet Power." Inasmuch as such prayers publicly and solemnly performed in the name of God "may react upon the religious prejudices of the masses and may produce in them a frame of mind hostile to the Soviet Power, these prayers appear to be agitation." Hence no such solemn prayers at important parts of the service "for known enemies of the Soviet Power can be permitted, and ministers of religion who stubbornly continue such prayers, thus emphasizing their solidarity with open counterrevolutionaries and producing in the masses hostility to the Soviet Power," would be recommended for exiling by administrative order for three years.[72]

This question was referred to the Commissariat of Justice in 1924. The answer was that in a circular of December 8, 1923, it had ruled that the commemoration of persons under trial for grave state offenses (especially "Citizen Belavin — Tikhon"), in public prayers or sermons, if clearly intended to stir up popular displeasure or to discredit the authorities, was a punishable act. Even if the prayers for Tikhon were not of a clearly demonstrative character, they might present grounds "for reconsidering the contract for the use of the church, as an expression of a disloyal attitude toward the decisions of the judicial authorities of the Republic." Even in April, 1924, ten months after the Patriarch had been released, a circular of the Commissariat of Justice stated that as the decision to drop the case was on the basis of amnesty and not acquittal, the circular banning public prayers for him was still valid.[73]

The severity of this rule posed a grave threat to Tikhonite parishes; it could, however, be avoided by simply omitting public prayers for Patriarch Tikhon. Another Soviet law that the old church faction could not easily evade was the provision that religious societies must register with the Soviet authorities in order to be permitted to function. On August 3, 1922, the Central Executive Committee and the Council of People's Commissars issued an important decree providing for the registration of nonprofit societies. Each was required to submit its bylaws, lists of members, and other information; upon receiving the required data, the provincial authorities should register the society if it conformed to the constitution and the laws of the land. If its actions appeared to be illegal, it might be closed by the authorities. Societies which did not register with the authorities were not to be permitted to function and should be closed. Those that were legalized, however, might hold provincial and national congresses and elect administrations at both levels.[74]

A detailed "Instruction as to the Method of Registering Religious Societies and of Issuing Permission to Hold Congresses of the Latter" was published in *Izvestiia* in April, 1923. The nature of the data requested from the founding members of such societies clearly indicates that the diocesan administration of the Tikhonite wing of the church could not secure the necessary registration.[75]

Thus, while the old section of the church, which remained loyal to Patriarch Tikhon, could and did maintain its existence on the parish level without much difficulty, the existence of its diocesan and central administrations was legally impossible. Moreover, the position of the bishops of this faction was precarious. Writers hostile to the Soviet regime have frequently charged that there was close co-operation between the Living Church or Renovationist authorities and the Soviet GPU, and that one Tuchkov, GPU official in charge of religious matters, was more than willing to arrest and exile bishops who blocked the path of the pro-Soviet church group.[76] Such writers have not submitted documentary proof of these allegations, nor has such documentation been available for this study, so that it is not possible to determine the correctness of these charges. Arrests, imprisonment, and exiling of Tikhonite bishops continued during 1922 and 1923, but in each case the authorities gave counterrevolutionary activity or anti-Soviet actions on the part of these hierarchs as the reason for their measures. Even if this was true, however, these punishments could not but help the Renovationists by eliminating opposing leaders.

In 1924 Valentinov in his collection of material on the Soviet "campaign against the church," printed a list alleging that six metropolitans, three archbishops, and fifty-four bishops were in prison or in exile, usually in remote corners of the U.S.S.R.; one had died in exile, and one had returned.[77] While data from the Soviet press are lacking for many of the bishops listed by him, Soviet reports indicate that the six metropolitans and the three archbishops, at least, were not free at that time and that many of the bishops likewise were in custody. It is quite possible that all the bishops listed by Valentinov were in prison or in exile at that time.

Soviet policy toward the Russian Orthodox church was thus based on the theory that the Renovationist church with its Higher Church Administration was loyal in acceptance of the Soviet regime and hence might be registered as a legally existing organization, while the old church headed by Patriarch Tikhon was disloyal and illegal. The actions of numbers of the leading churchmen during the revolution and the civil war, the pronouncements of the *émigré* clergy in the Karlovatskii Sobor, and the opposition of the Patriarch and his followers in regard to the use of the church's valuables for famine relief had apparently convinced the Soviet leaders that the Tikhonite prelates were implacable enemies of the Soviet regime whom it was not safe to leave at large. Whereas during the civil war period the Soviet authorities were too busy to take any definite action concerning the church, in 1922 they adopted a positive policy of curbing hostile clerics while giving considerable freedom of action to the friendly Renovationist grouping. While it is impossible to disprove the assertions of hostile writers that the Soviet rulers backed the split in the church in order to weaken it and make it easier prey, a more likely explanation seems to be that they struck at the older church group and gave limited support to the new in order to secure a church organization with which they could deal on a peaceful basis.

Comment in the Soviet press in 1922 and 1923 indicates that few of the Soviet leaders were enthusiastic about the Renovationists. In August, 1922, *Izvestiia* did go so far as to comment hopefully on the "progressive" clergy of the Living Church and to express the belief that the masses of the believers were more radical than the leaders.[77] By the summer of 1923, however, the attitude was that there was no revolution in the church nor even a reformation, but just a struggle for power between two groups, one of which, realizing the solidity of the Soviet regime, had adopted an approving attitude toward it. "Thus the workers' state has new fellow-travellers — of which one is the Renovated church. . . . This circumstance needs to be stated, and in reference to it we should build our policy in respect to the new church group." If, however, the circumstances should change, Soviet policy should change also.[78]

On the other hand, one writer specifically stated that the belief of the reformers that the Living Church was now the official Soviet church was quite wrong; the Soviets were merely following a policy of punishing their enemies, while leaving the loyal clergy alone.[79] Others went even further and expressed fear that the reformed church might become as bad an enemy as the old Tikhonite one. A writer discussing the attempt of Krasnitskii to reorganize the parishes said: "Any attempt to use the reorganization for political ends against the Soviet Power should be mercilessly unmasked and condemned," [80] and several months later another declared that "the Soviet Power has the right to demand that religious prejudices should not be used for political ends," and went on to say that the reformers themselves should not forget this.[81]

The veteran antireligious leaders were especially opposed to the Renovationist church. Iaroslavskii declared that it was proper to welcome the latter's support of the Soviet regime and program, but that a reformed, modernized religion might become more dangerous than the old.[82] A. I. Mezhov wrote in *Izvestiia* that while the state was neutral in religious matters, the Communist party was not and would fight the influence of any church, for ecclesiastical influence "stands in the way of liberating mankind from all idols and tyrants, earthly and heavenly, existing and imaginary." [83] Trotskii wrote that the Living Church was merely an attempt of the clerics to put on protective coloration, while pursuing essentially bourgeois aims,[84] while the influential Bonch-Bruevich wrote that the Communists must strike blow after blow against the church, always remembering that "the religious outlook itself is deeply hostile to our system of thought and that the proletariat and the intelligent peasants definitely do not need a 'living' nor a dead, neither a new nor an old church." [85]

Thus, as has been indicated, in 1922 the Soviet government experimented with a new policy of limited co-operation with those liberal clergy who were willing to accept the Soviet regime. At the same time it used its legislative and police powers to break up the administrative machinery of the old segment of the church, although it followed a moderate course toward the Tikhonite parishes. Particularly with the support of many of the parish clergy, eager to settle accounts with the bishops, the reform movement in the church went ahead rapidly in these years, with considerable prospects of full success. The Patriarch was in prison, awaiting trial, with a probable death sentence ahead. The situation, however, was to change greatly as a result of the remarkable events in the summer of 1923.

CHAPTER VIII

Failure of the Church Revolution

ONE OF THE LEADING POINTS of the Living Church program was the holding of a second Sobor to set the church's house in order and to deal with the reforms projected by the insurgent clergy. Early in the movement an important addition was made to the agenda for the Sobor: the ecclesiastical trial of the Patriarch for his sins in bringing the church to such a pass. In the light of these proposals as well as of the character of the reforming clergy, it was inevitable that the Sobor would be an important event. It was repeatedly postponed, however, "for technical reasons," and it was not until April 29, 1923 that it opened —[1] nearly a year after the Living Church movement had become active.

Although the leaders of the Living Church proclaimed that this Sobor would be much more representative than the first, its membership was carefully limited to exclude clergy and laymen who still followed Patriarch Tikhon. The election rules provided that in the cities the believers who wished to participate should be obliged to enroll with their parish priest and obtain a certificate of good standing from him. In addition, persons tried and convicted during the reform period were forbidden to take part — a provision that barred the Tikhonite clergy who had been ousted from their dioceses by the Higher Church Administration. Furthermore, the Sobor had a substantial number of ex officio or invited members, including the Higher Church Administration and the administrations of the Ukrainian and Siberian church districts, and the fifty-six diocesan commissioners of the Higher Church Administration.[2]

In spite of the voting restrictions, the Tikhonite clergy attempted to dominate the diocesan congresses that chose the elected members of the Sobor. In the diocese of Moscow they allegedly filibustered by singing prayers at frequent intervals, and it was only when they had left that business could be done.[3] In almost all the dioceses, however, the Renovationist group was in full control. The diocese of Nizhnii Novgorod was an outstanding exception; the diocesan commissioner of the Higher Church Administration had to close the meeting because of "the hostile attitude and the improper attacks" of an organized part of the gathering.[4] Archbishop Evdokim was late in arriving at the Sobor, because he had been sent to Viatka to deal with the clergy who opposed the reformers. He was able to bring the Viatka clergy into line, but only with considerable difficulty.[5]

Notwithstanding the careful selection of the delegates in the localities, much care was taken at the Sobor itself to exclude hostile elements. A detailed questionnaire was presented to all delegates, which asked their attitude toward the Soviets, their views regarding the activity of the Patriarch and the proposal to unfrock him, their former political activity, their feelings about the Patriarch's anathema of 1918, and other leading questions.[6] In spite of these fine screens, however, a small number of opposition churchmen and laymen did manage to attend, largely in the guise of "nonparty" members: there were some forty-five of them with voting rights, or about 10 per cent of the total.[7] Three of them actually managed to speak during the sessions of the Sobor.[8] Nevertheless, it was by no means a free body, accurately representing the views of the whole Orthodox church, for it had a carefully selected membership, speaking for only a faction of the church.

When the Sobor met on April 29 it had 476 members, of whom 430 had voting rights. Of these 122 were laymen and 308 were ecclesiastics (about 200 of the latter were deans). The Living Church, led by Krasnitskii, had 250 delegates; Vvedenskii's League of Congregations of the Ancient Apostolic Church (called SODATs from its initials) had 110; and Bishop Antonin's League of Church Regeneration had 45 delegates. There were 45 nonparty delegates (most of them Tikhonites), and there was a group of observers from the Free Laboring Church, without voting rights.[9]

All the leading speeches and the resolutions of the Sobor expressed ardent loyalty and support for the Soviet state. Krasnitskii

declared for "sincere recognition of the social revolution"; Vvedenskii demanded full severance of the church's ties with counterrevolution; and Antonin, as chairman of the Higher Church Administration, thanked the government for permission to meet, praised the
separation of church and state, and proclaimed: "to the Russian
Republic and its government, long life!" [10] At the second session,
upon the proposal of Vvedenskii, a strong resolution was adopted
expressing thanks to the government and greetings to Lenin and
hailing the October Revolution, "which has given life to the great
principles of equality and labor that are contained in Christ's teachings." The Sobor called on all honorable Christians to take an active
part in this "fight for human truth" and in all ways "to put into practice the great slogans of the October Revolution." The gathering also
expressed wishes for Lenin's speedy recovery in order that he might
once more "stand among the fighters for great social truth." [11]

In conformity with this attitude, the Sobor in its session of May 7
considered and condemned the Karlovatskii Sobor for its opposition
to the Soviets, its appeal for return of the Romanovs, its quest for
a new civil war, and its appeal to the Genoa Conference. With one
dissenting vote, all the members of the Karlovatskii Sobor were excommunicated by the Sobor of 1923.[12]

One of the main questions before the Sobor was that of ecclesiastical reform. On May 3 Vvedenskii urged dogmatic revision. Claiming
that the church needed a new stream of creative theology, he asked
that the Gospel and not the canons be taken as the higher law of the
church.[13] This appeal met little support in the Sobor, whose interests
were much better expressed by Dean Krasnitskii. He proposed a
program of confirming the provisions for a married episcopate, the
right of widowed priests to remarry, and greater control in the diocese by the parish clergy. These proposals were warmly supported by
the gathering, which howled down the feeble objections of a dean
and one of the bishops. The Sobor voted to approve white, married
bishops along with the earlier unmarried episcopate.[14]

The Sobor also adopted a resolution approving monasteries, provided they were working communities, far from city life, and devoted
to freedom, love, labor, equality and fraternity. Another resolution
approved the introduction of the Gregorian calendar.[15]

In general the Sobor took a highly unsympathetic attitude toward monastics and especially toward monastic bishops. Lack of esteem for the bishops was shown by a brief announcement of the chairman on May 4 that the conference of bishops then reviewing the question of unfrocking Patriarch Tikhon would not again convene upon their own initiative.[16]

The Ukrainian problem was also considered. The Living Church members from the Ukraine asked that they be granted autonomy, apparently in order to combat the Ukrainian Autocephalous church, which was dominated by Ukrainian nationalists. This question produced a heated and stormy debate, which was finally ended by a compromise decision to recognize autonomy as permissible in theory, but to leave the final decision to the next Sobor.[17]

The Sobor adopted a series of organizational measures. Dean Vvedenskii was made Archbishop of Krutitsy, administrator of the diocese of Moscow; Krasnitskii, after refusing the archepiscopate of Petrograd, took the title of Protopresbyter of the Orthodox church.[18] A new administrative organ of the church was set up — the Higher Church Council, of eighteen clergy and laymen. The Sobor at once elected the new members, most of whom were priests; it contained ten members from the Living Church, including Krasnitskii, six from the Ancient Apostolic Church (SODATs), headed by Archbishop Vvedenskii, and Metropolitan Antonin and one other from the League of Regeneration.[19]

The most significant move of the Sobor was the unfrocking of Patriarch Tikhon, who was still awaiting trial by the government. At the session of May 3 long speeches were made by Deans Vvedenskii and Krasnitskii, linking Patriarch Tikhon with counterrevolution, capitalism, and intervention, and calling for his unfrocking and for the abolition of the patriarchate. Antonin also spoke against him. Properly speaking, there was no trial, for the accused was neither present nor represented, and no evidence was furnished for the charges made. Instead, the Sobor at once adopted a series of resolutions condemning Tikhon's leadership as having plunged the church into counterrevolution, and the Patriarch himself "as a transgressor against the true commandments of Christ and as a traitor to the church." Tikhon was declared reduced to lay status and the patriarchate was declared abolished; the church would henceforth be run in conciliar fashion. This important decision was adopted with one dissenting vote and five abstentions.[20] The secretary of the Sobor did not report in his minutes whether there was debate upon the charges or the resolutions, so that full knowledge of the proceedings is lacking. The minutes of the Sobor show that the council of the bishops at the Sobor "unanimously" signed a resolution approving the penalty voted by the Sobor; the signatures, however, numbered fifty-four, while there were sixty-six bishops present, so that some must have refused to sign.[21]

On May 4 a special commission of the Sobor visited Tikhon in his rooms in the Donskoi Monastery to inform him of the decision of the Sobor. According to the official report, he signed the formal notification,[22] although some reports from abroad say that in signing he added the word "illegal."

Unquestionably this action against the Patriarch did not conform to the rules of the church regarding such punishment. There was nothing resembling a trial, and the decision was made by a body that was not truly representative of real church opinion. Hence the decision would stand only as long as the Renovationists were unchallenged in their control. When the Sobor ended its sessions on May 9, the Renovationists seem to have believed that they had finally established their regime and that, in spite of the continued opposition of the Tikhonites, its success was assured. These hopes were to be rudely disappointed.

The event that ruined the Renovationist plans was the release of Patriarch Tikhon from arrest and imprisonment. For over a year he had been imprisoned, awaiting trial on charges growing out of the trial of the Fifty-four and other court cases. For a long time no mention was made of the progress of his case, but on April 6, 1923, there was an announcement that the Trial Collegium of the Supreme Court would begin to hear the case of "former Patriarch Tikhon," Metropolitan Nikandr, Gur'ev, secretary of the Synod, and Archbishop Arsenii of Novgorod. Tikhon was the chief figure, as he was charged with "dealings with foreign powers, counterrevolutionary work directed toward overthrowing the Soviet order, opposition to decrees of the authorities, and using religious beliefs and prejudices for creating a disobedient and rebellious attitude among the masses." He was accused of having opposed the Soviet regime from the beginning, of having supported the Whites, of dealing with the Karlovatskii Sobor, and of being individually responsible for the violent opposition to the use of the church plate for famine relief. It was declared that during the preliminary investigation Tikhon had admitted his guilt on almost all of the above counts. These comments and the fact that the judges were named and Krylenko, foremost Soviet prosecutor, was assigned to the case,[23] indicated the importance attached to it.

The Soviet press gave further indications of the imminence of Tikhon's trial. When Lord Curzon, with the support of the Archbishop of Canterbury, included the imprisonment of the Patriarch in his ultimatum of May, 1923, bitter editorials promised that Tikhon's disclosures in court would prove the justice of the charges against him.[24] The chief newspapers reprinted numerous articles against Tikhon from the local press, and a series of resolutions condemning him adopted by lower clergy, workers, Red Army men, and peasants, also showed that his position was precarious.[25] On April 24, however, it was announced that Tikhon's trial would be postponed in order to combine it with that of Bishops Feodosii of Kolomna; a special announcement would name the day of the hearing.[26] According to Spinka, the postponement appeared very mysterious, as tickets of admission to the trial had already been issued.[27]

The mystery, however, was cleared up when on June 27 the press published Tikhon's statement to the Supreme Court, made on June 16:

In making this appeal to the Supreme Court of the R.S.F.S.R., I regard it as my duty according to my pastoral conscience to state the following:

Having been raised in a monarchist society and being until my very arrest under the influence of anti-Soviet persons, I was actually hostile to the Soviet Power, and, moreover, my hostility at times changed from a passive condition to active deeds, such as: the proclamation on the subject of the Peace of Brest in 1918; the anathematization of the government in the same year and, finally, the appeal against the removal of church valuables in 1922. All my anti-Soviet acts, except for a few inaccuracies, are set forth in the indictment of the

Supreme Court. Recognizing the correctness of the court in bringing
me to trial according to the articles of the Criminal Code indicated
in the indictment, I repent of these actions against the state order,
and I ask the Supreme Court to . . . free me from arrest.

At the same time I declare to the Supreme Court that henceforth
I am not an enemy of the Soviet Power. I am finally and decisively set-
ting myself apart from both the foreign and the internal monarchist
White-Guard counterrevolutionaries.

Signed: PATRIARCH TIKHON

(VASILII BELAVIN)

16 June

Whereupon the Trial Collegium for Criminal Affairs of the Supreme
Court, on June 25, ruled: "To grant the request of Citizen Belavin,
. . . to end . . . his retention under arrest." [28]

A supplementary statement by the jurist Galkin asserted that Tikhon had been arrested because of his unceasing counterrevolutionary
activity. His current declaration of loyalty toward the Soviet Power
removed the need for his arrest. "The decision of the Supreme Court,
of course, changes nothing in the procedure of Tikhon's case, the
investigation of which will continue its course." [29]

The Soviet government never explained its motives for freeing the
Patriarch, against whom it had a long reckoning. An editorial in
Izvestiia on June 28 provides a partial explanation. It states that Tikhon's confession of guilt would confound the enemies of the Soviets
and their knavish tricks, as well as prove that the revolutionary
state did not persecute religion, as charged by Lord Curzon. The
Soviet Power had shown magnanimity "and by this act it has under-
scored the fact that in its attitude toward Tikhon it was not at all
guided by motives of vengeance or in general by any persecution of
the church and of individual ministers of religion as such." [30]

Doubtless there were other reasons as well, but certainly the wish
to disprove charges abroad that they were martyring the Patriarch
was a factor. Likewise the anti-Soviet churchmen within the country
would be greatly taken aback and might even drop some of their
hostility. Another possible motive was suggested by a cartoon in a
Moscow workers' newspaper, which showed a hand-to-hand fight
between the Patriarch and another cleric, presumably a Renovationist, with a grinning worker, hands in pockets, watching. The caption

was: "While two are engaged in a struggle, the hands of the third are free." [31]

This newspaper, however, expressed the proletarian viewpoint, and did not necessarily indicate government policy. Indeed, it is possible that the government was seeking something quite different — namely, peace between the ecclesiastical factions and their merger on the basis of the full acceptance of the Soviet regime, in keeping with Tikhon's appeal to the government. Efforts along these lines (to be discussed later) were made and came close to succeeding; their failure does not seem to have been caused by Soviet actions.

Patriarch Tikhon himself did little to clarify the question of why he submitted to the Soviet authorities. In an interview with a reporter of the *Manchester Guardian* he was quoted as saying that he had never fought the Soviet government, but had merely opposed some of its laws. Now the old clergy, headed by him, were not opposing the government, but only the Living Church. He explained his release by the fact that the authorities, through study of his case, had become convinced that he was not a counterrevolutionary and had suggested that he sign a letter saying so.[32] If he was correctly quoted, his statement was in conflict with his earlier appeal to the Soviet authorities, which had contained a clear admission of guilt. The indictment in his case, published in Moscow in 1923, stated that documentary proof had been obtained that the disorders over the confiscation of church valuables had been organized according to directives from counterrevolutionaries abroad, that Tikhon had been in communication with anti-Soviet clergy such as Metropolitan Antonii Khrapovitskii and Archbishop (later Metropolitan) Evlogii, whose political views he well knew, and that from them he had learned of the calling of the Karlovitskii Sobor, for which he and the Synod had sent their blessing. Later he was informed of the actions of this Sobor through Metropolitan Evlogii. This correspondence, according to the indictment, had been carried on via the Estonian diplomatic mission in Moscow; the testimony of Archbishop Nikandr, Secretary Gur'ev, and other witnesses allegedly corroborated these charges.[33] If these charges and the others in the indictment alleging anti-Soviet actions during the civil war period were sound (and Patriarch Tikhon admitted in his appeal that they were substantially true), it would be incorrect to say that he had not been hostile to the Soviets, but only to some of their laws. Probably the most correct explanation is that the weight of the evidence shown to him during his imprisonment was so convincing that he, fearing to suffer the fate of Metropolitan Veniamin, listened to the arguments of his captors and secured release by admitting guilt. There is reason to believe that Tikhon at times was swayed by those around him (as, for example, when he turned over some of the administrative matters of the church to a group of liberal priests whom he had no reason to trust or like), and that, isolated in prison from his conservative advisers, he felt that his course of opposition to the Soviets had been an error. Moreover, he may have believed, as many conservative churchmen also reasoned, that in order to save the church from further repression and disaster and from the triumphant Renovationists it was his duty to submit.

Upon his release Patriarch Tikhon returned to the Donskoi Monastery, where he gave an interview to a Soviet reporter. He was quoted as saying that he had been well treated in prison and that reports that he had suffered torture were entirely false. He declared firmly that he had made a complete break with counterrevolution: "I stand completely on a Soviet platform." He felt, however, that the church should remain apart from politics. As for the Renovationists, he refused to recognize their action in unfrocking him and intended to resume his ecclesiastical functions.[34] On Sunday, July 1, he officiated in the church of the Donskoi Monastery before a dense throng and later performed service in the courtyard before those unable to enter the church. He spent several hours blessing the faithful. During the service he gave a short talk on the need for the church to stay outside politics, which rule it had failed to observe before. He refused to recognize the Renovationist Sobor of 1923 and declared it completely uncanonical.[35]

Tikhon also issued a long message to the faithful in which he strongly condemned the Sobor of 1923 and refused to recognize its rulings. He admitted that he had been against the Soviets in the first years after the revolution, but excused himself by citing his earlier training and the attitude of the Sobor of 1917. Later, he said, he had not been anti-Soviet, for he had rebuked the Karlovatskii Sobor for its reactionary utterances. In another passage he admitted the truth of his confession of guilt, declaring that henceforth "I decisively condemn any attack upon the Soviet government, no matter from where it comes. Let it be known to all foreign and domestic monarchists that I am not an enemy of the Soviet government." [36]

A second proclamation of the Patriarch, printed in *Izvestiia* early in July, 1923, was the most explicit of any in its admissions:

Having now the possibility of renewing my interrupted activity of serving the Holy Orthodox church, and recognizing my guilt before the Soviet Power, consisting of a number of our passive and active anti-Soviet actions, as was stated in the charges of the Supreme Court — i.e., in opposing the decree concerning the removal of church valuables for aid to the starving, anathematizing the Soviet Power, in the proclamation against the Peace of Brest, and so on — we, according to the duty of a Christian and archpastor, repent of these things and grieve for the victims caused by this anti-Soviet politics. Essentially not only we are guilty, but also all that milieu that trained us, and those evil-minded persons who urged us to these actions from the very beginning of the Soviet Power. As foes thereof, they tried through our church to overthrow it, for which they even attempted to use me, as head thereof. Being helpless to fight the Soviet Power openly and directly, they wished to secure its abolition by indirect means, by resorting to the church and its pastors.

Admitting our guilt before the people and the Soviet Power, I wish that those who, forgetting their duty as pastors, entered into common action with the enemies of the working people — the monarchists and White Guards — and, wishing to overthrow the Soviet Power, were even not averse to entering the ranks of the White armies, might do likewise. Grievous though it is to admit this crime, still we must speak this bitter but correct truth. We now condemn such actions and declare that the Russian Orthodox church is nonpolitical and henceforth does not want to be either a Red or a White church; it should and will be the one Conciliar Apostolic Church, and all attempts coming from any side to embroil the church in political struggle should be rejected and condemned.

The Patriarch concluded with a statement warning the members of the Karlovatskii Sobor that they should admit their guilt, submit to his orders, and repent; otherwise he would call them to Moscow for trial.[37]

The latter proposals appear to have been completely unrealistic, as it was highly improbable that Metropolitan Antonii, Archbishop Anastasii, and their fellows would be willing to come to Moscow for trial; nonetheless, this proclamation was the most concrete in its profession of repentance and of loyalty to the Soviet state that Patriarch Tikhon had yet made.

Apparently these appeals of the Patriarch to his followers failed to have the desired effect, for in August under the title "Around Former Patriarch Tikhon," *Izvestiia* printed excerpts from a proclamation signed by Patriarch Tikhon and Archbishops Serafim of Tver and Tikhon of the Urals, and Bishop Ilarion, announcing that the church was definitely separating itself from all counterrevolution. Return to the old order was impossible, and the church should not be the handmaid of tiny groups of men at home or abroad who wanted to use it for selfish political ends. "The church recognizes and supports the Soviet Power, for there is no power but from God. The church pronounces prayers for the Russian land and for the Soviet Power." The prelates stated that the church would return to normal only when the canonical system of administration was restored and when the believers observed with exactitude the state laws affecting the church. The laws of the state were the obligatory basis for the organization of the church. Hence the church as a whole and especially its leaders should display as much feeling for the church as possible.

> Priests are obliged to explain in detail both to themselves and to their flocks that the Russian Orthodox church has nothing in common with counterrevolution. It is the duty of the pastor to bring to the comprehension of the wide masses of believing people the fact that henceforth the church has set itself apart from counterrevolution and stands on the side of the Soviet Power.[38]

This message bears the earmarks of sincerity, and it seems probable that Tikhon was genuine in this attitude toward the Soviet regime in spite of the allegations of convinced reactionaries that this was merely *pro forma* submission. Metropolitan Antonii Khrapovitskii in Yugoslavia wrote that there was no need to be disturbed over it, as the Patriarch was merely reiterating his statement of 1919 that the church should avoid politics. He was making peace with the Soviet authorities "in an outward manner," not for his own safety but for that of the church.[39] Father Mikhail, who stated that he talked with the Patriarch both during and after the latter's stay in prison, declared that Tikhon made peace only because he mistakenly believed that the Renovationists were making great inroads into the church.[40] Father Kirrill Zaitsev, another conservative cleric, asserts that Patriarch Tikhon issued his instructions to pray for the Soviets as a result of Soviet pressure, but permitted them to remain a dead letter — "this, of course, with the knowledge and silent blessing of the Patriarch. . . ."[41] While it is, of course, impossible to prove that Tikhon was sincere in his submission, his subsequent actions indicate sincerity. There is no doubt, however, that considerable sections of his church were highly displeased by his repentance and refused to obey his injunctions. A Soviet antireligious writer later stated that an opposition group within the church actually accused him of betrayal of the church. Although the reactionaries did not dare defy him, they followed a policy of passive resistance against professing loyalty to the Soviets.[42]

Evidence of the strength of the reactionary element in the Tikhonite church was given by a message posted on the churches of Moscow early in 1924 by Bishop Ilarion, administrator of the diocese. It complained that near churches where the Patriarch performed there were frequent fierce quarrels and encounters and even violence; counterrevolutionary speeches had also been made. This was declared to be completely intolerable, as there was no place for enemies of the state, for Black Hundredites, near the Patriarch. "Evil and unneeded political talk, and even more any violence done near a church, abuses the church and throws a shadow of suspicion on the holy church and its servitors." Hence Bishop Ilarion asked the Orthodox not to misbehave, especially near churches. Persons with strong political passions should stay at home; he threatened that the Holy Eucharist would be denied to stubborn violators of the peace, as they disgraced the holy church.[43]

Whether or not Patriarch Tikhon was sincere in his professions respecting the government, in March, 1924, the latter found it possible to quash the still-pending case against him. The reasons given were his public repentance of his counterrevolutionary actions and the fact that "among the wide masses there is evident an intensified movement from religious superstitions to the side of science and enlightenment," with the result that the influence of the Orthodox church upon the workers and peasants had been greatly reduced; hence the former Patriarch and those arraigned with him no longer appeared socially dangerous.[44] In spite of the far from cordial tone of the announcement, the Patriarch expressed deep thanks for the gracious attitude toward his past activity and assured the government "that it will find in me a most loyal citizen of the Soviet Union, who fulfills conscientiously all the decrees and rulings of the Soviet Power." The Soviet press agency added that *Te Deums* of thanksgiving were performed in all churches of Moscow as a result of this action of the government.[45]

Apparently because of the loyal attitude of the Patriarch, the authorities gave him greater freedom in organizing the administration of the church, with an aim to uniting the warring factions of the Orthodox. (The attempts to heal the schism will be discussed subsequently.) In May, 1924, it was reported that he had instructed the bishops to organize diocesan councils on the basis approved by the Sobor of 1917.[46] Tikhon also took steps to organize a Synod and a Higher Church Council. These moves proved to be abortive, however, as the peace with the Renovationists did not succeed.

Thus the relations between the government and the Tikhonite church showed considerable improvement after his release, even though to the Soviet press and the authorities he was still "former Patriarch Tikhon," and public prayers for him were still forbidden. On the other hand, there was no release of any substantial part of the considerable number of priests and bishops serving prison sentences or terms of exile, and, indeed, bishops and other clergy continued to be sentenced by the courts on charges of hiding church treasures and for alleged moral offenses.[47] Fifteen churchmen at the Pecherskaia Lavra (a famous monastery at Kiev) were arrested after the police reported the finding of a large quantity of precious stones, gold, and silver hidden in the cellars, along with counterrevolutionary correspondence with Patriarch Tikhon, Metropolitan Antonii, "and other noted anti-Soviet figures."[48]

The Patriarch, in a letter to the editors, hastened to deny complicity in the concealment of the valuables. He stated that he had had direct authority over the Pecherskaia Lavra for only a brief time and knew nothing about the concealment of treasures. As for the counterrevolutionary documents, "we have not been and are not in communication with foreign counterrevolutionaries, nor with counterrevolutionary groups within the USSR, and we do not know anything about 'the counterrevolutionary political work' of the monks of the Lavra." [49]

But while Patriarch Tikhon composed his differences with the Soviet regime, he was far from compromising with the Renovationist church. On July 15/28, 1923, he issued a statement describing the origin and nature of the Renovationist movement, which he now declared was completely uncanonical and schismatic. As long as he had been under arrest, he said, he could do nothing about it, but now he called on the faithful to shun it and demanded of those who had adhered to it that they cleanse themselves through repentance. [50]

This message gave added impetus to a decline that was well under way. The Renovationist movement had reached its peak during the Sobor of 1923, when, for example, it held all but the four or five Moscow churches that remained loyal to the Patriarch. [51] Shortly thereafter events demonstrated that the Renovationist movement, and especially the Living Church section, had weak foundations. "The predominance of class interests over the ideological ones of the church, the lack of tolerance toward other views, the proneness to violent means of struggle" alienated many who might have been well disposed to a genuine liberal movement. Here lay the "original sin" of the insurrection — "its separation from the masses of the church." [52] Consequently, when Patriarch Tikhon once more appeared to head the church, a great wave of believers flowed out of the Renovationist church back to the Patriarch. Where the parish priest wanted to stay in the Renovationist church there was often harsh friction and at times even violence between the excited laymen and the priest and his supporters. The Renovationist Synod, headed by Metropolitan Evdokim, published a circular to the dioceses warning them what to expect from the Tikhonites. The latter, it stated, sometimes burst into churches at time of service, made appeals to the disturbed believers with pogrom speeches, caused all sorts of disorders, seized churches by force, spread monstrous rumors concerning their opponents, and used other unseemly tactics.[53]

In a later article Metropolitan Evdokim repeated his accusation. The monks and nuns evicted from monasteries frightened the ignorant with stories of the coming of Antichrist, of the speedy end of the world. In the parishes a secret political battle was in progress. The bourgeoisie and the disgruntled intelligentsia flocked into the churches, allegedly saying: "We must begin our [anti-Soviet] work with the church." Thus the church became the nucleus for the dispossessed who were fighting for their former privileges and wealth. The clergy who supported this campaign were well regarded, while the opponents of the former privileged class — the Renovationist clergy — received curses, threats, deprivation.[54]

While the patriarchal church undoubtedly became an ideological haven for anti-Soviet elements, there also were many believers who renewed their allegiance to Tikhon for reasons of devotion. A number of ecclesiastics, high in Renovationist councils, made public repentance as the Patriarch demanded and were accepted back into the fold. Bishop Artemii, Living Church head in Petrograd, Archbishop Konstantin of Kostroma, and Archbishop Serafim of Irkutsk, who had been made Metropolitan of Belorussia by the Renovationists, were among those who made their peace with Tikhon.[55] One of the most important was Metropolitan Sergii of Iaroslavl, who had so ardently praised the Living Church movement in 1923 — although, as already stated, he had soon turned against it. In January, 1924, after a brief stay in prison, he settled in Novgorod. In March he was called to Moscow, where, according to the *émigré* clergy, the Renovationists hoped to set up a new church to unite the newly formed Renovationist congregations. When he arrived, he made public repentance as a simple monk before the Patriarch, who raised him from his abasement, blessed him, and put on him the white cowl of a metropolitan.[56]

There were several attempts to reunite the Renovationists and the supporters of the Patriarch. One of these occurred in the fall of 1923; Metropolitan Evdokim of the Renovationists conferred with Archbishop Ilarion, Archbishop Serafim of Tver, and Archbishop Tikhon of the Urals, who had been delegated by Patriarch Tikhon. The discussions lasted from August to November, but ended without result.[57] In 1927 Bishop Gervasii of Kursk, Renovationist, told of attending, in the fall of 1923, a meeting of Tikhonite bishops in Moscow, who thought he was one of them. Archbishop Serafim, who had just held a two-hour conference with Metropolitan Evdokim, had agreed that Tikhon would appear before a Sobor and declare his retirement and relinquish control of the church. The Renovationists would then vote him back into office. After a lengthy discussion, however, the majority decided that the Renovationists were schismatics; if they wanted to end the schism, let them go to Canossa.[58] On the other hand, supporters of the Patriarch alleged that the negotiations failed because the Renovationists wanted to retain their privileges.[59] Another version is that, when the talks were just getting started, Evdokim sent out a false communiqué on the negotiations, which so irritated the Tikhonites that they broke off the *pourparlers* on November 10.[60]

The latter version was supported by a report in *Izvestiia* mentioning a letter from Metropolitan Evdokim to the *émigré* Metropolitan Antonii Khrapovitskii, relating that a mixed commission of bishops had sent Tikhon a resolution by the hand of his close supporter, Archbishop Ilarion, "to surrender all his powers, to retire to a monastery, to await the judgment upon him of a sobor of bishops." [61] Evdokim gave the same report to a Renovationist congress in Odessa, for it resolved: "The congress heard with especial pleasure the communiqué of Metropolitan Evdokim that Patriarch Tikhon, recognizing his political mistakes before the Soviet Power, had found in himself humbleness and wisdom, and also readiness to submit himself to a fraternal court of bishops." [62] An interesting view of the negotiations was given by Protopresbyter Krasnitskii, who declared that the failure of the discussions was caused by disagreement as to whether the reunited church should be headed by Tikhon or Evdokim.[63]

Whatever the explanation, the talks were broken off in November, 1923. A few months later, however, Tikhon made another attempt. According to the often well-informed Miliukov, when Tikhon asked the Soviet authorities for permission to hold a Sobor, he was told that he must drop his counterrevolutionary associations and prove

his good intentions by merging with the Living Church, with acceptance of Krasnitskii as the first step. Tikhon agreed to take him in as
vice-chairman of the church administration.[64] In July Krasnitskii
told an *Izvestiia* reporter that in the middle of March he had been
invited to Moscow for an important conference with Metropolitans
Peter Krutitskii, Serafim of Tver, and Tikhon of the Urals about ending the split in the church and the calling of a Sobor. The next day he
was received by Patriarch Tikhon, with whom he reached an agreement about a Sobor.[65] On May 19 Krasnitskii appealed to Tikhon
to readmit him and his group into the fold and to pardon all his sins
during the Renovationist period. Tikhon agreed to receive him into
communion "for the sake of peace and the good of the church" and
proposed that the Synod make him a member of the Higher Church
Administration. On May 21 the Synod decreed the organization of
this body, consisting of the Synod, chosen by Tikhon, and the Higher
Church Council, with Krasnitskii a member. This ruling was signed
by the Patriarch and Metropolitans Tikhon, Serafim, and Peter.[66]

On May 24 Krasnitskii issued a statement saying that he had joined
Tikhon, who had come around to his position concerning the Soviets.
Tikhon had promised the Living Church group half of the seats in
the central administration of the church and in all the diocesan
administrations. The Higher Church Council had already been
formed, with Krasnitskii and five members of his group in it. The
purpose of this merger, Krasnitskii said, was to fight "the church
counterrevolution" which divided the church. Tikhon planned to call
a Sobor and purge the church of reactionary elements.[67] Later, according to Miliukov, a provisional bureau was formed to prepare for
the Sobor; five of the twelve were appointed by Tikhon, while the
rest came from the Living Church. Full power in the church was to
rest with a Synod of bishops and the Patriarch.[68]

Before long, however, signs of difficulties appeared. On June 20
Izvestiia printed a statement by a Professor Pokrovskii to the effect
that an agreement to unite the two factions had been reached, but
Tikhon put off signing and finally refused outright. The moderate
Tikhonites laid this development to reactionary influences in the
church and were much disappointed in Tikhon, who, they felt, was a
waverer, without a firm will of his own. Many were reported to be

saying that the patriarchate would die with him.[69] Krasnitskii, however, continued to insist that all was well. In a statement printed in July he told a reporter that Tikhon had dropped his hostility to the Soviets, wanted to combat the reactionary *émigré* clergy, and in principle was not against the white, or nonmonastic, episcopate and the remarriage of widowed priests. The merger was completely arranged, and rumors to the contrary came from reactionaries. Krasnitskii added that the congregations of the church were much pleased by the developments.[70]

The Living Church leader did protest too much. A few days later Patriarch Tikhon told a reporter that he and Metropolitan Peter stood by the signed agreements with Krasnitskii and that everything was settled. He added, however, that the Synod and the Higher Church Council were unable to function, as they had no office space or quarters for members of the Synod. Metropolitan Peter said that everything was now very difficult, as the Synod, which formerly had had fifty million rubles, now had almost no money.[71]

Finally, in September Krasnitskii gave a public report on what had happened. In 1923, he said, the Tikhonites and the Renovationists (Vvedenskii's group) had reached a general understanding on most points, but could not agree on the man to head the church; some wanted Tikhon, others, Evdokim. Later, Tikhon made peace with the Living Church, declaring that he was not a foe of the Soviets nor of ecclesiastical reform. New administrative organs had been set up (obviously with the permission of the civil authorities), but the reactionary party stirred up the masses of believers against the Living Church, and on June 26, 1924, Tikhon annulled the resolution of agreement. At this point Krasnitskii's statement was challenged, but he was able to produce evidence that as late as August 8 Tikhon had expressed approval of the merger.[72] This account agrees with that of Miliukov, who stated that the failure of Tikhon's agreement with Krasnitskii was caused by intense opposition within the patriarchal church, which finally compelled Tikhon to announce that the whole scheme was a failure. Krasnitskii and his supporters resigned from the new grouping, and the government withdrew its support.[73] Further corroboration was given by a letter to *Izvestiia* from a Professor Belolikov, who was to have been a member of the Higher Church Council. He stated that he had become disgusted by the inactivity of the new ruling bodies, as three months had elapsed since their formation had been announced. According to him, patriarchal circles were explaining that these institutions did not operate because Tikhon had renounced them.[74]

This strange incident sheds considerable light upon relations between church and state at this time. For one thing, Patriarch Tikhon's willingness to negotiate, first with the Renovationists of Metropolitan Evdokim and Vvedenskii and then with Krasnitskii, shows that Tikhon and many of his followers wished to establish good relations with the Soviets. Krasnitskii, the strongest supporter of the white clergy against the monastic bishops, by his testimony at the trial of Metropolitan Veniamin of Petrograd had contributed to the sentencing and execution of Veniamin, an adherent of Tikhon, and at the Sobor of 1923 he had had much to do with the unfrocking of Tikhon. Yet the latter was willing to enter into close relations with him, with the approval of many of the Tikhonite bishops. On the other hand, it is quite understandable that many of Tikhon's church could not stomach Krasnitskii and opposed the measure, as did the group of bitter-end reactionaries within Tikhon's following.

The Soviet authorities seemed quite willing to approve the patriarchal church and legalize it, provided it gave an earnest of good faith by merging with one of the insurgent groups. The government apparently wished to end its feud with the Patriarch on any basis that would guarantee full acceptance of the Soviet regime on the part of his church.

As for the Renovationists headed by Metropolitan Evdokim and Vvedenskii, their position had declined. By approving a merger of Krasnitskii and Tikhon the Soviet authorities had shown a lack of interest in the now dominant Renovationist group. Moreover, the Renovationists were losing great numbers of laymen to Tikhon, often by whole parishes. So the Renovationists, weakened by the decline in Soviet sympathy and by defections, settled down to a long-drawn defensive battle. Thanks to their willingness to compromise on the married episcopate and their greater efforts to win the laymen, they were able to stabilize their position. Plans for a new Sobor were made at a conference in Moscow in June, 1924, which was attended by 466 delegates, including 83 bishops.[75]

In May, 1924, a declaration of the Renovationist Synod signed by sixty-five bishops asserted that Tikhon's negotiations with Krasnitskii showed the falsity and inconsistency of the Patriarch and the shame of his conduct. The declaration appealed to his followers to throw over the Patriarch and join the Renovationists in restoring unity.[76] Nevertheless, several members of the conference tried to establish contact with the Patriarch in order to promote church unity, but without success. Thereupon the conference resolved "to continue the irreconcilable fight against the Tikhonites and to regard any compromise with them as equally damaging from both the political and the ecclesiastical points of view." [77]

Although the Renovationist church was inferior in numbers to the patriarchal church, it had certain strategic advantages. In 1924, at the request of the Synod, fighting for control of church property in New York, the Central Executive Committee of the U.S.S.R. issued a testimonial stating that, as the Synod had been elected by the Sobor of 1923, in accordance with Soviet law, it was "recognized by the People's Commissariat of Justice as the organ of the Orthodox church within the framework of the said legislation of the U.S.S.R." [78]

Moreover, in one respect the positions of the Renovationist or Synodal church improved in 1924. Whereas in 1924 most of the Eastern Patriarchs had sided with Tikhon, in 1924 the new Patriarch of Constantinople suggested that Tikhon resign his patriarchate, which had been obtained under abnormal circumstances and was an obstacle to church unity. Tikhon indignantly accused the Patriarch of Constantinople of meddling in Russian church affairs. As for the schism in the Russian church, the Renovationists should end it by submitting.[79] Whereupon the Patriarch of Constantinople issued a declaration that he had removed Tikhon from the administration of the Russian church for not heeding the repeated urgings of the Eastern Patriarchs to restore unity in the Russian church. He also recognized the Synod as the true head of the Orthodox church in Russia.[80] The other Eastern Patriarchs also vacillated, first backing Tikhon, then later siding with the Synod party.[81] This development, however, seems to have had little effect, either in Russia or abroad.

By the beginning of 1925 the Renovationists claimed to have 170 bishops within the territory of the U.S.S.R. and 17,650 priests, serving 13,650 churches.[82] Another more detailed statement made at the same time gave a slightly higher number of churches. In Russia and Siberia there were 10,049 Renovationist churches with 9378 priests, and 19 monasteries. In the Ukraine there were about 3000 churches that recognized the Synod; in Belorussia, about 500; and in the Far Eastern Region, about 400, or an estimated total of about 14,000 churches.[83] If these figures were correct, the Renovationists controlled about one third of the Orthodox churches (as of 1914) in the territory of the U.S.S.R.

Thus by the beginning of 1925 what had started out in May, 1922, as an irresistible revolution sweeping the Russian Orthodox church had dwindled into a lingering defensive movement of the insurgents, who were now trying to save part of what had been won. The civil authorities, who apparently had at first hoped to secure in the Living Church a religious organization willing to live in peace with the Soviet regime, now were ready to accept a compromise with the patriarchal church. As long as Patriarch Tikhon was in power, however, it seemed probable that neither the Renovationists nor the Soviet authorities could secure the desired settlement. Consequently both churchmen and civil officials settled down to wait until Tikhon should die, when, it was hoped, a change in church leadership would bring an opportunity for a solution of the problem. The period of waiting proved to be of short duration.

CHAPTER IX

Metropolitan Sergii
Makes Peace

THE STALEMATE in the Russian church was broken in the spring of 1925 by the death of Patriarch Tikhon. Born in 1866, he had not yet lived his allotted span of years, but, as he had been seriously ill before, his death was not entirely unexpected. On February 23, 1924, he had had an attack of sclerosis, for which his physicians prescribed complete rest;[1] disregarding medical advice, however, he had continued to busy himself with the negotiations with Krasnitskii and apparently had fully recovered. In January, 1925, another attack sent him to the Bakunin hospital for treatment. When he began to recover he made trips from the hospital on business in spite of the protests of the doctors. Finally, on April 7, he returned from a long meeting of the Synod in a state of exhaustion, and late at night he had a heart failure. Neither his regular physician nor four others called in for consultation could save him.[2] His body was taken to the Donskoi Monastery, where after lying in state, it was buried with a solemn funeral at which five metropolitans, sixty-three bishops, and a host of priests officiated before a great crowd of people.[3]

Thus ended the stormy career of the first Russian patriarch since the days of Peter the Great. After leading the ecclesiastical forces that opposed the Soviets during the civil war period, and later heading the opposition to the use of consecrated vessels of the church for famine relief, he had reversed himself by admitting his anti-Soviet activity. It is interesting to note that P. G. Smidovich, high Soviet official in charge of ecclesiastical affairs, told Dr. Spinka that at first he had

thought that Tikhon was dishonest, but later he had come to feel that
Tikhon was an honorable man, sincere in his profession of loyalty.
Smidovich, however, felt that many of the Patriarch's associates were
opposed to his pro-Soviet policy and often were able to thwart it;
Tikhon, he believed, was too weak a personality to compel obedience
in this respect.[4]

The plausibility of this estimate of the Patriarch's position was supported by Tikhon's sensational Testament, prepared by him just before his death and published in *Izvestiia* at the request of Metropolitans Peter Krutitskii and Tikhon of the Urals. In it he declared that
the Soviet Power, which by the will of God had come to head the Russian state, had issued the declaration of separation of the church from
the state and of freedom of conscience, which he felt gave the Orthodox church the necessary rights for its existence. Hence he called on
the people and the clergy to join him in welcoming the workers' and
peasants' government. While he refused to make the slightest concessions or compromises in matters of faith, "we should be sincere in relation to the Soviet Power and the work of the USSR for the general
good, bringing the order of external church life and activity into conformity with the new state system, condemning all community with
the enemies of the Soviet Power and open or secret agitation against
it." He also called on all beloved sons of the Orthodox church "to
unite with us in fervent prayer to the All-Highest to send down help
to the Workers' and Peasants' Power and its labors for the common
good." Of the parish congregations and their executive organs he demanded that they prevent the infiltration of ill-intentioned persons
who might plan activity against the government and that they should
not nurture hopes of restoring the monarchy, but should be convinced
that the Soviet regime was the government of the people and hence
firm and unshakable. He urged them to elect to the parish councils
worthy men, honorably loyal to the church, and not dabblers in politics. The church should not fight the Soviets, but the true foes of Orthodoxy — sectarians, Roman Catholics, Protestants, Renovationists,
and the Godless.

Continuing his message, which he said came as he was "by the grace
of God recovering from illness, entering once more upon the service
of the church of God," he condemned "all opposition to the govern-

ment, evil-intentioned planning against it, rebellions and all sorts of hostility thereto" and urged his followers to join in working for the peace and well-being of the church. Particularly, he condemned those who, forgetting what is God's and abusing their position in the church, "give themselves over without measure to human, frequently crass politics, sometimes even having a criminal character," and hence he announced the formation of a special commission to investigate and remove from office those clerics who persisted in their errors and refused to repent of them before the Soviet Power. He also voiced sharp condemnation of the émigré clergy, particularly of the Karlovatskii Sobor, and threatened them with deprivation of the right of divine service and with trial before a Sobor. He warned Metropolitans Antonii and Platon that continued refusal to submit would compel him to judge them *in absentia*.

Finally, after denying allegations that he was not free in his dealings with his flock, but was subject to some sort of compulsion, Patriarch Tikhon called on his clerical and lay followers to submit to the Soviet Power from conscience, remembering the words of the Apostle that "there is no power not from God." If clean and sincere relations were once established, he was confident that the authorities would deal with them in full trust and would permit the church to teach its children the Law of God, to have theological schools, and to publish books and journals in defense of the Orthodox faith.[5]

Needless to say, this uncompromising message caused much fluttering in the dovecotes of the émigré clergy, who hastened to brand it as a forgery, on the grounds that it was dated by the Gregorian calendar and from the Donskoi Monastery on the day of Tikhon's death, although he lived in the hospital until the end. However, the submission of the document by two metropolitans close to the Patriarch and the fact that he felt he had recovered and would return home that day, support the presumption of authenticity. Also the facsimile of his signature published along with the text of the document was recognized by Professor Kartashev, who knew Tikhon well.[6] Consequently the strongly anti-Soviet clergy and laymen were reduced to claiming that the Patriarch had been compelled to sign it by the political police or that the two metropolitans had been forced to vouch for it.[7]

The Soviet position, as shown by an editorial in *Izvestiia*, was that the Patriarch, once an archenemy of the Soviets, had by the logic of events come to adopt a loyal attitude, in which he was apparently sincere. The Soviets did not need Tikhon's support, as they were strong in the support of the people; nevertheless, his testament gave the lie to foreign outcry about persecution of the Patriarch and would be a severe blow to all foes of the Soviet regime.[8]

Before his death the Patriarch had drawn up a new provision for his succession, naming Metropolitans Kirill, Agafangel, and Peter as his choices for the post of Locum Tenens. As both Kirill and Agafangel were still in exile, Metropolitan Peter Krutitskii was proclaimed acting head of the church before a gathering of sixty bishops. A Sobor was to be held within forty days to elect a new patriarch. It did not meet, however. The churchmen asserted that too many bishops were in exile to hold it; Smidovich, Soviet official in charge of religious matters, told Dr. Spinka that the churchmen had never asked for permission to hold it and had made no attempt to arrange it.[9]

The death of Tikhon greatly encouraged the Renovationists, who had regarded him as the chief obstacle to ending the schism. Consequently, almost immediately their Synod issued a message urging all churchmen to join in a new Sobor for that purpose, whether they recognized the authority of the Synod or not. The members of the Synod declared that they were willing to surrender their positions and that "the Holy Synod does not regard itself as an irreplaceable authority of the church." All were asked to forgive and forget the past and to join in fraternal labors for the good of the Orthodox church.[10] As Metropolitan Peter's grouping did not reply to this overture, the Renovationist Synod continued its preparation for the Sobor without them. On June 13, 1925, it made a warm appeal to all churchmen to end the schism and restore the unity of the church.[11] The diocesan and parish clergy of the Renovationist faction were told to approach the Tikhonite bishops and, failing them, the parish clergy and laymen, in order to draw them into preparations for the Sobor, whose chief purpose was to restore church unity.[12]

The Renovationists also carried on private talks with Metropolitan Peter; he, however, said that he, being only Locum Tenens, lacked the power to heal the breach. The matter would have to be submitted to the bishops; as, however, numbers of them were in prison or in exile, the Renovationists should take it upon themselves to secure their release. The Renovationists replied that this was a political matter outside their competence. Thus the conversations ended.[13] Later, on July 28, Peter issued a long message to the Orthodox, in which he enumerated the enemies of the church — the Catholics, the Uniats, the Baptists, and the Renovationists. He especially warned his followers not to have anything to do with the Renovationists, who should restore the unity of the church by repenting of their sins and discarding their uncanonical innovations such as married bishops and remarried priests. At the same time Peter sought to mollify the Soviet authorities by instructing his flock to submit to the civil authorities and to refrain from political conflict.[14]

Peter's flock obeyed his instructions by boycotting the Sobor, which met in October, 1925. Only a few Tikhonite laymen appeared at its meeting, where they demanded that the Renovationists admit their errors and return to the true church.[15] The Renovationists, headed by Metropolitan Vvedenskii, blamed the failure of the move for unity upon Metropolitan Peter and the other Tikhonites, who, they charged, were still working for a monarchist restoration. Nevertheless, the Sobor appealed to the masses of the Tikhonite church to move for peace and unity.[16] The Renovationists also adopted a very cautious policy toward the questions of married bishops, remarried priests, and the Gregorian calendar, in order that these matters should not be an obstacle to ending the schism.[17]

Thus the Sobor of 1925 failed to achieve its purpose, allegedly because of the reactionary, counterrevolutionary attitude of Metropolitan Peter and his followers. The Soviet authorities held this view, for an October 1 *Izvestiia* published an article stating that the Tikhonites were dabbling in politics, as shown by documents in the possession of the Renovationist Synod. The Tikhonites had done nothing to punish the clergy of the Karlovatskii Sobor, and, far from slackening their political activity, were busily engaged in inflaming the masses against the Soviets. The editor held that it was highly significant that Metropolitan Antonii Khrapovitskii, who at first had refused to recognize Metropolitan Peter as Locum Tenens, now favored him.[18] After the failure of the Sobor of 1925 *Izvestiia* returned to the attack, stating that the Renovationist clergy held that Peter was leaning on the reactionary *émigré* clergy and wished to win their trust and support. At the Sobor of 1925 it had been stated that Peter had sent a letter abroad recognizing the Grand Duke Kirill, Romanov pretender. The editor did not completely accept these charges, which were not without bias; but he stated that several actions of Metropolitan Peter had given grounds to think that there was much truth in this characterization. Consequently it depended upon Peter to refute these suspicions and upon the churchmen themselves "once and forever to put an end to the Black Hundred machinations of those persons who direct church life." [19]

Metropolitan Peter did not succeed in making his peace with the Soviets, for on December 23, 1925, he was arrested, along with a group of Moscow bishops close to him. The *émigré* spokesmen of the church charged that there was no justification for the arrest.[20] The Soviets did not publish their case against him; in August, 1926, however, Dr. Spinka had an interview with Smidovich, the official in charge of religious matters, and asked him about the case. Smidovich said that government agents abroad had gathered proof against Peter before his arrest, with the result that the case against him was so complete that he had already confessed that he had been in contact with monarchist organizations abroad and had sent his blessing to the Grand Duke Nikolai Nikolaevich. Moreover, Smidovich said, Peter had already signed his confession and had appealed to the court for mercy. However, Dr. Spinka was not shown the documents in the case, which were to be published later.[21] Later in the summer of 1926 Metropolitan Peter was exiled to Siberia.

After the warning article in *Izvestiia* in November, 1925, a group of Tikhonite bishops, led by Archbishop Grigorii of Ekaterinoslav, visited Peter and asked him to disprove the charges by answering them and to call a meeting of clergy in Moscow to consider the state of the church. Metropolitan Peter at first refused, but finally, according to Grigorii, he promised to draw up a declaration and communicate it to the bishops. Before this could be done, however, Peter was placed under arrest. Hence, on December 22, 1925, Grigorii's group called a gathering of bishops in the former patriarchal quarters in the Donskoi Monastery, at which a Temporary Higher Church Council of six, headed by Archbishop Grigorii, was formed and bylaws adopted. The new body was to function until a new Sobor of bishops, priests, and laymen should meet, not later than the summer of 1926. Thus a new revolt of part of the patriarchal church made its appearance. The Grigorievtsy, as the new following was popularly called, declared, however, that they had nothing in common with the Renovationists or other dissidents, but remained true to the traditions of the church.[22] Furthermore, they did not oppose Metropolitan Peter, claiming that they were merely acting for the church while he was not able to function.

Metropolitan Peter, however, had already taken steps to provide a replacement for himself by issuing a decree that if he were deprived of power to act in the church, Metropolitan Sergii of Nizhnii Novgorod should be Deputy Locum Tenens; three other hierarchs were named as alternates.[23] Thus at the moment when Archbishop Grigorii's group was forming the Temporary Higher Church Council, Metropolitan Sergii was given the powers of Deputy Locum Tenens. Archbishop Grigorii later told the Soviet press that his group had received a letter from Sergii notifying them that he was now head of the church. Wishing peace in the church, they had invited Sergii to come to Moscow to negotiate a merger. He refused and issued a decree forbidding the bishops associated with the Temporary Higher Church Council to administer their dioceses and perform divine service. Grigorii and his followers disregarded this ban.[24]

In this struggle Metropolitan Sergii received the support of most of the Tikhonite bishops, who, after some wavering, rallied around him. But the government refused him permission to come to Moscow to take over the affairs of the church, so his activity was severely limited.[25]

Thanks to the loyalty of the Grigorievtsy to the government they obtained the legalization of their organization on January 2, 1926, and also secured legalization for all who recognized them. This gave them the right to set up a conciliar administration of the church, to preach their faith freely, to open religious schools, and to publish religious books.[26] Armed with this powerful weapon, Archbishop Grigorii and his aides visited Metropolitan Peter in prison and persuaded him that, thanks to their legal position, they could secure peaceful and sound relations with the Soviet Power for the Russian church — something that Metropolitan Sergii apparently could not do. Much impressed, Peter issued a decree annulling Sergii's powers as Deputy Locum Tenens and bestowed these rights upon Archbishop Grigorii's group.[27]

Metropolitan Sergii wavered, but finally decided to defy the decree of Metropolitan Peter and, with the support of most of the Tikhonite group, refused to give up his position as temporary head of the church.[28] Likewise, when Metropolitan Agafangel of Iaroslavl returned from exile in April, 1926, and sought to resume his functions as Locum Tenens, which Patriarch Tikhon had given him in 1922, Metropolitan Sergii refused to withdraw.[29] A long struggle ensued, with Metropolitan Peter supporting Agafangel. Sergii, however, was upheld by many of the bishops, and finally Agafangel withdrew his claims and Metropolitan Peter again ordered the church to obey Metropolitan Sergii as Deputy Locum Tenens.[30]

The *émigré* church circles that reported these developments added that Agafangel had been egged on to act thus by Renovationists and also by Tuchkov, official of the political police. No proof of this assertion, however, was presented.[31]

Whether or not the Soviet authorities had any part in the actions of Archbishop Grigorii and Metropolitans Peter and Agafangel, there is no doubt that they favored the former as loyal and strongly distrusted Metropolitan Sergii. The latter was arrested early in 1926 and brought back to Moscow; in March he was sent back to Nizhnii Novgorod and released.[32] Even after this incident, during which he doubtless was investigated and questioned by the authorities, who must have decided that he was not immediately dangerous, he was regarded as the leader of the right wing of the patriarchal church. Bishop Boris, a supporter of Archbishop Grigorii, alleged that one of Sergii's charges against the Grigorievtsy was that they had officially approached the civil authorities — which charge probably did not please the latter.[33] On June 1 *Izvestiia,* discussing the confusion in the church in a manner favorable to Archbishop Grigorii, mentioned Sergii, "who has united around himself the reactionary elements."[34] Support for this opinion of Sergii was lent by the fact that he at this time was warmly supported by the archreactionaries around Metropolitan Antonii Khrapovitskii.[35] In 1928 the well-informed antireligious writer Kandidov doubtless gave the official view when he wrote that, in spite of

Sergii's repeated expressions of loyalty to the Soviet government, he had continued to "carry on correspondence with White Guards and to communicate to them concerning his uncompromising attitude toward the Soviet government," which had caused the *émigré* press to state that Sergii and his church stood firmly and decisively against "the godlessness of communion with the Soviet authorities." [36]

As a result of this feeling on the part of the Soviet leaders, they again summoned Sergii to Moscow. *Émigré* sources reported that he was given an ultimatum to dissolve the Church Synod Abroad (formed by the Karlovatskii Sobor), to unfrock and anathematize the hierarchs allied with it, and to adopt the Gregorian calendar. Sergii apparently refused, and consequently he was arrested on December 13, 1926. He had already made provision to turn his power over to any one of three archbishops, of whom the third, Serafim, assumed the functions, the other two having been deprived of freedom.[37]

At this moment the fortunes of the patriarchal church stood at a very low level; it was under attack from both the Renovationists and the Grigorievtsy, and of eleven hierarchs who had been named as Locum Tenens, ten were in prison or in exile. The *émigré* clergy seemed entirely correct in their assertions that the Soviet authorities were well on their way to success in an obvious aim to smash the organization of the Orthodox church.

Events, however, showed that both sides wished to reach a compromise. Metropolitan Peter had already shown a desire to secure a legalized administration for the church by his willingness to turn power over to Archbishop Grigorii. Likewise, the influential Archbishop Ilarion, administrator of the diocese of Moscow, late in February, 1926, signed an appeal, apparently to the Soviet government, in which he dwelt on the necessity for having a temporary administrative body to head the church and to call a truly representative Sobor, which would indicate "its complete lack of participation in and sympathy with all politically untrustworthy tendencies." Later he wrote: "I do not know whether among our hierarchy and in general among the thinking members of our church there are persons so naïve and shortsighted as to have ridiculous illusions about a restoration. . . ." [38]

Metropolitan Sergii himself took a similar stand. He was approached by the government for the purpose of securing a *modus vivendi* between church and government and was asked to ascertain the views of his church. In his appeal to the People's Commissariat of Internal Affairs (NKVD) and his draft of a declaration to the church, dated June 10, 1926, he asked the legalization of the church with himself as head and also of diocesan organizations and for the right to call a conference of bishops. He further asked permission to print a *Journal of the Moscow Patriarchate* and to have theological schools. In his declaration to his flock he stressed that legalization, sought by Patriarch Tikhon, was vitally needed by the church; it could be secured only by loyalty — that is, by a definite aversion from all parties and tendencies hostile to the Soviets. In spite of all the contradictions between the church point of view and Communist materialism, a church member could be a useful citizen; indeed, the majority of them were. Sergii himself, while refusing to be responsible for the politics of all members of the church, renounced politics. As for the hostile churchmen abroad, he could not punish them, but he would cast them out.[39]

For a time Sergii was apparently sure that his views were acceptable to the government, for his message to the faithful announced that an understanding had been reached. The agreement was not realized, however, and Metropolitan Sergii was again arrested late in 1926. Nevertheless, a new request for legal recognition of the church soon appeared — the so-called "appeal of the Solovetskii Bishops," an anonymous message addressed to the Soviet authorities, which circulated in manuscript form. It was believed in church circles to have come from a considerable number of bishops in exile at the Solovetskii Monastery in the White Sea. In general its content was much like that of Sergii's appeals, although it complained about the unfairness of the Soviets in supporting the Renovationists and in undeservedly punishing the Tikhonite clergy. But, while as long as the government had a Communist outlook there could be no fundamental harmony between church and state, the church was willing to live in peace with any government. The bishops promised to be completely neutral in political matters and to submit to all laws and civil decrees. Political questions would not be dealt with either in the parish councils or in the higher levels of the church. In return, they hoped that the Soviet authorities would permit the organization of the diocesan and central church administrations, the election of a Patriarch and a Synod, and the calling of a Sobor, and that the government would not attempt to hold the church in leading strings.[40]

Metropolitan Sergii remained under arrest from December, 1926, to April, 1927, during which time negotiations with the NKVD were proceeding. In the end, the repeated expressions of loyalty to the Soviet regime bore fruit. In May, 1927, shortly after his release, he summoned a conference of bishops and organized a Temporary Patriarchal Synod to assist him in his work. The proposal of Sergii and the Synod for legalization was then approved by the Administrative Section of the NKVD.[41] On June 10 Sergii sent a petition to the NKVD from Nizhnii Novgorod asking that he be registered as temporary head of the church and permitted to organize a chancellery, which should be moved to Moscow. He also asked that the local organs of the church be registered in order that the local steps for calling a Sobor might be taken. Sergii also asked for permission to hold small gatherings of bishops, and to have an ecclesiastical publication and theological educational institutions.[42]

Some of these concessions were granted fairly soon (Metropolitan Sergii was permitted to move to Moscow, and the *Journal of the Moscow Patriarchate* began publication in 1928), while others were long in coming — no theological seminaries were opened for many years, and Metropolitan Sergii did not call a Sobor until 1943 — but he and his Synod proclaimed publicly that they were unreservedly loyal to the Soviets. On June 29 a long proclamation to the Orthodox told of the changed state of affairs in the church. It stated that Patriarch Tikhon had long hoped for legalization of the church, but foreign enemies of the Soviets, many of them churchmen, had aroused "natural and justified distrust of the government toward the church leaders in general." Later the task fell to Sergii, and success was in sight, but foreign foes acted; killings, forgeries, raids, explosions, "and similar manifestations of underground warfare are before our eyes." Hence it was even more necessary for those who loved the church to show that "we, the church leaders, are not with the foes of our Soviet state and not with the senseless tools of their intrigues, but with our people and our government."

Sergii went on to announce that in May the Temporary Patriarchal Synod had been organized and had received permission to begin its functions. Thus the church had a legal central administration and hoped that legalization might soon be extended to the lower administration. "We express to the whole people our gratitude to the Soviet government for such attentiveness to the spiritual needs of the Orthodox people, and together with this we assure the government that we shall not use the trust confided in us for evil."

Vast problems remained ahead — of which one was to prove by deeds that true Orthodox as well as nonbelievers could be loyal citizens of the Soviet Power. While remaining Orthodox, they wished to recognize the Soviet Union "as our secular native land, whose joys and successes are our joys and successes, and whose failures are our failures. Every blow aimed at the Union, whether it be war, boycott, any public calamity or a simple assassination like that in Warsaw is regarded by us as a blow directed against us." [43] The effort to be both true sons of the Orthodox church and loyal Soviet citizens would succeed unless they failed to realize the changes that had occurred. Earlier, many people had regarded the Soviet regime as temporary, an accident of history, and held that the Orthodox should not break with the monarchy and the old regime. "Such was the attitude of well-known church circles, which was expressed, of course, both in words and deeds, and which drew the suspicion of the Soviet Power and hampered the efforts of the Most Holy Patriarch to establish peaceful relations between the church and the Soviet government." Sergii reproved such persons for thinking that they could avoid contact with the Soviets and called on them either to reverse their former attitudes by dropping politics and concerning themselves only with faith, or at least not to interfere with those at the helm and temporarily to retire from church affairs.[44]

Sergii also addressed himself to the clergy of the Karlovatskii Sobor, which still retained its fiercely monarchist, anti-Soviet attitude. In another message of July 29 he declared that he had demanded written pledges from them of full loyalty to the Soviets; if they refused or violated such pledges once given, they would be excluded from the jurisdiction of the Patriarchate of Moscow.[45]

In addition, Sergii gave an interview to a reporter from *Izvestiia,* in which he stressed loyalty to the regime. While earlier pronouncements, he said, had condemned hostility to the Soviets, they were halfway measures and had had little effect. Under him the church was establishing working relationships with the government, and none of the clergy should do anything to undermine the Soviets. He believed that the sensible majority as a whole would join him in this. "Ten years of the existence of the Soviet Power have, of course, taught them something." While he recognized that some of the die-hards retained their hostility to the Soviets, he felt that this would matter little. He and his Synod "recognize the Soviet Power as a normal and lawful authority, and we submit to all its rulings with full sincerity. In case of war our sympathies are entirely on the side of the Soviet Union: for we serve our native land, and all interventionists fight only in their own interests. . . ." He hoped that the moderates among the *émigré* clergy would accept this attitude.[46]

While the editors of *Izvestiia* devoted much space to these announcements of Sergii and his Synod, they expressed their opinion on these developments in a somewhat grudging manner. The tenor of their comment was that Sergii was no better than the rest of the clergy who had long fought the Soviets, but he and his followers were intelligent enough to realize that the former policy of outright opposition was bankrupt and that public opinion would not permit it. *Izvestiia* stated that ". . . the adoption of Soviet coloration compelled by the frame of mind of the workers and the peasants, the attempt to delay a full rupture between the people and the church — in this is the basic meaning of the proclamation of the churchmen. . . ."[47]

In spite of the lack of warmth in the Soviet press, Metropolitan Sergii continued to emphasize his loyalty to the regime. In October he and his Synod issued an order that the clergy should ask prayers at divine service for Metropolitan Peter, Locum Tenens, and for Sergii, and should also proclaim: "For our country and its authorities, to God we pray"; and in another part of the service, "And again we pray for our country and for its authorities, and may we live a quiet and undisturbed life in all righteousness and purity."[48]

At the same time Sergii made a report to the faithful in which he declared that good relations had been established with the Soviet authorities, thanks to which diocesan councils were gradually beginning to open and had already begun to function in at least eight dioceses. Empty sees were being filled, and ecclesiastical problems were brought to solution by the Synod. Not only had communion been established with the Eastern Patriarchs, but also messages of support had been received from churchmen in Japan and the Baltic states, and from most of the clergy of Western Europe, headed by Metropolitan Evlogii, while the churches in Finland and Poland had expressed a desire to recognize his authority.[49]

Opposition to Sergii's pro-Soviet policy remained, however. The right wing of the episcopate, headed by Metropolitan Iosif and two vicarian bishops of Petrograd, broke with Sergii over this decree, and in Iaroslavl Archbishop Serafim and, for a time, Metropolitan Agafangel came out in opposition, along with other hierarchs.[50] The revolt does not seem to have assumed serious proportions, however, as most of the parishes and the great majority of the bishops accepted Metropolitan Sergii's instructions. It does, however, seem to have had the effect of indefinitely postponing the much postponed Sobor.[51]

The great majority of Russian Orthodox believers apparently gave Sergii's policy at least passive acceptance, and in some cases active support. Many ecclesiastics took part in the celebration of the tenth anniversary of the October Revolution; in Perm the churchmen as a group took part in the torchlight procession on November 6 and the demonstrations of the next day.[52]

Opinions differ sharply as to the effect on the church of Metropolitan Sergii's policy. The view of the right wing of the *émigré* clergy was expressed in a book by Father Mikhail Pol'skii, who declared that Sergii had delivered the church into the hands of the GPU, the political police. The latter controlled the appointment of bishops, so that only weak and pliable men were named; the remainder were arrested and exiled. Thus the Soviet authorities used the legalization of the church to its undoing; its last state was worse than the first.[53] On the other hand, the moderate Stratonov, an ardent supporter of Patriarch Tikhon, held that Sergii's course was the only possible one and that the church was greatly strengthened thereby.[54] An article published in Paris late in 1928, which claimed to have come from "an exceedingly authoritative and informed person," was most enthusiastic about the results of the agreement with the Soviets. It stated that Sergii's position in the church was very strong; he enjoyed the support of all Orthodox Moscow and was eagerly sought to perform service in parish churches. The episcopate was rapidly returning to normal as the exiled bishops, who with rare exceptions warmly approved Sergii's policy, returned. Most of the early opposition to his moves had died out, and the dissidents had returned to the fold with the exception of Metropolitan Iosif and two vicarian bishops. Likewise Grigorii's faction was almost extinct, with only a few bishops and a handful of followers. The Renovationists also were declining in numbers.[55]

A year later, in February, 1930, Metropolitan Sergii gave two interviews to the Soviet press in which he remarked on the good condition of the church. Its administration was functioning successfully, with no oppression; the church had about thirty thousand parishes administered by 163 bishops.[56] At the same time, according to Miliukov, Sergii presented to Smidovich, Soviet official in charge of church affairs, a "Memorandum on the Needs of the Orthodox Patriarchal Church," which allegedly contained a long list of complaints. Churches were heavily taxed and burdened with high insurance rates, as well as compelled to make obligatory contributions to funds for industrialization. Priests were loaded with high taxes and suffered discrimination in respect to living quarters and the education of their children. Churches were closed by the government at the request of atheist groups.[57] A report on the state of the Russian church, apparently smuggled from Moscow to Paris in March, 1930, gave an even more dismal account. Allegedly the church was dominated by the political police, while clergy who were not sufficiently pliable were arrested and exiled. Impossible taxes and rents were loaded on the clerics, and churches and monasteries were often closed by the authorities in arbitrary fashion.[58]

Probably there was some exaggeration in both the rosy and the gloomy estimates cited above. On the whole, in spite of unfair measures against the clergy and the church, there is reason to feel that the church gained by the Soviet willingness to grant it legalization. In spite of the greatly intensified propagandistic efforts of its foes from 1929 on into the 1930's, the church survived — albeit in diminished estate — until the Second World War, when the government gave it much greater recognition. Hence the prophecies that agreement with the Soviet authorities would mean fatal domination of the church by hostile forces which would corrupt and sap it, were not borne out.

Metropolitan Sergii thus steered a skillful course between ecclesiastical enemies on both the right and the left. Among the latter, along with the unpacified followers of Archbishop Grigorii, Sergii also faced the still active Renovationists, who, he held, were in schism. His attitude was that they could make their peace only by full repentance and submission.[59]

For the Renovationists the years following the death of Patriarch Tikhon were marked by decline in spite of the internal dissension of the Tikhonites. Perhaps their position was too advanced politically for most of the believers, while presumably the strong supporters of the Soviets often went even further and broke with religion entirely. Whatever the reason, the Renovationists never recovered the ground lost after the freeing of Patriarch Tikhon. Whereas in their heyday they had control of almost all the church with its nearly forty thousand parishes, by October 1, 1925, their data, far from complete, gave them 12,593 churches in 108 dioceses.[60] The year 1926 seems to have been disastrous. Metropolitan Nikolai, reporting to the Renovationist Synod in January, 1927, spoke of the stabilization of the situation, in spite of the aggressive Tikhonites; this "kept our cause from collapse." While he was still optimistic, he admitted that the current situation for many localities was "downright tragic. It is fully understandable that many, surrounded by the realities, are ready to lose heart." [61] In one year they lost 2794 parishes, declining from 9039 to 6245 (apparently not including the Ukraine or Belorussia). Thus the Renovationists had 21 per cent of all the Orthodox parishes of the Russian Republic (R.S.F.S.R.), with their chief strength in outlying regions. These heavy losses were caused by several factors, among them the successful activity of Tikhonite bishops who had returned from exile, disappointment at the failure to reunite the church, and the dependence of the pastors upon their parishes.[62]

In 1927, although the Renovationists presented no figures, they claimed a small net gain in parishes, and Metropolitan Vvedenskii asserted that there was an irresistible popular movement toward them.[63] In 1928 they also expressed optimism, claiming no recent losses and some gains.[64] Vvedenskii even stated that they were approaching victory, with the Tikhonites fighting among themselves.[65]

Vvedenskii's optimism was not well founded, as the Renovationist movement continued to decline. At the end of 1928, however, it still seemed strong and enjoyed one advantage over its rivals — that of having theological education and a greater number of religious periodicals. In 1928 theological academies in Moscow and Leningrad had nearly one hundred students each, while the Kiev Theological School had fifty. Pastoral training courses existed in Voronezh, Vologda, Kursk, Kazan, Ufa, and several other cities.[66] Three religious periodicals were published by the central authorities of the Renovationists in addition to several diocesan organs.[67]

In the Ukraine the Renovationists had to adapt themselves to meet the competition of the Ukrainian Autocephalous church. In May, 1925, a Second All-Ukrainian Sobor proclaimed the autonomy of the Ukrainian (Renovationist) church; this action was approved by the Renovationist Sobor of 1925.[68]

As for the Ukrainian Autocephalous church, in 1924 it appealed to the Soviet authorities for legalization, claiming that it was fully loyal to the Soviet regime and had for years opposed the bourgeoisie and capitalism, and had upheld socialism.[69] The petition apparently was granted. According to later Soviet charges, however, this church was a stronghold of anti-Soviet Ukrainian nationalism, harboring the remnants of the nationalist movement of Petliura, which burst forth in 1926, during a requiem for the writer Ivan Franko, which turned into a demonstration for Petliura. But, although this church allegedly played an important part in the nationalist work against the Soviet regime, it was only in 1930 that the government moved against its leaders.[70] This will be discussed subsequently.

While the Soviet government thus permitted the existence of several Orthodox groups, to say nothing of other denominations — sectarians, Roman Catholics, Hebrews, and others — the official attitude on the local level was also important. Were the parish churches permitted to perform service freely; were the buildings sequestered wholesale; were the parish priests harassed; to what extent was religious instruction of children permitted? The following cases from Soviet lawbooks give some indication of the answers to these questions.

It must be said that the Soviet legal authorities, as Communists, regarded religious belief as an error, as a survival of prejudices implanted by ignorance. Nonetheless, they continued to be guided by the earlier laws providing that the free performance of religious rituals was permitted except where it violated public order. When in 1924 a group of workers of Vladimir complained that not only was their factory church closed by the authorities (as a result of the ban on institutional chapels), but they were also forbidden to hold religious discussions and prayer meetings on holy days, the central authorities explained to the local authorities that it was necessary "to have a tolerant and attentive attitude toward the religious prejudices of the worker and peasant population, combating them by means of agitation and propaganda and not by means of compulsion and prohibition." Hence it was suggested that the workers and white-collar workers be permitted to gather and perform the usual ceremonies of the cult. When another group complained that the closing of their factory chapel left them without a church, the Commissariat of Justice approved their proposal to move an abandoned church building to their vicinity.[71] Likewise the authorities issued a ruling in 1925 that facilitated the securing of permission to have outdoor public performances of *Te Deums,* religious processions, and other public ceremonies.[72]

In 1925 the Commissariat of Internal Affairs found it necessary to issue a circular stating that "performance of religious ceremonies within the homes of believers, like the religious ceremonies in churches, is permitted without hindrance, without special permission." The law required, however, that written permission be secured for public religious ceremonies such as processions and *Te Deums* on a cathedral square.[73]

Even freedom of preaching within somewhat restricted limits was upheld. In 1925 *Izvestiia* reported an incident which was later cited in the lawbooks as a model case. In a village of the province of Tula the local "enlightenment group" staged a play, "Out of Darkness into Light," in one act of which an ikon was ceremonially removed from a home. The next Sunday the local priest preached on this subject, terming the school where the play had been given "a home of debauchery," and called on the parishioners not to attend such plays or let their children attend them. He was brought to trial for this utterance and the provincial court sentenced him to three years' imprisonment for counterrevolutionary propaganda. He appealed to the Supreme Court, which declared that his utterances to the believers were not counter-revolutionary and dismissed the charges.[74]

The authorities continued to discourage the predilections of the local authorities to close parish churches. A circular of the Commissariat* of Justice of the R.S.F.S.R. in 1925 advised that "the closing of buildings of a cult in the possession of believers should in general not take place except in cases of extreme state need, when the satisfaction of the latter is impossible by other means." In such cases the laws should be carefully observed, to ensure the legality and desirability of such closings. Moreover, interested persons had the right to appeal to the Presidium of the Central Executive Committee.[75] Similar rules were adopted by the Presidium of the Central Executive Committee of the Ukraine in 1924. Even if real need dictated the requisitioning of church buildings, they should not be taken unless this was approved by a majority of the working people of the settlement, as shown by resolutions and decrees of public meetings, and only in case the believers would be able to satisfy their religious needs in another prayer meeting of the same denomination. Furthermore, such decisions required the confirmation of the central authorities.[76]

These reminders were definitely needed. In 1924 it was officially stated that the All-Union Central Executive Committee had been receiving complaints that at political meetings, antireligious gatherings, or during the discussion after antireligious lectures, the local authorities had proposed resolutions to close certain churches and had taken a mere majority vote at such unrepresentative gatherings as a mandate to close them. It was declared that "the Soviet authorities, which proclaimed in the decree of the separation of church from state the right of free performance of religious ceremonies . . . cannot permit a majority of votes to trample on the rights of freedom of conscience and free performance of ceremonies which belong even to a mere minority." [77] When local Communists and Young Communists arbitrarily seized a churchyard and property in it, when believers complained that their church bells had been confiscated, and when it was proposed to use a bell tower for a water tank, the central authorities reversed the decisions of the local officials and protected the interests of the believers.[78] In 1928 Iaroslavskii, leader of the Godless, wrote that in the past administrative pressure had been used in closing churches and that insufficient care had been used in securing of resolutions to close them, which had sometimes been adopted by a mere minority of the population. He stated that now, however, after ten years of the Soviet regime, it was different; no administrative pressure was used, and the resolutions were freely adopted.[79] (It was not long, however, before the same charges of improper methods of closing churches were again heard.)

At this period the central authorities were likewise moderate respecting rent and taxes on churches. The local officials were instructed that no rent should be charged for church buildings, although they might be subject to the tax on buildings, and the land plots of the churches were subject to rent.[80] The land-rent rates as set in 1923 proved to be moderate. For a plot one hundred feet square they ranged from one ruble per year in a county town to six rubles in Moscow; no land rent was charged in the villages.[81] In urban communities the church buildings were subject to the local tax, which was in proportion to the cost of the building. In 1923 the Commissariat of Finance ordered that the total cost of the church, often very ornate, should not be used as the basis of computation, but merely the cost of the four walls and the roof, without including the cost of the internal construction. The tax should be ½ per cent of the value. In 1924 this figure was reduced to ¼ per cent, and for 1925, ⅛ per cent.[82] A sharply worded circular of the Commissariat of Finance in 1925 warned that the assessments on churches in many cases were too high and often were insupportable for the small groups of believers using them, so that some reduction should be made by using the low insurance assessment.[83]

As for the members of the clergy, they were required to pay taxes and rent on the same basis as doctors and lawyers;[84] they were entitled to receive housing and land on the same basis as the rest of the population.[85]

Soviet laws also took account of the religious beliefs of the citizens when setting official holidays. The local trade unions were permitted to put the weekly day of rest on Sunday if desired, and to have ten additional holidays according to local custom, figured by the Julian calendar, although the Gregorian calendar was in official use.[86]

In respect to religious education, however, concessions were rare. No formal courses of catechism were permitted for persons below the age of eighteen; they might receive religious instruction only in the home. In 1924 it was explained that "at home" might mean either in the home of the child or in that of the priest or other instructor; the important thing was that the instruction should not develop into group exercises. Not more than three children might be taught together; they need not, however, all be of the same family. To be a teacher of religion did not require special pedagogical training.[87] In the Ukraine the rulings were more drastic, although apparently there was no ban on private religious instruction.[88]

It is difficult to sum up Soviet treatment of the Orthodox church in the years after the death of Patriarch Tikhon. Nevertheless, the facts presented seem to permit the conclusion that the authorities had both a short-term and a long-term policy toward religion and the Russian Orthodox church and that the short-term policy consisted of seeking a satisfactory *modus vivendi* with the church. Provided the church would drop its hostile attitude, the civil authorities were willing to grant it considerable rights, and they made consistent efforts to induce the churchmen to unite on a policy of loyalty to the Soviet regime. The performance of normal religious ceremonies was permitted at all times. At the same time, the long-term Soviet policy remained one of seeking the dying out of "religious prejudices" through a campaign of antireligious propaganda. In fact, during the latter part of the decade under consideration the antireligious campaign, as will be seen, was greatly intensified and reached new heights just as the compromise with Metropolitan Sergii was coming to fruition. The securing of a better legal status by no means ended the tribulations of the church.

CHAPTER X

The Storming of Heaven

THE COMMUNIST DRIVE against religion began well before the October Revolution, for, as has been said, Lenin insisted that the church was a firm ally of the tsars and that all religion by its very nature was implacably hostile to Communist materialism. After the Soviet seizure of power atheism continued to be a fundamental part of the Communist party program. As this party dominated Soviet life, its growth in strength brought a great increase in the antireligious influences at work in Russia. While the government took the attitude that religion was a private matter, it was sympathetic to the Godless movement, and one of its divisions, the Commissariat of Public Education, encouraged antireligious teaching in its schools. For a time, in fact, the Commissariat of Justice published antireligious propaganda of a specific Godless nature.

In spite of Lenin's conviction that religion was basically hostile during the civil war, he and many of the other Communist leaders regarded it as a question of secondary importance. Little was done to implement the party program by propagating ideas directed explicitly against religion; this, however, was because the Soviet leaders had vastly more important things to attend to rather than because of any changed attitude toward religious belief. Their utterances continued to display hostility to religion. In 1918 Lenin wrote that it was not enough to decree separation of church from state; the Communist party should strive to secure "actual liberation of the laboring masses from religious prejudice" by organizing extensive scientific, educative, antireligious propaganda. As before, however, he cautioned against irritating the religious feelings of the believers, as this would stimulate fanaticism.[1] Late in 1918 in an address to a congress of women workers he warned against harshness in combating religion, as it might infuriate the masses and promote disunity instead of the needed unity. "The deepest source of religious prejudice is poverty and ignorance; against this evil we must fight." [2] Paragraph 13 of the Program of the Communist party adopted in 1918 paraphrased these remarks of Lenin, calling for systematic antireligious propaganda to free the masses from their prejudices, but without irritating the feelings of the believers.[3]

Bukharin, for many years the official theoretician of the Communist party, declared that religion had been a tool of the exploiting classes, and hence the Soviet regime had been much more consistent in its separation of church from state than any of the bourgeois governments. Moreover, the Orthodox faith had allied itself with monarchy and had fought the revolutionary order. Hence the Soviets should organize extensive antireligious propaganda, stressing the general spreading of scientific knowledge, which "slowly but surely undermines the authority of all religion." The opening of relics was a fine weapon against the church, for it exhibited church deceit to the masses.[4]

In December, 1919, Latsis, a high official of the Cheka, proposed official support for a progressive group of clergy who had turned against the reactionary policy of the Patriarch. Krasikov, head of the Eighth Division of the Commissariat of Justice, indignantly repudiated this suggestion. He declared that the only path for religion and its agents was "into the archives of history," for the clergy were really not progressive, and their apparent change of heart had been dictated by circumstances. Hence to support any religious organization would be contrary to the basic principles of the proletarian dictatorship.[5] But while Krasikov's view prevailed in 1919, the policy of co-operating with a willing section of the church was soon to receive a trial.

Lunacharskii, Commissar of Education, devoted much thought to the nature and methods of antireligious propaganda. In 1919 he wrote that it was the duty of every Communist to carry on antireligious propaganda. The party itself should strive to "fight religious prejudices and antiquated beliefs" not only by its own efforts, but also by using the educational system. On the one hand, antireligious propaganda must avoid flirting with reformist groups and on the other must not antagonize by headlong attacks on the churches. The middle course was the correct one — that of enlightening the peasants.

Natural science and history must be used in the fight against "religious darkness." An ethical approach would also help by showing that the clergy often did not live up to what they taught and also that Christ's teachings were unrealistic and lured the masses away from seeking their own interests. In addition, discussion of the history of Christianity would show that the early equalitarianism of the church had been undermined and that the proletarians had been taught to hope for justice, not on earth, but in the hereafter.[6] Another writer was somewhat more concrete: "The school, the book, the political platform, the theater, the cinema — all should be drawn into the struggle against the religious prejudices and superstitions of the people."[7]

Actually, during the civil war little was accomplished. No use was made of the cinema except in documentary films, and the theater also was little used for antireligious purposes, as experience and dramatic vehicles were completely lacking. Likewise, while in the schools Communism (basically antireligious) was substituted for religion — in itself no mean task — little was done to promote propaganda specifically antireligious. Only a few teachers tried to carry on overt antireligious propaganda — without experience, without textbooks; most of the teachers were either believers or neutral.[8] On the other hand, antireligious books and brochures were published during those years, and *Revolutsiia i Tserkov'* (*Revolution and the Church*), organ of the Eighth Division of the Commissariat of Justice, regularly published articles on such themes as woman under religion and under Communism, and the heathen origin of Christian holidays, as well as unceasing anticlerical outpourings. Furthermore, the Red Army served to bring antireligious ideas to the general public, as the Communists claimed that the enlisted men, both as a result of experiencing the hostility of the clergy and as a result of the propaganda carried on in the barracks, often became antireligious.[9]

A propaganda method widely used, sometimes with indifferent success, was antireligious lectures and debates. On December 19, 1917, Lunacharskii, Commissar of Education, gave a lecture in Petrograd, "The Legend of Christ and Socialism,"[10] and he continued to speak throughout the civil war years. Such lectures did not always win converts, for, as an ardent antireligious writer later stated, the peasants and the petty bourgeois would agree that often the priests were deceivers and immoral and that relics and miracles were frauds — but their faith in God remained unshaken. The writer claimed, however, that the factory workers were largely antireligious.[11]

The other side was also heard. V. F. Martsinovskii, a very devout man, was permitted to deliver a series of lectures on religion in a student dining room in Moscow during the spring of 1920, and another in Samara. In addition, he spoke at a lecture delivered by Lunacharskii and later arranged a debate with him.[12] In fact, there were many debates between priests and antireligious workers, in which the clergy frequently enjoyed the sympathy of the audience and the unbelievers often came out second best. Finally, a conference of Communist party members decided to stop these debates.[13]

Throughout the years of civil war antireligious activity was hampered by a variety of factors, including lack of money, personnel, experience, and directives. This was the first attempt of the Bolsheviks to try systematic antireligious activity, so that everything had to be done *de novo*. Moreover, during the conflict, according to a Communist leader, "religion became a matter of tenth-rate importance"; many Communists had a happy conviction that it would die out automatically, so that no effort was needed. Consequently, antireligious literature was published in small quantities; handbooks and guidance for antireligious activities were rarely provided for local workers, and oral agitation was not carried on at all, or if it was, it chiefly took the form of crude anticlericalism. Naturally the work suffered.[14] Although Lunacharskii, Iaroslavskii, and several others participated in antireligious work, most of it centered in the Eighth (later the Fifth) Division of the Commissariat of Justice. During 1919 and 1920 Krasikov, head of the division, and two others delivered 411 lectures, of which 318 were in Moscow and 62 were in the province of Moscow. They also spoke to a number of local Soviet congresses and to Communist party groups. Their publishing activities were also scanty: five issues of *Revoliutsiia i Tserkov'*, totaling 140,000 copies; five antireligious booklets (285,000 copies); and 40,000 copies of one poster. Thus, although the demand allegedly was great, little was done to satisfy it.[15] During 1921 a total of 203 lectures was given;

220,000 copies of *Revoliutsiia i Tserkov'* were published, and 100,000 copies of a brochure. Even this material rarely reached the masses, as an organized distribution system was completely lacking.[16]

In the Ukraine, which did not come under firm Soviet control until about 1920, the state of antireligious propaganda was even more primitive.[17]

While overt antireligious activity was slight during the civil war, it increased considerably after it. Whereas the resolutions of the earlier congresses of the Communist party scarcely mentioned religion, the Tenth Congress, in March, 1921, listed as one of the seven tasks of the party's propaganda agency the organization of antireligious agitation and propaganda among the masses and ordered that it should further this cause by publishing journals, books, and textbooks, by arranging lectures, and by using the cinema.[18] The Eleventh Congress a year later also devoted a few lines of its forty-eight pages of minutes to a resolution that the propaganda agency should take up the work of publishing popular, agitational, antireligious Marxist literature.[19]

Much of the impetus for the increase of antireligious activity seems to have come from Lenin, in spite of his illness. In his letter of 1922, "On the Significance of Militant Materialism," he urged that a Marxist periodical should, among other things, be an organ of militant atheism, to lead this work, which was being carried on in very sluggish fashion. It should translate or review all foreign atheistic literature, including that of the eighteenth century, preparing it for mass distribution by adding suitable commentaries. The masses, he held, needed antireligious material of a varied nature, to approach them from all sides and awaken them from the religious dream. Even bourgeois works like Arthur Drews's *Myth about Christ,* while unsound in approach, were highly useful if properly interpreted.[20] According to Nadezhda Krupskaia, his wife, Lenin felt that it was not enough to strike at surface manifestations of religion, but that there must be deep penetration to the very roots of religion among the masses. He was exceedingly hostile to all theories of a compromise between the rival ideologies.[21]

In line with Lenin's advice and the decisions of the party congresses, the Central Committee in September, 1921, issued a series of rules

concerning religion. Members of the Communist party were ordered
to break completely with religion or be expelled. On the other hand,
directives should be issued to all Communist party organizations that
antireligious propaganda should not be overemphasized; the chief
aim was "re-establishing real agreement between the proletariat and
the petty-bourgeois masses of the peasantry, who are still imbued with
religious prejudices." More specifically, the party should not stress
antireligious debates, but should concentrate on "serious scientific
cultural and enlightening work, setting a foundation of natural science
under a historical explanation of the question of religion." [22] An All-
Russian Conference of the Communist party in August, 1922, went
even further in advising caution. Although religion was not specifically mentioned, the resolution urged that the party organizations
must show cordiality toward each separate group that showed signs
of willingness to co-operate with the Soviet regime. "The Party
should do everything it can to help the crystallization of those tendencies and groups that disclose an actual wish to help the workers'
and peasants' state." [23] This policy, which, expressed in religious
terms, was one of co-operation with the Living Church group, obviously imposed limitations upon antireligious propaganda.

The difficulty of securing suitable personnel for antireligious work
was another limiting factor. In 1921 and 1922 most of the work centered around the Fifth Section of the Commissariat of Justice and its
workers like Krasikov and Galkin. Few of the other Communists had
had any experience in this field, and most of those who had joined
during the civil war were uneducated. As suitable literature was lacking, most of the work was carried on orally on an exceedingly limited
scale.[24]

The lack of proper antireligious literature was especially difficult to
remedy. During the civil war a number of popular works were published to prove that the church was reactionary and deceived the people, but little to attack the bases of religion. Translations of Kunow
and Bebel's works on the origins of religion were the first steps. After
the civil war more was done. The Atheist publishing house, founded
in 1922, translated a number of outstanding foreign works, notably
those of Drews's, and Frazer's *The Golden Bough*. Several writers such
as Gorev, Paozerskii, and Lukin wrote on the church's opposition to

the revolution, while Skvortsov-Stepanov wrote popular works for the general public. In 1922 five Moscow publishers and four in other centers started systematic publication of antireligious propaganda, including the works of the French materialists of the eighteenth century, some of which had never before been printed in Russian.[25]

In the schools the shortage of proper books was especially troublesome. The old books from the imperial period were full of religious ideas, prayers, and phrases, and had to be discarded. Just at the moment when the Soviet regime was in dire distress, with its economic life at low ebb, new schoolbooks were demanded, and it was only with great difficulty that they could be supplied.[26] For some years the emphasis in the schools was on eradicating religion from them, with no attempt to make them overtly antireligious. While there was much antireligious propaganda supervised by Lenin among the teachers during 1921 and 1922, which won converts to atheism, many of the good teachers were sincerely religious. Consequently, until a new generation of teachers could be trained, the most that could be done was insist that all religion be eliminated from instruction. The emphasis was on introducing scientific explanations of natural and social phenomena; the pupils were taught that bad harvests, epidemics, and other calamities were due to natural causes and not to God's wrath and that sanitation was more important than prayer in controlling disease.[27]

While, in general, the antireligious movement in 1921 and 1922 was marked by caution, the activities of the Komsomol (Young Communist League) were more aggressive. These young people, who had helped to carry out the decree of separation of church from state and had served on the fighting fronts, now found themselves with reduced outlets for their enthusiasm; hence many threw themselves into the antireligious struggle. This development was warmly approved by a special conference of Communist antireligious workers.[28]

The initial Komsomol activity was the staging of an antireligious Christmas carnival in December, 1922. The first organized public antireligious demonstration, it was hastily conceived and received little support from the Communist party organizations. The literature to be used for the occasion was late in arriving. Moreover, in many cases the individual Komsomols faced strong opposition from family custom and authority and needed much courage to undertake this work. Many wavered and at the last minute stayed at home by the warm stove on Christmas Eve.[29]

In spite of these difficulties, the Komsomols in a number of places succeeded in staging their carnivals; the one in Tsaritsyn was typical. After antireligious meetings in the clubs and local centers, the youths proceeded to the central city squares with hundreds of torches, lighted stars, and caricatures: "The Entente," "The Kulak," "The Christmas Goose," "The Suckling Pig," and the main theme of the carnival, "fallen gods"; here were Marduk, Osiris, Jupiter, Allah, a Hebrew Jehovah, the Christian God. From the main square the procession accompanied by brass bands and the singing of parodies on religious chants swept through the city to the squares before the churches, where a play, *The Liberation of Truth,* was given. The procession ended only at dawn at the graves of the revolutionary dead. The images of the gods were burned in a mock ceremony, to signify the dying out of religion.[30]

Another campaign was put on at Easter, 1923, after a careful study of the results of the Christmas carnival. Elaborate preparations were made, under the guidance of the leading antireligionists; but this time the nature of the campaign was different; it was made more propagandist in character, and carnivals and processions in the streets were not encouraged.[31]

The results of the Komsomol campaigns were far from what had been intended. Although the enthusiasm of the Komsomols had been stimulated and although they drew great crowds to their spectacles, often greatly reducing church attendance, their youthful exuberance was not matched by good taste and tact. Communist spokesmen began to announce that "the unwise, incautious, and frequently quite outrageous approach" had had the effect of "arousing the religious feelings of believers and facilitated the development of religious propaganda." In some cases the unwise actions assumed the form of ducking priests in wells or the removal of cupolas from churches used by believers, or holding debates in churches. Administrative measures were used, such as closing churches arbitrarily, or prohibiting religious processions, which "thus produced in the local population displeasure with the Soviet Power." "Jokes," demonstrations, and administrative measures produced natural antagonism on the part of the believers, aroused the mass of the peasantry against antireligious propaganda, and gave the impression of persecution of religion.[32]

The unsatisfactory state of antireligious work was sufficiently important to cause the Twelfth Congress of the Communist party in April, 1923, to formulate a long pronouncement, "The Setting of Antireligious Agitation and Propaganda." It proclaimed that, while the revolution had shaken the religious prejudices of the masses and destroyed the old regime, religion still flourished and would disappear only when the peasants had been freed from dependence on nature and when the capitalist relations in the cities had ended. Indeed, while the older religions had been shaken, newer ones, more adaptable, were flourishing. Hence the antireligious work of the party must take the form of deeper, more systematic propaganda, to show the workers and peasants that their interests were not served by religion and to give them a scientific outlook in place of religious conceptions. Care should be taken, however, not to irritate the feelings of the believers by ridicule of articles of faith or by harsh measures, which merely aroused fanaticism.

What was especially needed was the publication of a great quantity of popular brochures, understandable to the average worker or peasant, to give him answers to questions about the origin of the world and of life and to show the evolution, class position, and role of the church and of religion in general. Special attention should be paid to organizing attractive lectures on a wide scale by naturalists, materialists, and other specialists. This, in turn, required that numbers of agitators and propagandists be trained in Communist universities, special courses, and seminars, to know the history, content, organization, and political and social activity of the various religious bodies. But in any event, final victory over religion would come only when the populace had been made literate and had received a materialist and scientific knowledge of nature. Hence the organization of the school system and the training of school teachers, along with the establishment of a wide network of village reading rooms, was necessary. Only when that had been done and when the Soviet government had raised agriculture and industry to new levels would the ground be prepared for "the final and full rooting out of religious prejudices from the minds of millions of citizens of the republic." [33]

Two months later the central committee of the trade-unions issued a circular on the subject of antireligious methods (June 9, 1923) in which they reported "absurd forms" of antireligious action — resolutions to close all churches, changing the day of rest from Sunday, and occasionally, expelling union members for religious adherence or even church marriages. The trade-unions were intended to unite all workers, irrespective of nationality or religion, and to raise their class consciousness and their cultural level by a long process of education against "the vestiges of spiritual slavery, darkness, ignorance, and superstition." This could not be done by compulsory methods, but by a long, systematic campaign of materialist enlightenment, carried on by clubs, groups, lectures, reports, Sunday universities, and schools for adults. It must be achieved without outraging the religious feelings of "those who had not freed themselves from the spiritual heritage of the past" or driving them from the union.[34]

A similar cautious attitude marked the rulings of the Thirteenth Congress of the Communist party in the spring of 1924. It strongly condemned administrative measures, such as arbitrary closing of churches. In the villages antireligious propaganda should deal exclusively with a materialistic interpretation of social life, and of the phenomena of nature with which the peasant came in contact such as rain, hail, drought, insect pests, the quality of the soil, and the action of fertilizer. Such antireligious work should center around the school and the reading room under Communist guidance. Above all, extreme care should be taken "in order not to outrage the religious feelings of the believers, over which victory can be won only by very long enlightening work, lasting for years and decades." [35] Trotskii, still important in 1924, on July 17 told a conference of club workers, "We shall drive out the mystics by materialism, . . . and on this basis we shall deal, where necessary, direct blows at religious prejudices. Full liquidation of religion will be attained only with an extensive socialist order, i.e., with such a technique as will free man from degrading dependence upon nature. . . ." [36]

In spite of the caution and restraint of the period, 1923 saw the real beginning of an organized antireligious movement. Late in 1922 the newspaper *Bezbozhnik* (the *Godless*) was started to serve as organ of the movement and to furnish inspiration. Although it was issued only once a week in a two-page format and had a limited circulation, it was warmly received by antireligious workers throughout the country, many of whom became contributors. In the autumn of 1924 these correspondents and subscribers met in Moscow and organized into a society, "Friends of the Newspaper *Bezbozhnik*." This organization held its first congress in April, 1925; in June it renamed itself "League of Militant Godless." [37] According to a leading Soviet writer, the organization took shape not as a result of orders from above, but spontaneously; it was "in the full sense of the word a child, a product of the revolutionary creativeness of the masses themselves." [38]

Membership in the new organization was relatively small during this period. Statistics, available from 1926 on only, show the following changes:[39]

Date	Cells	Members
January 1, 1926	2,421	87,033
January 1, 1927	3,121	138,402
January 1, 1928	3,900	123,007
January 1, 1929	8,928	465,498

The 1929 total was made up of approximately 30 per cent each of Communists and Komsomols, and 40 per cent of nonparty members. Workers formed about 40 per cent, peasants, 30, and white-collar workers, 20 per cent. Only about 20 per cent were women.[40]

The organization was financed almost entirely by the dues of members, amounting to five kopecks per month. Its central committee was maintained exclusively by the funds of the Bezbozhnik publishing house, although the local organizations gave portions of their dues for the propaganda work of the central organization. In addition, the fifty or more paid workers (instructors, lecturers, and organizers) were in part supported by the trade-unions, the Political Enlightenment organization of the Communist party, and by other organizations, as well as by the central committee of the League of Godless. The latter was constantly troubled by financial difficulties, as the members did not pay their dues properly.[41]

More important than the shortage of funds was the incorrect attitude of many Communists toward the antireligious struggle. Some held that the rulings of the Thirteenth Congress meant that little could be done at that time; the long, intensive campaign of education and materialism must first bring forth its fruits, and the socialist order must be set up, before the masses would listen to direct attack on the church and religion in general. The warning not to antagonize the feelings of the faithful was regarded as justification for no antireligious propaganda at all, as any preaching against religion would be sure to antagonize believers.[42] This "liquidationist attitude" went so far in the Ukraine in 1924 that many Communist organizations, disturbed by the bad results of earlier antireligious activity, put an outright ban on it, and it was only later that opposition to antireligious activity began to disappear.[43]

While Iaroslavskii and the other leaders of the League of Godless fought against this "rightist deviation," they also had to combat "leftist" errors — the view that anticlericalism was enough, if prosecuted vigorously, and that the long campaign of materialist education, directed against the religious world outlook, was unnecessary. These disputes as to policy came to the fore at the antireligious congresses of 1924 and 1925, and it was only at the Communist party conference on antireligious propaganda in April, 1926, that the problem was decided in favor of Iaroslavskii's position.[44]

The new rules on problems and methods of antireligious propaganda called for a many-sided approach, adjusted to the circumstances of the moment. Success in antireligious work depended on proper understanding of the nature of religion both as a system of ideas and as an influence in political and economic matters. Such work could succeed only if closely linked to economic matters and the class struggle. The following practical conclusions were drawn from this detailed and varied consideration of the problem:

1. Wide antireligious propaganda was necessary, both among the new workers and among the peasants. The Communist party alone could not do the job, which would need the participation of large numbers of nonparty personnel, organized in local Godless groups.

2. The Communist party organizations should co-operate closely

with the Godless groups, participate in their work, and give them guidance, as well as help by organizing special seminars to train their personnel.

3. The Godless should work with the trade-unions, the Political Enlightenment Section, the workers' clubs, peasant groups, and similar bodies.

4. There should be more antireligious work in schools and universities for the purpose of training agitators.[45]

These decisions did much to defeat the theory that antireligious activity should not be carried on, or was unimportant, although it proved difficult to induce the local Communist organizations to embrace the antireligious cause. It was especially against this reluctance that Stalin spoke in his interview with an American workers' delegation in 1927.[46] When asked if the Communist party could be neutral in respect to religion, he declared that it could not. While the law of the land permitted freedom of conscience, there was nothing to forbid propaganda against all religions. The party carried on propaganda against all religion because *it* (the party) stood for science; religious prejudice was contrary to science. Propaganda against these prejudices was an important means of undermining the influence of the clergy, who supported the exploiting classes and preached submission to them. The party could not be neutral toward "the reactionary clergy, who poison the minds of the laboring masses," and had suppressed them. "The only pity is that they have not been wholly liquidated." Antireligious propaganda was the way to finish the work of liquidating the reactionary clergy. He also remarked that it was very good when the party expelled those of its members who hampered the widest possible development of antireligious propaganda, for they had no place in the party.[47]

Stalin also remarked briefly at the Fifteenth Congress of the Communist party in December, 1927, that in addition to weaknesses in respect to housing, unemployment, the rise of anti-Semitism, and other failings, there was weakening of the antireligious struggle. He declared that all these failings must be eliminated.[48]

These directives were supported by a circular of the Agitation and Propaganda Section of the Communist party, which declared that the local organizations of the party were insufficiently active in the antireligious field and that they should intensify antireligious activity on all levels, as well as urge the trade-unions, the local Soviets, and other social organizations to do likewise. The party organizations also were asked to provide systematic guidance of the work of the units of the League of Godless.[49] Similarly, the central committee of the trade-unions insisted that the unions cease their neglect of antireligious activity, which should be integrated with their club work, their libraries, entertainments, and other functions. Club libraries should carry a liberal supply of antireligious literature and should strive to circulate it. The clubs should be especially active at religious holidays in order to induce the masses not to attend church. Above all, the directive insisted that the antireligious work should not be in the form of a spasmodic campaign, but should persistently and patiently explain to the masses the bases of the Marxist materialist outlook as the foundation of antireligious propaganda.[50]

Thus for the first time a centrally directed, integrated antireligious program began to function. The movement did not at once gain momentum, however; much effort had to be spent in arousing those who had earlier opposed antireligious work. In addition, the League of Godless lacked real central control and until 1929 remained a loosely knit collection of local leagues, often quite independent of the central committee. The latter chiefly provided guidance in respect to methodology and also handled the publication of suitable material. But by the end of 1928 much of the necessary organizational work had been done.[51]

Between January, 1926, and the end of 1928, much was done to prepare antireligious personnel. On January 1, 1927, there were 68 antireligious seminars, 9 study groups of propagandists, and several evening courses. There were also 15 reference centers for antireligious workers. In addition, fifteen Communist organizations had 266 study groups on lower levels. Some local organizations developed their work independently; the Briansk provincial Soviet organized a correspondence course and published a series of letters for self-instruction, "Teach Yourself to Be Godless."[52] The Red Army also helped by preparing antireligious personnel to work in the villages after discharge. Other village workers were trained in a special six-month course of the Communist party, with 233 persons enrolled.

The periodical *Antireligioznik* offered nine different correspondence courses in 1927: for Red Army men, for peasants, for study-group leaders, for teachers, and others. In 1928 seven more varieties were offered. Finally, in the summer of 1928 chairs for the study of religion were opened in the Communist Academy and the Institute of Red Professors; academic antireligious instruction was also started in the universities. An "antireligious university" opened in Moscow.[53]

Antireligious publication, too, forged ahead. Between 1923 and the end of 1928, besides the original *Bezbozhnik* there appeared *Antireligioznik,* a monthly journal, more scholarly and methodological than the others; another *Bezbozhnik,* a weekly, for popular consumption; *Bezbozhnik u Stanka (The Godless at the Machine),* a satirical journal especially for workers, and *Ateist,* a popular monthly journal.[54] Other periodicals were *Derevenskii Bezbozhnik (The Village Godless),* and *Bezvirnik (Nonbeliever,* in Ukrainian, published in Khar'kov).[55]

Numerous books were published, some of them in serveral editions of hundreds of thousands of copies. Iaroslavskii was author of several widely distributed works — *Communists and Religion* and *The Bible for Believers and Unbelievers;* Demian Bednyi produced a book *Fables* and many poems and plays satirizing priests, monks, and saints; Mikhail Gorev wrote about clerical counterrevolutionary activity; I. N. Skvortsov-Stepanov had several volumes on contemporary religious developments like the Living Church; and A. V. Lunacharskii and I. Lobachev discussed the question of whether Christ really existed. This they denied; the account of Christ, they held, was derived from the legends about Apis and Osiris, Adonis, Dionysus, Marduk, Melkarth, Ahura-Mazda, Mithras, and other heathen gods. There were many other works. Comparative religion, the Spanish Inquisition, the Russian church under the tsars and in the Soviet period, ecclesiastical opposition to Galileo, Copernicus, Giordano Bruno, Darwin — all furnished subjects for antireligious writers. Foreign works also were supplied in translation — among them Sinclair Lewis's *Elmer Gantry,* books by Haldeman-Julius and Upton Sinclair, and others.[56]

Much of this publication was done by the central committee of the League of Godless, which also published pamphlets to the number of several hundred thousand in 1926 and thirty-four million in 1929.

Local publishers were also hard at work; there were, for example, numerous Ukrainian publications and also some in Belorussian. The Godless leaders, however, were far from satisfied with the state of antireligious publishing at the end of 1928.[57]

The actual methods of carrying on antireligious work among the people assumed very diverse forms. In the cities, where the workers were often radically minded, the chief effort was to induce them to renounce some religious observance or practice. They were urged to continue working on a religious festival because the country needed more production or because the traditional holiday drinking bout was bad for health and impeded competition with another factory. Removal of ikons from workers' homes was another objective. In 1924 *Izvestiia* reported that the men and women of one factory had brought over one hundred ikons to the local Communist cell, which organized an antireligious meeting at which more than six hundred witnessed the ceremonial burning of the ikons.[58] Other goals were refusal to observe a given religious holiday and agreement to use the money saved for buying an agricultural implement for the community, or a group pledge not to receive the priest when he made Easter visits to the homes of the workers. Still other objectives were group petitions to remove church bells from the belfries or to close churches.[59]

Often these goals were not easily achieved and required long preparation by means of lectures, discussions, question-and-answer sessions, plays, concerts, readings, and other group activities, as well as by individual persuasion. The lectures and other work before audiences in turn required preparation — of posters, of visual aids, of the subject matter. Follow-up work was done by the clubs and reading rooms and by articles in newspapers. Plays and songs were regarded as especially valuable, as they drew people away from church attendance and, if arranged like vaudeville, could often obtain wide participation by the audience.[60]

In the villages, where the people clung more firmly to tradition, different methods were used. In addition to the lectures, readings, questions and answers, and other devices mentioned above, there was a strong emphasis on science; competitions were arranged between christened and unchristened infants as to health and growth, or a "godless field," scientifically worked and planted with selected seed, was matched against the field of a believing peasant, worked in the usual way and blessed by the priest. Excursions to the experimental field of a collective farm or to a meteorological station were also arranged. The hatching of incubator chicks at Easter was recommended as an antidote to Easter eggs. "Godless meteorology" was another device to interest the peasants, and to challenge the belief that the saints brought the weather. Simple chemical experiments could produce "godless miracles." In addition, godless christening and marriage ceremonies, marked by much formality, moralistic precepts, and group cordiality toward the principals in the ceremony, were encouraged. Amusements of various kinds were also put to antireligious uses: the radio, the cinema, the puppet theater, plays, songs, and the reading of drama and satires.[61]

In spite of the fact that the churches used color, singing, and brilliance to attract the people as late as 1928, little had been done to mobilize artists against them; in fact, most of the latter sympathized with religion. In December, 1928, Iaroslavskii spoke of "the extreme weakness of godless art" to a gathering of artistic workers. He could cite no outstanding production in painting, music, literature, sculpture, cinema, or theater.[62] Likewise the use of museums in the campaign against religion had not as yet made much progress. The first were opened in 1924, but did not treat anything but ancient religions. In 1925, a number of museums were opened in former monasteries or in provincial centers, and 1926 saw the founding of a large Godless museum in Moscow, with the church and the revolution as its theme. But until 1929 lack of quarters and other obstacles hampered the work.[63]

The Komsomols, with their energy and enthusiasm and their influence over other youth and the younger children, were important in the antireligious drive. Although official disapproval of their antireligious carnivals in 1923 seemed to many like a douche of cold water, and the prescribed long and careful campaign of enlightenment made little appeal to the restless spirits, the more steadfast and devoted members accepted the new rules and continued their work, less spectacular though it was. They played a large part in the growth of the League of Godless from 1925 on, organizing cells and carrying on persistent propaganda. In 1928, a year when the Soviet regime pushed strongly ahead toward socialism, the Eighth Congress of the Komsomol deplored the weakening of its antireligious activity and urged its members to throw themselves into this work as part of the campaign to socialize the country. The masses of the peasantry, in spite of the efforts of churchmen and sectarians, were to be drawn into the new economic and political life. The younger people were to be brought into the movement for socialism by organizing campaigns against drunkenness, by promoting self-education, by wide use of the cinema and radio, and similar methods. It was hoped thus to unmask the clergy as defenders of the kulaks and to induce the peasants to cease their financial support for religion.[64]

Antireligious activity in the schools also passed through several stages. In the early years after the civil war there was some antireligious propaganda in the schools, but on an individual basis, with little or no centralized support or guidance. The more moderate attitude in the 1920's resulted in a policy of emphasis on scientific and materialistic instruction, not specifically directed against religion. In 1925 the State School Council issued a letter on methods entitled "Nonreligious Education in the School," stating that "special implanting of antireligiousness in the soul of the child is not needed." Although the letter did urge proper antireligious propaganda and spoke of implanting atheism in the schools, most of the teachers took the unqualified term "nonreligious education" to mean neutrality toward religion. Some felt that religion would die out automatically. The Commissariat of Education theoretically stood for antireligious education, but did nothing to emphasize it, and thus the less militant concept of nonreligious education dominated for several years.[65] One official of the commissariat even took the position that, as there was no scientific basis for believing in the existence of God, naturally there was no need to mention Him. "There is no need to struggle against what does not exist. . . ."[66]

The revolutionary forces latent in the Soviet regime soon moved the schools off this dead center. In the spring of 1927 the League of Godless remarked on the bad state of antireligious work in the schools and started a campaign to revise the concept of nonreligious education. Much support was received from teachers of various lo-

calities. For a whole year the issue was heatedly fought out in the
pages of the *Teachers' Gazette* and in educational circles, with many
teachers arguing that a more active policy was not needed and might
produce antagonism. Even the Commissariat of Education strongly
defended the term "nonreligious education." But the pressure of
what seemed to be a strong majority and the fact that religion in the
schools was not dying out carried the day, and at the end of the school
year 1927–1928 the term "nonreligious education" was dropped from
official use. With the encouragement of the League of Godless, local
teachers began to undertake antireligious instruction, and early in
1929 the Commissariat of Education issued a letter on methods of
instruction of this sort.[67] Thus the school fell into line beside the
other Soviet institutions actively combating religion.

It cannot be said, however, that the antireligious campaign always
went smoothly. The religious groups, especially the sectarians, were
very skillful in attracting the young. Children who in the schools were
subject to antireligious propaganda, at home were under very great
pressure from their families to remain religious, exerted even by
threats and physical punishment. Some of the teachers were actively
religious, and even more were passive or neutral. Even some of those
who were hostile to religion lacked training in combating it.[68] The
churchmen also were active among the workers newly come from
the villages and succeeded in winning many of them, especially the
women. The trade-unions often failed to develop their antireligious
work with sufficient care.[69] In the villages, Communists declared,
churchmen sometimes could control the local Soviets and manipulate
them in their favor.[70]

At the same time, until early 1927 the Communist authorities of
the Ukraine disapproved of the League of Godless, and the Red
Army did not permit the formation of Godless cells in its units. Several provinces refused to approve the bylaws of the League — notably Nizhnii Novgorod, Viatka, and Irkutsk.[71] Opposed to the Godless, *Pravda* saw 50,000 churches with 250,000 ministers, and 100,000
monastics organized in spurious "working collectives." Furthermore,
each church had its parish council of twelve who likewise were devoted religious workers. Hence the Godless were faced by a numer-

ous and well-organized foe with centuries of experience in gaining influence over the populace. Moreover, *Pravda* claimed, anti-Soviet elements such as Socialist Revolutionaries, Mensheviks, and even Trotskyites, had taken refuge in church organizations as a useful underground asylum.[72]

Even where the Godless met no obstacles to their propaganda, they often encountered difficulties, sometimes of their own making. In 1926 a Godless writer warned against antireligious debates with local priests, which eager Communists loved to arrange. Too often, he said, the Communist, theoretically trained, lacked the ability to catch the attention of the peasants and made no progress, while the priest, speaking before a large and friendly audience and knowing his subject perfectly, made his opponent look foolish. The latter usually would become angry and shout, thus losing all influence over his audience. While experienced Godless propagandists were lacking, any priest could cite sonorous passages that appealed to the village public. "If you try to disprove the Immaculate Conception, he will say, 'What is impossible for man is possible for God.'" The Godless author recommended stopping such debates entirely.[73] Another writer cited by an *émigré* publication complained of the halfhearted way in which propaganda was sometimes presented. His duties required him to visit dozens of clubs on Easter night to supervise Komsomol Easter activities. Usually he found a cold, damp hall, half lighted, with old posters on the walls and the floor strewn with rubbish. There would be a dry, uninteresting lecture on the origin of Easter, usually an hour or more late. Small wonder that the audience became cold and bored, so that an old man might get up and, spitting on the floor, say to his wife: "Let's go to St. Nikita the Martyr's; there's tea there, it's more interesting, and it's warmer." Rarely were plays or music presented to catch the interest of the audience, so that the round was lost by default.[74]

Nevertheless, in spite of obstacles and lapses, the antireligious movement reached new heights in 1928 and was obviously rapidly gaining momentum. The Soviet authorities, who had succeeded in reaching a working arrangement with the Russian Orthodox church, were giving much attention to the long-range objective of eliminating religion as an influence over the people. Both in organization and methods the antireligious movement was greatly strengthened for far greater efforts in the years to come. The church was shortly to be confronted with an antireligious campaign of unparalleled intensity.

CHAPTER XI

The Results of Eleven Years

DURING THE PERIOD between the October Revolution and the end of 1928 the relations between the Russian Orthodox church and the Soviet government had altered profoundly. On the one hand, the church, which during the early years had strongly fought the Soviet regime, and which, in turn, had suffered severe blows, had finally accommodated itself to the new order and had reached a partial compromise with it. On the other hand, the antireligious activity sponsored by the Communist party, after a slow beginning, had reached a new height and was tending toward still further intensification. It is extremely difficult to evaluate the general effect of these developments and to reach a net balance for the condition of the Russian church. Statistics on the number of believers are almost completely lacking, for Soviet law forbade any mention in legal documents of the religious faith of citizens. Hence when data were needed, even the Soviet press and the League of Godless were reduced to guesses or the use of fragments of information. Furthermore, there is the familiar qualitative problem of what constitutes a believer. Should some criterion as to church attendance be used, or the highly elusive factor of inner conviction? These obstacles are enough to make any exact answer as to the state of Russian Orthodoxy in 1928 impossible.

On the other hand, the question demands an answer. Fortunately there is evidence, fragmentary and qualitative though it is. Although it comes from both the Godless and the believing camps, it seems to be in essential agreement, and thus it is possible to draw tentative conclusions from it.

One such scrap of evidence is the growth of the Communist party, the Komsomol, and the League of Godless, of which the last had

465,000 members at the end of 1928. Bukharin was quoted as saying that for every member of the Godless there were one hundred nonbelievers, which, if true, would mean 46,500,000 nonbelievers. Iaroslavskii, however, stated that if one computed the number of persons who had broken with religion and the church, no such impressive total would be obtained. The combined number of Communists, Komsomols, and Pioneers (aged ten to fourteen years) was more than five million, which led him to reckon the number of nonbelievers who had severed religious ties at significantly more than ten million.[1] While this is a large number it by no means represented a majority of the population, which, at the time he wrote (1929), was some one hundred thirty million. On the other hand, it would not be safe to regard all who had not "broken with religion" as believers.

In spite of this relatively small number of full converts to atheism, Iaroslavskii was filled with qualified optimism. In March, 1928, he declared that during the preceding three years great things had been accomplished among the masses of peasants and workers. This did not mean that the influence of religion had been destroyed, but it did signify "that we have driven a breach into the religious consciousness of the laboring masses." To complete the task, he said, would be a difficult matter, not the work of a day or a year, but of years to come, and even of a decade.[2]

Indirect evidence of the persistence of Orthodox practices was given in 1928 by a complaint of *Komsomolskaia Pravda* (*Komsomol Truth*) that the Moscow Consumers' Co-operative had baked 36,000 pounds of *kulich* and over ten thousand *paskhas* (two Easter delicacies) adorned with all sorts of ornaments, even "the Lord Jesus," and that many of the provincial co-operatives did the same.[3] And at the end of 1928 *Pravda* expressed regret over the numerous signs of the Christmas spirit: piles of Christmas trees for sale, stores decorated with Christmas emblems, and religious supplies prepared by state enterprises. At the factories, absenteeism had a bad effect on working discipline over the holiday.[4]

But while the Soviet press showed displeasure at the signs of religion, the Orthodox press abroad pointed out that the church was not as strong as formerly. In 1925, before the antireligious campaign of the League of Godless had really gathered momentum, an Orthodox periodical in Paris printed an unsigned "letter from Russia" on the state of the Russian church. The letter asserted that the character of the congregations had changed markedly since the revolution. In the cities one outstanding development had been the turning of the older intelligentsia to the church in large numbers. There were few soldiers in church, but in the suburbs a number of workers, and everywhere a stratum of tradesmen. While there were many believers in Russia, it was impossible to say whether they were a majority or a minority of the population. Most churches were full, but not to overflowing, while many, especially those of the Renovationists, were almost empty; fewer people were going to church than before the revolution and the number, the Orthodox author stated, was not growing. Many people had turned from the church during the civil war period, but in 1925 fewer were turning away.

In the villages observed — chiefly along the railways — the same author stated:

> you are struck by the emptiness of the churches. Women and old men are almost the only ones who go to church. The young have learned the lesson of atheism. The middle generation, which lived through the war, . . . has come out with a distressing portion of skepticism, or at all events, indifference to religion.

While the peasants still clung to certain outward observances of religion — church weddings, christenings, funerals, and the traditional holidays — they were much affected by the Communist newspaper, the reading room, revolutionary drama, and the songs of the young. The author felt that perhaps in the backwoods villages this had not occurred to such an extent, but nonetheless all Russia had been affected by the changes since 1917.[5]

Similarly, Father Michel d'Herbigny, S.J., who visited Moscow in the fall of 1925, stated that, according to information received from all factions of the Orthodox church, while the diffusion of atheistic propaganda based on science had had little effect upon adults, the young had been profoundly affected. Especially in the larger cities the children of workers had come to believe that religion was a deceit that had outlived its time, but was able to survive thanks to support from capitalism, which needed its influence in order to dominate mankind. In the rural areas the peasant children were less indoctrinated with these views, although there also they had begun to penetrate.[6]

Reports from Soviet sources also indicate that antireligious propaganda was having some effect. A study made in 1927 in one district in Moscow by the local Godless stated that the parish churches were not well attended except on Easter and the parish saints' days. In one church at late morning service on March 20 there were only two old women; in another, thirteen persons. In many churches on Sundays the choir was a substantial part of those present. On the other hand, in some especially popular churches, with a skillful preacher and a fine choir, six or seven hundred came on ordinary Sundays. On Easter the churches were filled to overflowing, but the congregation included some who were merely curious, as well as believers; some of the former were seen going to clubs (Communist-sponsored social centers) after the service. Likewise on the parish saints' days there were big congregations, which were, however, obtained in part at the expense of other parishes by the attraction of a fine choir, the presence of a bishop, and a religious procession. The study also analyzed the composition of the congregations, which contained many shopkeepers, artisans, domestic servants, along with the intelligentsia of the old regime and the dispossessed privileged classes of tsarist times. Few of the churchgoers were factory workers. Most of them were women of middle age, often accompanied by younger children.[7]

Another Soviet report, published in 1930 — shortly after the end of the period covered by these chapters — gave the results of an investigation of religion in Belorussia made by the Belorussian Academy of Sciences, using a sampling technique in 20 cities and 225 villages. The workers, the report stated, were 98.5 per cent nonbelievers, and the farmers of the collectives were over 80 per cent nonreligious. On the other hand, many of the villages (perhaps not so collectivized) were very devout. On the whole, the population was found to be 65.4 per cent nonreligious, with the men much less religious than the women.[8] An announcement by the Commissariat of Internal Affairs of the Ukraine late in 1924 was even more sweeping in its claims. It declared that the young had "completely abandoned religion," and

— somewhat inconsistently — that their participation in religious societies had "declined sharply." These societies, which were composed almost exclusively of old people, had only 3 per cent of their members from the workers. The announcement also stated that in many provinces the clergy were voluntarily giving up the cloth — a process that had embraced over 20 per cent of the priests in Volhynia.[9]

On the other hand, in 1929 an antireligious publication pointed out with dismay that religion was still strong among workers in the Urals. In Perm 69 per cent of the workers had ikons in their homes, while in other places the percentages ranged from 66 to 85.[10]

Several quantitative investigations among Red Army men showed that antireligious propaganda had considerable effect upon this portion of the population. According to their answers to questionnaires, some 70 per cent of the new recruits were religious; after several months or a year over 60 per cent were nonbelievers. Unfortunately, the brief articles providing this information give no indication as to the phrasing of the questionnaires or the method used in obtaining the answers.[11]

Studies of the extent of religious belief among school children indicated, however, that religion had by no means died out. In the city of Voronezh, some 36 per cent of 3685 elementary pupils were absent from school on January 7, 1928 — the Orthodox Christmas Day. In some schools the absentees formed over 50 per cent of the total. In general, in village schools absenteeism on religious holidays amounted to around 23 per cent.[12] During the 1928–1929 school year it was indicated by unsigned questionnaires and other unspecified methods that in the district of Balashov about 30 per cent of the elementary-school pupils were religious, and about 20 per cent of the secondary pupils. Even in the teachers' training schools about 15 per cent of the students were believers.[13] Anonymous responses to a questionnaire answered by 500 pupils in Perm in 1928 indicated that, although there were ikons in 70 per cent of their homes, about 28 per cent of the first-grade pupils prayed and went to church; 21 per cent of the fourth graders both believed and took part in religious ceremonies; another 13 per cent did not believe, but performed rites; and 66 per cent did neither. The remarks of some of the pupils suggested that the chief influence upon the pupils in favor of religion was not the priest but the mother or grandmother, who used strong measures of persuasion to make the children religious.[14]

Three investigations of the religious question in Moscow schools in 1927, 1928, and 1929 indicated that many of the pupils were religious. In October and November of 1927 a group of 615 pupils of the seventh grade answered questionnaires; their responses showed that 42 per cent were believers. The girls were far more religious than the boys. Significantly enough, almost all the children were from working-class families, and almost all from schools in which there was an active Godless group.[15] Another investigation in 1928 disclosed that about 50 per cent of the pupils of another Moscow district were religious and that a model seven-year school graduated pupils in 1928 who were 92 per cent religious.[16] In 1929 the noted educator Blonskii found that 61 per cent of some 89 pupils of the first three grades were religious; but out of over 100 fourth graders, only 24 per cent believed, while 76 did not. Eighty-nine per cent of 46 seventh-grade pupils did not believe. Blonskii, however, distrusted this last figure, as he felt that the pupils sometimes hid their real views; moreover, many of the pupils — possibly more religious than the rest — had left school before reaching the seventh grade. Nevertheless, he felt that a large proportion of the seventh-grade students were not religious.[17]

A little light upon the question of the extent of religious belief was shed by the statistics supplied by the Moscow Registry Office as to the proportion of births, marriages, and deaths marked by religious ceremonies, as shown in the following table: [18]

Births	1925	1926	1927	1928
		(In per cents)		
No religious ceremony	41.6	40.4	33.0	38.1
With religious ceremony	55.9	59.2	59.7	57.8
Unknown	2.5	0.4	7.3	4.1
Burials				
No religious ceremony	40.7	41.1	30.0	33.3
With religious ceremony	57.5	58.9	66.8	65.7
Unknown	1.8	—	3.2	1.0

Marriages	1925	1926	1927	1928
	(In per cents)			
No religious ceremony	77.3	78.4	81.6	86.3
With religious ceremony	21.1	21.6	15.6	11.8
Unknown	1.6	—	2.8	1.9

According to Soviet writers, the remarkable constancy of the proportion of religious christenings and burials was largely the result of the influence of the older, more conservative members of the family groups; the nonreligious marriages represented the views of the generation of marrying age.

Additional evidence of the vitality of the Russian Orthodox church was given by statistics of the church organization. In October, 1925, according to the Commissariat of Internal Affairs of the R.S.F.S.R., in the forty-eight provinces of the R.S.F.S.R. there were 28,381 Orthodox congregations, of which 81 per cent were of the Tikhonite following.[19] In 1927 a Godless periodical reported that there were 8324 churches (apparently Orthodox) in the Ukraine, which was 23 per cent less than in 1914.[20] This number, added to the 28,381 congregations of the forty-eight provinces of the R.S.F.S.R. in 1925, makes a total of 36,705. If it is assumed that the Belorussian S.S.R. had the same number of churches per 100,000 inhabitants as did the Ukraine, some 1400 churches for the Belorussian S.S.R. would have to be added. A further 1000 churches may be assumed to have existed in other parts of the U.S.S.R. (most of them with large non-Russian populations). Thus the estimated number of Orthodox churches in the U.S.S.R. in 1928 would be approximately 39,000. When comparison is made of this exceedingly inexact estimate with the 40,437 Orthodox parish churches in the same area in 1914, it indicates that only a relatively small proportion of parish churches had been closed since the revolution. Data for twenty-nine provinces only, in October, 1925, support this conclusion. In these provinces there were 20,421 Orthodox churches in use, while 1003 had been closed. Only one per cent of the Orthodox congregations in existence at that time lacked churches.[21]

A few scattered reports from individual localities also indicated that a relatively small part of the Orthodox churches had been closed. An investigation of the province of Samara in 1929 disclosed that there had been a gradual decline in the number of Orthodox parishes since the 1897 census and that the average number of believers per congregation had diminished by about one fifth.[22] The 460 Moscow churches were almost all in use early in 1927; only a small number had been closed because of lack of members to support them.[23] In 1928, a year of intensified antireligious activity, 354 churches and 28 monasteries ceased to function in the whole U.S.S.R. — [24] a relatively small number, which indicates that the attempt to get rid of all religion was far from a complete success.

Extremely scanty data about the ecclesiastical hierarchy likewise show that the church was still strong. In 1927 the periodical of the Karlovatskii Synod listed by name and location 272 Orthodox bishops in Russia, of whom 35 were said to be in exile within the country and 9 in prison.[25] And in 1927 *Antireligioznik* stated that in the Ukraine there were 95 bishops and 10,647 priests; in both categories, especially the former, these figures represented increases over the numbers in 1914.[26] Finally, in 1930 Metropolitan Sergii told a reporter that the Orthodox church had 30,000 parishes, 163 bishops, and several tens of millions of believers.[27]

The pieces of information concerning the state of the Russian Orthodox church at the end of 1928 are so fragmentary and often so vague in presentation that it is well nigh impossible to draw any exact conclusions. Nevertheless, certain broad general trends can be observed: The Orthodox church continued to function throughout this period, and at its end the number of its parish churches had declined by only a relatively small fraction from the prerevolutionary number. While the workers in the Russian cities had largely turned away from religion, important nonproletarian elements in the cities were still strongly religious, and the peasants probably had not turned against religion to any great degree. On the other hand, by the end of 1928 the antireligious campaign in the schools had begun to turn considerable numbers of the pupils, in the cities at least, against religious faith. In this fact lay a grave threat to the Russian Orthodox church.

How the early Soviet period had affected the church can best be realized by comparing the church at the beginning of the revolution with the church at the end of 1928. Unquestionably as an organization it was weakened economically. It was stripped of its lands and is investments; its treasures of gold and silver articles and gems had in part been taken from it for famine relief; and it had lost the appropriations from the state treasury. Its taper factories and printing establishments had been nationalized. The church, from parish priest to Locum Tenens, was almost entirely dependent upon the donations of the faithful. In education, also, it had lost greatly. On the eve of the October Revolution it enjoyed the favor of the government, and although its elementary schools had been nationalized under Kerenskii, religious education was still the rule in all schools, public and private, and the church still had hopes of recovering its parochial schools. By late 1928 it existed as a tolerated organization, but without schools, except a few theological institutions of the Renovationists. Religious education of children was rigorously limited, being confined to small-scale, private instruction.

Above all, the church's position vis-à-vis the government had changed markedly. At the end of 1917 the churchmen gathered in the Sobor felt that the church would save Russia from Bolshevik anarchy. The Patriarch anathematized the Soviet rulers, while his supporters repeatedly organized great religious demonstrations that challenged the new authorities. Even in 1922 the Patriarch defied the government over the issue of the treasures of the church, and some of his supporters aroused violence against it; undoubtedly some ecclesiastics hoped, like the Karlovatskii Sobor, that the church would cause the downfall of the hated regime. But well before 1928 the church had to change its course and trim its sails to the new winds that were blowing. The failure of the demonstrations to overturn the regime, the arrests, exilings, and exemplary executions by the Soviet authorities, and, above all, the failure of the people to seek the fall of the Soviets convinced all but a few of the most stubborn that the church must accommodate itself to the regime it had anathematized in 1918. And so it did; in 1928 it was praying for this regime. This defeat of the initial church policy indicated the strength of the government, for the fundamental policy of the latter respecting religion had changed little since the revolution.

On the other hand, the church organization had survived and had exhibited unexpected powers of endurance and adaptability. In spite of the rash and stubborn policy of many of its influential members and the stern retaliation of the Soviet government in 1922 and after, and notwithstanding the schisms and internal confusion in the church from 1922 on, its central organization and the allegiance of its members remained for the most part firm. By the end of 1928, in spite of serious inroads made upon the younger generation, the number of parishes and the size of the hierarchy had not greatly diminished. Those who wavered in their faith had fallen away; those who remained presumably were sincere in their devotion.

It should be strongly emphasized, however, that the Soviet leaders at no time sought to smash the church once and for all. They regarded it as a problem of relatively minor significance and, from 1922 on, readily adopted a policy of seeking a viable arrangement with it. When they failed to obtain this through the Living Church, they eventually secured such a compromise through Metropolitan Sergii. Between 1926 and 1929 the Orthodox church was enabled to improve its legal position thanks to official moderation.

But while Soviet short-term policy consistently prescribed a working agreement with the Orthodox church that would minimize friction with the large numbers of believers, the fundamental Communist hostility to religion remained. Marxism held that religion was basically opposed to the materialistic world outlook essential to Communism, as the church preached that the good life would come, not in this world as a result of revolutionary effort, but in heaven through divine grace. This doctrine, the Communists held, sought to make men satisfied with their lot on earth, so that they would accept their station in life rather than seek to change it at the expense of their masters. Thus religion, according to the Marxists, was basically reactionary and counterrevolutionary. Not only was it hostile to the science and materialism so dear to the Communist heart; it also supported the privileged classes who were the sworn enemies of the Soviet regime. Hence the Communist authorities encouraged antireligious propaganda, which began to expand greatly as the Five-Year Plan drew near. This was, however, to be not a sudden campaign to smash religion, but a long-drawn, consistent and determined effort to eradicate religious belief through education and conviction. The organization of this intensive effort to fight religion in the U.S.S.R. was only beginning in 1928, and the results were far from complete.

The history of Soviet dealings with the Russian Orthodox church during this period is intelligible only when the dual nature of Soviet religious policy is borne in mind. Just as Soviet diplomats sought working relations with other countries, while Communists of the Third International with varying degrees of intensity sought world revolution, so did Soviet officials seek a working basis for their relations with the church at the very time that Stalin was calling for the eventual eradication of all "religious prejudice" and when the League of Godless was beginning to expand with great rapidity. This dual approach, which has had a remarkable duration, was evolving in the years from 1917 to 1928.

CHAPTER XII

Fishers of Men

WHEN IN OCTOBER, 1928, the First Five-Year Plan went into effect, there began an intensive effort to replace the nonsocialist elements with socialized forms in commerce, industry, and agriculture. Inevitably religion and the Russian Orthodox church were affected. Not only did the church face a mounting antireligious campaign; it also was touched by the elimination of nonsocialist elements.

For the peasantry the plan set goals of 30 per cent collectivization, and suppression of the kulaks or more wealthy peasants by means of punitive taxation and confiscation of their grain surplus. The kulaks naturally fought back with a wide arsenal of weapons. Consequently, in 1929 and early 1930 the Soviet leaders changed from a policy of partial collectivization to one of complete collectivization and of liquidation of the kulaks as a class. To the Russian church this brought a fresh shock, for the kulaks — the most successful, prosperous peasants of the villages — had often played an important role in the church, the sole non-Soviet institution to which they — no lovers of the Soviet regime — might belong. The Soviet rulers probably felt that the religious organizations would be an obstacle to the fulfillment of their drastic plans, for the unfolding of the First Five-Year Plan was accompanied by a series of measures intended to undermine the power of religion.

A significant step in this direction was taken by the law of April 8, 1929, which dealt with the legal position of religious organizations. In part this measure granted a favorable status to the church, as it gave legal recognition to local and central organizations of the church, permitted religious congresses at all levels, and allowed parish representatives to enter into contractual relationships.[1] More-over, the members of the parishes were permitted to collect and keep funds and to build new houses of prayer. While provincial authorities were still authorized to take over church buildings and to put them to other uses, the believers were granted a two-week period in which to appeal against such decisions to the All-Union Central Executive Committee; action was thereupon suspended until the central authorities handed down a decision.[2] On the other hand, the law expressly forbade the religious organizations to engage in any activity but performing divine service. They were forbidden to establish mutual-aid funds and co-operatives, to organize young people's and women's gatherings, Bible or religious study groups, literary or handicraft groups, circles, or meetings, to organize excursions and playgrounds, and to open libraries and reading rooms. Only the necessary service books might be kept in the church building.[3] No teaching of religion to children or to adults was permitted "in state, social, or private educational institutions," and according to the editor of the lawbook cited, this annulled the right of parents to have their young children given religious instruction by the priest; now only the parents might give religious instruction to their children. The only exception to this rule was the provision for special theological courses for citizens of eighteen years of age or more.[4]

A further provision limited the activity of a minister of religion to the area inhabited by the members of his parish and containing the house of prayer. As for ministers, preachers, and instructors of religion without regular parishes, their activity "is restricted to the area in which the believers belonging to the said religious units regularly live."[5] The latter provisions seem to have been designed to limit the functioning of circuit-riding clergy.

Many of the above restrictions appear to have been more detrimental to the rapidly growing sectarians, Protestant in character, than they were to the Orthodox church, which seldom engaged in nonritual activity and was more conventional in its organization. Indeed, Dr. Matthew Spinka, an American theologian then in the U.S.S.R., states that he had been told on excellent authority that the restrictions in article 17 had been inspired by an Orthodox priest, formerly a missionary among the sectarians, who told the authorities that the earlier legislation operated greatly to the advantage of the sects.[6]

In addition to this set of rules, on the same day the Presidium of the All-Union Central Executive Committee decreed the establishment of a Standing Commission on Questions of Cults, attached to the Presidium and headed by Smidovich, a Communist. The commission comprised representatives of the Commissariats of Internal Affairs, of Justice, and of Education, all of the R.S.F.S.R., and of the All-Union Central Council of Trade-Unions.[7] The significance of this measure, however, is not readily apparent.

Additional tightening of the restrictions upon the religious bodies was accomplished by the amendment of the Constitution of the R.S.F.S.R. to eliminate the right of religious propaganda. The new article read: "For the purpose of assuring real liberty of conscience to the workers, the church is separated from the state and the school from the church, and liberty of confession and of antireligious propaganda is granted to all citizens." [8]

The first years of the Five-Year Plan introduced heavier taxation and fiscal burdens for all, which hit the clergy with especial severity. Ecclesiastics who depended solely upon the income from their priestly functions were regarded by the government as not engaged in socially useful labor and hence were subject to various discriminations. In 1928 it was decreed that the single agricultural tax paid by such individuals was to be levied on all sources of income and in proportion to their actual income, on the basis of the information available to the fiscal authorities rather than according to any set rules.[9] That this method of assessment sometimes caused injustices was admitted in a subsequent article in the Communist party periodical *Bol'shevik*, which asserted that the local officials had been warned to avoid inequities. The author estimated that the average increase in such taxation had been 31.58 per cent. He further stated that almost all the taxpayers so assessed had complained, and that more than half of the complaints had brought redress.[10] Further light on the taxation of the clergy was shed by a directive issued by the Commissariat of Finance in 1931. It ordered that the homes of ministers of religion should not be taxed more than 100 per cent above similar homes of working people. The agricultural tax on a member of the clergy was not to exceed his previous tax by more than 75 per cent, unless his sources of revenue had increased. If the priest had to pay the self-assessment tax (a locally voted tax), it was not to exceed 100 per cent of the agricultural or income tax that he paid.[11] The same directive ordered that houses of prayer were subject to the usual insurance premiums, the local building tax, and payment of ground rent for the land on which they stood; no other imposts or fees were to be levied upon them.[12]

While some of these measures were largely directed against the more prosperous peasants and only incidentally against the clergy, in 1930 one of the Godless writers mentioned with some satisfaction that "the taxation policy of the Soviet authorities strikes the pockets of the servitors of religious cults especially painfully." [13]

Nor was this all. In 1928 members of the clergy and other "non-laboring elements" were ordered to pay increased rent for their quarters. Those with taxable incomes above 3000 rubles per year were to pay rent ranging from 13.20 to 22.00 rubles for a room ten feet square in small towns, and from 19.80 to 44.00 rubles in large towns; if they were fortunate enough to occupy larger quarters the rents were in proportion. Those with smaller incomes were to pay from 7.70 to 11.00 rubles for one hundred square feet.[14] These rentals, while perhaps not exorbitant, were nevertheless substantially higher than those paid by members of the working classes.

As for the clergy who still lived in former manses (now nationalized property), they too paid higher rents. Whereas workers residing in these buildings paid rent on the basis of amortization of the cost of the building (one per cent if it was brick, 2 per cent if wooden), priests paid the amortization rates plus interest on the value of the building up to 10 per cent a year, depending on local conditions and the ability of the priest to pay.[15]

In 1929, as the vast influx of workers into the Soviet cities created a terrific housing shortage, the authorities took the further drastic step of evicting all nonworking people — which included the clergy — having incomes of over 3000 rubles per year from all nationalized and municipally owned dwellings in cities.[16] On January 3, 1930, *Pravda* printed an article indicating that *all* disenfranchised persons (among them the clergy) were to be expelled from all socialized housing: from municipal and nationalized housing, and from that belonging to state institutions and enterprises, to co-operatives in cities and workers' suburbs, and to similar institutions.[17]

These measures must have brought considerable hardship and privation to many ecclesiastics. Nevertheless, there still remained a substantial quantity of privately owned houses in which the clergy might find quarters. Nonlaboring elements must have found homes, for in December, 1932, the Soviet government decreed the establishment of a single internal passport system "with the aim of better control of the population of cities, workers' settlements, and newly built towns and for the purpose of relieving these settled places of persons not connected with production and the work in institutions or schools and not occupied in socially useful work. . . ."[18]

An additional burden on the clergy was the creation of difficulties in the way of their procurement of food and other necessities. The Central Co-operative Union in 1930 ordered that disenfranchised persons were to be provisioned only if they paid a special deposit. Their children, however, should receive equal treatment with other children.[19]

It should be noted that if ecclesiastics entered employment in the government and other agencies open to them they acquired the rights of citizens performing socially useful labor. Even this solution of their difficulties, however, was endangered, for in 1929 the central authorities decreed that the local officials might deprive of their positions all persons whose work had proved harmful to the interests of the working class.[20] Shortly thereafter one of the leading Godless reported that his organization had discovered that in some of the museums religious propaganda was being carried on, which led to the dismissal of the culprits; a professor of the Agricultural Academy had been dismissed because he continued to attend religious services.[21]

Eventually, however, the discrimination against disenfranchised persons went so far that it produced an official reaction. In March, 1930, the Presidium of the Central Executive Committee, as a result of numerous complaints, ordered "the unconditional elimination" of additional restrictions upon the disenfranchised and their families, "such as expulsion from their homes and their towns; wholesale deprivation of medical aid; prohibition of building; expulsion of their children from schools"; and other deprivations.[22]

In spite of this instance of moderation, however, the position of the clergy and other disenfranchised persons was unenviable. For not only were they subject to the disabilities already discussed, but they were also under the threat of severe penalties for actions regarded as dangerous to the Soviet regime. For propaganda or agitation directed toward stirring up national or religious hatred or dissension or for distributing printed matter for this purpose the penalty was loss of freedom for as much as two years. Propaganda or agitation urging the overthrow, undermining, or weakening of the Soviet regime was punishable by imprisonment for six months; if for this purpose use was made of the national or religious prejudices of the masses the penalty might range from three years' imprisonment to execution.[23] Furthermore, penalties of not more than one year of compulsory labor might be imposed for "the teaching of religious belief to young children and persons under age, in state or private educational institutions and schools," and likewise for "the commission of acts of deceit, with the purpose of encouraging superstition among the masses of the population and with a view to deriving profit of any kind therefrom." For the "enforced collection of contributions" to religious organizations and for the assumption of administrative, judicial, and other legal functions by ecclesiastical organizations, the penalty was imprisonment up to six months and a fine.[24] Finally, the OGPU (the political police, earlier known as the GPU) enjoyed wide powers in dealing with enemies of the regime, including the right to impose terms in concentration camps.[25]

A number of instances reported in the Soviet press show that these penalties were actually applied. In a rural parish of the province of Stalingrad a group of church members and the parish priest were tried for concealing church valuables in a secret place under the chancel, for counterrevolutionary activity and propaganda and for nonpayment of taxes. The priest was acquitted, while several of the laymen were sentenced to from one to two years' imprisonment. The author of the newspaper article about the case declared bitterly that the sentences were far too lenient.[26] In Tashkent a priest and several laymen were charged with illegal hoarding of a considerable sum of silver coins in the cellar of their church and with counterrevolutionary propaganda; after a trial the priest and two of the laymen were sentenced to be shot.[27] *Pravda* reported that in dealing with a large number of hoarders, the OGPU had shot eight of the worst offenders, who had also carried on counterrevolutionary propaganda; among them were two ministers of religion of unspecified denomination.[28] In June, 1929, two priests were arrested with other citizens on charges of refusing to give up their surplus grain, and their property was confiscated. Their friends collected a crowd before the village Soviet, demanding the release of the accused and restoration of their property; bricks were thrown at local officials. The priests and one of the laymen were sentenced to be shot.[29]

In another instance, a priest and his psalmist persuaded two women to secure signatures on a petition against the imminent closing of their church. The women stirred up the peasants; the priest was arrested, whereupon a mob formed demanding his release. The priest and the psalmist were each sentenced to one year of confinement.[30] More serious was the case of another priest and a psalmist and two laymen accused of antigovernmental propaganda. They allegedly opposed the compulsory grain deliveries to the government, using threats to intimidate the peasants. They were even convicted of having set fire to the homes of their Godless adversaries. The priest and the psalmist, along with one of the laymen, received death sentences.[31] A similar sentence was passed upon a village priest of the province of Moscow. According to the Soviet press, after the local peasants had voted to close the church and convert it into a school building, the church members became excited and agitated against the decision. Somewhat later some officials came with a cart to remove a broken bell lying near the church for use as scrap metal. A bell hanging in the church was rung to summon a mob, which beat the officials; the rioters were told that war would soon come and the Soviet regime would be overthrown. Subsequently the priest and some of his supporters were arrested and tried.[32]

While these were purely local incidents, not involving the higher authorities of the Orthodox church, in a few cases bishops also were accused. In Ivanovo Bishop Avgustin was charged with participation in a counterrevolutionary plot centering around one of the churches. Subversive literature, weapons, and incriminating correspondence allegedly were found in homes of participants, and members of the clergy were charged with oral incitement. The outcome of the case was not reported in the source.[33] Bishop Domitian of Arzamas was tried for counterrevolutionary activity, with charges of sexual profligacy thrown in. He was sentenced to eight years of solitary imprisonment.[34]

Metropolitan Sergii and the central administration of the Russian Orthodox church were not implicated in these charges and were never mentioned in the numerous items in the Soviet press. The Ukrainian Autocephalous Orthodox church, however, was denounced in the Soviet courts and press as a tool of the Ukrainian nationalist "League for the Liberation of the Ukraine," in which Metropolitan Lipkovskii and other dominant church leaders were active. After the conviction of the heads of the league, the Autocephalous church held a special council in 1930, at which the leading churchmen signed a document admitting that their church had for ten years carried on anti-Soviet propaganda with counterrevolutionary intent. The council consequently decreed the dissolution of the church; the parish priests were to continue their functions without guidance from a central administration.[35]

The increased intensity of legislative and penal measures against religion and the church was, however, only part of what Iaroslavskii, head of the League of Militant Godless, termed an "antireligious attack on an extended front." The Communist party, which through the Five-Year Plan had set out to achieve the triumph of socialism, obviously regarded religion and the church as an obstacle. Included in the "extended front" were the public schools, for, as has been noted earlier, the battle to replace the *nonreligious* outlook of the school system with an *antireligious* attitude had been won in 1928, and the effects of antireligious emphasis in the schools began to be felt during the period of the Five-Year Plan. In spite of the religious outlook of so many of the older teachers and the difficulty of replacing them with younger teachers trained in the antireligious viewpoint and able to stand up to the fierce opposition of believers in their communities, Iaroslavskii sought not only to have the school children indoctrinated against religion, but also to have them fired with a desire to combat religion outside the school, and above all in their own families — a difficult task, and one that could be accomplished only by patient persuasion.[36]

In some cases the effort to enlist the pupils as active participants achieved remarkable results. In the city of Iaroslavl groups of Godless pupils with much success visited all the shops and offices of one of the factories during an anti-Christmas campaign in order to sell subscriptions to the newspaper *Bezbozhnik (Godless)*.[37] A general account of educational developments during this period states that there was a vast antireligious activity on the part of the children. They campaigned among the general public against the observance of religious holidays and especially against the drunkenness and brawling often observed on those occasions. In the villages they sought to demonstrate that calf blindness could be prevented by letting light into the barn rather than by prayers; cabbage worms were fought with poison more successfully than with prayers and holy water.[38]

Organized labor in the U.S.S.R. also took part in the antireligious movement, for in March, 1929, the Eighth Congress of Trade-Unions adopted a resolution emphasizing the struggle against religion as an important part of the trade-union activity. The resolution was implemented by a circular calling for extensive antireligious work in trade-union clubs, Houses of Culture, libraries, and reading rooms, and ordering the training of antireligious personnel by means of the courses offered by the League of Militant Godless.[39]

Similarly, the Eighth Congress of the Komsomol, in 1928, urged that antireligious work be intensified to win the peasants away from the religious organizations to active participation in social and political life, and sponsored healthy amusements for them, a fight against drunkenness, and wide introduction of the radio and cinema into the villages. The Komsomols were urged to unmask the clergy as defenders of the kulaks, to prepare volunteer antireligious workers, and to carry on propaganda and agitation among the peasants to induce them to refuse money for religious purposes. This led to great activity by the Komsomols, beginning in 1929. Their efforts, however, were not properly led and suffered from deviations from the correct course.[40]

Finally, the League of Militant Godless itself expanded rapidly during these years. In 1928 its members numbered 123,007, in 3980 cells. During the succeeding months its growth was phenomenal; by January, 1930, there were 35,000 cells with 2,000,000 members.[41] Obviously, the antireligious tide was rising fast.

Quite early, however, it became obvious that all was not well. Iaroslavskii and other leaders repeatedly had to urge caution and moderation and to defend themselves against impatient zealots. While some wanted to declare the trade-unions completely antireligious, Iaroslavskii termed this harmful. The trade-unions "should also admit those who have not broken with religion, while working on them, helping them to free themselves from this religious, petty-bourgeois ideology. . . ."[42] The veteran Communist Mikhail Kalinin rebuked those who were indignant that believing workers had been given prominent posts in social work in the factories: "If the person belongs to the working class, if he already is beginning to take an interest in social work, we must believe that it is a good sign and that with time, sooner or later, he will pass over to the viewpoint of the Godless. . . . This will happen as inevitably as the fulfillment of the physical laws of nature. In the long run all religious feeling will disappear."[43] When Iaroslavskii was asked whether churchmen and sectarians had the right to bar speakers of the Godless from addressing their gatherings, the Godless leader replied that it was impossible to deny this right, just as it was out of the question to let priests address the Godless. "Really this boils down to one basic question — do we permit the existence of religious organizations or not? If we do not permit them, then we can do anything we wish, but if we permit them, then we cannot demand freedom of access for our agitators."[44]

In respect to the closing of churches Iaroslavskii, while gratified that it was assuming a mass character, questioned whether this fact actually represented the will of the people or was not perhaps the result of administrative pressure; ". . . where there is no sort of serious antireligious preparation, when the masses are unprepared, where the closing of a church arouses serious conflict, such a closing of a church is sometimes dangerous and harmful, when they don't take account of the opinion of the mass of the inhabitants and force through the closing of the church, not halting before open conflict." [45]

He also cautioned against changing the calendar in imitation of the French Jacobins of 1793. In his opinion, it was enough to refer to events "of our era" instead of "of the Christian era." Only when workers all over the world had come to feel that the October Revolution was the central event of history would it be possible to date time from it. [46]

Iaroslavskii's attitude did not, however, satisfy some of the Godless, and one of the Komsomol leaders objected to his moderation in closing churches and his insistence on the need for cultural work among the masses and for careful preparation before antireligious acts might be undertaken. Iaroslavskii answered: "Can we give the newspaper *Bezbozhnik* for reading to a person who is illiterate? Can we propagandize a person who thinks that worms are produced by mud? A person who thinks that the Prophet Elias rides across the heavens and from this come thunder and rain — can he be subjected to antireligious propaganda?" When the Komsomol newspaper proposed "to annihilate . . . the basic seats of religious deceit . . . ," he answered: "What does this mean? If you speak openly, *it signifies closing all religious organizations,* since these are the seats of religious propaganda. If we thus posed the question, it would be a matter of fierce struggle with at least sixty or seventy million working people. Would that be correct or not?" [47]

Actually, a strong drive against churches was in progress, as well as a campaign against the use of church bells. Early in 1929 the Komsomol press urged the confiscation of church bells to provide copper and tin for industrialization and to supply funds. [48] Another article from Khar'kov complained that the bells of the cathedral interfered with the radio program. [49] *Pravda* reported a general pulling down of bells in the province of Pervomaisk on November 7 for purposes of industrialization, with peasants playing a leading part. [50] According to one of the Godless periodicals, a wave of demands for removal of bells swept over the country during 1929, with the populace often in advance of the local authorities. Stalingrad was one of the first cities to eliminate bells; by the end of 1929 "hundreds of villages and a number of towns" had stilled their clangor.[51]

Iaroslavskii, however, advocated caution. While he felt that the ringing of bells was often troublesome, especially for a worker on the night shift who wanted to sleep during the day, he warned against arbitrariness in imposing an illegal ban on bells. "We must prosecute a campaign among the working class, prepare them, we must in the last analysis convince the masses. . . . This has been a privilege of the dominant church. Do we need to keep it or not? It seems to me that we do not. But we must carry on serious explanatory work in this direction." [52]

One of the most striking features of the antireligious movement during the First Five-Year Plan was the closing of great numbers of churches. Iaroslavskii termed this a mass movement.

> Actually masses of real workers, and in places of peasants, not only of unbelievers, but also of believers, took part in adopting resolutions for closing churches. We must stress this: *that such resolutions were adopted not only by unbelievers, but also by believers.* . . . It is necessary that not only unbelievers, but also believers be interested in the clubs that we are constructing, in the crèches and reading rooms. . . . If unbelievers succeeded in getting believers to sign that they support our measures, this would be a victory. *In some places we have such a victory.* For example, in Egor'evskaia, when a campaign was in process to close three churches, many believers signed the resolution, giving the reason that there were other churches where they could pray, and these churches were needed for cultural institutions.[53]

The Soviet press reported in 1929 that the Moscow Provincial Soviet had organized a traveling antireligious cinema, accompanied by lecturers, which visited twenty villages within one month. As a result, the peasants of these villages voted to close fifteen churches, and one of the priests publicly renounced holy orders.[54] *Izvestiia* reported that during the Christmas season of 1929 churches were closed in Taganrog and Leningrad, and demands for closing churches were made in Voronezh and Kazan. The City Soviet of Nezhin voted to take all the bells from the town's churches.[55] A peasant congress of a county near Tver on the Volga was reported to have voted that by spring the county should be free of kulaks, priests, and traders.[56]

The drive to close churches was closely linked with the rapid collectivization of the peasants; where the latter was successful, many churches were eliminated. Iaroslavskii optimistically announced in *Pravda* that the peasants were learning to overcome nature by applying modern farming technique and that within several years they would have freed themselves from the influence of religion. In one county the peasants had closed two out of every three churches, putting them to their own use — as mills, as houses of socialist culture with auditoriums, as libraries and cinemas. This was a result, he said, of almost complete collectivization.[57] In his report to the central leaders of the Godless movement in January, 1930, Iaroslavskii stated that Godless work, like collectivization, was proceeding much faster than had originally been planned. Opposition had resulted, which was to be expected. The struggle against the church was "one of the forms of class warfare, of most fierce class warfare." He could not cite exact figures as to the number of churches closed, but in some counties it amounted to 50 per cent. In areas of complete collectivization the peasants raised the question as to whether they should have a kolkhoz (collective-farm) church. He reported them as saying: "We are organizing kolkhozes. That means we must finish with the church."

Iaroslavskii continued: "It seems to me . . . that the process of collectivization is linked with the liquidation, if not of all churches, then, in any case, of a significant part of the churches, with the cutting at least in half of the numerical expression of all sorts of religious organizations and, doubtless, of the influence of these religious organizations. . . . If the main regions are collectivized, then in them the influence of the church organizations will be cut at least in half."[58]

In the effort to strike at the church through the kolkhoz the creation of "Godless kolkhozes" was important. These were collectives that by a majority vote had decided to declare themselves Godless and usually had taken a Godless name. This was usually the result of long and careful preparation and propaganda by the League of Godless.

In these Godless collectives the peasants were often persuaded to re-nounce religious holidays, and sometimes to burn their family ikons; often the local churches were closed and used for social purposes.[59] In 1929 the Second Congress of Godless adopted a directive ordering the following: "The League of Godless should be an advance detach-ment on the front of socialist construction. . . . Cells and councils of the Godless should be pioneers in the work of organizing collective farms, in the work of improving them. The cells of the Godless should strive for the organization of Godless collectives, the pur-chase of machines and tractors for the collective working of the land." [60]

Concurrent with the closing of parish churches there occurred the closing of many of the remaining monastic institutions. A report in *Pravda* early in 1930 told of a decree in the Ukraine ordering the clos-ing of 6 monasteries or convents in the Don region and the eviction of the last 48 monks from the Pecherskaia Lavra at Kiev.[61] In Voro-nezh several thousand people were reported to have unanimously voted a resolution asking the closing of 41 monastic institutions of the province, which were inhabited by over 1000 monks and nuns.[62] Another news item told of the blowing up of the Simonov Monastery (place not indicated) and the voluntary work of one thousand citi-zens in clearing away the rubble.[63] In spite of these assaults upon the monasteries, however, some of them always seem to have survived.

The collectivization of agriculture struck a blow at religion; in industry a similarly shrewd blow was dealt by the introduction of the continuous work week. On August 26, 1929, this innovation was de-creed by the Council of People's Commissars of the U.S.S.R. on the grounds that it would make for more efficient production and speed up the realization of the Five-Year Plan. The workers were promised the retention of the seven-hour day and the same number of rest days per year.[64] Shortly thereafter the All-Union Trade-Union Council issued a long explanation of this measure. It provided for the intro-duction of uninterrupted operation of industry and construction, with no general rest day for all alike; instead, the rest days of the workers would be staggered, so that some would have Monday off, some Tuesday, and so on. While the main purpose of this was economic, the message explained that the elimination of Sunday holidays and saints' days "will inevitably lead to fundamental changes in the old traditions of life in the workers' existence." It added that this measure would facilitate work in political training of the workers "and a more successful struggle against religion and other survivals of the old way of life." [65]

To the Godless leader Iaroslavskii this seemed to be "the most important decision of the year, which strikes a crushing blow at religion and religious ideologies rooted in the way of life of the workers and the peasant masses. . . ." He declared that the measure, which wiped out the difference between Saturdays, Sundays, and Mondays, made it possible to force out religious beliefs, "which are nourished by religious holidays." As a result of the universal adoption of this practice "there will undoubtedly occur the rooting out of the religious way of life on a gigantic scale." He warned, however, that this result would not follow automatically, but would require "colossal work" on the part of the Godless and other organizations.[66] A cartoon in *Pravda* supported this view. It portrayed a worker at a bench telling a newcomer that he would find it easier if he would drop from his back his pack containing an ikon, playing cards, a vodka bottle, and a cross, labeled "Sunday, religion, old life." The accompanying article reported that the workers of Kostroma were doing excellently on the new basis and were demanding the closing of all local churches.[67] On the other hand, the workers' newspaper *Krasnaia Gazeta* (*Red Gazette*) reported that some workers opposed the continuous work week, feeling that it would deprive them of overtime pay, and that the number of absentee workers on Sundays was greater than on other days.[68]

The continuous work week apparently facilitated the campaigns against Easter and Christmas, although the results were not always gratifying. An antireligious leader in *Izvestiia* reported that in the industrial town of Slaviansk the anti-Easter campaign was nothing but a demonstration of hooligans, who sought to break up the church services by throwing stones at the churches and shooting at the cross, which brought retaliatory stone-throwing by the congregations. During the anti-Christmas campaign a group of militant churchgoers succeeded in breaking into an antireligious social gathering and completely disrupting it.[69] On the other hand, during the 1929 anti-

Christmas campaign (January 7, 1930, New Style) there were reports from Leningrad, Moscow, Kiev, Tver, and many other cities telling of great popular enthusiasm for the demonstrations, which were accompanied by a minimum of absenteeism from work, by the ceremonial burning of ikons, and demands for closing churches.[70] One account told of a district in which during the preceding two years only 12 churches out of 320 had been closed; during the anti-Christmas campaign of 1929–1930 over one hundred were closed. Another district had 14 churches functioning out of 36 while a third had only 5 out of 22. There were mass burnings of ikons at Tver, Tula, and other towns, and in one locality alone eighteen priests renounced the cloth.[71]

Thus during the first eighteen months of the First Five-Year Plan the Godless movement seemed to be advancing with its wheels in high gear and churning into the dust the feeble churchmen who sought to bar its path. It was soon apparent, however, that although real and lasting successes had been achieved, many workers and especially peasants had been alienated by harsh methods and compulsion, which embittered the believers and often disgusted those who were wavering in their faith. Moreover, to a surprising degree the church proved able to adapt itself to the unfavorable milieu in which it now found itself.

As has already been indicated, in 1929 Iaroslavskii had warned of mistakes in the fight against religion. In January, 1930, in a letter to Maxim Gor'kii, Stalin agreed with the writer that in questions of antireligious propaganda "there reigns great confusion." He added: "Sometimes supernatural stupidities are permitted, which pour water on the mill of our enemies" — a failing that in his opinion would require much corrective work.[72] At the Sixteenth Congress of the Communist party its Central Committee took action against these defects. The highly important resolution, "On the Struggle against Distortions of the Party Line in the Kolkhoz Movement," devoted its sixth section to the antireligious situation.

Finally, the Central Committee feels it necessary to note some completely inadmissible distortions of the Party line in the sphere of the struggle against religious prejudices. . . . We have in mind the *administrative* closing of churches without the acquiescence of the predominant majority of the village, which leads usually to the strengthening of religious prejudices. . . .

Such action of the Communists of the Left, it was stated, aided counterrevolution and was not in harmony with the "Party line."

The first six recommendations accompanying this resolution dealt with the peasant problem; the seventh was devoted to the antireligious movement, in the following words:

> 7. Decisively to end the closing of churches in an administrative manner fictitiously disguised as the public and voluntary wish of the population. *To permit* the closing of churches only in the event of the actual wish of the predominant majority of the peasants and only with the confirmation by the provincial executive committees of the rulings of the village meetings. For abusive actions in respect to the religious feelings of peasant men and women, to bring the guilty to strict accountability.[73]

The Communist party was still insistent, however, on combating religious influences, for the congress adopted a resolution stating: "The Party should strengthen and develop the considerable successes attained in the work of liberating the masses from the reactionary influence of religion."[74] On the other hand, forty-one pages of resolutions were adopted, with twenty inches of column to a page; the above resolution measured one half inch only. This fact indicates that to the Soviet hierarchy the struggle against religion was of relatively little importance.

Several instances of the improper sort of tactics occasionally used were given by Iaroslavskii in a report to the central council of the Godless, on March 20, 1930. In the Volga German area a determined Godless member felt it necessary to close the local church. Of those present at the meeting, 23 were for closing, 13 were opposed, and nine abstained. The church was closed, but the next morning there were 70 resignations from the collective farm. "We ask you, which is more important — seventy persons who will stay in the kolkhoz even though they have not broken with religion, or the disorganization of the kolkhoz, even though the church is closed?"[75] In another passage he declared that the church was an obstacle in the way of collectivizing agriculture, but that perhaps preparation for the closing of the church should be undertaken for a year or two.

. . . why should that very obstacle be destroyed, and destroyed in such a way that for a very long time thereafter no kolkhoz can be organized in its place? We cannot put the question of the church first in the organization of collective farms.

In the village of Beresovo, . . . when the kolkhoz was organized, they seized the priest, compelling him to take off his cassock and to close the church. The priest immediately started agitating, and the kolkhoz was destroyed.[76]

Repeatedly he insisted that the lack of careful preparation in such matters and a spirit of impatience produced undesirable results.

In the village of Strugova Buda . . . the local Soviet closed the church without preparation; the women requested that it be reopened. Whose victory was that? It was the victory of religion over our fools. . . . We give weapons into the hands of our enemies.

In the village of Komsak, . . . Orenburg province, the chairman . . . issued a written permission to close a church. The flag was raised amid triumphal shots from the revolver of Judge Ianarov. The judge and his companions escaped from the crowd of women with difficulty.

Here is the village of Gorodishche, Stalingrad province. At the meeting 128 out of 1575 voters were present. And all of a sudden, without any preparation, the question of doing away with the bells [of the church] was raised. Nine persons were for removing all the bells but one, 28 were against it, and the rest were silent. The village Soviet removed the bells.[77]

He took the same attitude toward the burning of ikons, citing examples. The peasants of one village publicly burned eight cartloads, in another, four cartloads. A third village burned 70 per cent of the ikons in the village. The workers of a town burned four thousand. He commented that this was fine when done as a result of a real mass movement, which was usually the case; "but I know individual cases where the shock brigades visited the peasant cottages and requisitioned the ikons. . . . we should severely punish those. . . . Here is a communication: 'They are acting like blockheads with the public burning of ikons, which creates suitable ground for anti-Soviet propaganda by churchmen and increases the religious fanaticism of the masses.' "[78]

An article in *Antireligioznik* warned against deviations both to the Left and to the Right. The Left deviation consisted of a superficial attitude toward antireligious propaganda and of resorting to administrative measures or ridicule or abuse of the clergy and the rites, and mockery and abuse of the believers rather than an attempt to win them away from error. Such persons sometimes went into churches with their caps on, smoked cigarettes, hung up Godless posters there, or defiled altars and cemeteries. Others showed their zeal by publicly burning or trampling on ikons. Others made life miserable for the clergy, blaming them for the survival of religion. Their antireligious propaganda was superficial, directed toward the feelings of the people, with little real content. It was easily combated by the churchmen. Some touched only the class aspect of religion, neglecting the scientific approach. Only a careful, thorough, persistent approach would secure results.

On the other hand, the article continued, the Right deviation also was dangerous. It held that religion would die out automatically, so that there was no need to fight it. Or the Right became panicky in the face of opposition and sought to pacify it by retaining churches and minimizing antireligious propaganda. Many were correct in their personal attitudes toward religion, but failed to combat it actively. Some even let their children be christened, although they were careful not to attend and thus could feign ignorance. They also were tolerant of their families' predilection for Christmas trees, Easter eggs, and ikons. They failed to insist on Red weddings or funerals for their families. Sometimes the Right deviationists approved of sectarians as "Communists." The antireligious propaganda of the Right was largely cultural and failed to stress the class struggle against religion.[79]

For a time early in 1930 there was a heated discussion among the Godless, with some of the leaders and also some of the Komsomols accusing Iaroslavskii of too much timidity in closing churches and of not enough aggressive antireligious propaganda. Iaroslavskii and his adherents carried the day, however, and both Right and Left deviations were condemned by the heads of the Godless.[80]

There is an interesting parallel between the development of the antireligious campaign during the first part of the Five-Year Plan and the movement to collectivize agriculture. Like the Godless movement, the collectivization campaign, after a relatively modest beginning, quickly burgeoned into a luxuriant if somewhat unhealthy growth. In each case, the Communist party suddenly interfered with a call for more sanity and moderation. The counterpart of the restraining resolutions on antireligious affairs was Stalin's famous speech, "Dizziness from Success," and the concrete measures which accompanied it. In neither instance, however, was there abandonment of the major objectives; the new course called only for a more careful approach and for precautions to avoid alienating beyond repair the masses of the people.

CHAPTER XIII

The Way Is Long

As A RESULT OF the demands of the Communist party in March, 1930, for an end to antireligious excesses, the "Left deviation" declined and largely ceased to be a problem. On the other hand, more danger now appeared from the Right. In June, 1930, Iaroslavskii stated that some of the Godless had interpreted the directive to mean that antireligious activity was no longer desired. Some antireligious propagandists tried to substitute for it the mere teaching of chemistry or some other scientific technique, or sought to merge the League of Militant Godless with scientific or antialcohol societies. In some factories it was felt that the Godless cells might be disbanded, as the trade-union leaders allegedly disapproved of their work.[1] Speeches at a regional conference of the Young Godless late in 1930 showed a distinct tendency toward relaxation of antireligious efforts. "Why should we make all this fuss about nothing! All the youth no longer believe in God as it is." "Why should antireligious propaganda be carried on in universities and technical schools? The students there are developed, educated people and therefore, of course, antireligious."[2] One of the rural areas stated that the Godless there were inactive and that the predominant attitude was that there should be no antireligious work at that time. "It is not the time for it, comrades. Now is the time for great numbers to join the collective farm. Why do you begin speaking about religion?"[3]

This attitude seems to have been widespread, for in 1931 *Antireligioznik* warned that little was being done to inculcate a scientific outlook and dialectical materialism in the minds of those who were giving up religion. The successes of collectivization, it was stated, would aid greatly in this respect, but the peasant who joined a collective did

not at once slough off his religious traditions. Hence there was a colossal need for antireligious propaganda.[4] The overoptimistic belief
in the decline of religion persisted, however, for in 1932 *Pravda* reported that in a factory of the province of Ivanovo the chairman of
the factory trade-union committee stated flatly: "We have absolutely
no thought of carrying on this work; there are no believers among
us." The Stalino radio center refused to organize an anti-Christmas
campaign, saying that "all were Godless" in the Donets Basin. The
trade-unions of Shcheglovka took the attitude that "antireligious
work will only remind the workers that religious festivals exist, and
therefore will only increase the number of absentees."[5]

In spite of these views, the leaders of the Godless continued to emphasize that the task was far from ended. The League of Militant
Godless was late in working out proper methods and content for the
antireligious effort; not enough women were enrolled in Godless
cells; there was not enough work being done among the believers.
Antireligious work among the children was in poor shape. In general the methodology was weak, with poor co-ordination of theory
and practice and insufficient organization and guidance in the local
sectors.[6] The need for more support from the local organs of the
public-school system, from the trade-unions, and from scientists was
stressed. Above all, emphasis was on thoroughgoing, persistent antireligious propaganda on a high theoretical level.[7] Iaroslavskii declared that much remained to be done in indoctrinating both workers and peasants. The latter did not automatically become Godless
upon joining a collective farm, while among the workers were many
former peasants who had not yet adopted a proletarian outlook. The
Godless should make contact with the new masses and answer their
questions. In addition, the Komsomols were far from properly
trained, and even the Communist party had been filled up with new
recruits, many of whom needed proper training. Consequently, the
need for careful, intelligent antireligious propaganda was greater than
ever.[8]

The League of Militant Godless also continued to grow, although
not at the rate scheduled in the Godless Five-Year Plan, which
called for four million members by the end of 1930, seven million by
the end of 1931, and seventeen million by December, 1933 — figures

presented in all seriousness.[9] Nevertheless, from 465,498 members in
1929 (month not specified), the enrollment mushroomed to 5,673,000
on May 15, 1932.[10] Women formed about 30 per cent of the membership, which included many of the country's diverse nationalities.
Nearly 60 per cent of the members had no party affiliations; nearly
25 per cent were Komsomols, and about 20 per cent were Communists. While the goals of the Godless Five-Year Plan had not been
realized, the prospects seemed bright; it was predicted that by 1934
there would be ten million members, and twenty-two million by
1937.[11]

A hint that these expectations were far too optimistic was given,
however, by the fact that by the end of 1932 there were serious ar-
rears in the payment of Godless dues.[12] In spite of efforts to improve
matters during 1933, only 45 per cent of the quarterly dues were paid
during the first quarter, and even less in the second quarter.[13]

In 1930 and 1931 a change was noted in the work of the Godless.
Iaroslavskii declared: "We must show how, in this transition period,
to set up our antireligious work so that it will be subordinated to the
problems of the class struggle, to the problems of socialist construction. . . ."[14] In answer to the efforts of ecclesiastical enemies at
home and abroad antireligious propaganda should strive for the creation of Godless collective farms, for the sowing of "Godless hectares,"
and for the organization of workers' Godless brigades, shops, and
factories.[15] In 1931 the Godless leaders were told that they "must
make clear how the League of Militant Godless as a whole, from the
lowest cell to the Central Council, by antireligious propaganda and
by direct participation in socialist construction, has helped the Party
and the Soviet land in the struggle for the tempos of socialist construction, for quality, for the further development of socialist
building."[16]

The trade-unions, which had been instructed by the Sixteenth Congress of the Communist party to improve their antireligious work,
undertook to do so late in 1930.

They called for special efforts to train antireligious workers and
more funds for antireligious activities; the press and radio facilities
of the trade-unions were also instructed to participate.[17] Similarly,
in 1930 the newspaper of the Communist League of Youth called for

renewed efforts to win the youth of the land away from the influence of religion,[18] and in 1931 the Ninth Congress of the Komsomol decreed that its antireligious work must increase, especially among the sectarians. "The Ninth Congress lays great stress upon the importance of developing an antireligious movement among the children and of instilling a materialistic viewpoint in them." [19]

Much of the antireligious effort among the industrial workers went into the formation of "Godless shock brigades" — squads of workers who had pledged themselves to set an example in fulfilling their tasks for the socialist cause, as well as carrying on antireligious work. These brigades had begun in 1929; by July, 1931, there were some thirty-two hundred of them helping to expand the industrial production in harmony with the thesis that "antireligion has a productional significance." In order to end the usual disruption of work at religious festivals the Godless leaders declared: "It is one of the obligations of the League of Militant Godless to popularize widely the idea of the productional significance of antireligious propaganda." [20] This meant that where antireligious work was well done there was a sharp reduction in absenteeism on Easter in comparison with ordinary working days; where it was weak, the number of holiday absences was considerable. Many of the Communist League of Youth were eager participants in this sort of work. The Komsomols in a Moscow furniture factory at Easter, 1931, were reported to be competing to set new records as well as enrolling new members of the Godless and creating Godless shock brigades.[21]

In addition to efforts to boost production, the Godless sought to improve the living conditions of the workers. Noting that life in barracks had a demoralizing effect on the workers, the Godless at a construction site in the Urals undertook to clean up one of the barracks and to organize proper recreation for the inmates. As the work progressed, the barrack adopted the title of "Godless," organized a library, and fought drunkenness and card-playing. Antireligious lectures were organized, as well as drama, musical, and other groups. Some of the Godless undertook to make the dining room neat and to adorn it with flowers. The laundry and the sanitary facilities were also taken in hand. Especial efforts were made to interest the women of the enterprise in discussions, reports, antireligious plays or moving pictures, the reading of newspapers and periodical articles, picnics, and similar activities.[22]

An article in the antireligious press in 1932 illustrates the largely non-Godless activity of the Godless:

> We must learn to live in a cultured manner, to spend our leisure hours in a cultured manner, to enjoy ourselves in a cultured manner. In the new order of life there is no room for drinking, card-playing, hooliganism. There is also no room for religious rites and superstitions. The Godless must struggle for the socialist transformation of life, for the building up of new institutions: crèches, children's corners, common dining halls, mechanical laundries, and so on. . . . The tasks facing the Godless of the cities are of peculiar importance: they must reconstruct the whole way of life. The Militant Godless must be in the first ranks for the economic reconstruction of the life of the city. Each Godless member must be attached to a certain street, and his aim should be to make that street exemplary. In our cities we often find an old church standing side by side with a club. Therefore an enlightening, explanatory effort must be organized for closing all centers of these black, demoniacal forces. The Godless must be active warriors against dirt, against antisanitary conditions in our streets and apartments, our eating houses, bathhouses, hairdressers'.[23]

While these passages still breathed hostility to religion, the chief emphasis is on attaining the economic and social goals of the period, with the antireligious struggle relegated to a minor place.

In the agricultural sphere a similar trend may be observed. In 1930 an article in *Pravda* stated that the organization of collective farms had raised the problem of freeing the peasants from a petty-bourgeois world outlook, of freeing them from all religion. At the same time, collectivization had created the conditions necessary for solving this problem: for, it was declared, the collective-farm system freed the peasants from dependence upon nature, thanks to the new technique that it introduced. This, in turn, eliminated the basis for religion, which is largely a result of the inability of the ignorant to cope with the forces of nature. The demise of religion would not, however, take place without the assistance of the Godless; indeed, the kulaks and their priestly allies would fight the collectives with every weapon in their armories, so that a fierce struggle against religion was necessary in order to break the opposition to collectivization.[24]

By the summer of 1931, however, the emphasis was on economic matters. The Godless press urged its readers to be "in military readiness for the harvest campaign." They were to join collective farms, enroll peasants in them, or start new collectives. During the farm year the Godless were to form shock brigades to repair farm equipment, to sort and disinfect seed, and to retain the snow on the fields; at sowing time they were to form shock brigades of sowers and sow "Godless hectares." Antireligious work was required of them also — to discuss questions like "Lenin on religion," to secure antireligious printed matter for the kolkhoz, or to hold antireligious entertainments on holy days. During the harvest season the Godless were to push the work of getting in the crops, by seeking to get everyone into the fields on religious holidays, by organizing shock brigades, and by drawing others into the effort. And in season and out, they were to propagandize among the mass of the peasants by all mediums available. Special stress was to be given to winning the women over by praising the new way of life brought by crèches, kindergartens, and group meals.[25]

During 1932 the economic aspect of the work of the Godless was especially evident. Although the bulk of the peasants had joined the collective farms, during the harvest of 1932 the government experienced great difficulty in securing the compulsory deliveries of grain. In midsummer high government, Communist party and Soviet institutions had to concentrate on gathering and threshing the harvest. The Godless were included in this mobilization. Their leaders charged that the difficulties were caused by the furious opposition of kulak and priest to the new order of life, so that it was the duty of the Godless to expose this opposition and to lead the collective farmers to redoubled efforts in getting in the crops. Where antireligious work was weak the clergy intensified their efforts. Hence the militant atheists were to seek to fight idleness and drunkenness on religious holidays, to explain the latest concession of the government to the peasants, and to expose the eternal hostility of religion to the socialist order.[26]

Additional tasks assigned to the Godless were fighting illiteracy[27] and selling government bonds for the financing of socialist construction during the First Five-Year Plan.[28]

While much of the above activity of the Godless was economic in character, with little direct bearing upon religion, the effort to combat the celebration of religious festivals was both antireligious and economic in character. Year after year at the Christmas season and at Eastertide immense campaigns were organized to attract workers and peasants away from churches to social gatherings, pageants, moving pictures, plays, puppet shows, concerts, dancing, games, and other amusements, most of which were probably antireligious in flavor. A highly important part of the campaigns was the attempt to persuade workers and peasants to report for work on the festival days and to signify their hostility to God by working with extra zeal. On the whole, the Godless and their fellow workers among the Komsomols and the trade-unions announced gratifying successes; at Easter, 1930, many factories reported that they had fewer absentees than usual, and at a number of collective farms the plowing and the sowing proceeded without interruption.[29] Similar claims were made for the Christmas and Easter seasons in 1931 and 1932.

On the other hand, dismayed articles told of factories and collective farms where the antireligious work was slack, the clergy were active, and the number of absentees from work was greater than usual. In rural areas when religious festivals and Sundays were observed, drunkenness and brawls were frequent; crime and serious incidents increased at such times. As religious holidays were numerous during the summer, field work suffered.[30] Even members of a collective farm named "Bezbozhnik" (Godless) erred and strayed like lost sheep: they were very late in preparing for the 1932 sowing season, and many did not report for work on Easter Sunday and Monday — which facts caused the local reporter to question their right to the name of Godless.[31]

Perhaps absenteeism on religious grounds, along with the general slackness of labor discipline at this period, was partly responsible for a decree of November 15, 1932, punishing one day's unauthorized absence from work with deprivation of the right to ration cards for food and other articles and to use of the housing facilities of the enterprise concerned.[32] While a worker so punished could easily obtain another job and with it the rights he had lost, this legislation must have made observance of religious days more difficult.

The emphasis on economic efforts by the Godless did not, however, eliminate the direct attack upon religion. During 1930 and 1931 night-school courses known as "workers' antireligious universities" were set up in leading cities to train antireligious leaders and propagandists; they ran for two or two and one half years. Although they were greatly handicapped by lack of proper buildings, instructional materials, and instructors, these institutions numbered 44 in 1930 and 81 in 1931. There were also 3 "peasants' antireligious universities" in 1931. Their enrollment, not large at best, suffered heavily from withdrawals, but they did much to meet the pressing need for trained antireligious workers.[33] By 1933, however, there were only 27 of these antireligious universities.[34] In addition, antireligious training was given in some of the leading universities and in special institutes for that purpose.[35] Antireligious courses were widely given at lower levels; in 1933 there were 5020 elementary courses with 144,161 students, and 255 secondary courses with 4135 students.[36]

Antireligious work among school children continued. In 1931 Godless leaders from various parts of the country reported on their efforts to draw the children into this work in terms so optimistic as to indicate a great deal of enthusiasm among them. Indeed, the chief complaint was that they were left without proper guidance, so that sometimes their efforts were misdirected.[37] The authorities of the Commissariat of Education seem to have been remiss in their antireligious teaching and guidance, for an article in the newspaper *Bezbozhnik* in 1932 was highly critical of their failings.[38]

Development of antireligious museums reached a new peak during the First Five-Year Plan, with 44 in operation in 1930, many of them in once-famous churches and monasteries. Iaroslavskii reported that in 1929 the Central Antireligious Museum in Moscow was visited by 263,000 persons.[39] In 1932 an elaborate museum was set up in the Kazan Cathedral, one of the leading churches of Leningrad.[40]

The publication of antireligious printed matter likewise increased sharply after 1928. By 1930 the number of antireligious periodicals had risen from four in 1925 to twenty. The newspaper *Bezbozhnik,* with an average monthly circulation of 63,100 in 1928, distributed

473,000 copies per month in 1931. Similar, although smaller increases were obtained by the magazines *Bezbozhnik* and *Antireligioznik* (*Antireligious*). In the years 1927–1930, inclusive, these three periodicals published 43,600,000 copies.[41] In 1931 Iaroslavskii stated that the issue of nonperiodical antireligious literature had increased from 700,000 printed sheets in 1927 to 50,000,000 (800,000,000 pages) in 1930. He added that the shortage of paper had compelled the Godless to curtail the publication of newspapers and books, so that the demands of the masses could not be met.[42]

In the ten years ending in 1932 some 40,000,000 copies of antireligious books and pamphlets were published, always in editions of at least 10,000 copies. Outstanding achievements were the issuing of a *Workers' Antireligious Textbook,* which in 1931 went into its sixth edition of 100,000 copies, and the *Peasants' Antireligious Textbook,* whose sixth edition in 1931 consisted of 200,000 copies.[43]

The latter work, of 383 pages, was a very skillfully written text for the use of antireligious agitators and study groups. The first part, "Religion and Its Class Role," expounded the standard Godless theory that religion has always served the privileged classes to the detriment of the interests of the laboring masses; especially during the collectivization of agriculture in the Soviet Union the clergy allegedly exerted every effort to prevent the success of the collective farms. The second section dealt with the conflict of science and religion, charging that religion had always combated true science and that there could be no compromise between them. The text then launched into an explanation of the universe and of life on earth based on materialistic concepts. For its explanation of the development of forms of animal and vegetable life the book drew heavily on Darwin. The question of the existence of a soul in man was answered by an explanation of the working of the nervous system, the brain, instincts, conditioned reflexes, and the ductless glands. The final part of the book treated the history of religion and the church, seeking to show that religion evolved out of attempts to explain natural phenomena and that Christianity was simply a later and more complex form of earlier religions. The Gospel and the Bible, it asserted, lack any historical validity. The church inevitably became an ally of kings and emperors and assisted in the exploitation of the people. Invariably it fought progressive ideas, not stopping at the most frightful tortures. Other religions — Buddhism, Judaism, Islam, Lamaism — were no better; they all are hostile to socialism and the efforts of the people to build a better life, especially during the Five-Year Plan. But science and technique would overcome nature and destroy the foundations on which religion rests. It was the aim of the Godless to hasten the achievement of this goal.[44]

The extensive publication of antireligious printed matter did not, however, signify that it was always of high quality, nor was its effectiveness always great. In 1931 *Pravda* surveyed the antireligious efforts of some of the provincial newspapers and concluded that the provincial editors were failing badly, both quantitatively and qualitatively. In particular, many of the papers held that the growth of the collective-farm movement would automatically lead to the dying out of religion.[45] In 1932 *Pravda* even attacked the newspaper *Bezbozhnik* for having failed to organize well-planned, systematic agitation and resorting to spasmodic "campaigns" and "attacks." An unexpected "defeat" in midwinter was followed by a one-month "storm attack" to overcome the defeat; but the attack was not properly pushed, so that the editors were forced to admit that "the results of the month's campaign are so unsatisfactory that it is necessary to raise the alarm." But after this they were silent, and it was not until six weeks later that they recalled the campaign, stating that "the storm month is again a failure." *Pravda* added that the newspaper was prone to abstract slogans and neglected to give concrete materials.[46]

Even *Pravda* itself was open to criticism. In 1930 it carried a goodly quantity of antireligious material, but in 1931 it had less than 100 inches of column on the subject. In 1932 the amount increased to 269 inches; but 107 inches of this dealt with non-Orthodox churches abroad, especially the Roman Catholic church; another 112 inches treated the domestic scene. The Russian Orthodox church was not directly attacked, and most of the domestic material consisted of reports on the progress of antireligious work. As the total column length of *Pravda* was about 208,000 inches, the 269 inches of antireligious material amounted only to .13 per cent.

It is not without significance that the Soviet periodicals rarely attacked the Russian Orthodox church, but rather centered their fire on the Pope, who had made utterances regarded as extremely hostile. In his report to the Central Committee of the Communist party in 1930, Stalin referred to the "furious howl" raised by their enemies — "the capitalists and their press, the Pope and all sorts of bishops, Social Democrats and 'Russian' Mensheviks. . . ."[47] A fiery editorial in *Antireligioznik* in 1930 declared that clergy and reactionaries abroad were preparing a new crusade against the Soviet Union, with the Pope as the most ardent leader.[48]

When one surveys the antireligious movement during the First Five-Year Plan, it becomes evident that this was a striking phenomenon. Rarely has anything like it been seen, either in scale or in the passion, enthusiasm, and drive of the participants. On the other hand, the momentum of the drive soon was spent and the heated passions soon cooled. In 1931 and 1932 complaints became more and more frequent in the Godless press that antireligious work was poorly organized and largely confined to campaigns at religious holidays. While in the cities there was often much activity, in the outlying areas liaison was ofttimes sketchy and little work was done.[49] The trade-unions were charged with neglect of antireligious work and failure to co-operate with the Godless cells.[50] Reports from a village in the Ukraine in 1932 indicated that antireligious work, once flourishing, had been forgotten, while the local priests were active and successful. Weakness was also noted in a village of Kazakhstan.[51]

In December, 1932, one of the Godless leaders told a conference that many of the Godless kolkhozes had taken a turn for the worse. "We know tens of Godless kolkhozes which in 1930 and 1931 worked quite well on the antireligious front, but with the end of 1931 and the beginning of 1932 complete collapse set in." The reasons, he stated, were that they were unable to adjust their propaganda to the changed conditions, and the older approach was no longer effective. There still were believers in the Godless collectives, and the struggle against religion was far from over.[52] The Stalino coal-mining region reported the decline of antireligious work and the revival of the activity of priests and sectarians. Although during the Christmas holidays there were many idlers, the trade-unions refused to organize antireligious work. Even some of the Communists and Komsomols celebrated Christmas with drinking parties.[53] Many of the Godless did not work during the religious holidays; at one enterprise, 36 per cent of the workers were absent from work at Christmas.[54]

Another complaint was that many of the antireligious groups existed only on paper. Iaroslavskii declared in 1930 that some of the towns and villages that had declared themselves Godless were well on the way to becoming so, "but when entire districts are declared Godless, in a county where there is nothing, no culture, no [antireligious] work — this is a joke. . . ."[55] In Novorossiisk the Godless, instead of the thousands claimed, had very few members, and in some cases no one knew whether a Godless cell existed or not. The City Council of the League of Militant Godless was able to find only 7 of its 17 members.[56] Likewise, although the records for the province of Leningrad listed 200,000 Godless in the rural areas, a tour of the province disclosed that antireligious work was sometimes unheard of, and when a Godless representative was finally located, he declared that religion was dying a natural death and that antireligious propaganda only hindered the process.[57]

The antireligious work of the trade-unions and the Komsomol also declined markedly, especially in 1931 and 1932. In the province of Moscow, although antireligious lectures were well attended, the workers' clubs rarely scheduled them, and the club libraries were ill supplied with antireligious reading matter; the trade-unions provided scant funds for these purposes.[58] The Komsomol was accused of limiting its antireligious activities to the anti-Christmas and anti-Easter campaigns. In 1930 a trade-union congress noted that "the antireligious work of the Komsomol has become more feeble during the last few years," and the Second Congress of the League of Militant Godless stated that in most of the Komsomol organizations there was no antireligious work.[59] In 1931 the lack of Komsomol antireligious work was again noted, and investigations showed that in many counties only 20 per cent of the Komsomols were members of the League of Militant Godless.[60] In 1932, some of the Komsomol organizations neglected antireligious propaganda among the new workers, many of whom were still religious. Some of the Komsomols failed to report for work on religious holidays.[61]

During these later years of the First Five-Year Plan the Russian church survived, albeit with difficulty. In one respect, however, it apparently fared better than before; there was a marked decline in reports of ecclesiastics punished for counterrevolutionary activity. The Godless press still accused the clerics of plotting, but cited few instances in which these charges were proved. Late in 1930 a priest of Stalingrad was tried for concealing church valuables and for carrying on counterrevolutionary propaganda, but was acquitted.[62] In 1931 there were reports of two substantial conspiracies in which ecclesiastics were allegedly implicated. In Ivanovo a monarchist organization with seven priests among the members, and Bishop Avgustin as leader, was reported to have its center in a church. The organization was charged with working for the restoration of a tsar. In the North Caucasus and the Ukraine a widespread conspiracy allegedly headed by Bishop Alexii Bui and numbering some twenty monks and priests among its members was accused of plotting against the Soviet regime and of encouraging opposition to taxation and grain collections. In neither of these instances was the outcome of the case indicated.[63]

While the press less frequently charged the clergy with overt counterrevolutionary acts, there continued to be reports of attempts to defeat some of the Soviet efforts. In a village of the Ural area the clergy allegedly warned that those who took part in the campaign to eliminate adult illiteracy would be barred from church, and nuns declared that any woman who went to the teaching center would be committing an unpardonable sin.[64] Accusations that the clergy and their supporters were continuing to combat the collective farms were especially widespread, with the opposition taking very diverse forms. One device frequently reported was the miraculous renovation of ikons, whose colors allegedly were secretly brightened by the application of acid — a phenomenon interpreted as a sign that God or the Virgin was present to lead against the Godless kolkhoz. In one county of Moscow over thirteen hundred ikons were allegedly so treated.[65]

Another device ascribed to the religious foes of the collective farms was the spreading of rumors. These were said to include reports that the Pope, after his utterances against Godless Russia in 1930, was sending troops to overthrow the Soviet regime; prophecies of the end of the world and of the appearance of Antichrist, who would put his seal on all who joined the collectives; warnings that on the collective farms the old people would be made into fertilizer; reports that St. Serafim had manifested himself to a nun, telling her that he who entered a kolkhoz would be struck down by a rain of fire from heaven; and many others.[66] When locusts appeared in the fields in the summer of 1931, priests and kulaks were reported to have declared that previously, hearing the prayers and the *Te Deums* of the people, God had banished the pests to the depths of the earth. "Now the fields are being plowed with the machinery of Antichrist and public prayers are no longer attended. No wonder that the pests have been brought back to the surface. . . ."[67] A priest taking a religious census of his parish allegedly asked his parishioners: "How shall I write: for God or for the kolkhoz?"[68] Or a destitute wanderer, asking for alms, told his benefactors that he had been brought to this pass by entering a collective farm, where he had been stripped of all his possessions. The effect of his remarks, according to Iaroslavskii, who related the story, had, however, been destroyed when it was proved that the pilgrim was actually the former deacon of a neighboring church."[69]

Iaroslavskii also cited the texts of "letters from Heaven," which, according to him, had made their appearance in widely separated places:

> Dear kolkhoznik [collective farmer] comrades: I send you a letter from the heavenly kingdom, in which I ask you to withdraw from the kolkhoz and to take upon yourselves the shock-work of ruining the kolkhoz. Who does not assume this task will go directly to Hell, while he who assumes it will be received by Me among the holy saints and will attain the heavenly kingdom.

Another letter read:

> I am thy Lord God, and I say unto thee: The moment has come when the Devil will lead the people astray into his nets — into the kolkhozes. Who is not seduced by the kolkhoz will be saved, but in the days to come I shall wipe out all the kolkhozniks. And I shall also wipe out those who do not wear the cross on their breasts.[70]

The truth or falsity of these allegations cannot be ascertained. It is equally impossible to check the validity of the reports that the Orthodox clergy were coming more and more to accept the existence of the Soviet regime and to adapt themselves to it, and in some instances to become its supporters.

As early as 1929 Iaroslavskii warned that in many places the clergy were making determined efforts to replace the kulaks in the parish vestries with poor peasants, or in the cities to elect workers as vestrymen.[71] This practice apparently became widespread, as the Godless writers repeatedly expressed alarm. Bishop Alexii of Rylsk was even reported to have told his clergy that they should see that farmhands and poor and middle peasants should be elected to the vestries, as the former members, largely kulaks or merchants, gave an obvious class character to the churches and frightened away the masses.[72] This attempt to give a proletarian tinge to the church did not, however, placate the Godless, who claimed that it was merely a trick to deceive the laboring people. "Behind the 'toiling' vestry stands the whole pack of kulaks." [73]

Some of the clergy also sought to retain the support of the women by giving them a greater role in the parish. Deaconesses were named; women became parish treasurers. Even the vestries were opened to women; in many cases they held more than half of the posts, and in some instances the entire vestry was composed of women.[74]

If the Godless are to be believed, many of the churchmen even gave their support to the collective-farm movement. Whether this was done for ulterior motives, as the Godless charged, or out of conviction cannot be ascertained. In Rossoshanskii county the local bishop told his clergy, under threat of unfrocking, to break their ties with the kulaks and to align themselves with the collective farmers. A parish priest was reported to have declared that the elimination of the kulaks was "a work blessed by God." Another urged his flock to devote a church festival day to preparation for sowing rather than to worship. Still another pastor declared he would confess only collective farmers; a fourth urged the peasants to join a kolkhoz, as it was pleasing to God.[75] Priests of a number of villages where collectivization was strongly entrenched allegedly told their parishioners that in the future they would receive only collective farmers at communion and confession; individual peasants were told to stay away.[76]

Antireligious sources also reported that ecclesiastics had supported various Soviet activities, such as the establishment of kindergartens, dramatic groups, and reading rooms. One priest helped prepare decorations for a reading room; another actually served as librarian. In another village the priest, in addition to officiating in church, allegedly performed with a Soviet dramatic group in a play against religion! Many priests were reported to have become leaders of choral groups organized in village clubs, reading rooms, and similar institutions. Other reports told of priests who aided the campaign to sell government bonds or in the collection of taxes. One cleric even organized religious concerts in church and bought bonds with the proceeds. The comment of the author who presented these examples was: "All this was done to create the impression that religion and the church are not hostile to socialist construction, that churchmen and sectarians are supporters of the Soviet regime." [77]

Other pro-Soviet priests were reported to have worked for higher production of farm commodities. One pastor urged the villagers to organize a brigade to kill woodchucks; another from the pulpit exhorted his flock: "In the name of the Holy Ghost, pay the installments on the tractors." Several cases were cited where priests urged their parishioners into the fields even on high religious festival days during the harvest season. A Soviet newspaper told of the clergy of a church in Slaviansk who sallied forth in a body to the fields of a collective farm, where, working as a shock brigade, they outdid all the rest in the harvesting.[78]

Other ecclesiastics supported industrialization during the First Five-Year Plan. A priest of the Urals warmly praised the progress made, and a number of others were reported to have willingly surrendered the bells of their churches to aid in the campaign to industrialize.[79]

Politically as well as economically some of the clergy, according to Soviet sources, adopted a pro-Soviet attitude. Several of the revolutionary holidays were celebrated by churchmen — notably the anniversary of Lenin's death, May 1, and November 7. Some priests were reported to have led groups of young people in singing the "International," and others used revolutionary and Soviet tunes as the airs for hymns. In Omsk, crucifixes were made with hammer and sickle imposed upon them, and the inscription: "Proletarians of all lands, unite!" In 1931, at the time of the election of new vestrymen, the home of a village priest was draped in red bunting and adorned with various slogans.[80]

Some of the clergy, especially the Renovationists, are alleged to have made efforts to prove that religion and communism were in harmony. A priest of the Central Black-Soil Region wrote: "In its essence, in earthly life Christianity is contrary neither to communism nor to the Soviet regime. The first Christian congregation was purely communist — one soul and one property for all." Another priest is reported to have urged restoration of the principles of Christian communism and to have stressed the "real, revolutionary character" of Christianity — especially its hatred of the rich. A third, calling himself a true follower of Marx and Lenin, preached: "The church and the priesthood are not against communism, industrialization, and collectivization, but on the contrary, the church, together with the Soviet regime, is passing through all the transitional stages of the struggle of the working class and together they will proceed to the collectivization of the country on the basis of co-operation and industrialization." [81] A Renovationist archbishop, Timofei of Chuvashia, is alleged to have petitioned for reduction of his taxes on the grounds that during his seven-year incumbency he "has observed his obligation to strengthen the authority of the Soviet regime, to protect it both from attacks of certain groups of churchmen and from distortions of the general line of the Party and the government on the part of individual workers of the governmental apparatus." [82]

If reports from Soviet sources are credible, a number of churchmen took up the study of Marxism, subscribed to Marxist periodicals, and in other ways sought to study the dominant philosophy. Archbishop Pavel Piatigorskii of Minsk, a follower of Metropolitan Sergii, sought to convince the antireligionists that the Soviet regime was not an opponent of religion in general, but only sought to suppress anti-Soviet and counterrevolutionary activity on the part of churchmen. He cited Marx in an effort to prove that the latter had not been hostile to religion as such, but had merely condemned clerical counter-revolution.[83]

These reports, which probably had some foundation, indicate the existence of a considerable tendency among the Russian Orthodox clergy to make their peace with the Soviet regime and even to support it. It is impossible to determine the motives for this trend — whether it was out of sincere conviction that the new regime was beneficial to the masses; whether it was a result of Soviet punitive measures against the clergy; or whether the clergy sometimes found that their parishioners were now reconciled to and even enthusiastic about the collective farms and other aspects of the new Soviet life. Possibly all of these factors played a part in inducing this attitude. In addition, it should be borne in mind that this pro-Soviet trend among the clergy was not new. Signs of it had appeared in 1919; the Living Church movement had been strongly in favor of the Soviet regime since 1922, and Patriarch Tikhon had several times urged loyalty to it. Metropolitan Sergii, Acting Locum Tenens, had even ordered prayers for the Soviet authorities because as Russians the churchmen should feel that it was *their* regime, that its griefs and joys were theirs. This policy on the part of Metropolitan Sergii continued during the First Five-Year Plan and subsequently.

In February, 1930, *Pravda* reported a press conference between Metropolitan Sergii and foreign newspaper correspondents in Moscow. He was asked how the church could continue to exist when the clergy and the active parishioners were disenfranchised and hence subject to deprivation of food cards and of their residences in Moscow. He replied that they were misinformed; most of the believers enjoyed full rights and rendered the churchmen sufficient support. He further declared that the churchmen were not discriminated against in respect to eviction from their homes. When asked about the recent charges of the Pope and the Archbishop of Canterbury regarding persecution of religion in the U.S.S.R., he replied that these utterances were attempts to whip up a war against the Soviet Union and should be condemned as contrary to the spirit of Christianity. The Pope, he added, was an open enemy of the Orthodox church. As to measures of the Soviet authorities such as curtailment of bell-ringing, the abolition of Sunday and other religious holidays, and the closing of churches, he stated that they had not caused any real damage to the church and that there was no shortage of worshipers.[84]

Shortly thereafter, Metropolitan Sergii gave an interview to members of the Soviet press. In response to questions he denied flatly that there was persecution of religion in the U.S.S.R. While churches were sometimes closed, this was done according to the wishes of the population. Punishment inflicted upon priests was not a result of their religious status, but was a consequence of the refusal of some of them to be loyal toward the Soviet regime. He admitted that the current condition of the church caused him anxiety, but said that "the Divine Light cannot be extinguished and that with time it will be firmly established in the hearts of men." While the state of the church had grown "more difficult," this, he believed, was a result of the radical changes the country was experiencing and would, he hoped, not lead to the extinction of faith. He was sharply critical of the utterances of the Pope, which, he said, were an attempt to stir up a war against the U.S.S.R. and which he condemned as contrary to the way Christ would have acted. The Orthodox of Russia needed no help.[85]

In 1931 Metropolitan Sergii again showed his loyalty to the Soviet regime in a letter to the Patriarch of Constantinople complaining of the latter's acceptance of Metropolitan Evlogii, administrator of the Russian churches in Western Europe, under his jurisdiction. For a time Evlogii had accepted the authority of Sergii, but he had broken away from this allegiance because of his unwillingness to observe Sergii's ban on political activity and especially on hostility to the Soviet regime. Metropolitan Sergii stated that he and the Synod had removed Metropolitan Evlogii from his position as head of the Russian Orthodox churches of Western Europe and had ordered him to submit to trial by a tribunal of Russian bishops. Sergii objected to the action of the Patriarch in harboring the defiant Metropolitan Evlogii.[86]

If Russian religious circles abroad may be believed, Metropolitan Sergii was actually not as pleased with the state of the Russian church as his published statements indicated, for, as stated earlier (Chap. IX) Russian sources in Paris printed what was termed a petition from Metropolitan Sergii to Smidovich, chairman of the Commission on Questions of Cults, dated February 19, 1930. The document protested against discrimination against the church and its clergy in respect to insurance rates, taxes, rents, housing, the closing of churches, and related matters.[87] Although the protest was presented by Professor Paul Miliukov and others close to the Russian church in Paris, there is no satisfactory evidence available as to its authenticity.

But, while the Orthodox clergy were testifying to their loyalty to the Soviet regime and the Godless were moderating somewhat the intensity of their campaign against religion, the struggle for men's minds continued. The church sought to hold its followers and, if possible, gain new ones from the rising generations; the Godless sought the complete disappearance of all religion. By 1932, what results had been achieved in this contest?

As has already been indicated, the League of Militant Godless had grown greatly. Although its membership never approached the figure of seven million by the end of 1932, and the goal of seventeen million by December, 1933, remained a dream, by May, 1932, the enrollment totaled over five and one half million. The closing of churches continued, although at a slower pace. While no over-all statistics exist, isolated examples suggest the extent of the change. Moscow, which before the revolution had had over 460 Orthodox churches, by January 1, 1930, had 224 functioning Orthodox churches, even though the population of the city had increased by nearly 50 per cent.[88] By the beginning of 1933 there were approximately 140 houses of worship, of which about one hundred were Orthodox.[89] The northern town of Kargopol had had 23 churches and 2 cloisters before the revolution; by 1932, "no churches with their tiresome bell-ringing exist any more," and the cloisters had been put to other uses.[90] A county of the central agricultural region, 80 per cent collectivized, had closed 8 of its 19 churches by the end of 1931, and 2 more were closed in January, 1932. Several of the remaining churches were usually rather empty. On the other hand, two large villages, only partially collectivized, kept 3 large churches filled with huge congregations. The commentator asserted that where collectivization was a real success, little religion survived; where the collectivization was weak, religion was strong.[91] On the whole, the scanty evidence seems to corroborate the estimate of Dr. Paul Anderson that by 1933, 50 to 60 per cent of the churches had been closed.[92]

Occasionally priests, under the influence of the times, renounced the cloth. In 1929 a Leningrad newspaper reported that within a fortnight three priests, each of whom had served for twenty years or more, had become laymen,[93] and in March, 1930, *Bezbozhnik* printed the names of twelve priests who had recently given up holy orders.[94] Occasionally this process, often a result of political or economic difficulties encountered, was ascribed to the conviction that the priestly function interfered with the efforts to build socialism. A Ukrainian priest who had served for nine years came to the conclusion that the church, which had defended the monarchy, had no more utility, "as it hampers the construction of socialism in one country." [95] Iaroslavskii in 1931 claimed that this abandonment of the cloth had assumed great proportions; ". . . of late years we have had a mass renunciation of their trade by priests (literally thousands of them)." [96]

Another indication that the Godless had achieved some success by 1932 is given by various evidence (although by no means fully reliable) as to the number of citizens who had broken with religion. In January, 1930, the antireligious section of the Institute of Philosophy attached to the Communist Academy made an investigation, using unsigned questionnaires, of the extent of belief among 12,000 workers of several Moscow factories. Unfortunately, only 3000 of those approached turned in completed questionnaires — a fact that severely impairs the reliability of the inquiry. Of those who did reply, 88.8 per cent declared themselves nonbelievers, and 11.2 per cent were believers. As might have been expected, the men were less religious than the women, and the younger workers were less so than the older ones. None of the Komsomols among them were believers. Nearly 40 per cent had ceased to believe before the Revolution of 1917.[97] The Godless of the city of Kremenchug presented statistics on the membership of the religious organizations in their city. In 1930 there were 22,511 members, over two thirds of them Orthodox; in 1931 the number had dwindled to 10,970, with nine tenths of them Orthodox.[98]

Service in the Red Army seems to have done much to shake the faith of the men. When the new recruits reported to a cavalry regiment, a questionnaire showed that nearly half were firm believers and 22 per cent were wavering in their faith. After a year's work by the cell of the Godless, numbering about forty persons, during which the men had been exposed to lectures, reports, antireligious social evenings, moving pictures, readings, and similar indoctrination, only 15 per cent were still definitely religious, while nearly two thirds of the contingent were nonbelievers.[99] This information, coming from Godless sources, is, of course, ex parte testimony. It does, however, suggest the sort of influence to which recruits were subjected, and it would be strange if it did not produce some result.

In 1930 S. Vol'fson, a Communist, published the result of his investigation in the somewhat backward area of Belorussia. As has been already stated in Chapter XI, he found the workers of twenty cities were 98.5 per cent unbelievers; 82.2 per cent of the collective farmers were nonbelievers, while the average for the whole population indicated that 65.4 per cent were nonbelievers.[100]

In 1932 *Antireligioznik* contained a long, relatively objective article on the relations between the collective farm and the church in the rather backwoods area of Luga, based on the personal observations of its author. He found that the collectives, which embraced about half of the peasants, were greatly furthering the dying out of religious practices. The earlier wave of closing churches had spent itself and had even done harm by causing a sympathetic revulsion against the forceful methods sometimes used. But the growth of the collectives had contributed to the decline of the local churches. The author cited one church which had not been under pressure and which was not affected by antireligious propaganda, as it was almost nonexistent there; the local teachers were indifferent toward religion. Nevertheless, the priest resigned his living, as his income had dwindled away as a result of collectivization. According to his article the author's conclusion was that where collectivization flourished the church withered. On a Sunday he visited the church in a village three quarters collectivized and found only three old women present at service, although it was a rest day for the kolkhoz. The older and stronger the kolkhoz, he decided, the less religious observance there was. On the other hand, he cited a newly formed collective which spent three days on a religious holiday at the height of the harvest season; during the resultant drunken brawls two persons were killed and one seriously wounded.[101] Here again the testimony is not free from bias, and yet it should not be disregarded.

Thus there is good reason to believe that by 1932 the Russian Orthodox church had suffered a considerable loss of members. Nevertheless, there is also strong evidence that religion was far from dead. In February, 1930, in his interview with foreign newspapermen, Metropolitan Sergii, as has been mentioned earlier, claimed about thirty thousand parishes and 163 bishops.[102] Thus, while the church had lost significantly, it still possessed a sizable organization. Even the losses, probably large, between 1930 and the end of 1932, did not by any means wipe out the church. Indeed, in one important respect it gained during these years; according to one of the Godless, the dissident groups like the Renovationists and the factions of Grigorii and Iosif had largely collapsed and their members had rejoined the patriarchal church.[103]

Moreover, in spite of the efforts of the Godless, the school children were by no means completely hostile to religion. An investigation by questionnaire of 67 elementary pupils in a region of the Middle Volga, made in 1931, indicated that perhaps 60 per cent were non-believers, but some categories of peasant children included 50 or 60 per cent of believers.[104] In another school the wall-newspapers (a sort of handwritten bulletin), run by religious pupils, urged the others to go to church on the First of May and to burn lamps before their ikons. The teachers in several widely separated localities attended church, refused to take part in antireligious education, or otherwise showed their religious attitudes.[105] In a school of the Belorussian S.S.R. a Komsomol brigade discovered that ikons, lamps, and paintings of saints were still hanging in the schoolroom, and on the eve of religious festivals the teacher, who tried to interest the children in religion, decorated the ikon corner and lighted the lamps.[106] An investigator in a rural county near Leningrad discovered that half the children openly professed their belief; in one village, all the children were religious.[107]

Even a few of the Komsomols were still not hostile to religion. Four Komsomol girls went regularly to church and even crawled beneath an ikon in the hope of curing ailments. Others were married in church.[108] In one village the secretary of the Komsomol cell even took part in voluntary Saturday work to repair a church, while in another locality a group of Komsomols attended the church funeral of one of their number. A certain "holy man" somehow gained great influence over one of the active Komsomols, who became a novice and later wore a crown of barbed wire, causing drops of blood to run from his brow.[109]

If occasional members of the Communist Youth were thus derelict, it is not surprising that workers just come from the villages were often religious. Iaroslavskii stated in 1932 that about one third of the women trade-union members were believers, and one quarter of the men. Even those who had broken with religion still retained religious habits or practices.[110] Often the religious outlook of the workers caused numerous absences from work during festivals, according to reports from all parts of the country.[111]

Far more than the factory, the village remained a center of religious influence. While the establishment of collective farms reduced the amount of belief, the peasants persisted in celebrating religious festivals at great length, especially at newly formed collective farms and among the individual peasants; the firmly established kolkhozes were less apt to stop work for religious holidays.[112] The peasants, whether members of collectives or not, often retained ikons in their homes. Even the wife of a candidate for the Communist party had one.[113] Many of the collective farmers who regarded themselves as emancipated from religion still kept ikons in their homes, saying: "I do not believe, but ikons harm nobody. Let them hang." Often they had their children baptized and their deceased buried with the rites of the church and had church weddings.[114]

On the other hand, sometimes the ikons were retained largely as decorations and occasionally stood side by side with pictures of Marx or Lenin; in one home, an ikon hung beside an antireligious poster.[115]

Like the antireligious poster and the ikon on the same wall, both the Godless movement and the Russian Orthodox church were in existence at the end of the First Five-Year Plan. The church had received some severe blows from the expanding Godless movement and from the momentous changes in Soviet life, and yet it had survived. The evidence strongly indicates, however, that, even though the Godless movement had lost momentum by 1933, the church had been more gravely weakened during the years from 1928 to 1933 than during any other period.

CHAPTER XIV

"Religion Is Very Long-lived"

IN THE YEARS between the First Five-Year Plan and the outbreak of war in 1941, the U.S.S.R. experienced momentous developments. The Second and Third Five-Year Plans achieved rapid industrialization and almost complete collectivization of agriculture. Foreign relations, already strained by Japanese aggression in 1931, were further impaired by the rise of a hostile Germany and by a fresh series of aggressions. Internally, Soviet life, which had become more normal after the rigors of the First Five-Year Plan, became involved in the great purges of 1936–1938, resulting from the accumulated stresses and animosities of earlier years. Then came World War II. During 1939 and 1940 the U.S.S.R., thanks to its apparent harmony with Hitler's Germany, was able to move into much of the border territory lost after the end of the First World War, only to be rudely shocked by the German onslaught in June, 1941.

A period of such vast importance was certain to have great effect upon the Russian Orthodox church. For several years there was no essential change in its situation. Legally the clergy were still disenfranchised, subject to substantial disabilities, including deprivation of the right to send their children to universities.[1] The OGPU, the political police agency, was abolished in 1934, but its functions were transferred to the NKVD (People's Commissariat of Internal Affairs);[2] the latter, although in theory subject to control by state prosecutors,[2] differed little from its predecessor, as it enjoyed the right to confine enemies of the regime (which might include members of the clergy) without formal trial. Likewise, the taxation system bore heavily on the clergy, who were in the nonworking category. A worker with three dependents would pay 117 rubles tax per year upon an income of 250 rubles per month; a priest under similar circumstances would pay 580 rubles. A worker with an income of 6000 rubles would pay a tax of 472 rubles, while a priest with the same income would be taxed 2620 rubles.[3]

By 1936, however, the government removed the ban on admission of children of nonlaboring persons into the institutions of higher education, so that the children of the clergy enjoyed the same educational rights as other children.[4] The so-called Stalin Constitution of 1936 even removed the distinction between "working" and "nonworking" citizens. All enjoyed the right to vote and other rights and privileges of citizens, "irrespective of race and national origin, religious profession, educational standing" and other charactcristics. On the other hand, the ban on religious propaganda remained unchanged, for article 124 stated: "With the aim of securing freedom of conscience for the citizens, the church in the USSR is separated from the state and the school from the church. Freedom of celebrating religious cults and freedom of antireligious propaganda is recognized for all citizens."[5] Stalin himself upheld electoral rights for the clergy, for he flatly rejected amendments that would have forbidden the performance of religious rites and deprived the clergy and other quondam foes of the regime of their right to elect and be elected. He declared that it was no longer necessary to deprive the clergy and similar groups of full rights, since many were now no longer hostile, and those that were still foes were not dangerous.[6]

One significant benefit that this change in climate brought was more favorable treatment in respect to income tax. Although the clergy were not as lightly taxed as were the workers and the artists and writers, they paid taxes equivalent to those on members of the "free professions" (doctors, lawyers, and others having private practices),[7] which in 1940 were moderate compared to the present American income-tax rates.

Another indication of a changed attitude toward the Russian Orthodox church was given in 1936. The noted poet Demian Bednyi had written an *opéra comique* one of the scenes of which was a burlesque of the christening of the people of Kiev in 987 by the Grand Prince Vladimir. The All-Union Committee on Affairs of the Arts on November 11, 1936, condemned this opera on several points, one of which was "an antihistorical abusive portrayal of the christening of Rus, which was actually a constructive step in the history of the Russian people, as it furthered the bringing together of the Slavonic peoples with peoples of higher culture." The committee referred to the adoption of Christianity as "one of the greatest historic events of Kievan Rus," whose significance was that it brought the Slavs into contact with the peoples of Europe and their higher culture. "It is very well known that the clergy, especially the Greek clergy, considerably furthered the spreading of literacy in Kievan Rus, of book learning, of foreign languages, and so on. The first translation of foreign books . . . was done in conjunction with the adoption of Christianity by the Slavs."[8]

This reappraisal of the historic role of the church was followed by further recognition that in earlier times the church had played a constructive role. Moving pictures and plays showed churchmen of old as ardent Russian patriots, encouraging national heroes like Alexander Nevskii and Dmitrii of the Don to fight for the fatherland. In 1938 *Izvestiia* printed a long article by one Professor Bakhrushkin stressing the value of Christianity to the rising Russian state of Grand Prince Vladimir.[9] This viewpoint was stated in greater detail in 1941 by the Godless leader F. Oleshchuk, in his book (in Russian) *Overcoming the Surviving Remnants of Religion*. He complained that antireligious lecturers felt Alexander Nevskii had no great historic merit merely because the church had canonized him; Oleshchuk insisted that the early monasteries in Russia had been a progressive force as centers of learning. While religion in general was always a reactionary, antiscientific ideology, sometimes the progressive movements of the masses had taken religious forms and hence it was incorrect to regard all aspects of religion at all times as reactionary.[10]

As this utterance suggests, the recognition of the Russian church as a partially useful institution, especially in stimulating patriotism, did not mean approval of the contemporary church. Similarly, when the seven-day week was again adopted in 1941, with Sunday as the day of rest,[11] this was probably done for purposes of industrial efficiency

rather than to facilitate churchgoing. Sunday was still so widely regarded as the traditional weekly holiday that it was perhaps desirable
to recognize that fact. Certain it is that until June, 1941, the Godless
movement continued to combat the influence of religion. The antireligious movement was weak when the church was still in strong
disfavor, and there was a revival of Godless activity after the concessions and the more favorable attitude toward the historic role of
the church. Moreover, after the relaxation of the legal disabilities
of the clergy in 1936, there was little evidence of further extension of
privileges to the church and its ministers.

There are abundant signs of an antireligious decline after the First
Five-Year Plan. In 1934 Iaroslavskii urged a checkup on the members
of the League of Militant Godless, which he admitted would probably
show a smaller enrollment, consoling himself with the remark: "but
why deceive ourselves with a great quantity of members who do not
work with us?"[12] Antireligious work in the public schools, in spite
of the efforts of the Commissariat of Education, was also in a bad
state in 1934, as most of the local officials took no interest in it. Although some of the teachers were continuing to combat religion, this
was done "in very few schools." As a result, usually only 5 or 10 per
cent of the pupils attended on religious holidays.[13]

Later reports spoke of the decline in antireligious work, which
Iaroslavskii ascribed to the great successes on the economic front,
where industry and collective agriculture seemed to be progressing
rapidly. Millions of people were turning from religion and the religious organizations were no longer trying to fight the collective farms.
Hence many of the Communists and the Godless felt that the battle
had been practically won and that there was no more need for the
League of Militant Godless. Unfortunately, he added, where the antireligious work slacked off the clergy and their followers raised their
heads.[14] In 1936 the Tenth Congress of the Komsomol was told of a
letter sent in by one of the girls of this organization: "Why write in
the [Komsomol] program that the Communist League of Youth
'patiently explains to the young the danger of superstition and religious prejudices.' For among the young there have been no believing
persons for a very long time."[15]

Oleshchuk, one of the Godless leaders, stated in 1936 that the antireligious movement had been declining since 1932. Some of the provincial organizations of the Godless had ceased to function and the overwhelming majority of the county organizations had also stopped work. Most of the city and village Godless cells had collapsed. The number of antireligious lectures, meetings, and other activities had fallen off sharply, and the antireligious press had declined markedly. In like manner, the preparation of new Godless workers had largely ceased, while many formerly active had shifted to other work.[16] In 1937 *Izvestiia* corroborated this analysis of the situation, pointing out that no one knew how many of the five million Godless members in 1932 actually remained; Iaroslavskii said there were two million in 1937, while Oleshchuk, responsible secretary, did not even name a total. The League of Militant Godless was experiencing "a marked organizational decline."[17]

The newspaper *Bezbozhnik*, which had had a circulation of 473,500 copies in 1931, closed late in 1934 — another sign of the slump in the Godless movement. It did not resume publication until 1938.[18] The two leading monthly periodicals of the Godless experienced a sharp drop in circulation at this time.[19]

In 1936, however, the situation changed. In February and March a plenum of the Central Committee of the Communist party stressed the need for intensive political activity (including antireligious work) by members of the party.[20] The Program of the Communist party was rewritten, with more emphasis on "the organization of antireligious propaganda, which will aid the actual liberation of the working masses from religious prejudices and the organization of the very widest scientific and enlightening and antireligious propaganda." The Program of the Komsomol was also rewritten to include a provision that the League "patiently explains to the youth the harm of superstition and religious prejudices, organizing for this purpose special groups and lectures on antireligious propaganda." Stalin himself proposed the wording of this passage.[21]

In response to these injunctions, several editorials in *Pravda* called for serious antireligious work, and *Izvestiia* also sounded the call. The League of Militant Godless, the trade-unions, the Communist League of Youth, and the Commissariat of Public Education were all rebuked for failing to give this matter proper attention.[22] As a result of this prodding, a conference of Communists of the city of Moscow adopted a strong resolution demanding intensification of mass political work, including antireligious propaganda, "which now has acquired exceptionally important significance." A congress of the Communist party of the Ukraine issued a directive: "The Congress devotes especial attention to the organization of antireligious propaganda, which at the present time is a completely forgotten part of our work." Many of the provincial committees of the Communist party also took up this work in intensive fashion.[23] Oleshchuk reported a revival of Godless activity in the second half of 1936,[24] while in 1937 he stated that the Komsomol, the trade-unions, and the organs of public education were seriously taking up antireligious work, and the press had greatly increased the number of its antireligious articles.[25]

Throughout most of the decade of the 1930's the League of Militant Godless and the Communist party continued to hold that the Russian Orthodox church was counterrevolutionary by nature as well as in fact. Such accusations, however, were rare from 1933 to 1937, and in the single instance encountered where specific charges were made, the counterrevolutionary manifestations alleged consisted of the intensive celebration of religious holidays at the height of the summer farm work.[26]

In 1937 the charges that Orthodox churchmen were engaged in hostile activity were more frequent, although at first unorganized, minor opposition was alleged, such as propaganda against collective farms, black-market speculation, the circulation of frightening rumors, and even attempts to use the newly granted electoral rights in order to elect priests to local soviets[27] (which would be entirely legal). Later in 1937 the charges grew more serious. The tension that had mounted after the killing of the noted Leningrad Communist, S. M. Kirov, in the fall of 1934, had finally produced the famous treason trials involving Zinoviev, Kamenev, and many other noted figures of the Soviet regime; Bukharin and Rykov, former members of the Right opposition, were soon to be put on trial. In this frenzied atmosphere it was not surprising that ecclesiastics, many of whom had opposed the Soviet regime, were involved. In November, 1937, a lengthy article in *Izvestiia* reported clerical participation in the widespread plots. A Bishop D—— was named as an active agent of the

German Gestapo engaged in building up a spying and terrorist organization near Moscow. The Renovationist Bishop B——, who, it was said, since 1934 had been connected with a fascist secret service, at its orders had sought to build up an anti-Soviet organization in the Ukraine; one of its members had planned to blow up an artillery depot. Bishop T—— in Siberia, a former supporter of Kolchak, had worked to form a sabotage group in industrial enterprises, under orders from a foreign secret service. Similar activities by Orthodox hierarchs were reported in Siberia, in the province of Kalinin, and in Voronezh and Smolensk.[28]

Subsequent accusations became more explicit. Metropolitan Feofan Tuliakov of Gor'kii (Nizhnii Novgorod) and two bishops were charged with organizing a widespread conspiracy for purposes of spying, killing Soviet workers, setting fire to the homes of collective farmers, wrecking the Gor'kii Automobile Factory, and similar counterrevolutionary acts — all, it was alleged, under orders of a foreign secret service received through an underground church "center" in Moscow, and in collaboration with Trotskyite and Bukharinite spies.[29] One Father Krylov, so the account read, admitted freely his connection with these anti-Soviet plots and confessed that his group had burned the homes of twelve active collective farmers. In the spring of 1937 in Orel a bishop and twelve priests, as well as laymen, were charged with collaboration with Trotskyites and Bukharinites to harm the Soviet regime. A Khar'kov newspaper reported that the head of the church in Kremenchug had been proved a German spy.[30] Another priest, in the province of Omsk, allegedly testified in court that his counterrevolutionary group of priests looked for a more moderate attitude toward the clergy after the victory of the Rightist opposition of Bukharin and Rykov.[31] The action taken against the defendants was not indicated by the press.

While these revelations of criminal prosecutions of churchmen indicate a revival of hostility to the ecclesiastics of the Russian Orthodox church, it is worth noting that nowhere was there any hint that the Patriarchal Locum Tenens, Metropolitan Sergii, was involved in the alleged machinations. Moreover, the published reports of the great treason trials are almost free from references to churchmen. Only in the last of the three great trials did Ikramov, one of the defendants, testify that in 1933 Bukharin had urged him and his fellow conspirators to organize the remaining kulaks and the priests for insurrectionary purposes. Moreover, Andrei Vyshinskii, the prosecutor, made no attempt to stress participation of the clergy in the plot under discussion.[32] While it was almost inevitable that some of the churchmen would be accused of treasonable acts during this period of extreme tension, on the whole the Orthodox clergy seem to have fared better than many other important segments of Soviet society, including the Communist party.

Late in 1938 the purges came to an end and by 1939 the trend was toward moderation in political life. Charges that members of the clergy had been engaged in counterrevolutionary acts disappeared from the metropolitan press and even the Godless ceased to charge the clergy with subversive activity, although they continued to reiterate that religion was fundamentally opposed to socialism.

The antireligious movement continued, however, and it even grew substantially between 1937 and 1941. In 1938, according to incomplete data, there were 1,944,047 members in 60,748 cells,[33] while by January 1, 1940, there were 2,992,038 members in 95,159 cells. By the beginning of 1941 there were about three and one half million members.[34] The latter figure was still well below the peak membership of 5,700,-000 in 1932; nevertheless, it indicates that there had been a considerable resurgency of the Godless movement from the earlier slump.

In other respects, also, the Godless movement had regained some of its former momentum. In 1940 nearly one hundred sixty thousand persons were attending courses giving antireligious training, and it was claimed that 239,000 antireligious lectures were delivered to a total audience of 10,755,000 persons.[35]

As before, much stress was put upon antireligious training in the schools. Although some success seems to have been achieved, the Godless leaders persistently demanded even greater efforts. In 1938 an antireligious textbook declared: "We must paralyze every influence of religion upon the coming generation. The struggle for the youth, for the children must be one of the problems not only of the League of Militant Godless, but above all, of the Komsomol and the Soviet school." [36] In 1940 and 1941 *Pravda* repeatedly demanded improvement of antireligious training. An order of the Commissariat of Education early in 1940 had warned that this work was being neglected in many schools, with unfortunate consequences. On the other hand, it was stated, where the Godless, the Komsomols, the teachers, and the parents joined in antireligious work, the successes achieved were remarkable.[37]

Apparently the antireligious museum had proved itself an effective means of combating religion. Iaroslavskii declared that in 1936 a total of 157,000 persons had visited the Central Antireligious Museum in Moscow. At that time there were about thirty such museums in the U.S.S.R.;[38] by 1941 there were forty-seven, some of them in provincial or even county seats of government.[39]

The publication of antireligious matter continued on a large scale. In the period from 1928 through 1940 the State Antireligious Publishing House produced 1832 titles for a total of 140,200,000 copies. In addition, in 1940 alone the locally published antireligious works totaled 640,000 copies. The plan of the state publishers for 1941 called for producing 67 titles with a total of 3,505,000 copies, of which two thirds would be pamphlets for popular consumption. In addition, the two magazines *Bezbozhnik* and *Antireligioznik* were to have a planned circulation for the year of 2,220,000 copies, and the newspaper *Bezbozhnik* would have an annual circulation of 3,640,000.[40]

Among the antireligious books published in the 1930's were two textbooks — one for use in the elementary schools, and one for more mature members of study groups or for self-instruction. Both of them were written very skillfully. While they strongly attacked religion as a sworn enemy of socialism, much of their content was devoted to refutation of the biblical explanation of the origin of the universe and of man. The refutation drew heavily on astronomy, zoology, chemistry, embryology, paleontology, botany, psychology, and other natural sciences. The analysis of the various religions — all of them termed contrary to science — made use of data on comparative religions, the higher criticism of the Bible, and ancient, medieval, and modern history. Copiously illustrated, they were persuasively written and provided their readers with a completely materialistic explanation of the natural, social, and historic phenomena that they would encounter. Both of them went through several large editions, so that the impact of their highly impressive argument must have been felt by large portions of the Soviet citizenry.[41]

This approach to antireligious work became the dominant one during the latter part of the 1930's. A comparison of the content of the newspaper *Bezbozhnik* for 1941 with that of 1931 reveals the marked change in antireligious propaganda during that time. In the earlier period articles attacking individual members of the clergy as counterrevolutionaries, foes of collectivization and industrialization, and persistent enemies of the Soviet regime, were common, but by 1941 they had given way to more subtle articles intended to show that Christianity was antiscientific and that it had always opposed science, particularly in the persons of Copernicus, Galileo, Giordano Bruno, and others. Comparative religion was used to show that the Christian faith was strikingly similar to many other beliefs of the Levant, and the natural sciences were used to explain natural phenomena that formerly had been ascribed to supernatural causes.

Throughout this period the Godless leaders continued to emphasize the necessity for unremitting antireligious propaganda. Although they asserted that more and more people were turning against religion, they insisted that this was not enough and that a complete victory could only be won by pursuing the same course indefinitely. Occasional warnings were given that, inasmuch as the U.S.S.R. was encircled by hostile capitalist powers, the religious element, with its basically antimaterialistic outlook and its ties with the non-Soviet world, was a danger.[42] More frequently the argument was that religious ideas died hard, even in a socialist environment, and that although many citizens had broken with the church and its viewpoint, they had not developed a materialistic world outlook to replace the traditional religious one. Until all Soviet citizens could be transformed into conscious fighters for Communism the religious influence would not have been eradicated and harm would be done by its survival.[43] The Godless repeatedly urged concentration of antireligious work among believers, who rarely attended antireligious lectures and often were not reached by ordinary propaganda. They should be approached individually, with patient, friendly understanding. "The only method is propaganda, persuasion, enlightenment. . . .

we must not forget that there are millions of religious persons and that we must convince them, work tolerantly, intelligently, persistently, without violent attacks." [44]

Thus the Godless leaders, who during the First Five-Year Plan had made such sweeping attacks on religion and the Russian Orthodox church, by 1941 had abandoned their hopes of a quick and easy victory and had prepared themselves for a long, slow campaign of unrelenting attrition. During these same years the Russian Orthodox church had not changed its policy of loyal acceptance of the Soviet regime. Even the Godless leaders, while warning that this loyalty was insincere, admitted its existence.

> Formerly the priest and the sectarian openly preached against the collective farms; then it was easy enough to reveal their activity. But now the priest and the sectarian declare that they are upholders of the collective farms, that they are ready to give absolution to the collective farmers even before all the others, because they are true toilers, and so on. At present, the priest and the sectarian declare that the Bolsheviks are angels; that they have been sent down from heaven and that is why they are so strong. All these are truly counterrevolutionary manifestations, only covert ones, more finely tempered, than the earlier ones. [45]

In 1934 Metropolitan Sergii, who at the suggestion of Metropolitan Alexii and many other bishops in that year took the title "Most Blessed Metropolitan of Moscow and Kolomna," [46] gave additional proof of his already well-established loyalty. He informed the Synod of his inability to secure the submission of the anti-Soviet émigré hierarchs of the Karlovatskii Synod: Metropolitan Antonii, Archbishop Anastasii, and others. The Synod resolved to take punitive measures against the recalcitrant hierarchs. [47] Although the punishment had no apparent effect, the Synod under Metropolitan Sergii had once more shown that it was unwilling to countenance anti-Soviet activity within the church.

Two developments relating to the church occurred in close succession. The first was the adoption of the Stalin Constitution in December, 1936, which according to the Godless leaders, by granting full citizenship rights encouraged the clergy to become more active. [48] The other event was the abortive census of 1937, which provided for listing the citizens of sixteen years of age and over as believers or non-believers. Another item called for the name of the denomination, if any.[49] The results of the census were never published, allegedly because of improper procedures used in taking it.[50] Outside the U.S.S.R. it was widely rumored that, among other things, the census had indicated an alarmingly large number of believers. The authoritative Soviet explanation was that through criminal negligence the census takers missed large numbers of people. There was no mention of the religious factor as a reason for throwing out the census.[51] It appears impossible to determine whether the questions on religion had anything to do with the voiding of the census.

Evidence regarding the activity of the Russian church after 1937 is very scanty. Its opponents continued to report that most of the ecclesiastics professed loyalty to the Soviet regime and continued to seek the support of exemplary workers and other citizens in good standing, rather than that of groups that might be under a cloud because of suspected disloyalty.[52] In 1938, after the last great treason trial, there were signs of extraordinary efforts on the part of several of the churchmen to avoid the stigma of disloyalty. The Renovationist Metropolitan Nikolai Platonov of Leningrad renounced his ecclesiastical calling in a public declaration and summoned other clerics of all denominations to follow his example. The chairman of a Renovationist vestry in Iaroslavl, according to the Godless press, was moved by an article in *Izvestiia* accusing a number of higher clergy of treasonable activity to demand the elimination of all metropolitans, archbishops, and bishops from the church so that the rank and file of the believers might be free from the stain of disloyalty. In the province of Ivanovo even the bishop sought to clear himself by disassociating himself from the higher authorities of the church through a declaration of diocesan autonomy.[53]

The Godless repeatedly declared that the clergy claimed that they favored the Soviets and communism. They allegedly asserted that religion and communism were compatible, that "Christ was the first Communist," and that their type of Christianity had been purified of the weaknesses charged by the Godless.[54] In 1941 it was stated that priests were declaring that belief in God was not contrary to science and that the Communists had succeeded because God had willed it.

The author of this report warned, however, that this priestly acceptance of communism was not to be taken seriously, as the sympathy
of the masses for the new order compelled such utterances.[55] Nevertheless, it should be noted that such an attitude toward the Soviet
regime and toward communism would be in harmony with the stand
taken by Metropolitan Sergii more than ten years before, when he
had ordered prayers for the Soviet government.

It is no easy matter to determine the results of the years from 1933
to June, 1941, for the Russian Orthodox church, especially since the
evidence comes almost exclusively from the antireligious side. Nevertheless, it is clear that the church continued to exist and, albeit under
difficult circumstances, to command the allegiance of an important
number of citizens. On the tenth anniversary of the League of Militant Godless in 1935 Iaroslavskii, after reports of vast successes in
propagating atheism, warned that as yet only half of the work had
been done; there were religious organizations still in existence, with
influence *over tens of millions of working people.*[56] In 1936 he declared that "ministers of cults of all confessions and ranks" in the
U.S.S.R. numbered about one hundred thousand.[57] In the following
year, in a survey of the antireligious situation, he referred to cities
like Magnitogorsk, Karaganda, Sverdlovsk, Cheliabinsk, Alma Ata,
Igarka, Kirovsk, and others, which were either completely new or so
vastly expanded as to be almost entirely new. In these cities no
churches had been built. He warned, however, that this did not mean
that they were devoid of believers; ". . . one must not conclude that
in the city of Stalinsk with 120 thousand inhabitants there are no
believers. There are no churches, but there are as many believers as
you want."[58] Four years went by, but the situation changed only in
degree. In 1941 Oleshchuk stated that, while the growth of socialism
had eliminated the deepest roots of religion, so that wide masses
had turned from belief, it would be a mistake to think that in the
U.S.S.R. religion was already finished. "Religious survivals are still
quite widespread and are still a mass phenomenon. Many workers and
especially many collective farmers continue to some extent to believe
in God, are under the influence of religious organizations, attend religious ceremonies."[59] In another passage he stated that although a
person might give up part of his religious practices, such as the ven-

eration of ikons, this did not by any means indicate that he had become Godless, for often he still retained religious attitudes and had not adopted a materialistic outlook. Oleshchuk felt forced to admit: "Religion is very long-lived." [60]

What particularly troubled the antireligious workers was that religion still had influence among the young. Investigations by questionnaire in 1933 and 1934 showed that over 50 per cent of the pupils' families had ikons at home and that approximately 40 per cent of the mothers believed.[61] Studies of preschool children indicated that nearly half were under religious influence and that over one quarter prayed at home or had been to church.[62] During 1936 and 1937 antireligious leaders deplored repeated instances of religious participation by boys and girls. In several North Caucasus churches in 1936 children of school age made up over half of the Easter congregations, and in villages in the Moscow area many of the children wore crosses and otherwise indicated religious adherence.[63] Iaroslavskii and others warned their followers that often priests succeeded in interesting the young in choir-singing; even Komsomols and Pioneers were found in church choirs.[64] As late as 1941 Iaroslavskii was still insisting that "we must paralyze all influence of religion upon the rising generation. The struggle for the youth, for the children, should be one of the problems not only of the League of Militant Godless, but first of all the Komsomol and of the Soviet school." [65]

Occasional statements of the Godless mentioned strong religious observance by women; the men were much less devout. A study made in 1937 of an Orthodox church in Irkutsk in Siberia reported that 866 of the total congregation of 911 were women, of whom about 40 per cent were workers. About 80 members of the congregation were between 18 and 27 years of age.[66]

Interesting data were presented in the antireligious press in 1938 concerning the finances of the central organizations of the two chief Orthodox groups and the incomes of their leaders. The accuracy of these figures is by no means certain, as the author wished to show that the leading churchmen lived lives of parasitical ease. Also, even if the author did not distort his evidence, it is impossible to determine how dependable his sources of information were. Nevertheless, the account indicates that the Godless regarded the church as an institution of considerable strength. According to the article, in 1936 the Synod of Metropolitan Sergii received 355,831 rubles from the dioceses and from other sources. Metropolitan Sergii received a total income of 48,000 rubles in pay and expense allowances; two other hierarchs had incomes of 38,000 rubles each. The Renovationist Synod had an even larger income — 441,935 rubles. The article also stated that Metropolitan Alexander Vvedenskii had an annual income of 53,600 rubles, in addition to that received from the church where he served.[67]

If these figures are accurate, they indicate that both branches of the Russian Orthodox church still enjoyed wide popular support, as the sums cited came from the believers. The credibility of this report is, however, somewhat reduced by the fact that the reported income of the Renovationist Synod exceeded that of the patriarchal Synod, although the latter group had for ten years or more been far stronger than the Renovationists. The author of the article estimated that Metropolitan Sergii's following had from 75 to 80 per cent of all Orthodox churches in the U.S.S.R., while the Renovationists had from 15 to 20 per cent, and Archbishop Grigorii's group had about 5 per cent.[68]

It would be a mistake, however, to conclude that the survival of the church and the decline of the Godless movement after 1932 meant that religion and especially the Russian Orthodox church had overcome the menace to its existence. Impressive evidence — most, but not all, from sources hostile to religion — indicates that the Russian people were more and more turning away from religion. In 1935 Iaroslavskii, head of the Godless movement, told the All-Union Conference on Antireligious Propaganda: "If we figure how many people do not now recognize the priest, the rabbi, the mullah, how many have broken or are breaking with religion, then I think that this figure possibly *will amount to fifty millions,* if not more." He based his computation on the claim that the majority of the twenty-five million school children were nonbelievers, as were most of the trade-union members, as well as the Communists and the Komsomol. A considerable part of the younger collective farmers also had no use for the priest.[69] He mentioned that there were villages that had never seen a priest and, after prompting from the floor, went on to say:

"Yes, there are new cities where there is not one priest: take Magnitogorsk — there there is a population of a quarter of a million, and not one priest, one church. This, comrades, is an entirely new phenomenon." [70] Late in 1935 Iaroslavskii claimed that "at least half of the population has either fully or partially broken with religion." [71]

That this was not empty boasting is shown by Dr. Paul B. Anderson, a lifelong student of Russia and extremely close to the Russian Orthodox church in Paris through his position with the YMCA. In his book *Russia's Religious Future,* published in 1936, he quotes the remarks of an unnamed foreigner who visited the U.S.S.R. in the summer of 1935:

> I had to travel for miles in a Ford truck, since the churches in the immediate neighborhood were closed. The service was attended by a mere handful of people. I talked with the local priest and the first question I put to him was this: "What is the future for religion in Russia?" And without a minute's hesitation the priest replied: "There is no future for religion in Russia." The offering at this particular church consisted of five pieces of black bread, four green apples and an egg. I asked the priest what he would do when he had eaten his bread, apples, and egg, and he unblushingly told me he would visit among the homes of the faithful and beg for food. [72]

Whether this view was overly gloomy or not, in 1936 the Godless seemed to be in extremely high spirits. At their tenth anniversary meeting in February, 1936, more than sixteen hundred persons were present in "a joyous crowd." According to the observer who reported the meeting, "the attitude of all is exalted, triumphant." [73] Similar optimism was shown at a seminar for antireligious speakers in January, 1936. In all 394 reports were given, 302 of them on work in the villages. "All reporters unanimously *noted heightened interest in antireligious reports and lectures,* especially in cases where the subject of the lecture was known in advance." Questions from the audience were now much more pertinent to the occasion than formerly. "In earlier years questions about the causes of provisioning difficulties were inevitable and, moreover, they presented these questions so unanimously that it was impossible to concentrate on the subject of the report, but now this does not happen." Another speaker asserted:

"The situation that we meet in the collective farms is extremely favorable for our work. To deliver lectures has become more pleasant." [74]

Apparently the situation continued to be favorable for antireligious work thereafter, for in 1939 an antireligious writer estimated that "in our country, in spite of the extreme neglect of antireligious work, in two Five-Year Plans . . . about half of the working people in the village and about three-quarters of those in the city have broken with religion." [75] In the same year an editorial in a Godless publication stated that the Russian Orthodox church, which once had had some eighty thousand churches, now had about twenty thousand.[76] No further claims of successes against religion have been found, but it seems likely that religion did not gain appreciably during 1940 and the first half of 1941, and probably continued to decline.

The numerous reports of a growing lack of clergy — all emanating from Godless sources — also lend credibility to the indications of a decline of the Russian church. In 1938 an analysis of eighty-three priests of the city of Moscow disclosed that only three were less than forty years of age. "Evidently this is explained by the fact that the priests had not succeeded in preparing their successors, no matter how hard they try." [77] Several of the Godless leaders reported that many congregations had no regular pastors, but were served by itinerant clergy, who might visit the parish once a year to perform a number of christenings, marriages, and funerals. In some cases self-consecrated priests filled the needs of the parishes. Sometimes the religious ceremonies were said in the homes instead of in churches.[78] The organization of secret church groups that met in private homes or other unofficial locations was reported by Godless leaders with considerable annoyance.[79]

Additional devices of the hard-pressed believers, as reported by antireligious workers, consisted of the use of women lay readers in place of priests, and the performance of religious rites *in absentia*. The lay readers were reported from the Orthodox parishes in Karelia, where at least ten churches had them perform some of the rituals, especially requiems. While the priests had been discarded for drunkenness and lack of propriety, these women, who did not claim consecration, enjoyed much authority. In other regions where priests, although few in numbers, were still sought after, it was sometimes necessary to have the priest perform the funeral rites over a little earth brought from the grave of the deceased, after which the earth was replaced on the grave. For christenings the priest blessed a bottle of holy water, which was later used by the relatives or godparents in a substitute christening. Wedding rings, blessed *in absentia,* were later put on the spouses who had been unable to secure the presence of a priest at their nuptials.[80]

These devices of the believers prove that religion was a vital influence in their lives and that a lack of clergy did not automatically eliminate it. On the other hand, the church was obviously in difficulties and seemed to be losing ground steadily. When one bears in mind that for nearly one thousand years it had been indoctrinating the Russians, the substantial successes achieved by the Godless in the twenty-four-year period between the Revolution of 1917 and the outbreak of the Russo–German war in 1941 appear quite impressive. While the Godless were cautious about setting a terminal date for the existence of religion in Russia, they felt confident that its end was not far off. Another twenty-year period of determined antireligious effort, they were sure, might well come close to reducing religion in Russia to a curiosity for museums. But the world was not yet to see whether their hopes and aspirations were to be realized, for with the outbreak of war in June, 1941, the status of religion in the U.S.S.R. began to change rapidly.

CHAPTER XV

Patriarch and Generalissimo

IN THE FIRST MONTHS of 1941 the state of the Russian Orthodox church appeared to be distinctly unfavorable, as the Godless movement, after a sharp decline, was again gaining strength. With the German attack on the U.S.S.R. on June 22, 1941, however, the situation changed radically.

From the day of the attack the leaders of the church lent their support to the cause. Metropolitan Sergii immediately sent a message to all Orthodox parishes telling of the aggression by "Fascist bandits," reminding his followers of the patriotic deeds of their ancestors, and closing with the words: "The church of Christ blesses all Orthodox in defense of the sacred frontiers of our fatherland." [1] At a solemn *Te Deum* on the evening of June 26 the Acting Patriarch declared it the duty of all to defend their country and warned that the church would suffer at the hands of the Germans.[2] Similar appeals were made by Metropolitans Alexii of Leningrad and Nikolai of Kiev, as well as by a host of lesser ecclesiastics.[3]

In January, 1942, Metropolitan Sergii published a message to the inhabitants of the areas under German control, warning them against purchasing well-being "by treason to church and fatherland" or even by faint-hearted subservience.[4] Another message, in June, 1942, "To the Whole Church," paid tribute to the highly patriotic work of the guerrillas in the rear of the enemy and called for all possible support for this movement.[5] And at Christmas, 1942, the Acting Patriarch addressed an encouraging appeal to the people of the occupied areas: "Endure yet a little while . . . and once more light will shine upon you." [6]

Another indication of the church's enthusiasm for the cause was given on Red Army Day, February 23, 1942, when the churches and the clergy of Moscow donated 1,500,000 rubles to the Red Army Fund.[7] This example was widely followed: At the beginning of 1943 the Acting Patriarch announced the opening of a campaign to secure contributions for a tank column named after the medieval hero Dmitrii Donskoi; the Patriarchy itself contributed 100,000 rubles.[8]

Until late in 1942 the messages of the prelates made no special mention of the Soviet government or of Stalin. On November 7 of that year, however, Metropolitan Sergii hailed Stalin as "the divinely anointed [sic] leader" of the nation, who would lead them to victory. The hierarch added: "May God bless with victory and glory your great deeds for the fatherland." Metropolitan Nikolai of Kiev wished Stalin long life and strength "to cleanse the Ukraine of the German filth."[9] On New Year's Day, 1943, the Acting Patriarch sent greetings to Stalin, which concluded: "In prayer I wish you health for the new year and success in all your undertakings, for the welfare of the country is entrusted to you."[10]

The heads of the Russian Orthodox church also showed their loyalty by the measures taken against those few hierarchs who sided with the invaders. One of these was Archbishop Polikarp Sikorski, for many years an enemy of the Soviets, who had come under Soviet rule when the U.S.S.R. annexed the territories taken from Poland in 1939. When the Germans overran the Ukraine, Archbishop Polikarp renounced his allegiance to Metropolitan Sergii and proclaimed a revival of the Ukrainian Autocephalous church, which welcomed the protection of Hitler. The Acting Patriarch published two messages condemning Polikarp for disloyalty and insubordination, on February 5 and March 28, 1942, and he was excommunicated by a council of bishops.[11] Most of the Ukrainian clergy seemed to have supported the patriarchal church, so that Polikarp's efforts had little effect.[12] He later fled to Germany when the Germans were driven out of the Ukraine. Similar action was taken in the case of Archbishop Sergii Voskresenskii of the Baltic, Bishop Nikolai Amasiiskii of Rostov-on-Don, and Metropolitan Feofil Buldovskii of Khar'kov, all of whom collaborated with the Germans. Metropolitan Feofil had be-

come a schismatic fifteen years before.[13] Thus Metropolitan Sergii
and his supporters made it clear that they condemned those who
sided with the enemies of the nation.

While the attitude of the leaders of the Russian Orthodox church
is not surprising, in the light of Patriarch Tikhon's loyalty after his
release in 1923 and that of Metropolitan Sergii from 1927 on, the wartime attitude of the Soviet government and the Communist party is
more remarkable. Upon the outbreak of war in June, 1941, antireligious propaganda was at once toned down and soon ceased alto-
gether. Although the dissolution of the League of Militant Godless
was never formally announced, its periodicals ceased publication in
September and October, 1941, and the antireligious museums were
either transformed into museums of church history or closed. No
further overt antireligious manifestations were reported throughout
the war against Germany.[14] Only one instance of the earlier attitude
came to light. The veteran Communist M. I. Kalinin told a meeting
of propagandists that he did not feel that it was outrageous for young
men in the army to laugh at middle-aged recruits who wore crosses,
although he warned against outright abuse in such cases.[15] At other
times, however, the Soviet leaders displayed a cordial attitude toward
the church that was in marked contrast to their previous one.

This new-found cordiality was shown in many ways. At Easter,
1942, the curfew in Moscow was lifted in order that the faithful might
attend midnight services.[16] The government named Metropolitan
Nikolai of Kiev and Galicia to the Extraordinary State Committee
for investigating the crimes committed by the invaders — [17] the first
official body to which a churchman had been named by the government since the revolution. In 1943 the government made the greatly
revered ikon of the Iverian Virgin available for worship by moving it
to the Sokol'niki Cathedral from its long confinement in the closed
Donskoi Monastery.[18]

In spite of these signs of a new official policy toward the Russian
church, in September, 1943, the world was surprised to learn that on
September 4 Premier Stalin and Molotov had received Metropolitan
Sergii, Patriarchal Locum Tenens, Metropolitan Alexii of Leningrad,
and Metropolitan Nikolai of Kiev and Galicia in the Kremlin. During the conversation Metropolitan Sergii informed his host that the

church leaders were planning to call a Sobor (council) of bishops in the very near future to choose a Patriarch and a Synod to aid him. According to *Izvestiia*, Stalin was sympathetic to this proposal and stated that the Government had no objection thereto.[19]

Three days later the Sobor met in Moscow. Nineteen bishops convened to elect Metropolitan Sergii as the second Russian Patriarch since the days of Peter the Great and chose a Holy Synod. The Sobor unanimously adopted a message proposed by Metropolitan Sergii expressing thanks to the government for its solicitude for the needs of the church. Another message, also adopted without dissent, urged the Christians of the whole world to unite in combating Hitlerism.[20] The Sobor also deplored the fact that a few clergy and laymen had greeted the enemy like welcome guests and had even betrayed partisans and other patriots to the foe. The prelates confirmed the punishments already decreed for such offenses — excommunication for laymen, and unfrocking for ecclesiastics.[21]

On September 12 the first issue of the *Journal of the Patriarchate of Moscow* (*Zhurnal Moskovskoi Patriarkhii*) appeared, after a lapse of ten years. Nor was this all. The official favor for the church was made even more evident by the arrival of the Archbishop of York, accompanied by two Anglican priests. They were met in Moscow on September 19, 1943, by Metropolitan Nikolai, who took them to the Patriarch. On September 21 they attended service in the Patriarch's cathedral and were invited into the chancel. The Archbishop of York gave a brief address stressing the unity of the two churches against the common foe.[22] This was a historic event, for never before had an Anglican archbishop been a guest of the Russian church. The most remarkable aspect was that it happened, not in the days of the Orthodox tsars, but with the permission of the unbelievers of the Soviet regime.

In October, 1943, the government's rapprochement with the church was given administrative form by the creation of a Council for Affairs of the Orthodox Church as an adjunct to the Council of People's Commissars. As its head, G. G. Karpov, explained in August, 1944, its functions and those of its more than one hundred local representatives were to ensure good relations between church and state and, where possible, to satisfy the needs of the church in respect to opening new churches, arranging for theological education, and drafting legislation relating to the church. He stated that there were more churches in operation than before the war, and more priests, as some of those who had resigned had returned to church duties. Petitions for opening new churches were rarely refused, he added.[23]

Organized theological instruction was restored in the U.S.S.R. in 1944. Late in 1943 the Synod considered a proposal to open a Theological Institute in Moscow, with a three-year course for training future bishops and other leaders, and two-year pastoral courses in the dioceses.[24] This plan bore fruit with the simultaneous opening of the Theological Institute and the Theological Course in the Novodevichyi Monastery in Moscow on June 14, 1944. The latter institution, with the function of a seminary, was to train priests from candidates chosen from all who volunteered.[25] Karpov, in the interview in August, stated that while this was the only theological seminary at the time, this was not because of restrictions by the government. Six months earlier his council had assented to the opening of a seminary in Saratov, but the Synod had failed to open it.[26]

Even the rules on the religious instruction of children were greatly relaxed. Karpov, asked about this by Religious News Service in September, 1944, replied that while religious instruction was not permitted in the public schools, the parents had the right to have priests give such training. Children of any number of parents might gather in groups to receive such instruction in the priests' homes.[27] This attitude, it should be noted, was in marked contrast to the original interpretation of the law of April 8, 1929, as described in Chapter XII, which had ruled that the parents had no right to delegate the religious instruction of their children to any person outside the family.

The improved position of the patriarchal church evidently impressed many of the believers outside the fold, for after the election of the Patriarch in 1943 many of the Renovationist clergy hastened to repent of their schism and humbled themselves before him. On November 5, 1943, Bishop Mikhail Postnikov, after public penance, asked readmission of the Patriarch, who received him into the church with his former rank of bishop.[28] Bishop Mikhail's example was followed by many other Renovationist ecclesiastics, including

Metropolitans Vitalii Vvedenskii and Mikhail Orlov. Often they had to accept rank much below that that they had held in the Renovationist church.[29]

The Russian Orthodox church also extended its influence in other directions, for late in 1943 it re-established communion and cordial relations with the Orthodox church of Georgia.[30] In December, 1944, the Patriarchate of Moscow played host to a group of Orthodox clergy from the Carpatho-Ukraine, who, having been under the jurisdiction of the Serbian Orthodox church, now asked that they and their coreligionists become part of the Russian church.[31]

While the hand of the Soviet government was not always visible in these developments, it seems certain that the government's new cordiality toward the church had no little part in these happenings. More obvious proof of the government's attitude was given by the awarding of medals to ecclesiastics for their part in the defense of the nation. In October, 1943, on the instructions of the Presidium of the Supreme Soviet, medals "For the Defense of Leningrad" were presented to Metropolitan Alexii and other clergy of that city.[32] On October 9, 1944, *Pravda* prominently displayed an item on the awarding of the "For the Defense of Moscow" medal to a group of clergy of Moscow and Tula, with Metropolitan Nikolai of Kiev heading the list.[33]

Throughout the war the Russian church continued to serve the nation. In September, 1943, Metropolitan Sergii, Acting Patriarch, reported that in answer to his appeals the faithful had donated eight million rubles,[34] much of it for the Dmitrii Donskoi Tank Column. When it was ready, early in 1944, Metropolitan Nikolai went to the camp of the tank unit, where, with a warmly patriotic speech, he bestowed the church's gift upon them.[35] On March 23, 1944, the clergy of Moscow wired Stalin that they, inspired by the latest victories, were donating an additional one million rubles to build planes and asked God to give him strength and health for the speedy victorious conclusion of the war.[36] The clergy of the provincial city of Sverdlovsk alone contributed 4,615,389 rubles during three and one half years of war, with three deans donating from their personal savings sums of 53,300 rubles, 103,280 rubles, and 364,720 rubles, respectively.[37] In all, by October 1, 1944, the clergy and faithful of the Russian Orthodox church had donated 150,000,000 rubles, in addition to gifts in kind.[38]

Perhaps more important than financial aid was the moral support that the church continued to give to the cause. At the Sobor of 1943 Metropolitan Alexii of Leningrad read a report on the duty of the Christian to church and fatherland during the war. He stated that it was the duty of all to help; Christians could serve, if in no other way, by inspiring the people and thus helping to inspire the troops. They should also give constant prayers for victory and serve in all ways possible.[39] This report was approved by the Sobor, which also sent the following message to the Soviet government:

> Deeply touched by the sympathetic attitude of our national Leader, the Head of the Soviet government, I. V. Stalin, toward the needs of the Russian Orthodox church and toward the modest labors of us, its humble servants, we bring to the government our common conciliar thanks and joyful faith that, encouraged by this sympathy, we may multiply our share of work for the national undertaking to save the fatherland.
> May the Heavenly Head of the church bless the labors of the government with His creative blessing and may He crown our struggle for the just cause with the longed-for victory and the liberation of suffering mankind from the dread bonds of fascism.[40]

The leading churchmen continued to give ardent support to Stalin. On November 7, 1943, while performing service at a solemn celebration, which was gladdened by the news of the liberation of Kiev, Patriarch Sergii uttered prayers "for our Divinely protected land, and for its authorities, headed by its God-given leader." [41] After Sergii's death in 1944, Metropolitan Alexii of Leningrad, the Patriarchal Locum Tenens, in announcing the sad event to Stalin, spoke of "the sincere love he cherished for you" and assured Stalin that *he* would be guided by the same "deep loyalty to country and to our government headed by you." He further urged the marshal "to trust in the feelings of deep love for you and in the gratitude that inspires all those associated with the church that I shall henceforth head." [42]

In addition, the Russian church, through its appeals to the Orthodox of the Balkans, sought to weaken the enemy. In November,

1942, Metropolitans Sergii and Nikolai appealed to the Rumanian soldiers to cease shedding the fraternal blood of the cobelieving Russian people, and one month later the Acting Patriarch appealed to the Rumanian Orthodox clergy and laymen to renounce their involuntary alliance with Hitler. Would Rumania, he asked, "continue . . . to fight against the Russian people, with whom the Rumanian people are bound by the ties of Christian brotherhood?" [43] At Easter, 1943, he published an appeal to the Christians of the Balkans, informing them that the Russian church was advancing together with the Russian arms and asking if Greeks and Serbs would long remain quiet under the fascist yoke.[44] After the Germans had fled from Rumania and the Rumanians had taken up arms against them, Metropolitan Alexii, Locum Tenens, sent a message to the Rumanian Orthodox clergy and believers, greeting them as allies and urging them to fight hard for victory.[45]

Even a scholarly denial of the Pope's claims to be the vicar of Christ on earth, which was published by Patriarch Sergii in 1944,[46] was in harmony with the policies of the Soviet government. Although there was no political motive apparent in what seemed to be a learned theological article that dealt with an ancient controversy between the churches, it was doubtless designed to weaken the influence of the papacy — an institution that the Soviet government regarded as unfriendly.

When Patriarch Sergii died on May 15, 1944, Metropolitan Alexii of Leningrad became Locum Tenens of the Patriarchal Throne. The church was not, however, to wait long for a new Patriarch, for in November, 1944, a conclave of bishops issued a call for a new Sobor, which duly met in Moscow from January 31 to February 2, 1945. Whereas the Sobor that had elected Patriarch Sergii in 1943 had comprised only some 19 bishops, the assemblage in 1945 was attended by the 3 metropolitans of the Russian church, 41 bishops and archbishops, and 126 representatives of the clergy and laity from various parts of the land. Furthermore, Patriarchs Christopher of Alexandria and Alexander of Antioch were also present, as were representatives of the Patriarchs of Constantinople and Jerusalem and of the Rumanian and Serbian churches. Kallistrat, Patriarch and Catholicos of Georgia, was also at the Sobor, as well as Metropolitan Veniamin of

North America and the Aleutian Islands. Metropolitan Alexii, Locum Tenens and successor designated by Patriarch Sergii, was unanimously elected Patriarch; on February 4 he was invested with magnificent ceremony, in the presence of the visiting clergy, including the two Eastern Patriarchs.[47]

Harmony between church and government was fully in evidence at the Sobor. The Soviet authorities provided suitable transportation for the visiting prelates, and G. G. Karpov, chairman of the Council on Affairs of the Orthodox Church, greeted the assemblage in the name of the government. He praised the church and its leaders for their patriotic service to the fatherland and promised that his council would promote good relations between the church and the civil authorities and would take all measures to ensure freedom of conscience. In turn, the Sobor approved a message to the government, full of thankful praise. It ended with the words:

> Raising to the Lord God thanks for the great victories of our valiant warriors and for the expulsion of the enemy from our territories, the Sobor earnestly prays to the Lord to give our dear Native Land . . . the most speedy and final victory over fascism and to increase the strength, health, and years of life of our beloved Leader of the Soviet State and Supreme Commander of our glorious troops, Joseph Vissarionovich Stalin.[48]

After the Sobor there were two important events. One was a concert of religious music in the Great Hall of the Moscow Conservatory of Music, performed by the Patriarchal Choir and by the Symphonic Orchestra of the U.S.S.R., under a noted conductor — [49] an occurrence that would have been unthinkable five years before. The other development was an appeal "to the peoples of the whole world," made by many of the churchmen who had been present at the Sobor. They declared that they "raise their voices against the efforts of those, particularly the Vatican, who, seeking by their utterances to shield Hitlerite Germany from responsibility for all the crimes committed by it," were allegedly aiding to perpetuate the anti-Christian Fascist doctrines after the war. The churchmen stated that they blessed the efforts of those who, seeking to exterminate this doctrine, were striving to establish a peaceful order on earth.[50] These developments showed that the collaboration between church and government was close.

During the months between the Sobor and the collapse of Germany in May, 1945, the position of the church remained much as before. On April 10 Premier Stalin and Molotov received Patriarch Alexii and Metropolitan Nikolai in the Kremlin,[51] thus indicating that relations with the church remained cordial. On May 2, after the fall of Berlin, the Patriarch sent Stalin a message of thanksgiving in which he stated that the church was praying "still more ardently for you, beloved supreme leader of our people, and for our Army. . . ."[52] After the end of the fighting the Patriarch officiated at a special service of thanksgiving in which he congratulated his followers on the victory over fascism and wished long life to the Red Army and its Supreme Commander.[53] The Patriarch also gave a special interview to a correspondent of *Izvestiia,* stating that the church, which had never doubted the victory of their righteous cause, had prayed without ceasing for victory over the forces of darkness. In addition, it had contributed over three hundred million rubles, as well as gifts in kind. "But the most important thing the Russian Orthodox church did in wartime was to demonstrate to the whole world its complete unity with its government." His remarks, which were exceedingly patriotic in tone, were highly laudatory of Stalin. Above all, he declared, he would "always thank God that He sent to us wise leaders of the country and headed it with its chosen leader of genius, Joseph Vissarionovich Stalin."[54]

Thus the church remained loyal to the Soviet government. It also continued its hostility to the Vatican, which had begun before the Sobor of 1945. Three strong articles in the church press charged that the Vatican had sinned against Christ by its claims for predominance and by its efforts to save the fascist instigators of war from just punishment.[55]

The efforts to extend the influence of the Patriarchy of Moscow, which have already been noted, also continued, with some measure of success. The good relations with the Serbian Orthodox church that were established at the Sobor of 1945 were strengthened by the visit of Russian churchmen, headed by Bishop Sergii of Kirovograd and Odessa, to Belgrade in April, 1945.[56] The relations between the Rus-

sian and the Bulgarian Orthodox churches were especially cordial.
After the Bulgars overthrew their king in September, 1944, and
aligned themselves with the Soviet Union, Metropolitan Stefan of
Sofia blessed the new government and expressed gratitude to the Russian people for having again liberated Bulgaria from a foreign yoke.
Acting Patriarch Alexii sent him his blessing.[57] Upon the ending of
the schism between the Bulgarian church and the Patriarchate of Constantinople in February, 1945, a Russian church delegation went to
Sofia to congratulate Metropolitan Stefan upon the recognition of the
autocephalous Bulgarian church. Warm speeches of mutual sympathy
were exchanged.[58]

The improved status of the Russian church in the U.S.S.R. also
increased its prestige in the Near East, as did the revival of close
ties with the Orthodox of the Levant before and during the Sobor
of 1945. In May, 1944, many of the Russian Orthodox monks and
nuns in Jerusalem accepted the authority of the Patriarchal Locum
Tenens, who assumed official administration of Russian ecclesiastical
property in the Holy City.[59] On November 7, 1944, the anniversary
of the Revolution of 1917, Patriarch Alexander of Antioch sent a message of congratulations to the Soviet minister to Syria and Lebanon.[60]
While this message was delivered to the civil authorities of the
U.S.S.R., the sympathy for the Russian cause displayed therein must
also have embraced the Russian Orthodox church.

Even in the West the Russian Orthodox church enjoyed considerable prestige at the end of the war. Many of the Russian *émigrés* in
France were strongly moved to restore ties with the country of their
birth; it was under the influence of this feeling that Metropolitan
Evlogii again accepted the jurisdiction of the Patriarch of Moscow,[61]
although his flock later renounced it.

On the whole, during the war the Russian church made a substantial recovery, in large part because of the more benevolent attitude of
the Soviet government. It is highly probable that the official attitude
was caused largely by the belief that the church enjoyed sufficient
popular support to make its good will valuable during the national
emergency. The resurgence of the church should not be overesti-
mated, however, for there is reason to think that it recovered only a
fraction of its earlier losses. The French–Polish scientist, Eve Curie,

who visited Russia during the first war winter of 1941–1942, stated that religion had lost its hold on the young. In Moscow, she said, there were only 18 or 20 churches functioning (other accounts spoke of 26 Orthodox churches in Moscow), whereas there had been about 600 churches in prerevolutionary Moscow.[62] While at the high festivals these churches were crowded, nonetheless they probably were attended by only a fraction of the population.[63]

In July, 1941, the Soviet embassy in London issued a statement indicating that there were over 8000 houses of prayer in the U.S.S.R., about 30,000 registered religious congregations, and 58,442 ministers of religion. The Orthodox churches numbered only 4225 —[64] little more than one tenth of the number before the Revolution of 1917. The latter figure seems suspiciously low. In June, 1945, G. G. Karpov stated that there were more than 16,000 Orthodox churches open at that time —[65] which seems a more plausible estimate than the earlier one. The church was still far below its original strength, however.

What was especially important was that observers repeatedly stressed that there were few young people in the congregations. At the service in Kuibyshev that Eve Curie attended in 1941 she noted: "None of these faces was young. It was as if an entire generation had vanished, had escaped — and as if only aged people had remained to pray for the missing, for the absent." She concluded that her observations "had in fact strikingly confirmed to me that, on the whole, the young Russian generations had parted with Christianity, that they had been converted to a new faith that left room for no other faith."[66] A visitor at Christmas service in Kuibyshev in 1942 stated that it was attended by members of the older generation;[67] and a description of the Christmas crowds in 1944 that filled the Moscow Cathedral to overflowing stated: "The people were a normal sample of Moscow's housewives and middle-aged men. A few uniforms were to be seen. . . . Indeed, not many of those present could have received their education since the revolution."[68] Maurice Hindus, describing a special service for victory held in 1943, with Patriarch Sergii officiating in the presence of the Archbishop of York, said of the vast crowd present: ". . . few were the young people present and fewer still the men. Overwhelmingly the congregation was made up of middle-aged women in white and black kerchiefs."[69] In an interview with Acting Patriarch Sergii in 1941 Wallace Carroll pointed out that he had noted few young people in church; the churchman agreed, although he said that there had been some increase in the attendance of the young since the outbreak of war.[70]

Another weakness of the church was that there were few young priests. Metropolitan Sergii admitted to Wallace Carroll that few young men sought to enter the priesthood;[71] Bishop Pitirim of Kuibyshev told Eve Curie that there were no young priests in Russia.[72] This situation may have begun to change in the later part of the war, however, as a result of the new facilities for training priests.

There were other signs of weakness. In October, 1943, Patriarch Sergii warned his church that often the parishioners were interested merely in having rituals performed in impressive fashion and cared little for the spiritual aspect of religion. Even unconsecrated persons were used for that purpose. He cited a report that in Central Asia the vestry of a certain parish had engaged for Easter service a man who frankly said that he did not believe.[73] The Sobor of 1945 found it necessary to publish a message which, after hailing the recent achievements, pointed out certain failings in church life. Many laymen, the message declared, were negligent in observance of divine worship and the fasts of the church. Many believers were charged with failure to solemnize their weddings with the sacrament of marriage.[74]

In the light of the evidence presented above, there is reason to think that the Russian Orthodox church, in spite of its recovery during the war years, was still in a weakened state. This boded ill for the future, since, especially in the latter months of the war, it became clear that the benevolent Soviet attitude toward religion, including the Orthodox church, was not a result of any fundamental reversal of attitude and that, indeed, the basic Marxist hostility to religion was unchanged, although it was not strongly in evidence. Reference has already been made to a statement by Kalinin in 1943, in which he did not condemn mild ridicule of religious recruits in the army. Toward the end of the war additional signs of the antireligious outlook were to be observed.

Actually the new trend in propaganda was not explicitly anti-religious, for it concentrated on "scientific and enlightening propaganda," with no direct mention of religion or the church. An important directive of the Central Committee of the Communist party in September,

1944, "On the Organization of Scientific Educational Propaganda," ordered a great increase in scientific propaganda with the object of "raising the cultural level of the wide masses of the working people, and the overcoming of the survivals of ignorance, superstition, and prejudice." [75] While this article did not mention church or religion, it was obviously antireligious in its philosophical approach. Similarly, an article by Academician S. Vavilov insisted that the intelligentsia had the obligation unceasingly to carry on scientific and enlightening propaganda about the origin of life, about nature and the development of society in order to "overcome the remnants of superstition and prejudice." In particular he praised a series of pamphlets published by *Molodaia Gvardiia* (*The Young Guard*), on topics such as *The Origin of Mankind, Learning and Superstition, Will There Be an End of the Earth?* and *The Development of Life on Earth*.[76] The antireligious, materialistic outlook of this article was clear.

Thus by the end of the Russo–German war the situation of the Orthodox church in the U.S.S.R. was becoming more clearly defined. On the one hand, it had gained remarkably during the war, largely because of the benevolent attitude of the Soviet government, which, if one may judge from appearances, seems to have felt that the unity of the country would be promoted by permitting a revival of religion. In addition, to have the Russian church (and other denominations) in flourishing condition would weaken enemy propaganda and would strengthen Soviet influence in neighboring lands. On the other hand, the Soviet and Communist party authorities still apparently retained their conviction that religion was essentially an opponent of socialism and communism and felt it necessary to prevent it from regaining a really strong position, especially among the younger generation. The succeeding years would show how far the opposition to further extension of the church's influence would go.

CHAPTER XVI
The Strange Alliance

> Those manifestations . . . in the mutual relations between church and state are not something accidental, unexpected, do not have a temporary character, are not a tactical maneuver, as some ill-wishers say. . . . These measures of the Soviet government relating to the life of the Russian Orthodox church are in full conformity with the Constitution of the USSR and bear the character of approval of the position that the church took toward the Soviet state in the last decade before the war and, in particular, during the war, for the most speedy achievement of victory over the enemy.[1]

THESE WORDS, spoken by G. G. Karpov, chairman of the Council on Affairs of the Orthodox Church, during the latter part of the war, were a promise that the benevolent attitude toward the church would not wither away at the war's end. This chapter considers the extent to which this pledge has been kept.

On the whole, the pledge has been well kept. In a number of ways the Soviet government has shown favor toward the church — among them, the awarding of medals to members of the clergy for wartime services. In August, 1946, Patriarch Alexii was given the Order of the Red Banner for his work during the war, and in 1947 the medal "For Valiant Labor in the Great War of the Fatherland" was awarded groups of clergy of the dioceses of Molotovsk, Kuibyshev, Astrakhan, Kamenets-Podolsk, and Rostov-on-Don.[2] Furthermore, the utterances by Karpov continued to be favorable. In June, 1945, he cheerfully reported to C. L. Sulzberger of the *New York Times* that the church, thanks to its recovery, now had more than 16,000 churches in operation. The purpose of his council was "to guarantee real freedom for the church and religion."[3] In July, 1948, he addressed the Assembly of

Churchmen convened in Moscow to celebrate the five hundredth anniversary of the autocephalous status of the Russian church, stating that the church was wholly free and that the government wanted it to be so; he reported continuing gains of the church.[4]

The actions of the government displayed the same spirit. According to an American authority, on August 15, 1945, a decree by the Council of People's Commissars granted the church the right to acquire objects needed for divine service and to build, rent, or acquire church buildings. The local soviets were required to assist the congregations to repair and improve church buildings.[5] On February 22, 1946, the government of the Russian Soviet Republic passed a law ending taxes on monastery buildings and lands.[6] Even more remarkable was an incident reported by V. Tereschenko, who served for fifteen months as UNRRA representative in the Ukraine. In 1946 or 1947 he was told by an attorney that he had just succeeded in recovering for a parish organization a small house that had formerly belonged to it, even though the dispossessed occupant was an organization of the Communist party![7]

During the years after the war the church continued to grow. By 1948, according to Karpov, the number of parishes had risen from 16,000 to 22,000. There were 89 monastic institutions in 1948.[8] Dean Andrei Sergeenko of Paris, who with Father Sergei Shevich visited Moscow for three months early in 1947, reported that there were 25,500 churches functioning, as well as 3500 houses of prayer.[9] In spite of the discrepancy of the two sets of figures, they both indicate a remarkable revival of the Russian Orthodox church. In 1914 the number of parish churches was approximately 40,000; in 1947, after thirty years of Soviet rule, there were still more than half that number in existence, albeit in a slightly larger area.

Another sign of the church's growth was an increase in the number of bishops, as a result of numerous consecrations as well as of the return of a number of Renovationists to the fold. According to references made to them in the *Journal of the Patriarchate of Moscow,* there were 73 diocesan bishops and archbishops in 1950, in addition to Patriarch Alexii and Metropolitan Nikolai of Krutitsy. In 1949 a birthday greeting to Stalin was signed by the Patriarch and 73 other prelates.[10] In 1947 the *Bol'shaia Sovetskaia Entsiklopediia (Great*

Soviet Encyclopedia) stated that there were 83 dioceses headed by bishops.[11]

Throughout the postwar period the church appeared to be in good financial condition. The ceremonies, the entertainment provided for visiting church dignitaries, indicated no lack of funds, and the extensive restoration of damaged church buildings must have required substantial sums. An article in the church press indicated that the diocese of Chkalov in the Ural area had ample funds, as during 1946 it donated 1,742,000 rubles, as well as gifts in kind, for the needs of the state, while in February, 1947, the diocesan congress appropriated 50,000 rubles for widows, orphans, and invalids of the war, 30,000 for religious educational institutions, and 20,000 for the restoration of the Troitse-Sergieva Lavra (a famous monastery near Moscow).[12] According to Bishop Adam, an American prelate who visited the U.S.S.R. in 1946, the professors at the theological academies and seminaries were paid salaries comparable to those in secular schools, while the students received scholarships from the church.[13] In 1949 a priest of the diocese of Molotov (in the Ural region) sent 10,000 rubles to the Patriarchate of Moscow for the scholarship fund at the Moscow Theological Academy.[14]

Church attendance, as reported by church sources and by lay observers, also showed that the church had received a marked rejuvenation. Tereschenko, the UNRRA representative previously mentioned, referred to enormous crowds at the Moscow Cathedral at Easter and other festivals, as did the American John Fischer.[15] Dean Sergeenko and Father Shevich were highly enthusiastic about the size and the fervor of the congregations they observed in the U.S.S.R. early in 1947. They spoke of "a sea of people and souls"; at another occasion the crowd was so dense that one "could not raise his hand to make the sign of the cross." During Lent and at Eastertide there was "an unbelievable overfilling of the churches." At the cathedral in Leningrad, where some four hundred thousand received Communion at Easter, the Metropolitan did not dare follow the religious procession around the church lest the pressure of bodies prevent him from reentering. At a rural church near Moscow the priest stated that almost all the collective farmers were parishioners and that few were unbelievers.[16] Understandably, the visiting ecclesiastics were eager to impress the Russians in Paris, for whom they wrote; but even if allowance is made for exaggeration, the evidence seems to indicate a marked religious revival. The *Journal of the Patriarchate of Moscow* also reported large congregations. A special service on the saint's day of Patriarch Alexii in 1949 filled the cathedral to overflowing, and in summer long lines of pilgrims, as of yore, visited the Troitse-Sergieva Lavra, many of them sleeping in the open.[17]

Another sign of the favorable state of the Russian Orthodox church was the ending of the Union of Brest, an act in 1596 when a sizable group of Orthodox clergy and laymen had accepted papal authority while retaining their Orthodox rites and practices. In 1946 some five million Uniats renounced the papacy and asked to be received under the jurisdiction of the Patriarch of Moscow — a request that was speedily granted. According to the Orthodox explanation, an "initiative group" of Greek–Uniat priests of the Western Ukraine first journeyed to Kiev and were taken into the Russian Orthodox church; two of them were consecrated bishops. The initiative group then returned to L'vov, where they called a Sobor of 204 ecclesiastics and 12 laymen. On March 8, 1946, the gathering voted unanimously to return to the faith of their fathers by joining the Russian church.[18]

The Vatican promptly declared this action null and void, charging that the four Uniat bishops of the area had all been arrested, while their clergy had been subjected to intense pressure.[19] The Moscow radio sharply denied these charges, quoting the newly consecrated bishops Antonii and Mikhail as saying that, while the Uniat Metropolitan Slepoi and four bishops had been arrested, it was not for religious reasons but because they had been guilty of treasonable collaboration with the German invaders during the war. No other arrests among the Uniat clergy, the bishops were quoted as saying, had been made.[20]

It is, of course, impossible to determine why the Uniat bishops were arrested. Obviously, however, the arrests facilitated the renunciation of papal authority by the Uniats and their return to the Russian church. It seems likely that the latter development would not have taken place without the approval of the Soviet civil authorities.

A somewhat similar development occurred in Carpatho-Ukraine in 1949, after intensive missionary activity by Archbishop Makarii of L'vov. Whether the missionary efforts were assisted by the power of the government is not indicated in the extremely scanty sources available on this matter.[21]

One of the most impressive illustrations of the favorable state of the Russian Orthodox church was the celebration of the five hundredth anniversary of its autocephaly in Moscow July 8–19, 1948. The gathering included not only the leaders of the Russian church, but also the Patriarch-Catholicos of the Georgian Orthodox church, the Patriarchs of the Rumanian and Serbian Orthodox churches, and Metropolitan Stefan, head of the Bulgarian Orthodox church. Representatives of the Patriarchs of Constantinople, Antioch, and Alexandria were also present. The Greek, Albanian, and Polish Orthodox churches were also represented, and Russian Orthodox churchmen came to Moscow from Czechoslovakia, Western Europe, the United States, Yugoslavia, Bulgaria, and China. The Catholicos-Patriarch of the Armenian church attended as a guest. While the gathering did not rank as an ecumenical council, it considered several questions of interchurch interest, such as relations with the Vatican and the Anglican church. Numerous religious ceremonies, marked by great pomp and luxury, were held in Moscow and at the Troitse-Sergieva Lavra, and in addition the visitors were taken for a cruise on the Moscow–Volga Canal and attended a special concert of religious music by the Patriarchal Choir in the Great Hall of the Moscow State Conservatory of Music. The welcome extended to the conclave by G. G. Karpov for the government merely spelled out what was obvious — that the Soviet government had made possible this elaborate celebration.[22]

A marked expansion of Orthodox theological education is also significant. Whereas in 1940 there were no seminaries or theological academies in the U.S.S.R., in 1946 a visitor from the United States reported the existence of the Theological Academies of Moscow and Leningrad and of four seminaries (Moscow, Leningrad, Odessa, and Zhirovtsi, in Minsk Oblast').[23] Other seminaries were opened later, in Kiev, Lutsk (Volhynia), Stavropol, Saratov, and Vilnius.[24] As indicated above, in 1948 Karpov stated that there were ten seminaries, so there is one unaccounted for.

The seminary courses lasted three years, although a fourth, preparatory year was offered for those without proper qualifications for entrance. During the year 1946–1947 the Moscow Seminary had 124 students, of whom 18 graduated at the end of the year. Eight accepted calls to parishes, while the others continued their studies. Karpov delivered one of the commencement addresses.[25] In 1950 the Moscow Seminary had a graduating class of 38, 24 of whom went to parishes.[26] In 1946 the Leningrad Seminary began full-scale instruction, with 74 students and 13 instructors.[27]

The training of priests in seminaries was a great step forward, but because of the urgent need for pastors it was not enough. One of the Orthodox prelates spoke in 1946 of the pressure to speed up the output of priests by curtailing their preparation; the lack of properly prepared candidates was another difficulty.[28] To meet the need, several of the dioceses organized short courses, of three or four weeks' duration, to train priests who, although serving parishes, lacked theological training. In 1948 the diocese of Minsk trained a group of 42 priests for one month, and in Pinsk 27 priests attended a similar course for three weeks.[29] In 1949 short courses for priests were given in the dioceses of Vinnitsa and Ulianovsk.[30]

Little information is available concerning religious instruction of children during the postwar period. The one report accessible states that, inasmuch as religious lessons might not be given in schools or in church buildings, priests often delivered special sermons for children and gave private lessons in religion.[31]

While the Soviet government continued its favorable attitude toward the Russian Orthodox church even after the war crisis had passed, the church was eagerly co-operating with the government. When war was declared on Japan in August, 1945, Patriarch Alexii composed a message to the faithful stating that it was a just war and asking them to support it; he called for God's blessing upon the Russian arms. This message, however, was never published, as Japan surrendered before it could be made public.[32] Two years later, on the thirtieth anniversary of the Revolution of 1917, Patriarch Alexii published a message to the church hailing the Soviet regime and asking God's blessing upon it. "Let us intensify our prayers for the divinely protected Russian power and for its Authorities headed by the wise Leader, whom the Will of God chose and set up to lead our Fatherland along the path of good deeds and glory." [33] The Patriarch's Christmas message in December, 1948, expressed enthusiasm for the regime that had aided the revival of the church. "We, indeed, with faith in the all-providing help of God will, just as formerly, firmly and unswervingly go along the path of loyalty to the commands of the Orthodox church and of loyalty to our beloved Fatherland, not sparing strength in the service of God and Fatherland." [34]

In June, 1949, Donald Dallas, Reuters' correspondent in Moscow, sent three questions to Patriarch Alexii, two of which had only limited importance. To the third, "Was there conflict between loyalty to the Soviet regime and to the Russian Orthodox church?" the Patriarch replied: "No conflict exists or can exist if the believers follow the teachings of the Gospels and the Apostles." [35]

During 1949, as the hostility between East and West became more intense, leaders of the Russian church displayed fiery patriotism. On Red Army Day (February 23) a special liturgy was sung in the cathedral at Vilnius, at which Archbishop Fotii preached on the power and heroism of the Soviet Army and the valiant deeds of its heroes, while asserting that the army was an influence for peace, not war.[36] Later in the year a long article in the church periodical, "The Flame of Inspired Love for the Fatherland," dealt with the patriotism of the Russian clergy throughout the centuries and their refusal to bow before the nation's foes. The author asserted that even now, while the kindlers of new wars were raging, "the church blesses and will bless the defense of the Fatherland." [37] And on November 7, anniversary of the revolution, Metropolitan Nikandr of Novosibirsk preached with enthusiasm for the Soviet regime. The flowering of the U.S.S.R. was the work of God, whose blessing of peace he invoked upon his land. All Christians, he concluded, have the sacred duty to work for and aid in the development.[38]

Much of the loyalty of the Russian Orthodox church centered around Stalin. At the end of the war with Japan Patriarch Alexii sent a most cordial message of congratulations saying that the loyal sons of the church were giving blessings to the Lord and "zealous prayers for your well-being and long life, dear Joseph Vissarionovich." The Patriarch closed with the wish: "May our beloved Fatherland flourish under your wise leadership and may the peace won by you serve as a guarantee of peace for all mankind." [39] "Warmest wishes for health, for unvarying success in Your great work for the good of the Native Land, for the happiness of its peoples" were sent by the Patriarch to "highly esteemed Joseph Vissarionovich, the Great Chief of our State" at the celebration of the eight hundredth anniversay of the city of Moscow in 1947.[40] At the thirtieth anniversary of the Soviet regime in the same year the Patriarch sent to "deeply esteemed Joseph Vissarionovich" and to the government "heartfelt congratulations and warm wishes."[41]

Similar enthusiastic greetings were sent to Stalin at the great church celebration in 1948,[42] and on the generalissimo's seventieth birthday in 1949. On the latter occasion Patriarch Alexii delivered an address at a special *Te Deum* in which he said of the premier:

> He is the Leader recognized by all peoples of the world, not only of the peoples of the Soviet State, but also of all working people; he is the first in the ranks of proponents and defenders of peace among peoples, peace in the whole world.
>
> . . . .
>
> May the Lord give him long life in health and prosperity to stand at the helm of rule of our native land, and may our country flourish under his wise guidance for many and many years, to the joy and happiness of its peoples. Amen.[43]

Prayers for Stalin's health were delivered in all Orthodox churches on December 21, 1949, and on his birthday he was presented with an "Address of Greeting from the Clergy and the Laymen of the Russian Orthodox Church," signed by the Patriarch and all the bishops. It was enclosed in a casket of finely carved wood bearing a gold plaque: "To Joseph Vissarionovich Stalin on his Seventieth Birthday, from the Russian Orthodox Church."[44]

Beyond the frontiers of the U.S.S.R. the Patriarchate of Moscow sought in the postwar years to secure the allegiance of all Russian Orthodox believers and to induce in them sympathy for the Soviet regime — or at least a nonhostile attitude. While the political motive was not necessarily the predominant one, the question of "a loyal attitude" toward the Soviet government was important in the negotiations. Great success attended the efforts of the Patriarch in 1945; dioceses and parishes of Orthodox Russian *émigrés* from Paris to Manchuria accepted the jurisdiction of Moscow, although substantial groups refused to make their peace. Metropolitan Evlogii of Paris brought a large following into the fold, but his successor, Metropolitan Vladimir, soon broke with Moscow. In the United States many Russian Orthodox refused to accept the Patriarch's authority. Nevertheless, the Patriarchate of Moscow gained and kept the allegiance of large numbers of believers in Paris, Berlin, Helsinki, Prague, Yugoslavia, and other areas.[45]

An illustration of this trend was given in an article in the *Journal of the Patriarchate of Moscow* by Dean Konstantin Zambrizhitskii, who for twenty-eight years had lived in foreign parts. In 1948 he returned to Russia in a Soviet ship and was warmly welcomed in Moscow, where he noted marked changes in the city. He was quickly appointed to a parish in Kostroma, much to his delight. In his article he strongly recommended that other Orthodox Russians abroad return to their native land.[46]

In the relations of the Russian Orthodox church with the sister Orthodox churches of the Balkans and the Near East it was not a question of bringing them under the sway of the Moscow Patriarchate, but of strengthening their ties with the Russian church and, where possible, of asserting the leadership of the Russian Patriarch. One of the most important forms of contact was the exchange of visits. At the close of the war delegations of Russian clergy continued the earlier series of visitations to the Balkan countries. On May 12, 1945, Bishop Ieronim of Kishinev brought the Rumanian Patriarch a message from Patriarch Alexii. This visit, the Russian church claimed, strengthened the relations between the two churches and reminded the Rumanians of their common effort against the Turks in 1877.[47] A year later, Patriarch Alexii flew to Bulgaria for a ten-day stay, during which he was lavishly entertained and honored by the Bulgarian Orthodox church.[48]

The outstanding visit was that of Patriarch Alexii to the Orthodox churches of the Near East. On May 27, 1945, accompanied by Metropolitan Nikolai of Krutitsy, Archbishop Vitalii of Tula, and a suite of lesser clergy, he flew in a Soviet plane to Teheran, Bagdad, and Beirut. After a visit with the Patriarch of Antioch, the two motored to Jerusalem, where they were welcomed by the Patriarch and by many of the Russian clergy living there. Never before had a Russian patriarch appeared in the Holy City. Patriarch Alexii's journey then extended to Egypt, where King Farouk and the Patriarch of Alexandria served as hosts. On the return trip Alexii again visited Beirut, where he was entertained by the Soviet Ambassador and by the Patriarch of Antioch. From there he drove to Damascus, whose patriarch gave him an elaborate welcome. Finally he flew to Moscow in a special Soviet plane.[49]

This ceremonial journey of the leaders of the Russian church doubtless increased the influence of the Russian Orthodox church in the Near East, for this was the first time that a Russian patriarch had visited the Levant. Probably the influence of the Soviet government, which had made the expedition possible, was also furthered thereby. It is significant that Patriarch Alexii rather pointedly omitted Constantinople from his itinerary. His relations with the Patriarch of Constantinople, like those of the Soviet government with Greece and Turkey, were not cordial at that time.

In passing, it should be noted that Metropolitan Nikolai had left the patriarchal party at Alexandria, where he embarked by plane for London. He was welcomed by the Archbishops of Canterbury and York and visited King George.[50]

Return visits to Moscow soon began. In June, 1945, Metropolitan Stefan of Bulgaria came to the Soviet capital, where he was warmly greeted by the Patriarch and Karpov, the government's representative. Before his departure he journeyed to Leningrad and to Kiev, where he received full honors.[51] In 1946, the Rumanian Patriarch paid a similar courtesy call.[52]

The year 1948 saw the Council of Heads of Autocephalous Churches in Moscow, held in connection with the celebration of the five hundredth anniversary of the autocephaly of the Russian church. It brought to Moscow great numbers of high Orthodox ecclesiastics and served to tighten the bonds among the churches. After it the visits of Orthodox clergy to Moscow continued. In 1950 the Russian Patriarch was host to Patriarch Iustinian of Rumania and an extensive suite and to the newly installed Archbishop Paisii of Tirana, head of the Albanian Orthodox church.[53]

By the end of World War II the Russian church had risen to eminence among its sister churches. It had always had by far the largest body of believers; now its prestige was vastly enhanced by the visible favor of the Soviet government, whose power had risen to new heights. Consequently, although by tradition the Ecumenical Patriarch of Constantinople was foremost among equals, the center of gravity in the Orthodox world had shifted to Moscow, and it is not surprising to find the Russian Patriarch making an open bid for pre-eminence. In September, 1947, he convoked in Moscow a conference of bishops from most of the Eastern Orthodox churches, to discuss the calling of an ecumenical council, which had not been held for many centuries. The Patriarch of Constantinople disputed the right of the Russian church to call such a council, declaring that that was *his* prerogative as Ecumenical Patriarch. As a result, the Patriarch of Moscow postponed the conference "until a more suitable time." [54]

The Moscow celebration in 1948 proved to be the awaited occasion. After the greetings, ceremonies, and lavish entertainment, the visitors and the heads of the Russian church convened in a Conference of Heads of Autocephalous Churches, at which several weighty matters were considered. Although no claim was made that this was an ecumenical council, in many respects it acted like one. With the marked abstention of the Patriarchate of Constantinople and the Orthodox church of Greece, the assembled dignitaries adopted a series of resolutions that supported the position of the Russian church in world affairs and through it, that of the Soviet government. A strong resolution condemning the political orientation of the Vatican, and a "Message to Christians of the Whole World," were adopted, both of them supporting the Russian position. Conditional willingness to recognize communion with the Anglican church was shown. On the other hand, the meeting in a sharply critical resolution refused to participate in the World Conference of Churches. [55] In general, the action taken was evidence of the success of the Russian church in securing support for its policies and those of the Soviet government.

The abstention of the representatives of the Patriarch of Constantinople and of the Greek church did not pass unnoticed. In his concluding speech Patriarch Alexii stated: "We are sorry that the heads of the Greek churches did not grant their delegates the power to participate in this conference, because we want unity. I hope that this will not be the last conference of this sort." Patriarch Iustinian of

Rumania moved that the concluding words of Patriarch Alexii be included in the resolution of the conference, which was done. Patriarch Gavriil of Serbia proposed a resolution, also adopted, that the conference ask Patriarch Alexii to ensure that the various Orthodox churches should pursue common policies, especially in respect to the rest of the world.[56]

Thus the Russian church revealed a tendency to seize primacy in the Orthodox world from the Patriarch of Constantinople. It was significant that when in 1949 the new Patriarch of Constantinople, Athanagoras, sent a long message to Patriarch Alexii announcing his investiture and asking support and good relations, the Russian Patriarch sent a brief and cool reply hoping that they might have good relations and that they might "jointly solve all misunderstood questions which, unfortunately, have not yet been settled." [57] An article in the *Journal of the Patriarchate of Moscow* on the Moscow Conference of 1948 stressed the support given to Patriarch Alexii by the other Orthodox churches; unfortunately, it added, the Greek ecclesiastical press was hostile, accusing the Patriarch of Moscow of usurping the primacy of the Patriarch of Constantinople.[58] Late in 1949, in an article condemning the efforts of some of the *émigré* Russian clergy to put themselves under the Patriarch of Constantinople, Metropolitan Serafim stated that the latter should be reminded that he had no authority over the Russian Orthodox in Western Europe. Serafim declared that Moscow was the center of the Ecumenical church, not Constantinople. The high-sounding title of the Ecumenical Patriarch of Constantinople was devoid, he said, of significance.[59]

Although the friction between the two patriarchs centered around ecclesiastical questions, it is extremely likely that it had important political content. The Patriarch of Constantinople lived in Turkey, which like Greece was aligned with the Western bloc and strongly hostile to the U.S.S.R., so that he probably was anti-Soviet. In addition, Metropolitans Vladimir and Anastasii, who sought his protection, were violently anti-Soviet; Anastasii had been a member of the Karlovatskii Sobor of 1922 and had supported Hitler against the U.S.S.R.; later he established himself in Munich, in the American Zone of Western Germany. In general, from 1948 on the various

Orthodox churches have split along political lines, with those in countries of the Western bloc refusing to support the Patriarch of Moscow.

A similar political content also colored the apparently religious controversy with the Vatican, which became especially heated at the Moscow Conference in 1948. Upon the initiative of Patriarch Alexii the conclave adopted a resolution sternly condemning the Papacy. After accusing the Vatican of distorting the apostolic doctrine and of breaking the unity of the church, it charged that the Vatican had always played politics, supporting the strong against the weak: "The Vatican is the center of international intrigue against the interests of peoples, especially of the Slavs; a center of international fascism"; ". . . the Vatican . . . was one of the kindlers of two imperialist wars and at present takes active part in kindling a new war and, in general, in political struggle against world democracy." The resolution, signed by the churchmen there present, concluded with the words, "All Christians, without distinction as to nation and faith, cannot but condemn on this account the policy of the Vatican as anti-Christian, antidemocratic, and antinational." [60]

In the *Journal of the Patriarchate of Moscow* the Russian prelates continued their attacks upon the Papacy. It was accused of having departed from the principles of Christianity through its opposition to socialism and its alleged support of the rich against the poor.[61] Archbishop Germogen charged that the Papacy was always striving for world domination; to this end, he alleged, Pope Pius XI had actively supported Mussolini and his conquest of Abyssinia. In Germany the Papacy had supported Hitler, and Pope Pius XII had allegedly blessed the attempted conquests of the two Fascist leaders. When these men fell, the Papacy came to depend on the United States, with Cardinal Spellman a key figure. The Vatican and the United States, the archbishop charged, were both striving to bring on a third world war, in order to crush the new, progressive forces in Eastern Europe.[62] In 1950, Archbishop Luka condemned the Vatican for its opposition to progressive movements, as shown by the denunciation of progress and Liberalism in the Syllabus of Errors. In particular, the archbishop accused the Papacy of siding with the oppressors of the landless peasants of southern Italy, of supporting the Colonial powers in Indonesia, Indochina, and Malaya, and of supporting Fascist groups in South Korea, Greece, and Spain.[63]

The hostility of the Russian Orthodox church toward the Roman church, which has existed for centuries, cannot be ascribed solely to the former's alignment with the Soviet government. Nevertheless, the reasons given for the latest wave of anti-Catholic agitation indicate that much of the inspiration for it derives from the political attitude of the U.S.S.R. Similarly, while the Russian church has always professed to love peace, its role in the current Soviet peace campaign leaves little doubt that it is collaborating with the secular leaders of the U.S.S.R.

One of the early moves in the peace campaign was an article by Dean Smirnov at Christmas, 1947, saying that the threat of a new aggression had appeared in Churchill's speech at Fulton, Missouri — an utterance that he regarded as the beginning of a furious ideological preparation of American public opinion for beginning a war against the Soviet Union.[64] A few months later Patriarch Alexii wrote to Archbishop Damaskinos of Greece, protesting against the "grievous events in Greece [the Greek civil war], in the face of which the Russian Orthodox church can no longer keep silent." The archbishop, however, replied curtly that the Patriarch did not know what he was talking about; the Greek civil war was a rebellion by a willful minority.[65]

At the Moscow Conference of Autocephalous Churches in 1948 the peace refrain swelled to a mighty chorus. The conference adopted a message "To the Christians of the Whole World," saying that, while the Orthodox East was inspired by the great principles of peace on earth and good will towards men, "the aggressiveness of the Western capitalist and imperialist world sharply strikes the eye." Hence the churchmen called upon all Christians "to stand as armor against all attempts and actions directed toward the violation of peace. . . ."[66] When a World Congress of supporters of peace was summoned, the Patriarch published a message stating that he "warmly supports and blesses this call." The Russian people, he said, hate war; the Russian church, while preaching peace, noted with sorrow that some in other countries were preaching and preparing for a new, more ferocious war. Hence Patriarch Alexii called on all lovers of peace to unite to defend peace.[67]

During 1949 and 1950 the church's support of the peace campaign reached new intensity, with messages to the people to participate, the ordering of special prayers for peace in all churches, and warm greetings to "deeply esteemed Joseph Vissarionovich Stalin, who inspires our peoples and all peoples of the earth in this struggle that brings peace and happiness to mankind." [68] Early in 1950 the Patriarch called the representatives of all the autocephalous Orthodox churches to "simultaneous efforts for the restoration of peace on earth." He suggested "your agreement to take steps simultaneously in defense of peace, to the organization of conferences of representatives of churches everywhere to work out a program of universal action to defend peace." [69] In July Patriarch Alexii urged the clergy and the laymen of his church to support the Stockholm Peace Petition for outlawing atomic weapons. "I call all . . . to join their voices in defense of peace by means of their signatures. . . . May our Lord Jesus Christ, Who is our peace (Eph. 2:14), bless the present holy work and give success to this undertaking for the realization of the triumph of eternal peace in all the world." [70]

The next move was the appeal of the Patriarchs of the Russian, Georgian, and Armenian churches to the Christians of all the world, made in August, 1950. The three conferred in Tbilisi in Georgia on new ways to promote peace, which was threatened, in spite of a wide movement for peace, by "the enemies of peace" who were "stubbornly preparing for war." They called on the Christians of the whole world, in the name of the Savior, to work for peace and to confound those who wished to bring on a new conflict. They urged all pastors — Protestant, Catholic, and Anglican — "to support the fight against war and atomic weapons, and to urge from the pulpit that all flocks pray for peace in the whole world." [71]

The outbreak of hostilities in Korea evoked from the Patriarch and his Synod a protest to the Security Council of the United Nations. After stressing the horrors of the destruction wrought by "brutal bombing," it stated that the Russian Orthodox church "cannot remain indifferent to the sufferings of the Korean people and raises its voice in defense of the right. It cannot but express its condolence to the suffering country and protests against American aggression in, Korea." The United States, it was charged, had intervened in the internal affairs of the Korean people, and its leaders were striving "to draw other states into these actions against the Korean people." "The Russian Orthodox church decisively condemns this interference and the resulting inhuman annihilation of the peaceful population of Korea by American aviation. It insistently calls, in the name of Christ, the Savior of the World, to end the violence and bombardments, for removal of foreign troops from Korea and for a timely ending of the unlawful war." [72]

While this appeal did not produce the desired results, the Patriarch continued to urge peace. On November 7, 1950, he sent a greeting to Premier Stalin containing the following passage:

Our church, always of one soul with the people, inevitably serves and always will serve in all ways the cause of peace, with deep esteem looking to you, who head and inspire the fighters for peace throughout the whole world.

May this your deed be blessed by God and may the warm strivings of all honorable persons to secure peace of the constructive work of each in his native land, be realized. [73]

Thus the co-operation of the Russian Orthodox church with the Soviet government remained close in matters of foreign policy. The Soviet leaders, however, were still Communists, and they had not forgotten the teachings of Marx, Engels, and Lenin that religion was opposed to the materialist outlook that they desired to inculcate in their people. Perhaps it mattered little if the older generation still believed and prayed, as their influence would grow less with the years. The young, however, must not fall under the illusory spell of religion. A revived church might attract more children and youth; hence, in spite of the complete co-operation and loyalty of the church, the postwar years saw a reappearance of antireligious propaganda.

While, as stated earlier, in 1944 an active campaign had started to stimulate "scientific and enlightening propaganda" for the purpose of eliminating "the remnants of ignorance, superstition, and prejudice," the campaign did not at first assume a frankly antireligious character.

An early sign of the specifically antireligious approach was the publication in 1946 of a book by the historian R. Iu. Vipper, *The Rise of Christian Literature* (*Vozniknovenie Khristianskoi Literatury*). It was a scholarly attempt to show the antecedents of Christianity and how the New Testament came into being. Although it made no attack on Christianity or the Russian church, it contended that Jesus Christ never existed and that there was no historical basis for Christianity.

A more outspoken article appeared in *Komsomolskaia Pravda* in 1947, rebuking the magazine *Molodoi Bol'shevik* for an article which had stated that, instead of forbidding its members to go to church, the Komsomol should explain to them the harm of religious prejudices and help them to adopt a proper attitude. To *Komsomolskaia Pravda* this was an ignorant "attempt to show the possibility of harmonizing materialism with priestdom." It went on to explain that it was the duty of each member of the Komsomol to explain to the young "the harm of superstition and religious prejudices," for no young person could be a Komsomol unless he himself was free from such prejudices. *Molodoi Bol'shevik* was rebuked for failing to "orient itself on aggressive ideological struggle against religious survivals" and because it did not comprehend "the incompatibility of religious convictions and membership in the Komsomol."[74]

The official attitude was set forth even more clearly in the volume of the *Great Soviet Encyclopedia* dealing with the U.S.S.R. The section "Religion and the Church" stated that the Communist party, while permitting full freedom of religion, had never concealed "its negative attitude toward religion." This policy, it explained, included "on the one hand, the furthering of the actual liberation of the working masses from religious prejudice by means of organizing very wide scientific and enlightening propaganda, and on the other, presenting completely unrestricted possibilities for religious societies to perform their cult." The Soviet state held that the business of the church was the performance of its rites, and nothing more. "Any sort of propagandist, moralizing, and educational activity (on a scale passing beyond the limits of the definite religious congregations) should not belong to the church, as a union of believers, created and existing only for performing the cult."[75]

The antireligious attitude found frequent expression in the Soviet press. In the summer of 1948 the *Teachers' Gazette* (*Uchitel'skaia Gazeta*) sounded a call for educating the students "in the spirit of a scientific world outlook." Although the children were subject to many influences outside the school, including those of capitalist remnants, religion, and so on, many teachers disregarded antireligious work or avoided it, or even "are themselves captives to religious error and at times observe religious rites." The school could not dodge the obligation to combat religious influences upon the young, and all false theories of nonreligious training instead of antireligious education and of the automatic dying out of religion should be strongly dealt with. "Work in training the student youth in a spirit of scientific world outlook, including active and consistent atheistic propaganda, demands first of all from the teacher himself deep training in ideas and a constant raising of the level of his Marxist–Leninist preparation." [76] Likewise the influential magazine *Bol'shevik* insisted that as part of their struggle against the reactionary, bourgeois ideology, the organizations of the Communist party "should definitely put an end to a scornful attitude toward scientific and enlightening propaganda among the working people, should systematically carry on propaganda against religious prejudices and superstitions." [77]

In 1949 the antireligious movement reached a new intensity, with the schools and the Komsomol taking the lead. An article in a pedagogical magazine, arguing that the Communist party expected the Soviet school to bring up the young in the spirit of communism, held that the school should combat the survival of moribund ideas, among them religion. Much had been done; the "overwhelming majority" had broken with religion, and only remnants of it survived. During the war, of course, most of the clergy had supported the Soviet cause and had been given medals for their patriotic work. This did not mean official approval of religion; "the policies of the Party and the Soviet regime concerning religion remain the same as they were — i.e., directed toward full liberation of the popular masses from religious influence, by means of explanation and persuasion. . . . The religious prejudices in the U.S.S.R. are only remnants. The disappearance of these remnants is inevitable, as they in fundamental fashion contradict the whole aspect of the Communist society being con-

structed among us." Hence, "the basic task of Communist training
and of overcoming the remnants of religiousness under our conditions consists of showing to the students . . . the full incompatibility
of science . . . and religion. . . ." [78]

The same note was struck at the Eleventh Congress of Komsomols
in March, 1949. N. A. Mikhailov, secretary of its central committee,
warned that the churchmen had become more active, while the Komsomol had relaxed. Some of the members even took part in religious
rites, without any reaction on the part of their organizations. He
continued: "The Komsomol must not maintain neutrality in respect
to religion. . . . Participation in religious rites is incompatible with
being in the ranks of the Komsomol." [79] Only a small fraction of
Mikhailov's speech dealt with religion; nevertheless, this unequivocal
directive was important.

While most of the antireligious activity centered in the Komsomol
and the schools, in November, 1949, the Moscow radio presented a
talk, "Science and Religion on the Origins of Man," which contained
the following passage:

"There will always be poor on earth" teaches the Bible. By quoting
the Holy Scriptures, the bourgeoisie is in a position to assert that
class society is inexorable and permanent, that the violation of the
laws of the capitalist state is tantamount to violation of Holy Writ.
. . . Another such holy book, . . . the New Testament, through its
principle "resist not evil," teaches man to bear without demur the
misfortunes and burdens of his earthly existence — poverty, hunger,
and persecution.[80]

Charges that religion is antiscientific and that it supports reaction
were contained in a long article in the *Teachers' Gazette* by the veteran antireligious leader F. Oleshchuk. "Communism is the banner of
revolution, of progress, of movement forward; religion is the banner
of reaction, of retrogression." Religion holds that labor is a curse,
not a blessing, takes a reactionary attitude toward women, and supports national hatreds and dissensions. "The Bolshevik Party and the
Soviet regime call for a struggle fully to overcome religious prejudices
and superstition, for bringing up all Soviet people in the spirit of a
scientific materialist world outlook, for transforming all the work-

ing people of our land into active and conscious builders of socialism."
In this struggle the teachers would have a leading role. "The Soviet
teacher . . . is obliged not only to be nonbelieving, but to be an active
propagandist of godlessness among others, to be a bearer of the ideas
of militant proletarian atheism. . . . The task of the teacher is to
bring up the young generation in the spirit of Marxist–Leninist
science, . . . which is completely incompatible with any religion." [81]

The duty of the school in combating religion was extended by an
article in *Narodnoe Obrazovanie* (*Public Education*). It was not
enough to educate the children in materialism; the school must induce the parents to stop putting religious ideas in their minds.

> The school should put before the believing parents the question
> of the extreme harmfulness from a pedagogical point of view, of the
> nonpermissibility of extending religious influence over the children.
> The experience of the foremost teachers shows that intelligent presen-
> tation of this question gives splendid results. Believing parents in the
> vast majority of cases realize that they do not have the right, that
> it is not in their interest morally to cripple the children, to put them
> in a divided position, bringing them up at home on religious preju-
> dices that definitely contradict the school instruction and training,
> which are truly scientific. [82]

The new campaign against religion continued in 1950. In March,
when a Komsomol asked whether it would be proper for him to
have a church wedding, *Komsomolskaia Pravda* answered that it
would not. "The Communist Party has never been indifferent to
religion. The Bolsheviks stand for science, while religion is opposed to
science. That is why the Party has always spread scientific knowledge
directed against all kinds of religious superstitions. Religion is deeply
alien to our philosophy." [83]

Finally, in August, 1950, the Leningrad radio announced that the
Society for the Dissemination of Political and Scientific Knowledge
had decided to launch an intense drive against "the medieval Christian outlook," which would be waged entirely on a scientific basis.
Propagandists would be sent to all the Soviet Republics with antireligious films, and 29,000,000 pamphlets would be distributed. "The
struggle against the Gospel and Christian legend must be conducted
ruthlessly and with all the means at the disposal of communism," the

chairman declared.[84] And in the same month the society's publication *Nauka i Zhizn'* (*Science and Life*) in an article "Can Religion Die Out by Itself under Socialism?" — answered in the negative. Religion, a remnant of bourgeois ideology, would survive in altered form and could only be eliminated by systematic and unrelenting propaganda. "Marxism-Leninism and religion are as irreconcilable as materialism and idealism. The struggle between them is particularly acute in our times." [85]

Thus the period under consideration closes with the Orthodox church in the U.S.S.R. affected by apparently conflicting tendencies. The Church has gained markedly since the outbreak of the Russo–German war in 1941 and now is in the most favorable position it has enjoyed for two decades or more. This state of affairs has come about, not in spite of the Soviet government, but with its approval and, in part, assistance. Since June, 1941, the government has lavished favors on the Russian Orthodox church, which, in turn, has strongly supported the government both at home and abroad. On the other hand, from 1944 on a contrary tendency has been noted. Even while honors and benefits were being bestowed on the church, the Communist party has undertaken a campaign of antireligious propaganda, based on the alleged incompatibility of science and religion — a campaign that has grown steadily more intense. How can these inconsistencies be reconciled?

Actually, the Soviet attitude toward religion has been quite consistent. From the beginning, Lenin and Stalin held that religion was incompatible with communism and that the demise of religion would come only after long, persistent antireligious propaganda. On the other hand, the religious problem was never regarded as one of great urgency, but as a matter that should be subordinated to other, more vital matters: the survival of the Soviet regime during the civil war, the collectivization of agriculture, the winning of the war with Germany. Even in the periods when the struggle against the Russian church was most intense, as in the famine of 1921–1922, Soviet policy sought to reach a *modus vivendi* with groups of accommodating churchmen rather than to destroy the church root and branch. Once reached, the compromise has endured. The clergy, except during brief periods of special strain, have not been interfered with, and divine worship has been carried on regularly. Because the question of religion and the church has been subordinated to more important problems, Soviet policy toward the Russian church has been flexible, leading, in the last decade, to the granting of considerable favor to the church. Since the interests of the U.S.S.R. would be currently furthered by a flourishing church, the church was aided to expand, to develop its theological schools, and to establish strong contact with Orthodox churches abroad. It reciprocated by supporting the Soviet government and its foreign policy.

But while the ideological opposition to religion and the Russian church has been restrained, and at times muted, it has not been ended. The Communist opposition to religion is a constant element. Religion must be eliminated, sooner or later, and above all it must not gain the younger generations. Hence the growing drive to indoctrinate the youth with a materialist, godless outlook, even while the Russian church is encouraged to expand its activities. Probably to the leaders in the Kremlin it matters little that some millions of middle-aged and elderly people still believe, as long as the rising generations are convinced materialists. The Russian church, and other religious bodies, can safely be permitted to linger on, for in a generation few but atheists and materialists will remain. Careful study of the evidence that has been presented in these pages has led to the conclusion that this is the estimate of the religious situation held by the leaders of the Communist party in the U.S.S.R. Only time will tell whether their estimate is a correct one.

Notes

NOTES TO CHAPTER I

1. Russia, *Vsepoddanneishii Otchet Ober-Prokurora Sviateishago Sinoda* . . . *za 1914 god,* pp. 4–7 and 67 of tables.

2. *Moskovskiia Tserkovnyia Vedomosti,* No. 3–4, 1917, quoted in B. Kandidov, *Tserkov' i Fevral'skaia Revoliutsiia,* pp. 16–17. Kandidov is one of the leading Soviet antireligious writers. In all cases in which it has been possible to check his citations they have proved accurate, so that although his interpretation is untrustworthy, his presentation of source material is reliable.

3. *Ibid.,* p. 16.

4. *Golos Tserkvi,* No. 4–5, 1917, p. 10, quoted in Kandidov, *op. cit.,* pp. 16–17.

5. *Tserkovnyia Vedomosti,* Feb. 25, 1917, pp. 168–169. All dates in this chapter are according to the Old Style.

6. B. V. Titlinov, *Tserkov' vo Vremia Revoliutsii,* p. 55; see also A. V. Kartashev, "Revoliutsiia i Sobor 1917–1918 gg.," *Bogoslovskaia Mysl',* 1942, p. 77.

7. Kandidov, *op. cit.,* p. 19.

8. A. Peshekhonov, *Pervye Nedeli,* in S. A. Alexeev (comp.), *Fevral'-skaia Revoliutsiia,* p. 451.

9. Titlinov, *op. cit.,* p. 57.

10. Kandidov, *op. cit.,* pp. 19–20.

11. Protopresviter Georgii Shavel'skii, "Tserkov' i Revoliutsiia," *Russkaia Mysl',* Apr., 1922, pp. 111–112.

12. *Rech',* Mar. 11, 1917.

13. *Ibid.,* Apr. 12, 1917.

14. I. I. Bliumental', *Revoliutsiia 1917–1918 gg. v Samarskoi Gubernii,* I, 71, 78, 99, 166, 241.

15. Kartashev, *op. cit.,* p. 77; *Rech',* Mar. 8, 1917.

16. Kandidov, *op. cit.,* pp. 24-25.

17. Kartashev, *op. cit.*, pp. 77–78; *Rech'*, Mar. 7, 10, 1917; *Vserossiiskii Tserkovno–Obshchestvennyi Vestnik* (hereafter cited as *Vser. Ts.–O. Vestnik*), Apr. 15, 1917.

18. *Rech'*, Mar. 14, 1917.

19. Kartashev, *op. cit.*, pp. 78–81; *Vser. Ts.–O. Vestnik*, Apr. 16, 1917.

20. Titlinov, *op. cit.*, pp. 76–78; Kartashev, *op. cit.*, p. 86.

21. Titlinov, *op. cit.*, pp. 79–80. Before the Revolution of 1917 there was a somewhat limited freedom to change religions. Nonbelief was not legally recognized; everyone was officially ascribed to some religious denomination.

22. *Ibid.*, pp. 80–82. Titlinov, a professor at the Petrograd Theological Academy and editor of the *Vserossiiskii Tserkovno–Obshchestvennyi Vestinik*, was a leader of the reformist section of the commission.

The Pre-Sobor Council was composed in part of members elected by different parts of the church (by the episcopate, by the monasteries, by the theological academies, and other parts of the church community) and in part of members appointed by the Synod. (*Tserkovnyia Vedomosti*, May 20, 1917.)

23. *Deianiia Sviashchennago Sobora Pravoslavnoi Rossiiskoi Tserkvi* (hereafter cited as Sobor, *Deianiia*), Kniga (Kn.) II, Vypusk (Vyp.) 2, pp. 190–193.

24. *Vser. Ts.–O. Vestnik*, Apr. 15, 1917; *Rech'*, Mar. 25, 1917.

25. A. I. Vvedenskii, *Tserkov' i Gosudarstvo*, pp. 33–35.

26. *Vser. Ts.–O. Vestnik*, Apr. 18, 1917.

27. Kartashev, *op. cit.*, p. 82.

28. *Vser. Ts.–O. Vestnik*, Apr. 14, 1917. According to Russian church tradition, only monastics might become bishops; thus it was practically impossible for the married parish clergy ("white" clergy) to enter the episcopate.

29. *Ibid.*, Apr. 16, 1917.

30. *Chrezvychainoe Eparkhial'noe Sobranie Dukhovenstva i Mirian Kishinevskoi Eparkhii . . . 19–25 Apr. 1917 g.*, pp. 50–53.

31. *Vser. Ts.–O. Vestnik*, Apr. 18, 1917.

32. Kartashev, *op. cit.*, pp. 83–84.

33. Shavel'skii, *op. cit.*, p. 108. The author did not indicate whether the clergy had a part in the archbishop's arrest.

34. Sobor, *Deianiia*, Kn. II, Vyp. 2, p. 103.

35. *Vser. Ts.–O. Vestnik*, May 21, 1917.

36. *Ibid.*, Apr. 18, 1917. One of the bishops was head of the diocese and the other a vicarian bishop.

37. Sobor, *Deianiia,* cited in Vvedenskii, *op. cit.,* pp. 166–167.

38. Kartashev, *op. cit.,* p. 78.

39. *Ibid.,* pp. 81–82. Kartashev does not indicate the relative weight of the clergy in these elections.

40. Titlinov, *op. cit.,* p. 90.

41. Vvedenskii, *op. cit.,* pp. 39–42.

42. *Birzhevyia Vedomosti,* Mar. 13, 1917.

43. Vvedenskii, *op. cit.,* pp. 42–43.

44. Kandidov, *op. cit.,* pp. 13–14.

45. *Vser. Ts.–O. Vestnik,* No. 28, quoted in Kandidov, *op. cit.,* p. 57.

46. *Ibid.,* pp. 61–62.

47. *Ibid.,* pp. 57–58.

48. Kartashev, *op. cit.,* p. 84.

49. *Vser. Ts.–O. Vestnik,* Apr. 18, 1917. The source does not indicate whether this was a local or a national gathering.

50. Kartashev, *op. cit.,* pp. 84–85; Vvedenskii, *op. cit.,* pp. 64–65.

51. *Ibid.,* p. 66.

52. N. K. Krupskaia, *Antireligioznaia Propaganda,* pp. 11–12.

53. Kartashev, *op. cit.,* p. 81; Titlinov, *op. cit.,* p. 66; Vvedenskii, *op. cit.,* p. 36; *Vser. Ts.–O. Vestnik,* May 21, 1917.

54. Kandidov, *op. cit.,* p. 91.

55. *Ibid.,* pp. 91–92; see also *Vser. Ts.–O. Vestnik,* Apr. 18, 1917.

56. Shavel'skii, *op. cit.,* p. 108.

57. Vvedenskii, *op. cit.,* p. 34.

58. *Vser. Ts.–O. Vestnik,* No. 95, cited in Vvedenskii, *op. cit.,* pp. 55–56.

59. Vvedenskii, *op. cit.,* pp. 44–46.

60. *Ibid.,* pp. 34–36; Titlinov, *op. cit.,* pp. 67–68.

61. Vvedenskii, *op. cit.,* pp. 51–53.

62. *Tserkovnyia Vedomosti,* July 22, 1917, pp. 231–233.

63. Kandidov, *op. cit.,* pp. 74–75.

64. *Tserkovnyia Vedomosti,* Aug. 19, 1917, pp. 263–264.

65. Kandidov, *op. cit.,* pp. 80–84.

66. *Ibid.,* p. 75.

67. *Ibid.,* pp. 43–45.

68. Vvedenskii, *op. cit.,* p. 55.

NOTES TO CHAPTER II

1. *Tserkovnyia Vedomosti,* May 20, 1917; A. V. Kartashev, "Vremennoe Pravitel'stvo i Tserkov'," *Sovremennyia Zapiski,* LII (1933), 379.

2. A. I. Vvedenskii, *Tserkov' i Gosudarstvo,* pp. 66–72.

3. *Tserkovnyia Vedomosti,* July 15, 1917; Sobor, *Deianiia,* Kn. I, Vyp. 1, pp. 97–133.

4. A. V. Kartashev, "Revoliutsiia i Sobor 1917–1918 gg., "*Bogoslovskaia Mysl',* 1942, p. 87.

5. Sobor, *Deianiia,* Kn. I, Vyp. 1, pp. 60–133.

6. *Ibid.,* Kn. I, Vyp. 2, pp. 25–28.

7. *Ibid.,* p. 33.

8. *Ibid.,* pp. 39–40.

9. *Ibid.,* pp. 34–36, 40–41.

10. *Ibid.,* pp. 54–55, 58–61.

11. *Ibid.,* pp. 62–63.

12. *Ibid.,* p. 67.

13. *Tserkovnyia Vedomosti,* Sept. 30, 1917, pp. 327–330.

14. *Ibid.,* pp. 311–313.

15. M. N. Pokrovskii and Ia. A. Iakovlev (eds.), *1917 g. v Dokumentakh i Materialakh, Gosudarstvennoe Soveshchanie,* p. 66.

16. Sobor, *Deianiia,* Kn. I, Vyp. 2, pp. 48–49.

17. *Ibid.,* p. 74.

18. Vvedenskii, *op. cit.,* pp. 98-99; Titlinov, *Tserkov' vo Vremia Revoliutsii,* p. 70.

19. Protopresviter Georgii Shavel'skii, "Tserkov' i Revoliutsiia," *Russkaia Mysl',* Apr., 1922, pp. 112–113.

20. Sobor, *Deianiia,* Kn. I, Vyp. 2, p. 29.

21. Kartashev, "Vremennoe Pravitel'stvo i Tserkov'," *Sovremennyia Zapiski,* LII (1933), 381. The Synod provided most of the funds for the Sobor out of its own resources.

22. Sobor, *Deianiia,* Kn. II, Vyp. 1, p. 92.

23. *Ibid.,* Vyp. 2, pp. 98–120.

24. S. P. Rudnev, *Pri Vechernykh Ogniakh,* pp. 180–181.

25. *Birzhevyia Vedomosti,* Sept. 29, 1917.

26. Sobor, *Deianiia,* Kn. II, Vyp. 1, pp. 72–74.

27. *Ibid.,* pp. 76–77.

28. *Ibid.,* pp. 77–79.

29. *Ibid.,* p. 83.

30. *Ibid.,* pp. 86–88.

31. *Ibid.,* Vyp. 2, pp. 128–129.

32. *Ibid.,* pp. 200–202.

33. *Ibid.,* p. 275.

34. *Ibid.,* pp. 335–336.

35. *Ibid.,* pp. 402–403.

36. *Birzhevyia Vedomosti*, Oct. 20, 1917.

37. *Ibid.*, Oct. 18, 20, 1917.

38. Kartashev, "Revoliutsiia i Sobor . . . ," *Bogosl. Mysl'*, 1942, p. 91.

39. B. V. Titlinov, "Piat' Let Bor'by za Tserkovnoe Obnovlenie," *Vestnik Sviashchennogo Sinoda Pravoslavnoi Rossiiskoi Tserkvi*, No. 4, 1927, pp. 12–13. Titlinov led the liberal forces in the Sobor of 1917.

40. V. F. Martsinovskii, *Zapiski Veruiushchego*, p. 35; *Birzhevyia Vedomosti*, Oct. 17, 1917.

41. *Birzhevyia Vedomosti*, Sept. 23, 1917.

42. Rudnev, *op. cit.*, pp. 173–174.

43. *Ibid.*, pp. 175–177.

44. *Izvestiia*, Aug. 10, 1922.

45. Vvedenskii, *Tserkov' i Gosudarstvo*, p. 102; Kartashev, "Revoliutsiia i Sobor . . . ," *Bogosl. Mysl'*, 1942, p. 94.

46. *Loc. cit.*

47. Vvedenskii, *op. cit.*, pp. 102–103.

48. Rudnev, *op. cit.*, p. 183.

49. Vvedenskii, *op. cit.*, p. 105.

50. Sobor, *Deianiia*, Kn. II, Vyp. 2, pp. 346–353, 355–359, 374–377.

51. *Ibid.*, p. 410.

52. *Ibid.*, Kn. III, pp. 1–2.

53. *Ibid.*, pp. 9–10.

54. *Ibid.*, pp. 38–41; M. Spinka, *The Church and the Russian Revolution*, pp. 87–89.

55. Sobor, *Deianiia*, Kn. III, pp. 52–56.

56. *Ibid.*, pp. 107–109.

57. Kartashev, "Revoliutsiia i Sobor . . . ," *Bogosl. Mysl'*, 1942, p. 91.

58. Vvedenskii, *op. cit.*, p. 107.

59. P. V. Verkhovskoi, *Patriarkh Tikhon*, pp. 3–5.

60. A. I. Vvedenskii, *Za Chto Lishali Sana Byvshego Patriarkha Tikhona*, p. 35.

61. *Birzhevyia Vedomosti*, Sept. 20, 1917.

62. Sobor, *Deianiia*, Kn. I, Vyp. 2, pp. 64–65; Kartashev, "Revoliutsiia i Sobor . . . ," *Bogosl. Mysl'*, 1942, p. 91.

63. Sobor, *Deianiia*, Kn. IV, Vyp. 1, pp. 158–159; Kartashev, "Revoliutsiia i Sobor . . . ," *Bogosl. Mysl'*, 1942, p. 96.

64. Vvedenskii, *Tserkov' i Gosudarstvo*, p. 109.

65. Rudnev, *op. cit.*, p. 213.

66. Evlogii, Mitropolit, *Put' Moei Zhizni*, p. 300.

67. Sobor, *Deianiia*, Kn. III, pp. 67–74.

68. *Ibid.*, p. 71.
69. *Ibid.*, p. 72.
70. *Ibid.*, pp. 76–77.
71. *Ibid.*, pp. 78–83.
72. *Ibid.*, p. 129.
73. *Ibid.*, pp. 185–187.
74. *Ibid.*, p. 176; pp. 253–254.
75. *Ibid.*, p. 254.
76. *Ibid.*, Kn. IV, Vyp. 1, pp. 130–131.
77. *Ibid.*, p. 114.
78. *Ibid.*, pp. 34–114 *passim.*
79. *Ibid.*, pp. 138–139.

NOTES TO CHAPTER III

1. Quotation from "K Kritike Gegel'evskoi Filosofii Prava," in *Mysli K. Marksa i F. Engel'sa o Religii*, p. 356.
2. *Ibid.*, p. 31.
3. Quotation from *La Lutte contre la Religion en Russie soviétique*, No. 2, Apr., 1931, p. 5.
4. V. Lenin, *Sochineniia*, IV, 353–354.
5. M. Enisherlov (ed.), *Voinstvuiushchee Bezbozhie v SSSR za 15 Let*, p. 93.
6. Russia, Gosudarstvennaia Duma, *Stenograficheskiia Otchety*, III Duma, Session II, Part 3, p. 2076.
7. Lenin, *op. cit.*, XIV, 76.
8. *Ibid.*, XIV, 402.
9. *Ibid.*, IV, 70.
10. *Ibid.*, XIV, 72, 75.
11. R.S.F.S.R., *Sobranie Uzakonenii i Rasporiazhenii Raboche-Krest'-ianskogo Pravitel'stva*, No. 18, pp. 272–273, quoted from J. Bunyan, and H. H. Fisher, *The Bolshevik Revolution, 1917–1918. Documents and Materials*, pp. 590–591. The text of the decree is as follows:

1. The church is separated from the state.
2. Within the territory of the Republic the passing of any local laws or regulations or interference with freedom of conscience or the granting of special rights or privileges to citizens because they belong to a certain faith, is forbidden.
3. Every citizen has the right to adopt any religion or to profess none at all. Every legal restriction connected with the profession of certain faiths or with the nonprofession of any faith is now abolished.

Note: Official documents shall make no mention of a citizen's faith.

4. State or semiofficial public functions are not to be accompanied by religious ceremonies or rituals.

5. Religious performances may be carried on freely in so far as they do not disturb public order or encroach upon the rights of citizens of the Russian Republic. The local authorities have the right to take the necessary measures to preserve order and to safeguard the rights of the citizens.

6. No one may refuse to carry out his civic duties on the grounds of his religious views. Exceptions to this rule may be made by special decisions of the people's court, provided that one civic duty is substituted for another.

7. Religious oaths are abolished. In case of necessity a solemn promise will suffice.

8. All civil acts are performed exclusively by the civil authorities of the department for the registration of marriages and births.

9. The school is separated from the church. The teaching of religion in state and public schools, as well as in private schools where general subjects are taught, is forbidden. Citizens may study or teach religious subjects privately.

10. Church and religious societies are subject to the same laws and regulations as private societies and unions. They do not enjoy any special privileges or subsidies from the state or from local institutions.

11. The levying of obligatory collections or imposts for the benefit of church or religious societies is forbidden. These organizations are also forbidden to coerce or punish their members.

12. Church and religious societies have no right to own property. They do not have the rights of juridical persons.

13. All property in Russia now owned by churches and religious organizations is henceforth the property of the people. Buildings and objects that are needed for religious services revert to the free use of religious organizations by special arrangement with the central or local authorities.

12. M. Spinka, *The Church and the Russian Revolution*, pp. 113–117, 140–143; B. Titlinov, *Tserkov' vo Vremia Revoliutsii*, pp. 109–118, 140–146.

13. In February, 1918, at the Synod building a Soviet official compelled the Synod officials to surrender the building and the capital reserves amounting to over forty-eight million rubles. The offices of the former Minister of Cults were also seized. (*Novaia Zhizn'*, cited by J. Bunyan and H. H. Fisher, *op. cit.*, p. 592.) On March 15/28 the Sobor was told

that forty-six and one half million in securities were confiscated, and over one million in cash. (Sobor, *Deianiia*, Kn. IX, Vyp. 1, p. 31.)

14. Osobaia Komissiia po Razsledovaniiu Zlodeianii Bol'shevikov, *Soobshchenie o Goneniiakh Bol'shevikov na Tserkov' v Donskoi Oblasti*, pp. 2–5; idem, *Svedeniia o Zlodeianiiakh Bol'shevikov v Otnoshenii Tserkvi i Eia Sluzhitelei v Stavropol'skoi Eparkhii*, pp. 3–6.

15. B. V. Titlinov, *Tserkov' vo Vremia Revoliutsii*, p. 130.

16. Evlogii, Mitropolit, *Put' Moei Zhizni*, p. 310; N. D. Zhevakhov, *Vospominaniia*, II, 40–43.

17. Sobor, *Deianiia*, Kn. IV, Vyp. 1, pp. 8–9, 57–59.

18. *Ibid.*, pp. 59–60.

19. A. I. Vvedenskii, *Tserkov' i Gosudarstvo*, pp. 114–116. It was originally intended to print one million copies of this message, but the printers refused, and it had to be circulated in multigraphed form. Also printed in *Tserkovnyia Vedomosti Izdavaemyia pri Vysshem Russkom Tserkovnom Upravlenii Zagranitsei* (hereafter cited as *Tserk. Ved. . . . Zagr.*), No. 9–10, 1925, pp. 18–19.

20. A. I. Vvedenskii, *Tserkov' Patriarkha Tikhona*, p. 45.

21. *Ibid.*, pp. 45–47.

22. Sobor, *Deianiia*, cited in Vvedenskii, *Tserkov' i Gosudarstvo*, pp. 116–128.

23. *Ibid.*, p. 147.

24. *Ibid.*, p. 153.

25. Sobor, *Deianiia*, Kn. VI, Vyp. 1, pp. 43–44.

26. *Ibid.*, pp. 71–73.

27. Titlinov, *op. cit.*, pp. 120–121.

28. *Tserk. Ved. . . . Zagr.*, No. 9–10, 1925, pp. 19–20. This *émigré* religious periodical reprinted many of the anti-Soviet messages of the Sobor and the Patriarch. As in several other instances the citations of the journal have proved accurate when checked against the original, where there is no reason to suspect ulterior motives its quotations have been regarded as genuine in the present study.

29. *Svoboda Rossii*, May 9, 1918, cited in J. Bunyan, *Intervention, Civil War and Communism*, p. 15; D. I. Doroshenko, "Getmanstvo 1918 g. na Ukraine," *Golos Minuvshego na Chuzhoi Storone*, N. 5/XVIII (1927), p. 161.

30. B. Kandidov, *Tserkov' i Grazhdanskaia Voina na Iuge*, p. 30; *Pravda*, No. 117, May 28, 1922.

31. R.S.F.S.R., *Obvinitel'noe Zakliuchenie po Delu Grazhdan: Bellavina . . . ; Fedomenova . . . ; Stadnitskogo . . . ; i Gur'eva . . .*, p. 14.

32. G. P. Fedotov, *The Russian Church since the Revolution*, p. 26. The author, who was professor of medieval history in the universities of Saratov and Petrograd, left Russia in 1925. He became active in the Russian Orthodox church in Paris headed by Metropolitan Evlogii and taught in the Russian Theological Institute in Paris.

33. Titlinov, *op. cit.*, pp. 121–122.

34. Sobor, *Deianiia,* cited in Vvedenskii, *Tserkov' i Gosudarstvo*, p. 150.

35. *Ibid.*, pp. 183–187.

36. *Ibid.*, pp. 191, 193.

37. Titlinov, *op. cit.*, p. 122.

38. Leaflet presented by Baron de Baye to the Bibliothèque de Documentation Internationale Contemporaine, Paris.

39. *Novaia Zhizn'*, Feb. 19, 1918, cited in J. Bunyan and H. H. Fisher, *The Bolshevik Revolution,* p. 592.

40. Sobor, *Deianiia,* cited in Vvedenskii, *Tserkov' i Gosudarstvo*, pp. 181–182.

41. *Ibid.*, pp. 202–207.

42. Fedotov, *op. cit.*, p. 24.

43. Titlinov, *op. cit.*, pp. 125–126.

44. *Ibid.*, p. 127; Fedotov, *op. cit.*, p. 24; Sobor, *Deianiia,* cited in Vvedenskii, *Tserkov' i Gosudarstvo*, pp. 194–195; Bunyan and Fisher, *op. cit.*, pp. 592–594.

45. *Tserk. Ved.*, . . . *Zagr.*, No. 3–4, 1927.

46. M. Gorev, *Protiv Antisemitov*, p. 99.

47. Sobor, *Deianiia,* Kn. IX, Vyp. 1, pp. 25–29.

48. *Ibid.*, pp. 27, 30.

49. *Ibid.*, p. 31.

50. *Ibid.*, pp. 31–32.

51. Titlinov, *op. cit.*, pp. 133–136.

52. *Tserk. Ved.* . . . *Zagr.*, No. 6–7, June, 1922, pp. 3–5.

53. Vvedenskii, *Tserkov' i Gosudarstvo*, p. 219.

54. *Ibid.*, p. 224.

55. *Ibid.*, pp. 222–224.

56. P. N. Miliukov, *Outlines of Russian Culture,* I, 165.

57. *Tserk. Ved.* . . . *Zagr.*, No. 6–7, 1922, pp. 2–3; Vvedenskii, *Tserkov' Gosudarstvo*, pp. 216–219.

58. *Izvestiia*, No. 81, Apr. 14, 1923.

59. Vvedenskii, *Tserkov' i Gosudarstvo*, pp. 225–226.

60. *Ibid.*, pp. 227–229.

61. *Ibid.*, pp. 226–227.

62. Bunyan, *op. cit.*, pp. 511, 520–611.

63. R.S.F.S.R., *Sobranie Uzakonenii i Rasporiazhenii Raboche-Krest'ianskogo Pravitel'stva. Sistematicheskii Sbornik Vazhneishikh Dekretov, 1917–1920*, pp. 20–21.

64. *Ibid.*, pp. 22–23.

65. Leaflet presented by Baron de Baye to Bibliothèque de Documentation Internationale Contemporaine, Paris.

66. *Tserk. Ved.* . . . *Zagr.*, No. 10–11, 1922, p. 7.

67. Vvedenskii, *Tserkov' i Gosudarstvo*, pp. 232–233.

68. Spinka, *op. cit.*, p. 146.

69. *Polozhenie o Vysshem i Eparkhial'nom Upravlenii Pravoslavnoi Tserkvi*, pp. 3–14.

70. Vvedenskii, *Tserkov' i Gosudarstvo*, p. 230.

71. *Tserk. Ved.* . . . *Zagr.*, No. 9–10, 1925, pp. 20–21.

72. Miliukov, *op. cit.*, I, 166.

73. Osobaia Komissiia, *Svedeniia o Zlodeianiiakh Bol'shevikov* . . . , p. 15.

74. *Ezhenedel'nik Chrezvychainykh Komissii*, No. 1, 1918, pp. 24–25, 31; No. 3, pp. 28–29; No. 5, pp. 25–26.

75. N. V. Krylenko, *Sudostroistvo R.S.F.S.R.*, pp. 97–110.

76. Vvedenskii, *Tserkov' i Gosudarstvo*, pp. 229–230.

77. *Revoliutsiia i Tserkov'*, No. 1, 1919, pp. 10–11.

78. *Ibid.*, p. 11.

79. M. Ia. Latsis, *Dva Goda Bor'by na Vnutrennom Fronte*, p. 20.

80. R.S.F.S.R., *Obvinitel'noe Zakliuchenie* . . . , pp. 17–18. According to *Whitaker's Almanack* for 1918, p. 677, the British consul general in Moscow was Oliver Wardrop; no other Oliver was listed among the fifty British consular agents in Russia.

81. *Kalendar' Antireligioznika za 1941 god*, p. 25.

82. Latsis, *op. cit.*, pp. 48–50.

83. *Revoliutsiia i Tserkov'*, No. 3–5, 1919, pp. 47–48.

84. *Ibid.*, No. 1, 1919, p. 45.

85. *Ibid.*, p. 28.

86. E. N. Trubetskoi, *Smysl' Zhizni*, pp. 276–277.

87. *Izvestiia*, No. 73, Apr. 4, 1919; Gorev, *op. cit.*, p. 99.

88. A. Viroubova, *Memories of the Russian Court*, pp. 323, 328; S. V. Markov, *How We Tried to Save the Tsaritsa*, pp. 150–156, 213–215; I. Koganitskii, "1917–1918 Gody v Tobol'ske — Nikolai Romanov-Germogenshchina," *Proletarskaia Revoliutsiia*, No. 4, 1922, pp. 3–15; *Revoliutsiia i Tserkov'*, No. 1, 1919, pp. 23–26.

89. S. V. Troitskii, *Chto Sdelal Patriarkh Tikhon dlia Tserkvi i Rodiny*, p. 13; A. Rozhdestvenskii, *His Holiness Tikhon, Patriarch of All the Russias*, p. 22.

90. Rozhdestvenskii, *op. cit.*, p. 25.

91. *Ibid.*, pp. 27–28.

NOTES TO CHAPTER IV

1. *Revoliutsiia i Tserkov'*, No. 1, 1919, pp. 1–5.
2. *Ibid.*, No. 6–8, 1919, p. 118.
3. *Izvestiia*, No. 84, Apr. 18, 1919.
4. *Revol. i Tserkov'*, 1919, No. 2, p. 41, and No. 6–8, p. 108.
5. *Ibid.*, No. 9–12, p. 71.
6. *Ibid.*, No. 2, 1919, p. 38.
7. *Ibid.*, No. 9–12, 1920, p. 104.
8. *Ibid.*, p. 103.
9. V. Shul'gin, *"1920 God." Ocherki*, p. 154.
10. *Revol. i Tserkov'*, No. 6–8, 1919, pp. 113–114.
11. *Ibid.*, No. 9–12, 1922, p. 106.
12. *Ibid.*, No. 2, 1919, pp. 44–47; No. 3, 1919, p. 66.
13. *Ibid.*, No. 6–8, 1919, p. 77; *Vlast' Sovetov*, Jan.–Feb., 1922, p. 4.
14. *Revol. i Tserkov'*, No. 2, 1919, pp. 42–43.
15. *Ibid.*, No. 9–12, 1920, pp. 88–89.
16. *Ibid.*, pp. 100–101.
17. *Loc. cit.*
18. R.S.F.S.R., *Sobranie Uzakonenii i Rasporiazhenii . . . Pravitel'stva*, No. 18, 1918, pp. 272–273.
19. *Idem, Sistematicheskii Sbornik Vazhneishikh Dekretov, 1917–1920*, pp. 20–21.
20. P. V. Gidulianov and P. Krasikov (eds.), *Tserkov' i Gosudarstvo po Zakonodatel'stvu RSFSR*, p. 27.
21. *Ibid.*, pp. 27–28.
22. *Ibid.*, p. 27.
23. *Ibid.*, p. 28.
24. P. V. Gidulianov (ed.), *Otdelenie Tserkvi ot Gosudarstva*, 1924 ed., pp. 207–208.
25. *Revol. i Tserkov'*, No. 2, 1919, p. 37.
26. *Ibid.*, No. 6–8, 1919, p. 115.
27. *Ibid.*, No. 2, 1919, p. 37.
28. *Ibid.*, p. 40.
29. *Ibid.*, No. 6–8, 1919, pp. 115–116.

30. Gidulianov and Krasikov, *op. cit.*, p. 12.

31. *Ibid.*, pp. 51–52.

32. *Revol. i Tserkov'*, No. 9–12, 1920, pp. 107–108.

33. Gidulianov and Krasikov, *op. cit.*, pp. 15 and 22.

34. *Izvestiia*, No. 84, Apr. 18, 1919.

35. *Ibid.*, No. 90, Apr. 29, 1919.

36. B. V. Titlinov, *Tserkov' vo Vremia Revoliutsii*, p. 161.

37. Gidulianov, *op. cit.*, 1923 ed., p. 14.

38. *Revol. i Tserkov'*, No. 2, 1919, pp. 38–39.

39. Gidulianov and Krasikov, *op. cit.*, p. 47.

40. Gidulianov, *op. cit.*, 1924 ed., p. 371.

41. *Revol. i Tserkov'*, No. 6–8, 1919, p. 115.

42. *Ibid.*, No. 9–12, 1920, p. 70.

43. Gidulianov and Krasikov, *op. cit.*, p. 42.

44. *Revol. i Tserkov'*, No. 1, 1919, p. 22.

45. *Izvestiia*, No. 84, Apr. 18, 1919.

46. *Loc. cit.*

47. *Revol. i Tserkov'*, No. 1, 1919, pp. 8–9.

48. G. P. Fedotov, *The Russian Church since the Revolution*, pp. 42–43.

49. *Revol. i Tserkov'*, No. 9–12, 1920, p. 83.

50. *Loc. cit.*

51. Gidulianov and Krasikov, *op. cit.*, pp. 81–82.

52. R.S.F.S.R., Narodnyi Komissariat Iustitsii, *Otchet IX Vserossiiskomu S'ezdu Sovetov*, pp. 48–49.

53. *Revol. i Tserkov'*, No. 3–5, 1919, pp. 12–13.

54. *Ibid.*, No. 9–12, 1920, pp. 83–84.

55. *Antireligioznik*, Mar., 1927, p. 41.

56. Fedotov, *op. cit.*, pp. 27–28.

57. *Vestnik Sviashchennogo Sinoda Pravoslavnoi Rossiiskoi Tserkvi*, No. 1, 1926, p. 18.

58. *Revol. i Tserkov'*, No. 1, 1919, p. 27.

59. *Ibid.*, No. 9–12, 1920, pp. 105–106.

60. *Ibid.*, No. 6–8, 1919, p. 120.

61. *Ibid.*, No. 2, 1919, pp. 43–44; No. 9–12, 1920, p. 85.

62. *Ibid.*, No. 9–12, pp. 72–82.

63. Circular of People's Commissariat of Justice, Aug. 20, 1920, published in *Revol. i Tserkov'*, No. 6–8, 1919, pp. 124–125.

64. *Ibid.*, No. 1, 1919, p. 42.

65. *Ibid.*, No. 6–8, 1919, p. 125.

66. *Ibid.*, No. 9–12, 1920, pp. 45–53.

67. Osobaia Komissiia po Razsledovaniiu Zlodeianii Bol'shevikov, *Svodka Materialov po Gorodu Khar'kova i Khar'kovskoi Gubernii*, pp. 11–16; *idem, Svedeniia o Zlodeianiiakh Bol'shevikov . . . v Stavropol'skoi Eparkhii, pp.* 10–13; *idem, Soobshchenie o Goneniiakh Bol'shevikov na Tserkov' v Donskoi Oblasti*, pp. 2–5.

68. *Tserk. Ved. . . . Zagr.*, No. 13–14, 1923, p. 10.

69. B. Kandidov, *Tserkovno-Belogvardeiskii Sobor v Stavropole v Mae 1919 g.*, pp. 69–71.

70. *Ezhenedel'nik Chrezvychainykh Komissii*, Oct. 20, 1918, pp. 20–21.

71. *Revol. i Tserkov'*, No. 6–8, 1919, p. 100.

72. *Ibid.*, pp. 100–101.

73. *Ibid.*, No. 3–5, 1919, pp. 39–44.

74. M. I. Chudnovtsev, *Politicheskaia Rol' Tserkovnikov i Sektantov v S.S.S.R.*, p. 70.

75. *Revol. i Tserkov'*, No. 1–3, 1922, pp. 55–56.

76. *Ibid.*, No. 9–12, 1920, pp. 89–91.

77. *Ibid.*, No. 6–8, 1919, p. 101.

78. *Ibid.*, No. 9–12, 1920, pp. 60–61.

79. Gidulianov and Krasikov, *op. cit.*, p. 47.

NOTES TO CHAPTER V

1. A. A. Valentinov (ed.), *Chernaia Kniga ("Shturm Nebes")*, pp. 160–161.

2. *Revol. i Tserkov'*, No. 3–5, 1919, p. 51.

3. R.S.F.S.R., *Obvinitel'noe Zakliuchenie . . .* , pp. 17–28.

4. N. V. Krylenko, *Za Piat' Let. 1918–1922 gg. Obvinitel'nye Rechi . . .* , p. 67; *Vlast' Sovetov*, No. 11–12, 1922, p. 29.

5. F. McCullagh, *A Prisoner of the Reds*, pp. 262–263.

6. *Revol. i Tserkov'*, No. 9–12, 1920, p. 56. This issue actually came out in 1921.

7. P. A. Krasikov, *Na Tserkovnom Fronte*, pp. 299–301.

8. P. Orlovskii, *Poslanie Patriarkha Tikhona k Arkhipastyriam i Pastyriam Tserkvi Rossiiskoi*, pp. 3–11; P. A. Krasikov, "Chetyre Manifesta Patriarkha Tikhona," *Revol. i Tserkov'*, No. 3–5, 1919, pp. 1–6; *Izvestiia*, No. 236, Oct. 22, 1919; Kirrill Zaitsev, *Pravoslavnaia Tserkov' v Sovetskoi Rossii*, p. 54.

9. *Tserk. Ved. . . . Zagr.*, No. 17–18, 1926, pp. 6–7.

10. *Izvestiia*, No. 269, Sept. 20, 1919. Zinoviev replied that no widespread repression of the clergy was intended and suggested that the metropolitan publicize his actions against any clergy thus disciplined by the church au-

thorities. He made no mention of intentions regarding the relics of St. Alexander Nevskii. (*Loc. cit.*)

11. See B. Kandidov, *Mensheviki i Popovshchina v Bor'be protiv Oktiabr'skoi Revoliutsii;* I. Brikhnichev, *Patriarkh Tikhon i Ego Tserkov';* B. Kandidov, *Iaponskaia Interventsiia v Sibiri i Tserkov';* Ia. Shipov, *Tikhonovskaia Tserkov' i Vrangel';* N. Burkin, *Monastyri v Rossii;* B. Kandidov, *Tserkov' i Kontrrazvedka;* A. S. Dolotov, *Tserkov' i Sektantstvo v Sibiri.*

12. *Tobol'skiia Eparkhial'nyia Vedomosti,* No. 34, Dec. 28, 1918, pp. 321–322.

13. B. Kandidov, *Religioznaia Kontrrevoliutsiia 1918–1920 gg. i Interventsiia,* pp. 42–43. The text of the proclamation, apparently slightly abridged, is published in *The Times* of London and the *New York Times,* both of Feb. 15, 1919.

14. "Razval Kolchakovshchiny," *Krasnyi Arkhiv,* No. 31, p. 74.

15. L. A. Krol', *Za Tri Goda,* pp. 195–196.

16. M. Enisherlov (ed.), *Voinstvuiushchee Bezbozhie . . . za 15 Let,* p. 320.

17. P. N. Krasnov, "Vsevelikoe Voisko Donskoe," *Arkhiv Russkoi Revoliutsii,* V, 223–224.

18. *Tserk. Ved. . . . Zagr.,* No. 3–4, 1927.

19. V. Volin, *Don i Dobrovol'cheskaia Armiia,* p. 36.

20. *Tserk. Ved. . . . Zagr., loc. cit.*

21. A. I. Denikin, *Ocherki Russkoi Smuty,* III, 261, 204, 206.

22. Krasnov, *op. cit.,* V, 271.

23. *The Times,* Jan. 11, 1919.

24. M. S. Margulies, *God Interventsii,* I, 181, 186, 288, 294.

25. Denikin, *op. cit.,* IV, 234–235.

26. B. Kandidov, *Tserkovno-Belogvardeiskii Sobor v Stavropole v Mae 1919 g.,* p. 63.

27. *Ibid.,* p. 54.

28. *Ibid.,* pp. 80–81.

29. Osobaia Komissiia po Razsledovaniiu Zlodeianii Bol'shevikov, *Svedeniia o Zlodeaniiakh Bol'shevikov . . . v Stavropol'skoi Eparkhii,* pp. 7–9.

30. *Kubanskii Tserkovnyi Vestnik,* No. 22–23, 1919, p. 338.

31. Denikin, *op. cit.,* V, 157–158.

32. *Ibid.,* pp. 160–161; *Kubanskii Tserkovnyi Vestnik,* No. 22–23, 1919, pp. 339–343.

33. Denikin, *op. cit.,* IV, 94.

34. V. Shul'gin, *"1920 God,"* p. 36.

35. *The Times*, Sept. 9, 1919.

36. P. N. Wrangel, "Zapiski," *Beloe Delo*, VI, 22–25.

37. I. Kalinin, *Pod Znamenem Vrangelia*, pp. 122–123.

38. *Ibid.*, pp. 128–129.

39. *Ibid.*, pp. 127–128.

40. Margulies, *op. cit.*, III, 233.

41. V. A. Obolenskii, *Krym pri Vrangelia*, pp. 45–46.

42. *Revol. i Tserkov'*, No. 6–8, 1919, p. 104; *Izvestiia*, No. 288, Dec. 23, 1919.

43. *Vlast' Sovetov*, No. 11–12, 1922, p. 29.

44. *Revol. i Tserkov'*, No. 9–12, 1920, pp. 66–67.

45. *Ibid.*, No. 6–8, 1919, p. 61.

46. *Ibid.*, No. 9–12, 1920, pp. 55–56, 67.

47. *Ibid.*, p. 67.

48. E. E. Iaroslavskii, *Na Antireligioznom Fronte*, p. 19.

49. *Revol i Tserkov'*, No. 9–12, 1920, pp. 66–67.

50. *Ibid.*, p. 67; No. 6–8, 1919, pp. 104–106.

51. "Tserkov' i Bol'shevizm," *Russkaia Mysl'*, No. 5, 1922.

52. Denikin, *op. cit.*, II, 148.

53. F. McCullagh, *The Bolshevik Persecution of Christianity*, p. 86.

54. *Revol. i Tserkov'*, No. 2, 1919, pp. 35–36.

55. Enisherlov, *op. cit.*, p. 321.

56. *Revol. i Tserkov'*, No. 2, 1919, p. 37; No. 9–12, 1920, pp. 64–66.

57. Iaroslavskii, *op. cit.*, p. 21.

58. *Ibid.*, p. 7.

59. *Revol. i Tserkov'*, No. 9–12, 1920, pp. 64–66.

60. McCullagh, *The Bolshevik Persecution* . . . , p. 85.

61. A. I. Vvedenskii, *Tserkov' i Gosudarstvo*, pp. 239–240.

62. I. Stratonov, *Russkaia Tserkovnaia Smuta*, p. 14.

63. *Vlast' Sovetov*, No. 11–12, 1922, pp. 80–81.

NOTES TO CHAPTER VI

1. M. Spinka, *The Church and the Russian Revolution*, pp. 163–165; I. Stratonov, *Russkaia Tserkovnaia Smuta*, p. 44. The text of Patriarch Tikhon's appeal to his followers is given in Kirrill Zaitsev, *Pravoslavnaia Tserkov' v Sovetskoi Rossii*, pp. 91–94.

2. B. V. Titlinov, *Tserkov' vo Vremia Revoliutsii*, p. 184. The author did not indicate whether these were depreciated paper rubles or gold rubles.

3. P. V. Gidulianov and P. Krasikov (eds.), *Tserkov' i Gosudarstvo po Zakonodatel'stvu RSFSR*, p. 52.

4. *Izvestiia,* No. 19, Jan. 26, 1922.

5. *Loc. cit.* A *pud* is 36 pounds.

6. *Deianiia Russkago Vsegranichnago Tserkovnago Sobora,* pp. 8–14.

7. *Ibid.,* p. 24.

8. *Tserk. Ved. . . . Zagr.,* No. 2, 1922, p. 3.

9. *Deianiia Russkago . . . Sobora,* pp. 25–28.

10. Stratonov, *op. cit.,* pp. 27–31; *Deianiia Russkago . . . Sobora,* pp. 48–52.

11. *Ibid.,* pp. 37–38.

12. *Ibid.,* pp. 151–156; *Tserk. Ved. . . . Zagr.,* No. 3, 1922, p. 4.

13. *Deianiia Russkago . . . Sobora,* p. 3.

14. *Ukazy Sv. Patriarkha Tikhona,* pp. 3–5.

15. Stratonov, *op. cit.,* pp. 47–48.

16. *Izvestiia,* Feb. 12, 1922.

17. *Ibid.,* Feb. 15, 1922; Stratonov, *op. cit.,* p. 45.

18. *Izvestiia,* Jan. 29, Feb. 8, Feb. 9, Feb. 17, 1922.

19. *Ibid.,* Jan. 31, Feb. 10, Feb. 12, Feb. 18, Feb. 21, 1922.

20. *Ibid.,* Feb. 1, 1922.

21. *Pravda,* No. 33, Feb. 11, 1922.

22. *Izvestiia,* Feb. 12, 1922.

23. *Ibid.,* Feb. 24, 1922.

24. *Ibid.* No. 44, Feb. 26, 1922.

25. F. McCullagh, *The Bolshevik Persecution of Christianity,* p. 14.

26. A. A. Valentinov (ed.), *Chernaia Kniga,* pp. 253–254.

27. Spinka, *op. cit.,* pp. 179–182.

28. *Pravda,* No. 111, May 20, 1922.

29. P. A. Krasikov, *Na Tserkovnom Fronte,* pp. 200–201.

30. *Izvestiia,* Mar. 10, 1922.

31. *Ibid.,* Mar. 15, 1922.

32. *Ibid.,* Mar. 26, 1922.

33. *Tserk. Ved. . . . Zagr.,* No. 3, 1922, pp. 2–4.

34. Stratonov, *op. cit.,* p. 46.

35. Protopresbyter Georgii Shavel'skii, "Tserkov' i Revoliutsiia," *Russkaia Mysl',* Apr., 1922, p. 144.

36. Stratonov, *op. cit.,* p. 43.

37. P. Krasikov, "Chernyi Sobor, ili Zagovor protiv Rabochei-Krest'ianskoi Rossii," *Revol. i Tserkov',* No. 1–3, 1922, pp. 24–26.

38. *Izvestiia,* Mar. 28, 1922.

39. *Ibid.,* Feb. 24, 1922.

40. *Ibid.,* Mar. 25, 1922.

41. *Pravda*, No. 100, May 7, 1922.
42. *Izvestiia*, Mar. 29, 1922.
43. *Ibid.*, Mar. 15, 23, 31, 29, Apr. 22, 1922.
44. *Ibid.*, Mar. 29, 1922.
45. *Ibid.*, Apr. 1, 1922.
46. Stratonov, *op. cit.*, p. 60; *Tserk. Ved.* . . . *Zagr.*, No. 12–13, Sept., 1922, pp. 6–7.
47. R.S.F.S.R., *Obvinitel'noe Zakliuchenie po Delu* . . . *Bellavina* . . . , pp. 29–30.
48. *Izvestiia*, Mar. 28, 1922.
49. *Ibid.*, Apr. 4, 1922.
50. *Ibid.*, Apr. 28, May 6, 1922.
51. *Ibid.*, May 3, 1922.
52. *Ibid.*, May 5, 7, 1922.
53. *Ibid.*, May 6, 1922.
54. *Ibid.*, May 6, 9, 1922.
55. *Pravda*, No. 99, May 6, 1922.
56. *Izvestiia*, No. 100, May 7, 1922.
57. McCullagh, *op. cit.*, p. 17. None of the other authors who deal with this period mention such a circular.
58. *Izvestiia*, May 9, 1922.
59. *Ibid.*, June 1, 1922.
60. *Ibid.*, June 28, 1922.
61. *Ibid.*, No. 181, Aug. 13, 1922.
62. *Ibid.*
63. B. Kandidov, *Golod 1921 Goda i Tserkov'*, p. 35.
64. *Izvestiia, loc. cit.*
65. *Loc. cit.*
66. Valentinov, *op. cit.*, pp. 198–238.
67. P. A. Krasikov, *Na Tserkovnom Fronte*, pp. 283–296.
68. *Izvestiia, loc. cit.*
69. Valentinov, *op. cit.*, pp. 198–238.
70. *Izvestiia, loc. cit.*
71. *Ibid.*, Aug. 6, 1922.
72. *Loc. cit.*, Aug. 8, 27, 1922.
73. *Pravda*, No. 200, Sept. 7, 1922.
74. *Ibid.*, No. 158, July 18, 1922.
75. Kandidov, *Golod 1921 Goda i Tserkov'*, pp. 51–52.
76. *Ibid.*, pp. 52–59.
77. *Pravda, loc. cit.*, No. 166, July 27, 1922.

78. *Izvestiia,* Mar. 23, 1922.

79. *Ibid.,* No. 171, Aug. 2, 1922.

80. Valentinov, *op. cit.,* pp. 74–76.

81. R.S.F.S.R., Tsentral'naia Komissiia Pomoshchi Golodaiushchim, *Itogi Bor'by s Golodom v 1921–22 gg.,* pp. 20–21, 452–453. The amounts were given in Russian weights (*puds* and *funts*).

82. *Izvestiia,* No. 287, Dec. 19, 1922.

83. H. H. Fisher, *The Famine in Soviet Russia, 1919–1923,* pp. 318–320.

84. *Ibid.,* pp. 156–159.

85. I. Brikhnichev, *Patriarkh Tikhon i Ego Tserkov',* pp. 19–20.

NOTES TO CHAPTER VII

1. A. I. Vvedenskii, *Tserkov' i Gosudarstvo,* pp. 109–110.

2. *Ibid.,* pp. 241–242.

3. *Izvestiia,* Mar. 26, 31, 1922.

4. *Ibid.,* Mar. 26, 1922.

5. *Pravda,* No. 102, May 10, 1922.

6. *Loc. cit.,* No. 108, May 17, 1922; *Izvestiia,* No. 108, May 17, 1922. Both newspapers printed the account on their front pages.

7. *Izvestiia,* No. 106, May 14, 1922; *Pravda,* No. 106, May 14, 1922.

8. *Tserk. Ved.* . . . *Zagr.,* No. 11–12, pp. 1–2.

9. F. McCullagh, *The Bolshevik Persecution* . . . , pp. 38–40.

10. *Vestnik Sviashchennogo Sinoda Pravoslavnoi Rossiiskoi Tserkvi* (hereafter cited as *Vestnik Sv. Sinoda*), No. 2, 1925, p. 18.

11. S. V. Troitskii, *Chto Takoe "Zhivaia Tserkov',"* pp. 6–7.

12. *Pravda,* No.111, May 20, 1922.

13. *Ibid.,* No. 112, May 21, 1922; *Izvestiia,* May 21, 1922.

14. B. V. Titlinov, *Novaia Tserkov',* pp. 27–39.

15. *Vestnik Sv. Sinoda,* No. 4, 1927, p. 8, cited in W. C. Emhardt, *Religion in Soviet Russia,* p. 307.

16. *Vestnik Sv. Sinoda,* No. 9–10, 1927, pp. 42–43.

17. M. Spinka, *The Church and the Russian Revolution,* p. 207.

18. W. C. Emhardt, *Religion in Soviet Russia,* p. 307.

19. *Pravda,* No. 158, July 18, 1922.

19a. *Zhivaia Tserkov',* No. 1, 1922, p. 10.

19b. *Ibid.,* pp. 1–9.

19c. *Izvestiia,* May 13, 1922.

20. *Zhivaia Tserkov',* No. 2, May 23, 1922, p. 14.

21. *Izvestiia,* June 11, 1922.

22. *Zhivaia Tserkov',* No. 2, May 23, 1922, pp. 2–3.

23. *Izvestiia*, May 20, 1922.

24. *Ibid.*, May 21, 1922.

25. *Zhivaia Tserkov'*, No. 4–5, July 1–15, 1922, p. 1.

26. *Izvestiia*, July 7, 1922.

27. *Ibid.*, June 11, July 19, 1922.

28. *Zhivaia Tserkov'*, No. 4–5, July 1–15, 1922, pp. 18–19.

29. *Ibid.*, pp. 8–9.

30. *Ibid.; Izvestiia*, July 11, 1922.

31. I. V. Stepanov, *O "Zhivoi Tserkvi,"* pp. 14–15.

32. *Izvestiia*, No. 178, Aug. 10, 1922.

33. *Ibid.*, Aug. 15, 1922; *Zhivaia Tserkov'*, No. 8–9, 1922, p. 10.

34. *Pravda*, No. 184, Aug. 17, 1922.

35. *Izvestiia*, Aug. 5, 1922.

36. *Ibid.*, Aug. 6, 1922.

37. *Pravda*, No. 180, Aug. 12, 1922; *Zhivaia Tserkov'*, No. 8–9, Sept., 1922, pp. 7–8.

38. *Zhivaia Tserkov'*, No. 8–9, Sept., 1922, pp. 7–9.

39. *Izvestiia*, Aug. 15, 1922.

40. *Loc. cit.; Pravda*, No. 188, Aug. 23, 1922.

41. Fedotov, *The Russian Church since the Revolution*, p. 62.

42. *Izvestiia*, Aug. 5, 1922.

43. *Ibid.*, Aug. 15, Sept. 2, 1922; *Pravda*, No. 188, Aug. 23, 1922; *Zhivaia Tserkov'*, No. 10, Oct., 1922, pp. 1–2.

44. Titlinov, *op. cit.*, pp. 32–35; *Izvestiia*, Sept. 30, 1922.

45. *Izvestiia*, No. 238, Oct. 21, 1922.

46. *Ibid.*, No. 273, Dec. 2, 1922; No. 284, Dec. 15, 1922.

47. *Zhivaia Tserkov'*, No. 6–7, Aug., 1922, p. 3, cited in V. D. Bonch-Bruevich, *"Zhivaia Tserkov'" i Proletariat*, p. 33.

48. *Izvestiia*, Aug. 12, 1922.

49. *Zhivaia Tserkov'*, No. 8–9, Sept., 1922, p. 8.

50. *Izvestiia*, July 22, 1922.

51. Titlinov, *op. cit.*, pp. 20–21.

52. *Ibid.*, p. 51.

53. *Pravda*, No. 178, Aug. 11, 1922.

54. *Izvestiia*, No. 290, Dec. 22, 1922.

55. *Pravda*, No. 189, Sept. 5, 1922.

56. Metropolitan Evdokim, "Sobornyi Razum ili Edinovlastie?" *Khristianin*, No. 2–3, July, 1924, p. 2.

57. I. Bulatov, *K Raskolu v Russkoi Pravoslavnoi Tserkvi*, pp. 65–66.

58. "Dossier Américain de 'l'Orthodoxie Panukrainienne,' Dix-huit Docu-

ments Inédits," *Orientalia Christiana*, No. 4, July–Sept., 1923, pp. 87–215.

59. *Loc. cit.*

60. Uk. S.S.R., *Sbornik Tsirkuliarov po Narodnemu Komissariatu Iustitsii*, p. 104.

61. P. V. Gidulianov (ed.), *Otdelenie Tserkvi ot Gosudarstva v SSSR*, 1926 ed., pp. 41–45, 142–144.

62. *Izvestiia*, No. 226, Oct. 7, 1922; No. 84, Apr. 18, 1923.

63. Gidulianov, *op. cit.*, 1924 ed., p. 379.

64. *Ibid.*, pp. 195–196.

65. *Ibid.*, p. 55.

66. *Ibid.*, pp. 10–12.

67. *Ibid.*, pp. 12–13.

68. P. V. Gidulianov and P. Krasikov (eds.) *Tserkov' i Gosudarstuo* . . . , pp. 72–75.

69. Gidulianov, *op. cit.*, 1924 ed., pp. 128–129.

70. *Ibid.*, pp. 15–16.

71. *Ibid.*, p. 249.

72. *Vestnik Sv. Sinoda*, No. 1, Sept. 18, 1923, pp. 5–6.

73. Gidulianov, *op. cit.*, 1924 ed., pp. 28–29.

74. Gidulianov and Krasikov, *op. cit.*, pp. 31–41.

75. *Izvestiia*, No. 92, Apr. 27, 1923.

76. E.g., P. N. Miliukov, *Outlines of Russian Culture*, I, 174.

77. *Izvestiia*, No. 179, Aug. 11, 1922.

78. *Ibid.*, No. 103, May 11, 1923.

79. Stepanov, *op. cit.*, p. 3.

80. *Izvestiia*, Dec. 3, 1922.

81. *Ibid.*, No. 85, Apr. 19, 1923.

82. E. E. Iaroslavskii, *Razvernutym Frontom*, pp. 37–38.

83. *Izvestiia*, No. 147, July 4, 1923.

84. I. Bulatov, *op. cit.*, p. 59.

85. Bonch-Bruevich, *op. cit.*, p. 63.

NOTES TO CHAPTER VIII

1. *Zhivaia Tserkov'*, No. 10, 1922, p. 8; No. 11, 1923, p. 1; No. 12, 1923, p. 1.

2. *Ibid.*, No. 11, 1923, pp. 3–4; S. V. Troitskii, *Chto Takoe "Zhivaia Tserkov'*," pp. 16–18.

3. *Izvestiia*, No. 91, Apr. 26, 1923.

4. *Ibid.*, No. 83, Apr. 17, 1923.

5. *Ibid.*, No. 101, May 9, 1923.

6. *Ibid.*, No. 94, Apr. 29, 1923.

7. *Ibid.*, No. 117, May 30, 1923.

8. *Vestnik Sv. Sinoda*, No. 1, 1927, p. 7.

9. *Izvestiia*, No. 99, May 6, 1923; No. 117, May 30, 1923.

10. *Ibid.*, No. 96, May 3, 1923; Pomestnyi Sobor Rossiiskoi Pravoslavnoi Tserkvi 1923 god, *Biulleteni*, pp. 6–7.

11. *Ibid.*, p. 8; *Vestnik Sv. Sinoda*, No. 6, 1923, p. 3.

12. Pomestnyi Sobor, *op. cit.*, pp. 19–21; *Izvestiia*, No. 100, May 8, 1923.

13. *Loc. cit.*; Pomestnyi Sobor, *op. cit.*, p. 21.

14. *Ibid.*, pp. 13–15, 21–22; *Vestnik Sv. Sinoda*, No. 8–9, 1928, p. 13.

15. Pomestnyi Sobor, *op. cit.*, pp. 18–19; *Izvestiia*, No. 99, May 6, 1923.

16. *Loc. cit.*; Pomestnyi Sobor, *op. cit.*, p. 15.

17. *Ibid.*, p. 24; *Izvestiia*, No. 101, May 9, 1923.

18. Pomestnyi Sobor, *op. cit.*, pp. 16, 25.

19. *Ibid.*, pp. 23–28.

20. *Ibid.*, pp. 9–13; *Izvestiia*, No. 98, May 5, 1923.

21. M. Spinka, *The Church and the Russian Revolution*, p. 240.

22. *Izvestiia*, No. 102, May 10, 1922.

23. *Ibid.*, No. 76, Apr. 6, 1923.

24. *Ibid.*, No. 81, Apr. 14, 1923.

25. *Ibid.*, No. 85, Apr. 19, 1923; No. 87, Apr. 21, 1923.

26. *Ibid.*, No. 89, Apr. 24, 1923.

27. Spinka, *op. cit.*, p. 250.

28. *Izvestiia*, No. 141, June 27, 1923.

29. *Ibid.*, No. 142, June 28, 1923.

30. *Loc. cit.*

31. Spinka, *op. cit.*, p. 253.

32. *Ibid.*, pp. 253–254. The author has been unable to find the original interview.

33. R.S.F.S.R., *Obvinitel'noe Zakliuchenie po Delu . . . Bellavina*, pp. 29–32.

34. *Izvestiia*, No. 143, June 29, 1923.

35. *Ibid.*, No. 146, July 3, 1923.

36. *Ibid.*, No. 147, July 4, 1923.

37. *Ibid.*, No. 149, July 6, 1923.

38. *Ibid.*, No. 186, Aug. 21, 1923.

39. *Tserk. Ved. . . . Zagr.*, No. 13–14, July, 1923, p. 9.

40. Mikhail, Sviashchennik, *Polozhenie Tserkvi v Sovetskoi Rossii*, p. 14.

41. Kirrill Zaitsev, *Pravoslavnaia Tserkov' v Sovetskoi Rossii*, pp. 158–159.

42. *Antireligioznik,* No. 10, Oct., 1927, p. 28.

43. *Tserk. Ved. . . . Zagr.,* No. 3–4, Feb., 1924, pp. 13–14.

44. *Izvestiia,* No. 67, Mar. 22, 1924.

45. *Ibid.,* No. 68, Mar. 23, 1924.

46. *Ibid.,* No. 116, May 23, 1924.

47. *Ibid.,* No. 73, Mar. 29, 1924; No. 76, Apr. 2, 1935.

48. *Ibid.,* No. 4, Jan. 6, 1925.

49. *Ibid.,* No. 15, Jan. 18, 1925.

50. Spinka, *op. cit.,* pp. 256–260; R. J. Cooke, *Religion in Russia under the Soviets,* pp. 226–230. The author was a bishop of the Methodist Episcopal church. This message was not printed in the Soviet press.

51. Troitskii, *op. cit.,* p. 19.

52. B. V. Titlinov, *Novaia Tserkov',* p. 20. The author was a Renovationist leader.

53. *Izvestiia,* No. 295, Dec. 25, 1923.

54. *Khristianin,* No. 2–3, July, 1924, pp. 53–54.

55. *Tserk. Ved. . . . Zagr.,* No. 3–4, Feb., 1924, p. 8; No. 5–6, Mar., 1924, p. 10; No. 3–4, Feb., 1925, p. 10.

56. *Ibid.,* No. 7–8, Apr., 1924.

57. Troitskii, *op. cit.,* p. 25; I. Stratonov, *Russkaia Tserkovnaia Smuta,* pp. 98–99; *Vestnik Sv. Sinoda,* No. 4, 1927, p. 16.

58. *Ibid.,* pp. 23–24.

59. Stratonov, *op. cit.,* p. 99.

60. Troitskii, *op. cit.,* pp. 25–26.

61. *Izvestiia,* No. 244, Oct. 25, 1923.

62. *Ibid.,* No. 283, Dec. 11, 1923.

63. *Ibid.,* Sept. 21, 1924.

64. P. N. Miliukov, *Outlines of Russian Culture,* I, 186.

65. *Izvestiia,* July 5, 1924.

66. *Ibid.,* July 1, 1924.

67. *Ibid.,* May 24, 1924.

68. Miliukov, *op. cit.,* I, 186.

69. *Izvestiia,* June 20, 1924.

70. *Ibid.,* July 5, 1924.

71. *Ibid.,* July 10, 1924.

72. *Ibid.,* Sept. 21, 1924.

73. Miliukov, *op. cit.,* I, 186.

74. *Izvestiia,* Sept. 19, 1924.

75. *Vestnik Sv. Sinoda,* No. 3, 1925, p. 9.

76. *Izvestiia,* May 31, 1924.

77. Miliukov, *op. cit.*, I, 186–187.

78. *Khristianin*, No. 1, June, 1924, p. 54.

79. *Tserk. Ved.* . . . *Zagr.*, No. 7–8, Apr., 1925, p. 4.

80. *Izvestiia*, June 1, 1924.

81. Spinka, *op. cit.*, p. 279.

82. *Vestnik Sv. Sinoda*, No. 1, 1925, p. 3.

83. *Ibid.*, p. 16.

NOTES TO CHAPTER IX

1. *Izvestiia*, Feb. 28, 1924.

2. *Ibid.*, Apr. 9, 1925; Stratonov, *Russkaia Tserkovnaia Smuta*, pp. 124–125.

3. *Izvestiia*, Apr. 14, 1925; M. Spinka, *The Church and the Russian Revolution*, p. 283.

4. Spinka, *op. cit.*, p. 284.

5. *Izvestiia*, Apr. 15, 1925.

6. M. K. Gorkachov, *Vozbuditeli Raskola*, pp. 9–10.

7. *Ibid.*, p. 10; Mikhail, Sviashchennik, *Polozhenie Tserkvi v Sovetskoi Rossii*, p. 21; E. N. Trubetskoi, "Pamiati Sv. Patriarkha Tikhona," *Put'*, No. 1, Sept., 1923, pp. 118–119.

8. *Izvestiia*, Apr. 15, 1925.

9. Spinka, *op. cit.*, pp. 292–293; Stratonov, *op. cit.*, pp. 125–128; *Golos Litovskoi Pravoslavnoi Eparkhii*, No. 6–7, June–July, 1925, pp. 81–83.

10. *Vestnik Sv. Sinoda*, No. 2, 1925, pp. 1–2.

11. *Ibid.*, No. 4, 1925, pp. 2–3.

12. *Ibid.*, pp. 1–2.

13. P. N. Miliukov, *Outlines of Russian Culture*, I, 189; *Vestnik Sv. Sinoda*, No. 7, 1926, p. 5.

14. Ms. copy in possession of Professor Fritz Lieb of Basel.

15. *Vestnik Sv. Sinoda*, No. 6 (2), 1926, pp. 11, 13, 17.

16. *Ibid.*, pp. 13–14.

17. *Ibid.*, pp. 15–18.

18. *Izvestiia*, Oct. 1, 1925.

19. *Ibid.*, Nov. 15, 1925.

20. Stratonov, *op. cit.*, pp. 129–130; Miliukov, *op. cit.*, I, 191; *Tserk. Ved.* . . . *Zagr.*, No. 5–6, March, 1926, pp. 6–7.

21. Spinka, *op. cit.*, p. 312.

22. *Izvestiia*, Jan. 7, 1926.

23. *Tserk. Ved.* . . . *Zagr.*, No. 5–6, 1926, p. 7.

24. *Izvestiia*, Feb. 9, 1926.

25. Spinka, *op. cit.*, p. 310.

26. *Ob'iasnitel'naia Zapiska k Poslaniiu ot 12 Maia 1927 Goda Malogo Sobora Episkopov ili Vremennogo Vysshego Tserkovnogo Soveta,* in possession of Professor Fritz Lieb of Basel. The text of the decree of legalization is given in *Tserk. Ved. . . . Zagr.,* No. 5–6, Mar., 1926, p. 8.

27. *Izvestiia,* Feb. 9, 1926; the texts of Grigorii's report to Peter, and of Peter's ruling are given in *Tserk. Ved. . . . Zagr.,* No. 9–10, May, 1926, pp. 5–6.

28. *Tserk. Ved. . . . Zagr.,* No. 5–6, Mar., 1926, pp. 11–12. At this time this publication was strongly supporting Sergii and was hostile to the Grigorievtsy. While there is no proof that the text of this message, said to have been received from a reliable source in Russia, was genuine, there is no apparent reason to doubt its authenticity.

29. *Ibid.,* No. 11–12, June, 1926, pp. 4–6.

30. *Ibid.,* pp. 6–7; No. 15–16, Aug., 1926, p. 18; No. 5–6, Mar., 1927, pp. 1–2; Boris, Episkop, *O Sovremennom Polozhenii Russkoi Pravoslavnoi Patriarshei Tserkvi,* p. 13.

31. *Tserk. Ved. . . . Zagr.,* No. 15–16, Aug., 1926, p. 18; S. V. Troitskii, *Chto Takoe "Zhivaia Tserkov',"* p. 31.

32. *Tserk. Ved. . . . Zagr.,* No. 9–10, May, 1926, p. 6; No. 11–12, June, 1926, p. 32; G. P. Fedotov, *The Russian Church since the Revolution,* p. 75.

33. Boris, Episkop, *op. cit.,* p. 14.

34. *Izvestiia,* June 1, 1926.

35. *Tserkovnyia Vedomosti . . . Zagranitsei,* the organ of the Karlovatskii Synod, strongly favored Sergii against Grigorii, Agafangel, Peter, and the Renovationists.

36. B. Kandidov, *Tserkov' i Shpionazh,* p. 53.

37. *Tserk. Ved. . . . Zagr.,* No. 23–24, Dec., 1926, p. 9; *Ukazy Sv. Patriarkha Tikhona,* pp. 9–10.

38. *Vozrozhdenie,* No. 443, Aug. 19, 1926.

39. Stratonov, *op. cit.,* p. 63; Spinka, *op. cit.,* p. 312; Miliukov, *op. cit.,* I, 195; *Russie et Chrétienté,* No. 2, 1947, pp. 38–41. Sergii's proclamation is also contained in a typed document, *Obzor Glavneishikh Sobytii Tserkovnoi Zhizni Rossii za Vremia s 1925 g. do Nashikh Dnei,* which is described as a report written by a churchman in Moscow in 1930 and smuggled out to Metropolitan Evlogii in Paris. Metropolitan Evlogii gave this copy to General Denikin; after his death it was taken to Columbia University by Mme. Denikin. It has not been possible to obtain copies of these documents from Soviet sources.

40. *Vestnik Khristianskago Studencheskago Dvizheniia,* No. 7, cited in I. Stratonov, "Dokumenty Vserossiiskoi Patriarshei Tserkvi Posliedniago Vremeni," *Put',* No. 9, Jan., 1928, p. 64.

41. *Vestnik Sv. Sinoda,* No. 7–8, 1927, p. 5.

42. Stratonov, *op cit.,* pp. 175–176.

43. The assassination referred to was the recent one of the Soviet envoy to Poland, in a Warsaw street.

44. *Izvestiia,* No. 188, Aug. 19, 1927.

45. *Loc. cit.*

46. *Loc. cit.*

47. *Loc. cit.*

48. *Tserk. Ved.* . . . *Zagr.,* No. 1–2, Jan., 1928, Supplement, p. 1.

49. *Ibid.,* pp. 2–4.

50. *Ibid.,* pp. 4–5; No. 7–8, 1928, pp. 6–7; *Vestnik Sv. Sinoda,* No. 9–12, 1929, p. 3.

51. *Tserk. Ved.* . . . *Zagr.,* No. 23–24, Dec., 1928, pp. 6–7.

52. M. I. Chudnovtsev, *Politicheskaia Rol' Tserkovnikov i Sektantov v S.S.S.R.,* pp. 65–67.

53. Mikhail, Sviashchennik, *op. cit.,* pp. 23–28, 51–62.

54. Stratonov, *op. cit.,* pp. 178–180.

55. *Vestnik Russkago Studencheskago Dvizheniia,* No. 1–2, Jan.–Feb., 1929, pp. 38–41.

56. *Izvestiia,* Feb. 16, 19, 1930.

57. Miliukov, *op. cit.,* I, 203–204. The source of this document is not indicated.

58. Typed document, *Obzor Glavneishikh Sobytii Tserkovnoi Zhizni Rossii.*

59. *Vestnik Sv. Sinoda,* No. 7, 1926, p. 6.

60. *Ibid.,* No. 7, 1926, p. 2.

61. *Ibid.,* No. 2, 1927, pp. 18–19.

62. *Ibid.,* p. 16.

63. *Ibid.,* No. 2, 1928, pp. 7–8; No. 4, 1927, pp. 8–10.

64. *Ibid.,* No. 8–9, 1928, p. 2.

65. *Ibid.,* No. 10, 1928, pp. 3–4.

66. *Izvestiia,* No. 299, Dec. 25, 1928; Troitskii, *op. cit.,* p. 4, n.; *Vestnik Sv. Sinoda,* No. 1, 1927, p. 2.

67. *Loc. cit.*

68. *Vestnik Sv. Sinoda,* No. 4, 1925, pp. 6–8; No. 6, 1926, p. 26.

69. *Izvestiia,* Dec. 16, 1924.

70. *Antireligioznik,* No. 4, 1930, pp. 20–21.

71. P. V. Gidulianov (ed.), *Otdelenie Tserkvi ot Gosudarstva,* 1924 ed., pp. 13–14.

72. *Ibid.,* 1926 ed., pp. 53–54.

73. *Ibid.,* pp. 55–56.

74. *Ibid.,* p. 37; *Izvestiia,* May 13, 1925.

75. Gidulianov, *op. cit.,* 1926 ed., pp. 238–239.

76. *Ibid.,* p. 244.

77. *Ibid.,* 1924 ed., p. 131.

78. *Ibid.,* pp. 132–133; *Izvestiia,* Sept. 12, 1925.

79. *Antireligioznik,* No. 3, Mar., 1928, p. 19.

80. Gidulianov, *op. cit.,* 1924 ed., pp. 83–84.

81. *Ibid.,* p. 114. The rates ranged from 0.1 kopeck to 3.0 kopecks per sq. *sazhen.*

82. *Ibid.,* pp. 85–86; 1926 ed., pp. 202–203.

83. *Ibid.,* 1926 ed., pp. 210–211.

84. *Ibid.,* pp. 316, 323–324, 342–345.

85. P. V. Gidulianov and P. Krasikov (eds.), *Tserkov' i Gosudarstvo,* pp. 50–51, 80.

86. Gidulianov, *op. cit.,* 1924 ed., pp. 20–21.

87. *Ibid.,* pp. 203–205. This applies to the R.S.F.S.R. only.

88. *Ibid.,* 1926 ed., pp. 369–370.

NOTES TO CHAPTER X

1. V. I. Lenin, *Sochineniia,* XXIV, 100. In this chapter and subsequently the term "antireligious propaganda" is used in the sense that Lenin habitually used it. It refers to propaganda directed specifically against religion and concentrating against this influence. Although the general propaganda and activities of the Communist party were fundamentally antireligious, they have not been treated as antireligious unless they were overtly against religion.

2. *Ibid.,* XXIII, 285–286.

3. E. E. Iaroslavskii, *Kommunisty i Religiia,* p. 17.

4. N. Bukharin and E. Preobrazhenskii, *Azbuka Kommunizma,* pp. 150–155.

5. P. A. Krasikov, *Na Tserkovnom Fronte,* pp. 157–160.

6. *Revol. i Tserkov',* No. 1, 1919, pp. 13–15.

7. *Ibid.,* p. 12.

8. M. Enisherlov (ed.), *Voinstvuiushchee Bezbozhie v SSSR za 15 Let,* pp. 285–286.

9. *Ibid.,* pp. 413–417.

10. *Izvestiia,* Dec. 19, 1917.

11. *Antireligioznik,* No. 10, 1927, pp. 34–35.

12. V. F. Martsinovskii, *Zapiski Veruiushchego,* pp. 106–107, 114 ff., 96 ff.

13. *Antireligioznik,* No. 10, 1927, p. 36.

14. R.S.F.S.R., Narodnyi Komissariat Iustitsii, *Otchet IX Vserossiiskomu S'ezdu Sovetov,* p. 41.

15. *Revol. i Tserkov',* No. 9–12, 1920, pp. 97–100.

16. R.S.F.S.R., *op. cit.,* pp. 55–58.

17. *Antireligioznik,* No. 5, 1926, p. 39.

18. Vsesoiuznaia Kommunisticheskaia Partiia, *VKP (b) v Rezoliutsiiakh i Resheniiakh S'ezdov, Konferentsii i Plenumov TsK,* Part I, pp. 449–450.

19. *Ibid.,* p. 530.

20. Lenin, *op. cit.,* XXVII, 183–186.

21. *Revoliutsiia i Kul'tura,* No. 15, Aug. 15, 1928, p. 26.

22. E. E. Iaroslavskii, *Na Antireligioznom Fronte,* pp. 21–22.

23. Vsesoiuz. Kom. Partiia, *op. cit.,* pp. 556–567.

24. Enisherlov, *op. cit.,* pp. 369–371.

25. *Ibid.,* pp. 386–389, 432–434.

26. N. K. Krupskaia, "O Bezreligioznom Vospitanie v Shkole," *Antireligioznik,* No. 10, Oct., 1927, pp. 21–22.

27. *Loc. cit.;* Krupskaia, *Antireligioznaia Propaganda,* p. 29.

28. *Pravda,* No. 73, Mar. 31, 1922.

29. Iaroslavskii, *Na Antireligioznom Fronte,* p. 167.

30. Enisherlov, *op. cit.,* pp. 305–306; *Izvestiia,* Jan. 10, 1923.

31. Enisherlov, *op. cit.,* p. 306.

32. *Antireligioznaia Propaganda. K Postanovke Raboty,* p. 7.

33. Vsesoiuz. Kom. Partiia, *op. cit.,* pp. 618–620.

34. P. V. Gidulianov (ed.), *Otdelenie Tserkvi ot Gosudarstva,* 1924 ed., pp. 3–4.

35. Iaroslavskii, *Na Antireligioznom Fronte,* pp. 49–52.

36. *Izvestiia,* July 23, 1924.

37. Enisherlov, *op. cit.,* p. 326.

38. *Antireligioznik,* No. 10, Oct., 1927, p. 50.

39. *Antireligioznik,* No. 6, July, 1929, p. 112; the data for 1929 are from Enisherlov, *op. cit.,* pp. 344–345.

40. *Antireligioznik,* No. 6, July, 1929, pp. 112–113.

41. *Ibid.,* p. 114; *loc. cit.,* No. 1, Jan., 1927, pp. 45-46.

42. Enisherlov, *op. cit.,* p. 326.

43. *Antireligioznik,* No. 4, Apr., 1926, pp. 7-8.

44. Enisherlov, *op. cit.,* p. 326; F. N. Oleshchuk, *V Pokhod na Boga,* pp. 23-27.

45. *Antireligioznik,* No. 8, Aug., 1926, pp. 62-68.

46. Enisherlov, *op. cit.,* pp. 326-327.

47. I. V. Stalin, *Sochineniia,* X, 131-133.

48. *Ibid.,* X, 324.

49. *Antireligioznik,* No. 10, Oct., 1927, p. 128.

50. N. Orleanskii (comp.), *Zakon o Religioznykh Ob'edineniiakh RSFSR,* pp. 51-53.

51. Enisherlov, *op. cit.,* pp. 327-328.

52. *Ibid.,* p. 375.

53. *Ibid.,* pp. 376-377, 328.

54. *Tseli i Zadachi Soiuza Bezbozhnikov,* p. 56.

55. Enisherlov, *op. cit.,* p. 390.

56. *Ibid.,* pp. 391-394; A. V. Lunacharskii, *Lichnost' Khrista v Sovremennoi Nauke* . . . ; I. Lobachev, *Pravda o Khriste i Khristianstve.*

57. Enisherlov, *op. cit.,* p. 331.

58. *Izvestiia,* Mar. 22, 1924.

59. Enisherlov, *op. cit.,* pp. 199-204.

60. A. I. Golovkin, *Metodika Antireligioznykh Kampanii,* pp. 15-29.

61. I. V. Stepanov, *Kak Vesti Antireligioznuiu Propagandu v Derevne.*

62. Enisherlov, *op. cit.,* pp. 485-505.

63. *Ibid.,* pp. 462-464.

64. *Ibid.,* pp. 306-310.

65. *Ibid.,* pp. 289-290, 329-330; F. N. Oleshchuk, *Shkola i Vospitanie Aktivnykh Ateistov,* pp. 31-39.

66. *Revoliutsiia i Kul'tura,* No. 10, May 31, 1928, p. 22.

67. Enisherlov, *op. cit.,* pp. 291-295.

68. Oleshchuk, *Shkola i Vospitanie,* pp. 40-47.

69. *Izvestiia,* No. 211, Sept. 11, 1928; Oleshchuk, *V Pokhod na Boga,* pp. 20-22.

70. *Izvestiia,* No. 250, Oct. 26, 1928.

71. *Antireligioznik,* No. 10, Oct., 1927, p. 47.

72. *Pravda,* No. 299, Dec. 25, 1928.

73. *Antireligioznik,* No. 7, July, 1926, pp. 66-67.

74. Cited in *Vestnik Russkago Studencheskago Dvizheniia,* Jan. 1, 1927, p. 17.

NOTES TO CHAPTER XI

1. E. E. Iaroslavskii, *Razvernutym Frontom*, pp. 8–9.
2. *Antireligioznik*, No. 3, Mar., 1928, pp. 22–24.
3. *Ibid.*, No. 6, June, 1928, pp. 4–5. Probably the vast majority of Orthodox housewives baked their own.
4. *Pravda*, No. 299, Dec. 25, 1928.
5. *Put'*, No. 2, 1925, pp. 6–7.
6. M. d'Herbigny, *L'Aspect religieux de Moscou en Octobre*, p. 194.
7. *Antireligioznik*, No. 10, Oct., 1927, pp. 73–74.
8. M. Enisherlov (ed.), *Voinstvuiushchee Bezbozhie . . .* , p. 221. No details were given as to the technique of investigation, which was merely described as *vyborochnoe*.
9. *Izvestiia*, Dec. 31, 1924.
10. *Antireligioznik*, No. 11, Nov., 1929, p. 64.
11. *Ibid.*, No. 6, June, 1926, pp. 58–59; No. 1, Jan., 1928, pp. 61–62; No. 10, Oct., 1928, pp. 73–76.
12. F. N. Oleshchuk, *Shkola i Vospitanie Aktivnykh Ateistov*, pp. 40–43. The figure for absences in village schools is remarkably low, as most observers agreed that religion was stronger in the villages than in the towns. Perhaps the explanation is that the figure for city absences is for the important festival of Christmas only, while the village figure is for all religious holidays.
13. *Antireligioznik*, No. 9, Sept., 1929, p. 89.
14. *Ibid.*, No. 6, June, 1928, pp. 70–71. It is, of course, impossible to determine whether the remarks about family indoctrination were sincere or were made to please the examiners.
15. *Ibid.*, No. 3, Mar., 1928, pp. 57–62.
16. *Revoliutsiia i Kul'tura*, No. 23–24, Dec., 1928, pp. 64–65.
17. *Na Putiakh k Novoi Shkole*, No. 4–5, 1929, pp. 67–74.
18. *Antireligioznik*, No. 6, June, 1929, pp. 89–91.
19. R.S.F.S.R., Nar. Kom. Vnutrennykh Del, *Statisticheskii Obzor Deiatel'nosti Mestnykh Administrativnykh Organov* Vyp. 6, 1925, pp. 22–26. The forty-eight provinces covered were not specified. A Soviet report on administrative territorial divisions of the R.S.F.S.R. for 1922 indicates, however, that the forty-eight provinces there listed included almost all the Russian population, while the other areas contained chiefly non-Russian inhabitants. Hence the vast majority of the Orthodox believers would be found in the forty-eight provinces; on the other hand, a number of Orthodox parishes would doubtless be found in other parts of the R.S.F.S.R. not

included in the forty-eight provinces, notably the Maritime Province of the Far East, the Orenburg and Ural regions, and the Crimea.

20. *Antireligioznik,* No. 4, Apr., 1929, p. 115.

21. R.S.F.S.R., Nar. Kom. Vn. Del, *loc. cit.*

22. *Antireligioznik,* No. 2, Feb., 1928, p. 67.

23. M. Spinka, *The Church and the Russian Revolution,* p. 151.

24. *Izvestiia,* No. 66, Mar. 22, 1929.

25. *Tserk. Ved. . . . Zagr.,* No. 3–4, Feb., 1927, pp. 13–14; No. 5–6, Mar., p. 20; No. 11–12, June, pp. 14–16; No. 17–18, Sept., p. 8; No. 19–20, Oct., p. 8; No. 21–22, Nov., 1927, pp. 11–12.

26. *Antireligioznik,* No. 9, Sept., 1928, p. 24.

27. *Izvestiia,* No. 49, Feb. 19, 1930.

NOTES TO CHAPTER XII

1. R.S.F.S.R., *Sobranie Uzakonenii i Rasporiazhenii,* No. 353, 1929, arts. 1–24, in N. Orleanski (comp.), *Zakon o Religiozniykh Ob'edineniiakh,* pp. 6–12. Cf. K. Cramer (ed.), *Das Notbuch der russischen Christenheit,* pp. 91–92.

2. Orleanskii, *op. cit.,* pp. 16–21, arts. 36, 37, 45, 54.

3. *Ibid.,* p. 11, art. 17.

4. *Ibid.,* art. 18.

5. *Ibid.,* pp. 11–12, art. 19.

6. M. Spinka, *Christianity Confronts Communism,* p. 99.

7. Orleanskii, *op. cit.,* p. 25.

8. *Konstitutsii Soiuza SSR i Soiuznykh Respublik,* p. 22.

9. U.S.S.R., *Sobranie Zakonov i Rasporiazhenii,* No. 24, May, 1928.

10. *Bol'shevik,* No. 2, Jan., 1929, pp. 67, 75-76.

11. *Izvestiia,* No. 54, Feb. 24, 1931.

12. *Ibid.*

13. *Antireligioznik,* No. 1, 1930, p. 5.

14. Orelanskii, *op. cit.,* p. 57.

15. R.S.F.S.R., Nar. Kom. Vn. Del., *Biulleten',* No. 29, 1929, cited in Orleanskii, *op. cit.,* pp. 58–60.

16. R.S.F.S.R., *Sobr. Uzak.,* No. 33, 1929, quoted in Orleanskii, *op. cit.,* pp. 58–60.

17. *Pravda,* No. 3, Jan. 3, 1930.

18. R.S.F.S.R., *Sobr. Uzak.,* No. 516, 1932.

19. *Izvestiia,* No. 154, June 6, 1930.

20. *Ibid.,* No. 124, June 2, 1929.

21. *Pravda,* No. 133, June 13, 1929.

22. *Izvestiia*, No. 81, Mar. 23, 1930.
23. D. Karnitskii and G. Roginskii, *Ugolovnyi Kodeks RSFSR*, sec. 59, par. 7; sec. 58, par. 10.
24. *Ibid.*, secs. 122–125.
25. U.S.S.R., *op. cit.*, No. 248, 1930.
26. *Bor'ba*, No. 254, Nov. 26, 1930.
27. *Izvestiia*, Dec. 21, 1930.
28. *Pravda*, No. 260, Sept. 9, 1930.
29. *Izvestiia*, No. 25, Jan. 26, 1930.
30. *Bezbozhnik*, No. 11, Feb. 21, 1930.
31. *Ibid.*, No. 49, Dec. 1, 1929.
32. *Komsomolskaia Pravda*, No. 121, May 30, 1929.
33. *Antireligioznik*, No. 8, Aug., 1931, pp. 43–44.
34. *Krasnaia Gazeta*, No. 233, Oct. 7, 1932.
35. *Pravda*, No. 36, Feb. 6, 1930; No. 58, Feb. 28, 1930; No. 78, Mar. 20, 1930. Cf. Cramer, *op. cit.*, pp. 95–97.
36. E. E. Iaroslavskii, *Razvernutym Frontom*, pp. 52–58, 35.
37. *Bezbozhnik*, No. 3, Jan. 11, 1930.
38. M. Enisherlov (ed.), *Voinstvuiushchee Bezbozhie* . . . , pp. 296–298.
39. Orleanskii, *op. cit.*, pp. 53–55.
40. Enisherlov, *op. cit.*, pp. 309–310.
41. *Antireligioznik*, No. 1, 1931, p. 40.
42. Iaroslavskii, *op. cit.*, p. 60.
43. *Izvestiia*, No. 138, June 19, 1929.
44. Iaroslavskii, *op. cit.*, pp. 111–112.
45. *Ibid.*, pp. 50–51.
46. *Ibid.*, p. 66.
47. *Ibid.*, pp. 119, 86.
48. *Komsomolskaia Pravda*, No. 80, Apr. 7, 1929.
49. *Ibid.*, No. 111, May 18, 1929.
50. *Pravda*, No. 268, Nov. 18, 1929.
51. *Antireligioznik*, No. 2, 1930, pp. 12–22.
52. Iaroslavskii, *op. cit.*, pp. 62–64.
53. *Ibid.*, pp. 48–49.
54. *Komsomolskaia Pravda*, No. 283, Dec. 8, 1929.
55. *Izvestiia*, No. 8, Jan. 8, 1930.
56. *Pravda*, Jan. 19, 1930.
57. *Ibid.*, Jan. 15, 1930.
58. *Antireligioznik*, No. 3, 1930, pp. 6–7.
59. Enisherlov, *op. cit.*, pp. 199–200.

60. *Ibid.*, p. 335.

61. *Pravda*, Jan. 12, 1930.

62. *Izvestiia*, No. 8, Jan. 8, 1930.

63. *Ibid.*, No. 19, Jan. 19, 1930.

64. U.S.S.R., *op. cit.*, No. 502, 1929, quoted in Orleanskii, *op. cit.*, pp. 126–128.

65. *Ibid.*, p. 134.

66. *Antireligioznik*, No. 10, 1929, pp. 5–6, quoted in Enisherlov, *op. cit.*, pp. 332–333.

67. *Pravda*, Jan. 13, 1930.

68. *Krasnaia Gazeta*, No. 304, Dec. 3, 1929.

69. *Izvestiia*, No. 139, June 6, 1929.

70. *Pravda*, No. 8, Jan. 8, 1930; *Izvestiia*, No. 8, Jan. 8, 1930; *Antireligioznik*, No. 3, 1930, pp. 95–97.

71. *Antireligioznik*, No. 3, 1930, pp. 47–51.

72. I. V. Stalin, *Sochineniia*, XII, 176–177.

73. *Pravda*, No. 73, Mar. 15, 1930; Vsesoiuz. Kom. Partiia, *VKP (b) v Rezoliutsiiakh*, Part II, pp. 662–663.

74. Vsesoiuz. Kom. Partiia, *VKP (b) v Rezoliutsiiakh*, Part II, p. 404.

75. *Bezbozhnik*, No. 17, Mar. 25, 1930.

76. *Ibid.*, No. 18, Mar. 30, 1930.

77. *Ibid.*, No. 17, Mar. 25, 1930.

78. *Ibid.*, No. 18, Mar. 30, 1930.

79. *Antireligioznik*, No. 1, 1930, pp. 5–11.

80. *Ibid.*, pp. 67–84; *Pravda*, No. 172, June 24, 1930.

NOTES TO CHAPTER XIII

1. *Pravda*, No. 172, June 24, 1930.

2. *Bezbozhnik*, No. 69, Dec. 15, 1930.

3. *Ibid.*, No. 40, Aug. 25, 1931.

4. *Antireligioznik*, No. 6, 1931, p. 3.

5. *Pravda*, No. 138, May 20, 1932.

6. M. Enisherlov (ed.), *Voinstvuiushchee Bezbozhie*, p. 342.

7. *Pod Znamenem Marksizma*, No. 11–12, 1931, pp. 190–203.

8. *Antireligioznik*, No. 19–20, 1932, pp. 6–11.

9. *Ibid.*, No. 4, 1930, p. 3.

10. Enisherlov, *op. cit.*, p. 347.

11. *Ibid.*, pp. 350–352.

12. *Antireligioznik,* No. 1, 1933, p. 43.

13. *Ibid.,* No. 3, 1933, pp. 1–3.

14. *Ibid.,* No. 3, 1930, p. 10.

15. *Pod Znamenem Marksizma,* No. 3, 1931, pp. 33–35.

16. *Antireligioznik,* No. 4, 1931, p. 3.

17. *Bezbozhnik,* No. 72, Dec. 30, 1930.

18. *Komsomolskaia Pravda,* No. 88, Apr. 17, 1930.

19. *Bezbozhnik,* No. 16, Mar. 25, 1931.

20. *Antireligioznik,* No. 7, 1931, p. 3; *Pravda,* No. 116, Apr. 27, 1931.

21. *Komsomolskaia Pravda,* No. 100, Apr. 11, 1932.

22. *Antireligioznik,* No. 17–18, 1932, pp. 48–54.

23. *Bezbozhnik,* No. 13, Mar. 25, 1932.

24. *Pravda,* No. 223, Aug. 14, 1930.

25. *Antireligioznik,* No. 7, 1931, pp. 31–34.

26. *Ibid.,* No. 13, 1932, pp. 3–5.

27. *Ibid.,* No. 2, 1931, pp. 35–37.

28. *Ibid.,* No. 11–12, 1932, p. 40.

29. *Bezbozhnik,* No. 24, Apr. 30, 1930; *Pravda,* No. 110, Apr. 21, 1930.

30. *Bezbozhnik,* No. 24, Apr. 4, 1930; No. 49, Sept. 10, 1931; *Antireligioznik,* No. 11–12, 1932, pp. 3–5.

31. *Derevenskii Bezbozhnik,* No. 10, May, 1932.

32. U.S.S.R., *Sobr. Zakonov,* No. 475, 1932.

33. *Antireligioznik,* No. 4, 1931, pp. 43–50; Enisherlov, *op. cit.,* pp. 379–380.

34. *Antireligioznik,* No. 4, 1933, p. 38.

35. Enisherlov, *op. cit.,* pp. 379–380.

36. *Antireligioznik,* No. 4, 1933, p. 38.

37. N. Amosov, *Na Detskom Antireligioznom Fronte.*

38. *Bezbozhnik,* No. 12, Mar. 19, 1932.

39. *Pod Znamenem Marksizma,* No. 3, 1930, p. 51.

40. *Pravda,* No. 48, Feb. 18, 1932.

41. Enisherlov, *op. cit.,* p. 395.

42. *Pod Znamenem Marksizma,* No. 3, 1931, p. 51.

43. Enisherlov, *op. cit.,* pp. 391–393.

44. M. M. Sheinman, *Antireligioznyi Krest'ianskii Uchebnik.*

45. *Pravda,* No. 15, Jan. 15, 1931.

46. *Ibid.,* No. 138, May 20, 1932.

47. I. V. Stalin, *Sochineniia,* XII, 343.

48. *Antireligioznik,* No. 3, 1930, p. 3.

49. *Bezbozhnik*, No. 35, July 30, 1931; *Brianskii Rabochii*, No. 80, Apr. 11, 1931.

50. *Bezbozhnik*, No. 58, Oct. 25, 1931.

51. *Ibid.*, No. 4, Jan. 24, 1932.

52. *Antireligioznik*, No. 2, 1933, pp. 27–28.

53. *Loc. cit.*

54. *Antireligioznik*, No. 14, 1932, p. 36.

55. *Bezbozhnik*, No. 18, Mar. 30, 1930.

56. *Proletarskaia Chernomorka*, No. 75, 1931.

57. *Krasnaia Gazeta*, No. 100, Apr. 29, 1932.

58. *Izvestiia*, No. 304, Dec. 24, 1930.

59. *Komsomolskaia Pravda*, No. 328, Dec. 24, 1930.

60. *Ibid.*, No. 98, Apr. 4, 1931; No. 101, Apr. 12, 1931.

61. *Bezbozhnik*, No. 30, June 30, 1932.

62. *Bor'ba*, No. 254, Nov. 6, 1930.

63. *Antireligioznik*, No. 8, 1931, pp. 43–44; Enisherlov, *op. cit.*, pp. 130–131.

64. Enisherlov, *op. cit.*, p. 132.

65. *Bezbozhnik*, No. 46, Aug. 25, 1931; *Pod Znamenem Marksizma*, No. 11–12, 1931, p. 193; V. A. Shishakov, *Religiia na Sluzhbe Kapitalisticheskikh Elementov v SSSR*, p. 24.

66. Enisherlov, *op. cit.*, p. 135; *Pod Znamenem Marksizma*, No. 11–12, 1931, pp. 193–194; *ibid.*, No. 3, 1931, p. 48.

67. M. M. Sheinman, *Religion and Church in the USSR*, p. 34.

68. *Antireligioznik*, No. 8–9, 1930, p. 22.

69. *Pod Znamenem Marksizma*, No. 3, 1931, p. 48.

70. *Ibid.*, p. 47.

71. E. E. Iaroslavskii, *Razvernutym Frontom*, pp. 22–23.

72. P. Zarin, *Politicheskaia Maskirovka Religioznykh Organizatsii*, pp. 41–46; *Antireligioznik*, No. 10, 1931, p. 9.

73. *Izvestiia*, No. 4, Jan. 4, 1931.

74. Zarin, *op. cit.*, pp. 50–51; Enisherlov, *op. cit.*, p. 136.

75. *Antireligioznik*, No. 10, 1931, p. 16.

76. Zarin, *op. cit.*, p. 77.

77. *Ibid.*, pp. 67–70, 62.

78. *Ibid.*, pp. 63–65.

79. *Ibid.*, pp. 65–66.

80. *Ibid.*, pp. 30–31, 28–29.

81. *Ibid.*, pp. 86–87.

82. *Ibid.*, p. 97.

83. *Ibid.*, pp. 82–83, 95–96.

84. *Pravda*, No. 49, Feb. 9, 1930.

85. *Pravda and Izvestiia*, No. 46, Feb. 16, 1930. Cf. *Manchester Guardian*, Feb. 20, 1930.

86. *Poslednyia Novosti*, No. 3766, July 15, 1931.

87. P. N. Miliukov, *Outlines of Russian Culture*, I, 203–204; P. B. Anderson, *Russia's Religious Future*, pp. 41–43.

88. *Antireligioznik*, No. 8–9, 1930, p. 101.

89. *Ibid.*, No. 3, 1933, p. 14.

90. *Derevenskii Bezbozhnik*, No. 14, July, 1932.

91. *Antireligioznik*, No. 10, 1932, pp. 49–52.

92. Anderson, *op. cit.*, p. 19.

93. *Krasnaia Gazeta*, No. 307, Dec. 6, 1929.

94. *Bezbozhnik*, No. 14, Mar. 10, 1930.

95. Enisherlov, *op. cit.*, p. 128.

96. *Pod Znamenem Marksizma*, No. 3, 1931, p. 48.

97. *Pravda*, No. 355, Dec. 26, 1930.

98. *Bezbozhnik*, No. 46, Aug. 28, 1931.

99. *Antireligioznik*, No. 1, 1931, p. 60.

100. Enisherlov, *op. cit.*, p. 221.

101. *Antireligioznik*, No. 17–18, 1932, pp. 37–47.

102. *Izvestiia*, No. 49, Feb. 19, 1930.

103. Enisherlov, *op. cit.*, p. 125.

104. *Antireligioznik*, No. 8, 1931, pp. 59–61.

105. *Komsomolskaia Pravda*, No. 147, June 24, 1930; *Bezbozhnik*, No. 69, Dec. 15, 1931.

106. *Vozhaty*, No. 3, Feb., 1932.

107. *Krasnaia Gazeta*, No. 100, Apr. 29, 1932.

108. *Bezbozhnik*, No. 68, Dec. 15, 1931.

109. *Komsomolskaia Pravda*, No. 170, June 22, 1931.

110. *Bezbozhnik*, May 5, 1932.

111. *Ibid.*, No. 35, July 30, 1931; No. 27, May 20, 1931; *Bezbozhnik u Stanka*, No. 9, May 1, 1931; *Pod Znamenem Marksizma*, No. 3, 1931, p. 50.

112. *Ibid.*, pp. 49–50; *Antireligioznik*, No. 17–18, 1932, pp. 37–47, and No. 10, 1932, pp. 49–52.

113. *Ibid.*, No. 10, 1932, pp. 49–52.

114. *Ibid.*, No. 17–18, 1932, pp. 37–47; *Bezbozhnik*, No. 13, Mar. 25, 1932.

115. *Antireligioznik*, *loc. cit.*

NOTES TO CHAPTER XIV

1. R.S.F.S.R., *Sobr. Uzak.*, No. 226, 1934, art. 15; U.S.S.R., *Sobr. Zak.*, No. 87b, 1934.

2. *Ibid.*, No. 283, 284, 421, 1934; No. 94, 1935.

3. *Ibid.*, No. 211b, 1934.

4. *Ibid.*, No. 2, 1936.

5. *Konstitutsiia Soiuza Sovetskikh Sotsialisticheskikh Respublik* (1936), arts. 135–136, 124; E. E. Iaroslavskii, *Stalinskaia Konstitutsiia i (Vopros o Religii*, pp. 4–6.

6. I. V. Stalin, *O Proekte Konstitutsii Soiuza SSR*, pp. 32–34.

7. K. N. Plotnikov, *Biudzhet Sotsialisticheskogo Gosudarstva*, p. 280. A. Baykov, *The Development of the Soviet Economic System*, p. 382.

8. U.S.S.R., Vsesoiuznyi Komitet po Delam Iskusstv, *Protiv Fal'skifikatsii Narodnogo Proshlogo*, pp. 3–13.

9. *Izvestiia*, No. 75, Mar. 30, 1938.

10. F. N. Oleshchuk, *O Preodolenii Religioznykh Perezhitkov*, p. 31.

11. *Izvestiia*, No. 146, June 27, 1940.

12. *Antireligioznik*, No. 2, 1934, p. 3.

13. *Ibid.*, No. 1, 1935, pp. 31–32.

14. *Ibid.*, No. 4, 1935, pp. 8–14.

15. *Ibid.*, No. 3, 1936, p. 18.

16. *Ibid.*, No. 1, 1937, pp. 17–18.

17. *Izvestiia*, No. 60, Mar. 10, 1937.

18. See Chap. XIII; *Pravda*, No. 23, Jan. 24, 1941.

19. P. B. Anderson, *Russia's Religious Future*, p. 13.

20. *Antireligioznik*, No. 4, 1937, p. 31.

21. Iaroslavskii, *op. cit.*, p. 15; Pravda, No. 115, Apr. 22, 1936.

22. *Izvestiia*, No. 100, Apr. 27, 1937; No. 60, Mar. 10, 1937; No. 62, Mar. 12, 1937; No. 154, July 3, 1937.

23. *Antireligioznik*, No. 10, 1937, pp. 6–16.

24. *Ibid.*, No. 1, 1937, pp. 18–21.

25. *Ibid.*, No. 7, 1937, p. 11.

26. *Ibid.*, No. 4, 1935, pp. 16–17.

27. *Izvestiia*, No. 118, May 21, 1937; No. 187, Aug. 11, 1937; No. 222, Sept. 22, 1937; No. 275, Nov. 27, 1937; *Bol'shevik*, No. 4, 1937, pp. 34–35; No. 20, 1937, pp. 37–38.

28. *Izvestiia*, No. 271, Nov. 22, 1937.

29. *Ibid.*, No. 30, Feb. 5, 1938; *Antireligioznik*, No. 3, 1938, pp. 7–8.

30. *Ibid.*, No. 3, 1938, pp. 8–10; *Bol'shevik*, No. 20, 1937, p. 39.

31. *Pod Znamenem Marksizma,* No. 1, 1938, p. 40.

32. U.S.S.R., Nar. Kom. Iust., *Report of Court Proceedings in the Case of the Anti-Soviet "Bloc of Rights and Trotskyists . . . ,"* p. 347.

33. *Antireligioznik,* No. 11, 1939, p. 3.

34. *Bezbozhnik,* No. 14, Apr. 6, 1941.

35. *Loc. cit.; Antireligioznik,* No. 5, 1941, pp. 1–2.

36. M. M. Sheinman, *Antireligioznyi Uchebnik dlia Kruzhkov i Samoobrazovaniia,* p. 39.

37. *Pravda,* No. 128, May 9, 1940; No. 348, Dec. 17, 1940. *Bezbozhnik,* No. 20, May 18, 1941.

38. *Antireligioznik,* No. 2, 1936, p. 5.

39. *Ibid.,* No. 5, 1941, p. 7.

40. *Ibid.,* pp. 2–3.

41. A. T. Lukachevskii (ed.), *Antireligioznyi Uchebnik;* Sheinman, *op. cit.*

42. *Pravda,* No. 35, Feb. 5, 1938, cited in *Dvadsatiletie (XX-letie) Otdeleniia Tserkvi ot Gosudarstva,* pp. 20–24; Oleshchuk, *op. cit.,* pp. 12–17.

43. *Bol'shevik,* No. 7–8, 1941, p. 119; E. E. Iaroslavskii, *Kommunizm i Religiia,* pp. 3–21.

44. *Antireligioznik,* No. 5, 1941, p. 8; Oleshchuk, *op. cit.,* pp. 33–34.

45. *Antireligioznik,* No. 3, 1934, p. 38. Cf. No. 2, 1934, p. 2, and No. 4, 1935, pp. 15–16.

46. *Patriarkh Sergii i Ego Dukhovnoe Nasledstvo,* pp. 41–42.

47. *Zhurnal Moskovskoi Patriarkhii,* No. 9, 1945, pp. 9–12.

48. *Bol'shevik,* No. 16, 1938, pp. 35–37; *Izvestiia,* No. 154, July 3, 1937.

49. U.S.S.R., *Sobr. Zakonov,* No. 237, 1936; *Izvestiia,* No. 303, Dec. 29, 1936.

50. U.S.S.R., *Sobr. Zakonov,* No. 292, 1937.

51. *Bol'shevik,* No. 23–24, 1938, pp. 61–62.

52. *Ibid.,* No. 16, 1938, pp. 35–37.

53. *Ibid.,* p. 37. This account does not indicate whether the bishop was a Renovationist or a follower of the patriarchal church.

54. *Antireligioznik,* No. 7, 1938, p. 52; No. 6, 1939, pp. 1–5.

55. Oleshchuk, *op. cit.,* p. 23.

56. *Antireligioznik,* No. 6, 1935, p. 4.

57. Iaroslavskii, *Stalinskaia Konstitutsiia i Vopros o Religii,* p. 14.

58. *Antireligioznik,* No. 6, 1937, p. 8.

59. Oleshchuk, *op. cit.,* pp. 8–9.

60. *Ibid.,* p. 37.

61. E. I. Perovskii, *Antireligioznoe Vospitanie v Nachal'noi Shkole,* p. 17.

62. *Antireligioznik,* No. 1, 1935, pp. 27-31.

63. *Ibid.,* No. 3, 1936, pp. 19-20.

64. *Bol'shevik,* No. 4, 1937, pp. 33-34; No. 20, 1937, pp. 36-37; *Antireligioznik,* No. 6, 1937, p. 9.

65. Iaroslavskii, *Kommunizm i Religiia,* p. 32.

66. *Antireligioznik,* No. 6, 1937, p. 11.

67. *Ibid.,* No. 4, 1938, pp. 34-35.

68. *Ibid.,* p. 34.

69. *Ibid.,* No. 4, 1935, pp. 11-12.

70. *Ibid.,* p. 13.

71. *Ibid.,* No. 6, 1935, p. 2.

72. Anderson, *op. cit.,* p. 21.

73. *Antireligioznik,* No. 2, 1936, p. 19.

74. *Ibid.,* p. 23.

75. *Ibid.,* No. 5, 1939, p. 18.

76. *Ibid.,* No. 6, 1939, p. 5. The figure of eighty thousand Orthodox churches before 1917 is much too large.

77. *Ibid.,* No. 7, 1938, p. 51.

78. *Ibid.,* No. 6, 1937, p. 8; No. 6, 1939, p. 5; Oleshchuk, *op. cit.,* p. 24.

79. *Antireligioznik,* No. 2, 1940, p. 24.

80. *Ibid.,* pp. 24-28.

NOTES TO CHAPTER XV

1. *Pravda o Religii v Rossii,* pp. 15-17.

2. *Ibid.,* pp. 83-86.

3. *Ibid.,* pp. 98-111.

4. *Patriarkh Sergii i Ego Dukhovnoe Nasledstvo,* p. 90.

5. *Ibid.,* p. 85.

6. *Ibid.,* p. 90.

7. *Pravda o Religii v Rossii,* p. 168.

8. *New York Times,* Jan. 5, 1943.

9. *Ibid.,* Nov. 10, 1942.

10. *Ibid.,* Jan. 5, 1943.

11. *Pravda o Religii v Rossii,* pp. 129-142; *Patriarkh Sergii i Ego Dukhovnoe Nasledstvo,* p. 89.

12. B. Spuler, "Die Rechtsfrage der Orthodoxen Kirche in der U.d. SSR," *Ost-Probleme,* No. 12, 1949, p. 360.

13. *Patriarkh Sergii,* p. 89; *Zhurnal Moskovskoi Patriarkhii* (hereafter cited as *Zh. M. P.*), No. 3, 1943, pp. 5-6.

14. *New York Times,* Oct. 6, 7, 1941; N. S. Timasheff in W. Gurian (ed.), *The Soviet Union,* p. 184.

15. *Sputnik Agitatora,* No. 10, 1943, p. 8.

16. *Pravda o Religii v Rossii,* p. 216.

17. *Soviet War Documents,* pp. 155–157.

18. *New York Times,* Aug. 5, 1943.

19. *Izvestiia,* No. 210, Sept. 5, 1943, cited in *Zh. M. P.,* No. 1, 1943, p. 5.

20. *Ibid.,* p. 6.

21. *Ibid.,* p .16.

22. *Ibid.,* No. 2, 1943, pp. 18–23.

23. *New York Times,* Aug. 11, 1944.

24. *Zh. M. P.,* No. 3, 1943, pp. 22–24.

25. *Ibid.,* No. 7, 1944, pp. 10–18.

26. *New York Times,* Aug. 12, 1944.

27. *Christian Science Monitor,* Sept. 30, 1944.

28. *Zh. M. P.,* No. 3, 1943, pp. 8–9.

29. *Ibid.,* No. 4, 1944, p. 9; No. 1, 1945, pp. 7–8.

30. *Ibid.,* No. 3, 1944, pp. 6–10.

31. *Ibid.,* No. 1, 1945, pp. 5–10; *Izvestiia,* Dec. 14, 1944.

32. *Soviet War News,* Oct. 19, 1943.

33. *Russkii Golos,* Oct. 11, 1944.

34. *Zh. M. P.,* No. 1, 1943, pp. 8–9.

35. *Ibid.,* No. 4, 1944, pp. 12–17.

36. *Ibid.,* p. 5.

37. *Ibid.,* No. 1, 1945, p. 46.

38. *Ibid.,* No. 10, 1944, p. 3.

39. *Ibid.,* No. 1, 1943, pp. 9–12.

40. *Ibid.,* p. 13.

41. *Ibid.,* No. 4, 1943, pp. 13–14.

42. *Patriarkh Sergii,* pp. 135–136.

43. *Ibid.,* p. 90.

44. *Loc. cit.*

45. *Zh. M. P.,* No. 9, 1944, pp. 3–5.

46. *Ibid.,* No. 2, 1944, pp. 13–18.

47. *Patriarkh Sergii,* pp. 322–331.

48. *Zh. M. P.,* No. 2, 1945, pp. 10–11; *Izvestiia,* Feb. 4, 1945, No. 29.

49. *Zh. M. P.,* No. 3, 1945, pp. 27–32.

50. *Izvestiia,* No. 34, Feb. 10, 1945.

51. *Zh. M. P.,* No. 5, 1945, p. 3.

52. *Loc. cit.*

53. *Loc. cit.*

54. *Izvestiia,* No. 110, May 12, 1945.

55. *Zh. M. P.,* No. 4, 1945, pp. 7–9 and 19–21; No. 5, 1945, pp. 36–43.

56. *Izvestiia,* Apr. 13, 1945.

57. *Zh. M. P.,* No. 10, 1944, pp. 6–7.

58. *Ibid.,* No. 5, 1945, pp. 19–26.

59. *New York Times,* May 9, 1944.

60. *Izvestiia,* Nov. 23, 1944.

61. *Russkii Golos,* Mar. 10, 1945.

62. Eve Curie, *Journey among Warriors,* pp. 144–145. (Her figure of 600 churches in prewar Moscow seems high.) *New York Times,* Apr. 19, and 26, 1943. (An article in this newspaper for Jan. 8, 1944, stated that Christmas was celebrated in more than 50 churches.)

63. E. Briem, *Kommunismus und Religion,* p. 385.

64. S. Evans, *Soviet Churches and the War,* pp. 87–88.

65. *New York Times,* June 7, 1945.

66. Curie, *op. cit.,* pp. 143–144.

67. *New York Times,* Jan. 10, 1942.

68. *Ibid.,* Jan. 8, 1944.

69. *New York Herald Tribune,* Sept. 25, 1943.

70. W. Carroll, *We're in This with Russia,* pp. 150–151.

71. *Loc. cit.*

72. Curie, *op. cit.,* pp. 145–146.

73. *Zh. M. P.,* No. 2, 1943, pp. 3–5.

74. *Izvestiia,* Feb. 6, 1945. The publication of this purely ecclesiastical message by *Izvestiia* was a remarkable event.

75. *Propagandist,* No. 18, 1944, pp. 1–5.

76. *Izvestiia,* Dec. 14, 1944. Other examples are in *Pravda,* Oct. 28, 1944; *Moskovskii Bol'shevik,* Feb. 27, 1945; and *Vechernaia Moskva,* Feb. 27, 1945, as translated by Joint Press Reading Service, Moscow.

NOTES TO CHAPTER XVI

1. *Patriarkh Sergii,* pp. 308–309.

2. *New York Times,* Aug. 18, 1946; *Zh. M. P.,* No. 2, 1947, p. 37; No. 4, 1947, p. 37.

3. *New York Times,* June 7, 1945.

4. *Zh. M. P.,* Sp. No., 1948, pp. 10–11.

5. N. S. Timasheff in W. Gurian (ed.), *The Soviet Union,* pp. 156–157. (I have not been able to locate the text of this decree — J. S. C.)

6. *New York Times,* Feb. 24, 1946.

7. Gurian, *op. cit.*, p. 158.

8. *USSR Information Bulletin*, Jan. 28, 1949, pp. 54–56.

9. *Vestnik Russkogo Zapadno-Evropeiskogo Patriarshego Ekzarkhata*, No. 2, 1947, p. 13.

10. *Zh. M. P.*, No. 12, 1949, pp. 9–11.

11. *Bol'shaia Sovetskaia Entsiklopediia*, vol. *Soiuz Sovetskikh Sotsialisticheskikh Respublik*, col. 1787.

12. *Zh. M. P.*, No. 3, 1947, p. 53.

13. *Russkii Golos*, Dec. 1, 1946.

14. *Zh. M. P.*, No. 11, 1949, p. 12.

15. Gurian, *op. cit.*, pp. 168–170.

16. *Vestnik Russk. Zap.-Evr. Pat. Ekzarkhata*, No. 2, 1947, pp. 15–20 *passim*.

17. *Zh. M. P.*, No. 3, 1950, p. 2; No. 7, 1949, pp. 4–6.

18. *Patriarkh Sergii*, pp. 372–373; see also J. B. Barron and H. M. Waddams (eds.), *Communism and the Churches*, p. 29.

19. *New York Times*, Mar. 7, 13, 19, 1946.

20. *Ibid.*, Apr. 15, 1946.

21. *Zh. M. P.*, No. 10, 1949, pp. 6–10.

22. *Ibid.*, Sp. No., 1948.

23. *Russkii Golos*, Dec. 1, 1946.

24. *Zh. M. P.*, No. 6, 1947; No. 1, 2, 7, 1948; *Vest. Russk. Zap.-Evr. Pat. Ekzarkhata*, No. 2, 1947, p. 8.

25. *Zh. M. P.*, No. 7, 1947, pp. 35–38.

26. *Ibid.*, No. 8, 1950, pp. 68–69.

27. *Ibid.*, No. 7, 1947, pp. 44–46.

28. *Patriarkh Sergii, op. cit.*, p. 392.

29. *Zh. M. P.*, No. 9, 1948, p. 69; No. 7, 1948, p. 70.

30. *Ibid.*, No. 12, 1949, p. 59; No. 3, 1950, p. 62.

31. *Vest. R. Zap.-Evr. Pat. Ekzarkhata*, No. 2, 1947, pp. 18–19.

32. *Zh. M. P.*, No. 8, 1945, pp. 3–4.

33. *Ibid.*, No. 11, 1947, pp. 4–5.

34. *Ibid.*, No. 1, 1949, pp. 4–5.

35. *Ibid.*, No. 4, 1949, p. 1.

36. *Ibid.*, pp. 53–54.

37. *Ibid.*, No. 7, 1949, pp. 28–35.

38. *Ibid.*, No. 12, 1949, pp. 57–58.

39. *Ibid.*, No. 9, 1945, p. 3.

40. *Ibid.*, No. 10, 1947, p. 3.

41. *Ibid.*, No. 11, 1947, p. 3.

42. *Ibid.,* Sp. No., 1948, p. 13.

43. *Ibid.,* No. 12, 1949, pp. 7–9; No. 1, 1950, p. 4.

44. *Ibid.,* pp. 11–13.

45. *Patriarkh Sergii,* pp. 358–372; *Zh. M. P.,* No. 9, 1945, pp. 9–12; No. 1, 1948, pp. 13–24; No. 3, 1949, p. 8; No. 4, 1949, pp. 5–6; No. 8, 1949, pp. 11–12; No. 11, 1949, pp. 7–9; Gurian, *op. cit.,* pp. 159–160.

46. *Zh. M. P.,* No. 2, 1949, pp. 44–45.

47. *Patriarkh Sergii,* p. 349.

48. *Zh. M. P.,* No. 6, 1946, pp. 3–19.

49. *Ibid.,* No. 8, 1945, pp. 6–25; No. 9, 1945, pp. 16–25.

50. *Ibid,* No. 8, 1945, pp. 27–48.

51. *Ibid.,* No. 9, 1945, pp. 29–44.

52. *New York Times,* Oct. 22, 1946.

53. *Zh. M. P.,* No. 7, 1950, pp. 20–32; No. 9, 1950, pp. 21–25.

54. Gurian, *op. cit.,* pp. 161–162.

55. *Zh. M. P.,* Sp. No., 1948; No. 8, 1949, pp. 14–28.

56. *Ibid.,* Sp. No., 1948, pp. 35–37, 66.

57. *Ibid.,* No. 5, 1949, pp. 3–4.

58. *Ibid.,* No. 8, 1949, pp. 14–24.

59. *Ibid.,* No. 12, 1949, pp. 26–28.

60. *Ibid.,* Sp. No., 1948, pp. 23–25.

61. *Ibid.,* No. 9, 1949, pp. 52–57.

62. *Ibid.,* pp. 43–51.

63. *Ibid.,* No. 5, 1950, pp. 30–31.

64. *Ibid.,* No. 12, 1947, pp. 28–29.

65. Gurian, *op. cit.,* pp. 180–181.

66. *Zh. M. P.,* Sp. No., 1948, pp. 31–32.

67. *Ibid.,* No. 2, 1949, p. 3.

68. *Ibid.,* N. 5, 1949, pp. 12–33; No. 11, pp. 13, 3.

69. *Ibid.,* No. 3, 1950, p. 3.

70. *Ibid.,* No. 6, 1950, p. 3.

71. *Ibid.,* No. 8, 1950, pp. 5–7.

72. *Ibid.,* pp. 3–4.

73. *Ibid.,* No. 11, 1950, p. 3.

74. *Komsomolskaia Pravda,* No. 246, Oct. 18, 1947.

75. *Bol'shaia Sovetskaia Entsiklopediia,* vol. cited, cols. 1781–1784.

76. *Uchitel'skaia Gazeta,* No. 25, June 10, 1948.

77. *Bol'shevik,* No. 11, 1948, p. 36.

78. *Narodnoe Obrazovanie,* No. 4, 1949, pp. 18–21.

79. *Komsomolskaia Pravda,* No. 75, Mar. 31, 1949.

80. Barron and Waddams, *op. cit.*, pp. 30–31.

81. *Uchitel'skaia Gazeta*, No. 93, Nov. 26, 1949.

82. *Narodnoe Obrazovanie*, No. 4, 1949, p. 25.

83. *Komsomolskaia Pravda*, Mar. 21, 1950, quoted in *Current Digest of the Soviet Press*, May 6, 1950.

84. *New York Times*, Aug. 29, 1950.

85. *Current Digest of the Soviet Press*, Nov. 18, 1950, pp. 8–9.

$\mathcal{B}i\mathcal{B}liograp\mathcal{H}\gamma$

I. BOOKS

ALEKSEEV, S. A. (ed.). *Fevral'skaia Revoliutsiia.* Moscow, 1926.

AMOSOV, N. *Na Detskom Antireligioznom Fronte.* Moscow, 1930.

ANDERSON, PAUL B. *Russia's Religious Future.* London, 1935.

Antireligioznaia Propaganda. K. Postanovke Raboty. Khar'kov, 1925.

BARRON, J. B., and WADDAMS, H. G. (eds.). *Communism and the Churches. A Documentation.* New York, 1950.

BAYKOV, ALEXANDER. *The Development of the Soviet Economic System.* Cambridge (Eng.), New York, 1947.

BLIUMENTAL', I. I. *Revoliutsiia 1917–1918 gg. v. Samarskoi Gubernii Khronika Sobytii).* Samara, 1927.

Bol'shaia Sovetskaia Entsiklopediia, volume on *Soiuz Sovetskikh Sotsialisticheskikh Respublik.* Moscow, 1947.

BONCH-BRUEVICH, V. D. *"Zhivaia Tserkov'" i Proletariat.* Moscow, 1929.

BORIS, EPISKOP. *O Sovremennom Polozhenii Russkoi Pravoslavnoi Patriarshei Tserkvi.* Moscow, 1927.

BRIEM, EFRAIM. *Kommunismus und Religion in der Sowjetunion. Ein Ideenkampf.* Basel, n.d.

BRIKHNICHEV, I. *Patriarkh Tikhon i Ego Tserkov'.* Moscow, 1923.

BUKHARIN, N., and PREOBRAZHENSKII, E. *Azbuka Kommunizma* (3rd ed.). Odessa, 1923.

BULATOV, I. *K Raskolu v Russkoi Pravoslavnoi Tserkvi.* Vologda, 1922.

BUNYAN, JAMES (ed.). *Intervention, Civil War and Communism in Russia.* Baltimore, 1936.

BUNYAN, JAMES, and FISHER, H. H. *The Bolshevik Revolution, 1917–1918. Documents and Materials.* Stanford, Calif., 1934.

BURKIN, N. *Monastyri v Rossii, Ikh Eksplatatorskaia i Kontrrevoliutsionnaia Rol'.* Moscow, 1931.

CARROLL, WALLACE. *We're in This with Russia.* Boston, 1942.

Chrezvychainoe Eparkhial'noe Sobranie Dukhovenstva i Mirian Kishinev-

skoi Eparkhii, Sostoiavsheesia v G. Kishineve 19–25 Apr. 1917 g. Kishinev, 1917.

CHUDNOVTSEV, M. I. *Politicheskaia Rol' Tserkovnikov i Sektantov v S.S.S.R.* Moscow, 1929.

COOKE, RICHARD J. *Religion in Russia under the Soviets.* New York, Cincinnati, 1924.

CRAMER, KARL (ed.). *Das Notbuch der russischen Christenheit* (2nd ed., rev. and enl.). Berlin-Steglitz, 1930.

CURIE, EVE. *Journey among Warriors.* Garden City, N. Y., 1943.

Deianiia Russkago Vsezagranichago Tserkovnago Sobora, Sostoiavshagosia 8–20 Noiabria 1921 goda . . . . Sremski Karlovtsy, Yugoslavia, 1922.

DENIKIN, A. I. *Ocherki Russkoi Smuty.* 5 vols. Paris, 1921–1926.

DOLOTOV, A. S. *Tserkov' i Sektantstvo v Sibiri.* Novosibirsk, 1930.

Dvadtsatiletie (XX-letie) Otdeleniia Tserkvi ot Gosudarstva. Moscow, 1938.

EMHARDT, W. C. *Religion in Soviet Russia.* Milwaukee, 1929.

ENISHERLOV, M. (ed.). *Voinstvuiushchee Bezbozhie v SSSR za 15 Let.* Moscow, 1932.

EVANS, STANLEY. *Soviet Churches and the War.* London, 1944.

EVLOGII, MITROPOLIT. *Put' Moei Zhizni. Vospominaniia Mitropolita Evlogiia.* Paris, 1947.

FEDOTOV, G. P. *The Russian Church since the Revolution.* London, New York, 1928.

FISHER, H. H. *The Famine in Soviet Russia, 1919–1923: The Operations of the American Relief Administration.* Stanford, Calif., 1935.

GIDULIANOV, P. V. (ed.). *Otdelenie Tserkvi ot Gosudarstva. Polnyi Sbornik Dekretov RSFSR i SSSR, Instruktsii, Tsirkuliarov, i t. d.* Moscow, 1924.

GIDULIANOV, P. V., and KRASIKOV, P. (eds.). *Tserkov' i Gosudarstvo po Zakonodatel'stvu RSFSR.* Moscow, 1923.

GOLOVKIN, A. I. *Metodika Antireligioznykh Kampanii.* Ivanovo, 1930.

GORCHAKOV, M. K. *Vozbuditeli Raskola.* Paris, 1927.

GOREV, M. *Protiv Antisemitov. Ocherki i Zarisovki.* Moscow, 1928.

GURIAN, WALDEMAR (ed.). *The Soviet Union, Background, Ideology, Reality.* Notre Dame, Ind., 1951.

D' HERBIGNY, MICHEL. *L'Aspect religieux de Moscou en Octobre, 1925.* Rome, 1926.

IAROSLAVSKII, E. E. *Kommunisty i Religiia.* Moscow, 1931.

———. *Kommunizm i Regligiia* (4th ed.). Moscow, Leningrad, 1931.

———. *Na Antireligioznom Fronte. Sbornik Statei, Dokladov, Lektsii i Tsirkuliarov za Piat' Let, 1919–1924.* Moscow, 1924.

———. *Razvernutym Frontom*. Moscow, 1929.

———. *Stalinskaia Konstitutsiia i Vopros o Religiia*. Moscow, 1936.

Kalendar' Antireligioznika na 1941 god. Moscow, 1941.

KALININ, I. *Pod Znamenem Vrangelia. Zametki b. Voennogo Prokurora*. Leningrad, 1925.

KANDIDOV, BORIS. *Golod 1921 Goda i Tserkov'*. Moscow, Leningrad, 1932.

———. *Iaponskaia Interventsiia v Sibiri i Tserkov'*. Moscow, 1932.

———. *Mensheviki i Popovshchina v Bor'be protiv Oktiabr'skoi Revoliutsii*. Moscow, 1931.

———, *Religiöznaia Kontrrevoliutsiia 1918–1920 gg. i Interventsiia (Ocherki i Materialy)*. Moscow, 1930.

———. *Tserkov' i Fevral'skaia Revoliutsiia — Klassovaia Pozitsiia Pravoslavnoi Tserkvi v Period Fevral'–Avgust 1917 g.* Moscow, 1934.

———. *Tserkov' i Grazhdanskaia Voina na Iuge (Materialy k Istorii Religioznoi Kontrrevoliutsii v Gody Grazhdanskoi Voiny.)* Moscow, 1931.

———. *Tserkov' i Kontrrazvedka. Kontrrevoliuts. i Terrorist. Deiatel'nost' Tserkovnikov na Iuge v Gody Grazhdanskoi Voiny*. Moscow, 1930.

———. *Tserkov' i Shpionazh*. Moscow, 1938.

———. *Tserkovno-Belogvardeiskii Sobor v Stavropole v Mae 1919 g.* Moscow, 1930.

KARNITSKII, D., and ROGINSKII, G. *Ugolovnyi Kodeks RSFSR. Posobie dlia Slushatelei Pravovykh Vuzov, Shkol i Iuridicheskikh Kursov*. Moscow, 1935.

Konstitutsiia (Osnovnoi Zakon) Soiuza Sovetskikh Sotsialisticheskikh Respublik. Moscow, 1938.

Konstitutsii Soiuza SSR i Soiuznykh Respublik. Moscow, 1932.

KRASIKOV, P. A. *Na Tserkovnom Fronte (1918–1923)*. Moscow, 1923.

KROL, L. A. *Za Tri Goda (Vospominaniia, Vpechatleniia i Vstrechi)*. Vladivostok, 1921.

KRUPSKAIA, N. K. *Antireligioznaia Propaganda*. Moscow, Leningrad, 1929.

KRYLENKO, N. V. *Sudostroistvo R.S.F.S.R.* Moscow, 1923.

———. *Za Piat' Let. 1918–1922 gg. Obvinitel'nye Rechi po Naibolee Krupnym Protsessam, Zaslushannym v Moskovskom i Verkhovnom Revoliutsionnykh Tribunalakh*. Moscow, Petrograd, 1923.

LATSIS, M. IA. *Dva Goda Bor'by na Vnutrennom Fronte*. Moscow, 1920.

LENIN, V. I. *Sochineniia* (3rd ed.). 30 vols. Leningrad, 1935–1937.

LOBACHEV, I. *Pravda o Khriste i Khristianstve*. Samara, 1924.

LUKACHEVSKII, A. T. (ed.). *Antireligioznyi Uchebnik*. Moscow, 1933.

LUNACHARSKII, A. B. *Lichnost' Khrista v Sovremennoi Nauke i Literature.* Moscow, 1928.

McCULLAGH, FRANCIS. *The Bolshevik Persecution of Christianity.* London, 1924.

———. *A Prisoner of the Reds.* London, 1921.

MARGULIES, M. S. *God Interventsii.* 3 vols. Moscow, 1923.

MARKOV, S. V. *How We Tried to Save the Tsaritsa.* London, 1929.

MARTSINOVSKII, V. F. *Zapiski Veruiushchego. Iz Istorii Religioznago Dvizheniia v Sovetskoi Rossii (1917–1923).* Prague, 1929.

MIKHAIL, SVIASHCHENNIK. *Polozhenie Tserkvi v Sovetskoi Rossii. Ocherk Bezhavshego iz Rossii Sviashchennika.* Jerusalem, 1931.

MILIUKOV, P. N. *Outlines of Russian Culture.* 3 vols. Philadelphia, 1942.

Mysli K. Marksa i F. Engel'sa o Religii (2nd ed., rev. and enl.). Leningrad, 1929.

OBOLENSKII, V. A. *Krym pri Vrangelia. Memuary Belogvardeitsa* (2nd ed.). Moscow, Leningrad, 1928.

OLESHCHUK, F. N. *O Preodolenii Religioznykh Perezhitkov.* Moscow, 1941.

———. *Shkola i Vospitanie Aktivnykh Ateistov.* Moscow, Leningrad, 1928.

———. *V. Pokhod na Boga* (2nd ed., rev. and enl.). Moscow, 1930.

ORLEANSKII, N. (comp.). *Zakon o Religioznykh Ob'edineniiakh RSFSR i Deistvuiushchie Zakony, Instruktsii, s Otdel'nymi Kommentiariami . . . .* Moscow, 1930.

ORLOVSKII, P. *Poslanie Patriarkha Tikhona k Arkhipastyriam i Pastyriam Tserkvi Rossiiskoi.* Moscow, 1919.

OSOBAIA KOMISSIIA PO RAZSLEDOVANIIU ZLODEIANII BOL'SHEVIKOV. *Soobshchenie o Goneniiakh Bol'shevikov na Tserkov' v Donskoi Oblasti.* Rostov-on-Don, 1919.

———. *Svedeniia o Zlodeianiiakh Bol'shevikov v Otnoshenii Tserkvi i Eia Sluzhitelei v Stavropol'skoi Eparkhii.* Rostov-on-Don, 1919.

———. *Svodka Materialov po Gorodu Khar-kova i Khar'kovskoi Gubernii.* Rostov-on-Don, 1919.

Patriarkh Sergii i Ego Dukhovnoe Nasledstvo. Moscow, 1947.

PEROVSKII, E. I. *Antireligioznoe Vospitanie v Nachal'noi Shkole; Metodicheskoe Posobie dlia Uchitelei* (2nd. ed., rev. and enl.). Moscow, 1936.

PLOTNIKOV, K. N. *Biudzhet Sotsialisticheskogo Gosudarstva.* Moscow, 1948.

POKROVSKII, M. N., and IAKOVLEV, IA. A. (eds.). *1917 g. v Dokumentakh i Materialakh. Gosudarstvennoe Soveshchanie.* Moscow, 1930.

Polozhenie o Vysshem i Eparkhial'nom Upravlenii Pravoslavnoi Tserkvi. Warsaw, 1822.

Pomestnyi Sobor Rossiiskoi Pravoslavnoi Tserkvi 1923 god. *Biulleteni.* Moscow, 1931.

Pravda o Religii v Rossii. Moscow, 1942.

Rozhdestvenskii, A. *His Holiness Tikhon, Patriarch of All the Russias.* London, 1923.

Rudnev, S. P. *Pri Vechernykh Ogniakh.* Kharbin, 1928.

Russia, Gosudarstvennaia Duma. *Stenograficheskiia Otchety.* 37 vols. Petrograd, 1906–1916.

——, Sviateishii Sinod. *Vsepoddanneishii Otchet Ober-Prokurora . . . za 1914 god.* Petrograd, 1916.

R.S.F.S.R. *Sobranie Uzakonenii i Rasporiazhenii Raboche-Krest'ianskogo Pravitel'stva R.S.F.S.R.* Moscow, 1917——.

——. *Sobranie Uzakonenii i Rasporiazhenii Raboche-Krest'ianskogo Pravitel'stva. Sistematicheskii Sbornik Vazhneishikh Dekretov. 1917–1920.* Moscow, 1921.

——, Narodnyi Komissariat Iustitsii. *Otchet IX Vserossiiskomu S'ezdu Sovetov.* Moscow, 1921.

——, Narodnyi Komissariat Vnutrennykh Del. *Statisticheskii Obzor Deiatel'nosti Mestnykh Administrativnykh Organov.* Moscow. 1925.

——, Tsentral'naia Komissiia Pomoshchi Golodaiushchim. *Itogi Bor'by s Golodom v 1921–22 gg. Sbornik Statei i Otchetov.* Moscow, 1922.

——, Verkhovnyi Sud. *Obvinitel'noe Zakliuchenie po Delu Grazhdan: Bellavina Vasiliia Ivanovicha; Fedomenova Nikandra Grigor'evicha; Stadnitskogo Arseniia Georgievicha; i Gur'eva Petra Viktorovicha.* Moscow, 1923.

Sheinman, M. M. *Antireligioznyi Krest'ianskii Uchebnik dlia Antireligioznogo Aktiva i Antireligioznykh Kruzhkov* (6th ed.). Moscow, 1931.

——. *Antireligioznyi Uchebnik dlia Kruzhkov i Samoobrazovaniia.* Moscow, 1938.

——. *Religion and Church in the USSR.* Moscow, Leningrad, 1933.

Shipov, A. *Tikhonovskaia Tserkov' i Vrangel'. Istoricheskii Ocherk.* Moscow, 1923.

Shishakov, V. A. *Religiia na Sluzhbe Kapitalisticheskikh Elementov v SSSR.* Moscow, 1931.

Shul'gin, V. *"1920 God." Ocherki.* Sofia, 1921.

Spinka, Matthew. *Christianity Confronts Communism.* New York, London, 1936.

——. *The Church and the Russian Revolution.* New York, 1927.

Stalin, I. V. *O Proekte Konstitutsii Soiuza SSR.* Moscow, 1949.

——. *Sochineniia.* 13 vols. Moscow, 1946——.

STEPANOV, I. V. *Kak Vesti Antireligioznuiu Propagandu v Derevne.* Leningrad, 1930.

———. *O "Zhivoi Tserkvi."* Moscow, 1922.

STRATONOV, I. *Russkaia Tserkovnaia Smuta.* (*1921–1931* gg). Berlin, 1932.

SVIASHCHENNYI SOBOR PRAVOSLAVNOI ROSSIISKO TSERKVI. *Deianiia.* 15 vols. Moscow, 1918–1919.

TITLINOV, B. V. *Novaia Tserkov'.* Petrograd, 1923.

———. *Tserkov' vo Vremia Revoliutsii.* Petrograd, 1924.

TROITSKII, S. V. *Chto Sdelal Patriarkh Tikhon dlia Tserkvi i Rodiny.* Odessa, 1919.

———. *Chto Takoe "Zhivaia Tserkov'."* Warsaw, 1928.

———. *Razmezhivanie ili Raskol.* Paris, 1932.

TRUBETSKOI, E. N. *Smysl' Zhizni.* Berlin, 1922.

Tseli i Zadachi Soiuza Bezbozhnikov. Ul'ianovsk, 1928.

Ukazy Sv. Patriarkha Tikhona. London, 1927.

UK. S.S.R. *Sbornik Tsirkuliarov po Narodnemu Komissariatu Iustitsii.* Khar'kov, 1922.

U.S.S.R. *Sobranie Zakonov i Rasporiazhenii Raboche-Krest'ianskogo Pravitel'stva Soiuza Sovetskikh Sotsialisticheskikh Respublik.* Moscow, 1923–38.

———. *Soviet War Documents.* Embassy of the U.S.S.R., Washington, D.C., 1943.

———, NARODYNYI KOMISSARIAT IUSTITSII. *Report of Court Proceedings in the Case of the Anti-Soviet "Bloc of Rights and Trotskyists,"* . . . *March 2–13, 1938.* Moscow, 1938.

———, KOMITET PO DELAM ISKUSSTV. *Protiv Fal'sifikatsii Narodnogo Proshlogo.* Moscow, 1937.

VALENTINOV, A. A. (ed.). *Chernaia Kniga* ("*Shturm Nebes*"). Paris, 1925.

VERKHOVSKOI, P. V. *Patriarkh Tikhon.* Rostov-on-Don, 1919.

VIPPER, R. Iu. *Vozniknovenie Khristianskoi Literatury.* Moscow, Leningrad, 1946.

VIROUBOVA, ANNA. *Memories of the Russian Court.* New York, 1923.

VOLIN, V. *Don i Dobrovol'cheskaia Armiia. Ocherk Nedavnago Proshlago.* Rostov-on-Don, 1919.

VSESOIUZNAIA KOMMUNISTICHESKAIA PARTIIA. *Vsesoiuznaia Kommunisticheskaia Partiia* (*b*) *v Rezoliutsiiakh i Resheniiakh S'ezdov, Konferentsii i Plenumov Tsk.* 2 vols. Moscow, 1933–1936.

VVEDENSKII, A. I. *Tserkov' i Gosudarstvo.* Moscow, 1923.

———. *Tserkov' Patriarkha Tikhona.* Moscow, 1923.

——. *Za Chto Lishali Sana Byvshego Patriarkha Tikhona.* Moscow, 1923.

ZAITSEV, KIRILL. *Pravoslavnaia Tserkov' v Sovetskoi Rossii.* Shanghai, 1947.

ZARIN, P. *Politicheskaia Maskirovka Religioznykh Organizatsii.* Moscow, 1934.

ZHEVAKHOV, N. D. *Vospominaniia,* Vol. II. Novy Sad, Yugoslavia, 1920.

II. PERIODICALS

Antireligioznik. Moscow.
Arkhiv Russkoi Revoliutsii. Berlin.
Beloe Del. Berlin.
Bezbozhnik. Moscow.
Bezbozhnik u Stanka. Moscow.
Birzhevyia Vedomosti. Petrograd.
Bogoslovskaia Mysl'. Paris.
Bol'shevik. Moscow.
Bor'ba. Stalingrad.
Brianskii Rabochii. Briansk.
Christian Science Monitor. Boston.
Derevenskii Bezbozhnik. Moscow.
Ezhenedel'nik Chrezvychainnykh Komissii po Bor'be s Kontrrevoliutsii i Spekuliatsii. Moscow.
Golos Litovskoi Pravoslavnoi Eparkhii. Kaunas.
Golos Minuvshego na Chuzhoi Storone. Paris.
Izvestiia. Moscow.
Khristianin. Moscow.
Komsomolskaia Pravda. Moscow.
Krasnaia Gazeta. Leningrad.
Krasnyi Arkhiv. Moscow.
Kubanskii Tserkovnyi Vestnik. Stavropol.
La Lutte contre la Religion en Russie soviétique. Paris.
Manchester Guardian. Manchester.
Molodaia Gvardiia. Moscow.
Na Putiakh k Novoi Shkole. Moscow.
Narodnoe Obrazovanie. Moscow.
Nauka i Zhizn'. Moscow.
New York Herald Tribune. New York.
New York Times. New York.
Orientalia Christiana. Rome.

Ost-Probleme. Frankfurt am Main.
Pod Znamenem Marksizma. Moscow.
Poslednyia Novosti. Paris.
Pravda. Moscow.
Proletarskaia Chernomorka. Novorossiisk.
Proletarskaia Revoliutsiia. Moscow.
Propagandist. Moscow.
Put': Organ Russkoi Religioznoi Mysli. Paris.
Rech'. Petrograd.
Revoliutsiia i Kul'tura. Moscow.
Revoliutsiia i Tserkov'. Moscow.
Russie et Chrétienté. Paris.
Russkaia Mysl'. Paris.
Russkii Golos. New York.
Soviet War News. London.
Sovremennyia Zapiski. Paris.
Sputnik Agitatora. Moscow.
The Times. London.
Tobol'skiia Eparkhial'myia Vedomosti. Tobol'.
Tserkovnyi Vestnik Zapadno-Evropeiskago Patriarshego Ekzarkhata. Paris.
Tserkovnyia Vedomosti. Petrograd.
Tserkovnyia Vedomosti Izdavaemyia pri Vysshem Russkom Tserkovnom Upravlenii Zagranitsei. Sremski Karlovtsy, Yugoslavia.
Uchitel'skaia Gazeta. Moscow.
USSR Information Bulletin. Washington, D. C.
Vestnik Russkago Studencheskago Dvizheniia. Paris.
Vestnik Sviashchennogo Sinoda Pravoslavnoi Rossiiskoi Tserkvi. Moscow.
Vlast' Sovetov. Moscow.
Vozhaty. Moscow.
Vozrozhdenie. Paris.
Vserossiiskii Tserkovno-Obshchestvennyi Vestnik. Petrograd.
Zhivaia Tserkov'. Moscow.
Zhurnal Moskovskoi Patriarkhii. Moscow.

Index

OGPU. *See* GPU

Old Believers, 5

Oleshchuk, F., antireligious leader, stresses progressive role of early church, 1941, 274; admits decline of antireligious work, 1936, 275; warns of survival of religion, 1941, 284; insists that teachers must raise atheist generation, 1949, 322–323

Over-procuratorship, 4

PAPACY, aids Russian famine sufferers, 1922, 106–107; condemned by members of Sobor of 1945, 298; accused of collaboration with fascism, 299; charges that Uniats were compelled to join Orthodox church, 1946, 307; accused of Fascist tendencies by Russian clergy, 1948, 314–317

Parochial schools, dispute about nationalization of, 1917, 18–19; nationalized, 31–32

Peter the Great, 3

Peter, Metropolitan of Krutitsy, named as possible Locum Tenens, 1925, 178; negotiates with Renovationists, 178–179; termed a reactionary by *Izvestiia,* 1925, 179; arrested and exiled, 1926, 180; names Metropolitan Sergii as Deputy Locum Tenens, 1925, 181; turns control of the church over to Archbishop Grigorii, 181–182; recognizes Metropolitan Sergii as Deputy Locum Tenens, 1926, 182

Pitirim, Metropolitan, 12

Platon, Exarch of Georgia, retained in new Synod, 1917, 13; attends Congress of Clergy and Laymen, 16; preaches anti-Bolshevik sermon, July, 1917, 22; at Moscow State Conference, 30; Metropolitan, leads delegation of Sobor to Military Revolutionary Committee, 39–40; negotiates with Red commandant of Kremlin, 1917, 41; anti-Soviet activities in Odessa, 1919–1920, 97; member of Karlovatskii Sobor, 1921, 108

Pokrovskii, M. N., Vice-Commissar of Education, 78

Pomgol (Central Committee for Aid to the Starving), to receive contributions from the church, 1921, 107; Bishop Antonin invited to join, 1922, 116; reports on use of church treasure, 1922, 125

Pre-Sobor Council, formulates program, 1917, 19; prepares agenda for Sobor, 26–27

Provisional Government, 19

Public schools and religion, subject of a compromise, 1917, 19; Soviet policy during civil war, 213–214; difficulties of antireligious work in schools, 1918–1922, 202; developments, 1924–1928, 213–214; persistence of religion in schools, (1928) 221–222, (1931) 270, (1934–1941) 285; renewed insistence on antireligious work in schools, 1948–1949, 321–323

QUAKERS, 106

RAEV, N. P., 11, 12

Rasputin, Grigorii, dominates Synod, 1915–1916, 7; dismissal of his ecclesiastical supporters, 1917, 12–13

Red Army, carries on propaganda against religion, 1918–1920, 209–210; effect of antireligious work upon (1921–1928) 221, (1931) 268–269

Regiments of Jesus, 99

Relic frauds, 85–86

Religious instruction of children, rules, 1919, 76–77; liberal interpretation made, 1944, 294

Removal of church plate for famine relief, 1922, 116–117; riots against removals, 118–119, 121

Renovationists, oppose patriarchal church, 1922, 138–146; hold Sobor in 1923, 155–158; decline of after release of Patriarch, 167–168; lose bishops to patriarchal church, 168; receive official Soviet recognition, 1924, 173; supported by Patriarch of Constantinople, 173; statistics on Renovationist churches, 1925, 174; issue appeal for church unification, 178; negotiate with Metropolitan Peter, 178–179; hold Sobor in 1925, 179; decline of, 1925–1928, 189–190; leaders